Robert Cellem

Visit of His Royal Highness the Prince of Wales to the British North American Provinces

and United States in the Year 1860

VISIT OF HIS ROYAL HIGHNESS

THE PRINCE OF WALES

TO THE

BRITISH • NORTH AMERICAN PROVINCES

AND

UNITED STATES,

IN THE YEAR 1860.

COMPILED FROM THE PUBLIC JOURNALS,

BY

ROBERT CELLEM.

TORONTO:
PUBLISHED BY HENRY ROWSELL, KING STREET.

1861.

INDEX.

Portrait of the Prince, dedication, and introductory remarks	5
Address of the Legislative Assembly of Canada for a visit from Royalty	6
President Buchanan's letter of invitation	8
Reply of Her Majesty	9
Leaving Osborne, Isle of Wight	9
Embarkation at Plymouth	10
American view of the visit	11
Description of Newfoundland	13
Arrival at St. John's, Newfoundland	30
The landing and the reception	36
The levee	37
Miscellaneous incidents	39
Presentation of Newfoundland dog	40
Regatta	40
The ball	43
The *Hero*	47
Departure for Halifax and the landing	49
Address from the Mayor and reply	55
Address from the Executive Government and reply	58
The review	61
The ball	62
Address from Municipalities, Clergy, and other bodies	64
Progress through Nova Scotia	65
The review and ball	82
Lady Laura Phipps' poem	85
Departure from Nova Scotia	88
Arrival at St. John's, N. B.	91
Departure for Frederickton and enthusiasm along the river	92
The ball	99
Leaves for Charlottetown, P. E. I.	102
From thence to Gaspè	113
The St. Lawrence	117
The Saguenay	118
Quebec, and the address	120
The levee	137
Speakers knighted	140
Addresses and replies	141
The Montmorenci Falls	143
The ball	145
Officers, the pets of the ladies	146
Laval University	147
Leaves for Three Rivers	152
Reception and address	152
Arrival in Montreal and addresses	156
The Exhibition	161
Opening the Victoria Bridge	163
The levee	168
Address of the Clergy of Montreal and the reply	169
Address of the Grand Trunk Railway	170

The ball	172
Lachine rapids	174
The Firemen's gathering	174
The review	177
Visit to Isle Dooval	178
The cricket match	179
Hyacinthe	180
Sherbrooke	180
Lennoxville address	182
The levee at Hon. Mr. Galt's	182
Return to Montreal	183
Departure for Ottawa	183
Reception and canoe display	184
Mayor's address and reply	Appendix
Inauguration of the Government Buildings	186
Lunch by the Legislature	190
The Chaudiere slide	190
Canoe races	190
Leaving Ottawa	190
Brockville address and reply	191
Kingston	195
Belleville	197
Cobourg and the ball	204
Rice Lake	206
Peterborough	207
Port Hope and reception	208
Whitby and reception	212
To Toronto	212
The reception	213
Address of the Mayor and reply	215
Illuminations and arches	218
The levee	220
Osgoode Hall reception	233
The Cathedral and the Lord Bishop's sermon	236
The Prince in Toronto from an American view	244
Visit and return from Collingwood	249
Davenport and Weston	252
Thornhill and Richmondhill	252
King and Aurora	252
Newmarket and Holland Landing	252
Bradford, Barrie, Angus, and Sunnidale	253
Collingwood, and sail on the Georgian Bay	256
The Pittsburgh delegation	256
The fire-works in Toronto	257
Visit to the amphitheatre	260
The regatta	261
Inauguration of the park and address from Dr. McCaul and inscription	264
Review of Active Militia Force	268
Visit to University and address	269
Inauguration of Botanical Gardens, address and reply	272
Visit to the Normal School, address and reply	276
Visit to Knox's College	279
State dinner	279
The ball, and who he danced with	279
The Belleville address	283
The departure from Toronto	284
Brampton, the Credit, Georgetown, Guelph	288

Berlin, Petersburgh, and Stratford.. 288
London, address and reply.. 289
From an English view of his progress... 291
Sarnia, Municipal addresses and replies.. 297
Indian address and reply, with presentation of Indian curiosities........ 298
Artemius Ward's comic view.. 300
Ingersoll, Woodstock, Paris, Brantford... 304
Dunville, Colborne, Fort Erie, and Ottawa... 305
Arrival at Niagara Falls... 306
Militia order for assembling at Queenston Heights............................. 306
Illuminations at the Falls.. 307
Blondin's feat.. 308
Queenston Heights... 310
Militia Force—Committee... 311
    "   Veterans.. "
    "   Active Force... "
    "   Sedentary Force.. "
    "   Welland Companies.. "
Address on the Inauguration of Brock's Monument............................ 313
Niagara and his reception... 316
Port Dalhousie and his reception.. 317
St. Catharines   "   "   317
Address of the 5th Bat. Sedentary Militia.. 317
Hamilton and his reception... 319
The Levee, Exhibition, and Inauguration of Water Works................... 323
Address and reply of the Prince on leaving Hamilton for Detroit........ 326
English remarks... 329
Demonstrations at Windsor... 332
Reception in Detroit and address.. 333
Detroit to Chicago.. 336
In Chicago.. 338
Visit to a grain elevator.. 340
Departure and arrival at Dwight.. 343
The Prince as a sportsman.. 344
A French view of the Prince's visit... 345
At St. Louis—the fair.. 346
At Cincinatti—the ball... 351
At Pittsburgh—visits a coal mine.. 356
At Harrisburg... 359
Goes to Baltimore... 359
Reception at Washington by the President, and visit to the public
    buildings... 361
Trip to the South.. 368
The Tomb of Washington at Mount Vernon..................................... 369
Richmond.. 370
Return from thence... 370
Return to Baltimore and reception... 376
Visit to Philadelphia... 377
The opera... 382
Departure from Philadelphia and arrival at New York...................... 386
The review... 388
The Astor Library... 390
The ball... 392
Incidents of the visit... 400
Church services in New York... 400
New York to West Point... 403
West Point to Albany and Boston... 403

Boston to Portland and embarkation for England.................................. 418
English press on the visit 425
Incidents in the voyage and anxiety of the Queen............................ 426
Arrival at Plymouth.. 429
Remarks on the visit by His Grace the Duke of Newcastle................. 432
Letter from Lord Lyons, on behalf of Her Majesty the Queen, to President Buchanan and his Secretary's reply 433
Autographs of the Queen, &c., &c... 435
Concluding remarks 436

To

The Honourable Sir Allan Napier MacNab,

Colonel—Veteran Batallion,

Aid-de-Camp to Her Majesty the Queen,

This Upper Canadian Issue

of

The Prince's Tour

is respectfully dedicated.

Sir,

To you, as one of Her Majesty's Aid-de-Camps, I venture to presume to dedicate a compilation of the Tour of His Royal Highness in the North American Provinces. If it has any merit I shall feel much gratification in its publication—if otherwise, I shall deplore the introduction of your name; but, associated as you have been with the defence and legislation of Canada for nearly half a century, I venture to hope you will receive my compilation as a mark of deep respect.

THE COMPILER.

INTRODUCTORY REMARKS.

To those who have had the pleasure of witnessing the glorious and noble reception of our future King, it is needless to make any introductory remarks.

It is merely the object to compile, as accurately as possible, the most leading and correct representation of our Royal Guest's progress; and should omissions occur in it, it is hoped that no intentional neglect will be attributed to the compiler.

In after years, when the acclamation and excitement shall have gradually lulled, perhaps this memento of the ovation which has been paid to His Royal Highness, and through him to his Queen mother, may wile many a weary hour, and teach our children that the glorious institutions of England and Britain held sway yet, and dwelt in the hearts of their kindred equally in the British possessions as in the country of our cousins of the United States.

It would be an act of supererogation to make any concluding remarks to a compilation which has for its object a mere synopsis of the Prince's visit. The concluding remarks of our English journals as to the ovation shown is sufficient to exhibit how heartily the visit has been appreciated. It was a Canadian invitation, and a more glorious reception could not have been conceived.

Toronto, 4th Dec., 1860.

The invitation to visit Canada and the United States are necessarily introduced first, and are as follows :—

ADDRESS OF LEGISLATIVE ASSEMBLY.

MOST GRACIOUS SOVEREIGN,

We, your Majesty's most dutiful and loyal subjects, the Legislative Council and Assembly of Canada, in Provincial Parliament assembled, humbly approach your Majesty with renewed assurances of devotion and attachment to your Royal person and government.

We have long hoped that your Majesty would be graciously pleased to honour with your presence your Majesty's subjects in British North America, and to receive the personal tribute of our unwavering attachment to your rule ; and we trust, that, while your Majesty's presence would still more closely unite the bonds which attach this Province to the Empire, it would gratify your Majesty to witness the progress and prosperity of this distant part of your dominions.

The completion in 1860, of the Victoria Bridge, the most gigantic work of modern days, would afford to your Majesty a fitting occasion to judge of the importance of the Province of Canada ; while it would afford the inhabitants the opportunity of uniting in their expression of loyalty and attachment to the Throne and Empire.

We therefore most humbly pray that your Majesty will graciously deign to be present upon the occasion of the opening of the Victoria Bridge, with your Majesty's Royal Consort, and such members of your Majesty's august Family as it may please your Majesty to select to accompany you.

Legislative Council, 4th May, 1859.

This Address was presented to her Majesty by the Speaker of the House of Assembly, one of the gentlemen recently knighted by the Prince of Wales, Sir Henry Smith, and was most graciously responded to in the following terms :

Downing Street, *30th January*, 1860.

SIR,

As the two Houses of the Canadian Legislature will soon re-assemble for the despatch of business, it becomes my duty to inform you that the joint Address, to which they agreed at the close of their last Session, was duly presented to the Queen, and was most graciously received by Her Majesty.

In that Address, the Legislative Council and Commons of Canada earnestly pray the Queen to receive in person the tribute of their unwavering attachment to her rule, and to honour with her presence her subjects in British North America, upon the occasion of the opening of the great Victoria Bridge, accompanied by the Prince Consort and such members of the Royal Family as it may please Her Majesty to attend her on the occasion.

Her Majesty values deeply the attachment to her person, and the loyalty to her Crown which have induced this Address; and I am commanded to assure the Legislature, through you, how lively an interest is felt by the Queen in the growing prosperity of Canada, in the welfare and contentment of her subjects in that important Province of her Empire, and in the completion of the gigantic work which is a fitting type of the successful industry of the people.

It is therefore with sincere regret that Her Majesty is compelled to decline compliance with this loyal invitation. Her Majesty feels that her duties at the seat of the Empire prevent so long an absence, and at so great a distance, as a visit to Canada would necessarily require.

Impressed, however, with an earnest desire to testify to the utmost of her power her warm appreciation of the affectionate loyalty of her Canadian subjects, the Queen commands me to express her hope that when the time for the opening of the Bridge is fixed, it may be probable for His Royal Highness the Prince of Wales to attend the ceremony in Her Majesty's name, and to witness those gratifying scenes in which the Queen herself is unable to participate.

The Queen trusts that nothing may interfere with the arrangements, for it is Her Majesty's sincere desire that the young Prince, on whom the Crown of the Empire will devolve, may have the opportunity of visiting that portion of her dominions from which the address has proceeded, and may become acquainted with a people, in whose rapid progress towards greatness Her Majesty, in common with her subjects in Great Britain, feels a lively and enduring sympathy.

I have, &c.,
NEWCASTLE.

The invitation from the President of the United States forms a pleasing feature in this compilation, and is accordingly recorded; it is as follows :—

To HER MAJESTY QUEEN VICTORIA.

I have learned from the public journals that the Prince of Wales is about to visit your Majesty's North American dominions. Should it be the intention of His Royal Highness to extend his visit to the United States, I need not say how happy I should be to give him a cordial welcome to Washington. You may be well assured that every where in this country he will be greeted by the American people in such a manner as will prove gratifying to your Majesty. In this they will manifest their deep sense of your domestic virtues, as well as their convictions of your merits as a wise, patriotic and constitutional sovereign.

Your Majesty's most obedient servant,
- JAMES BUCHANAN.

Washington, 4th June, 1860.

REPLY.

Buckingham Palace, 22nd June, 1860.

MY GOOD FRIEND,

I have been much gratified at the feelings which prompted you to write to me, inviting the Prince of Wales to come to Washington. He intends to return from Canada through the United States, and it will give him great pleasure to have an opportunity of testifying to you in person that those feelings are fully reciprocated by him. He will thus be able, at the same time, to mark the respect which he entertains for the Chief Magistrate of a great and friendly State and kindred nation.

The Prince of Wales will drop all Royal state on leaving my dominions, and travel under the name of Lord Renfrew, as he has done when travelling on the continent of Europe.

The Prince Consort desires to be kindly remembered to you.

I remain ever your good friend,

VICTORIA R.

His Excellency Mayor Wood, on behalf of the Common Council of New York, through Mr. Dallas, the English Envoy, also conveyed an invitation to visit that city, and it was most graciously accepted. The details appear hereafter.

THE DEPARTURE FROM ENGLAND.

Osborne, 9th July, 1860.

This morning at 9 o'clock, their Royal Highnesses the Prince Consort and the Prince of Wales left Osborne to embark in the Royal yacht Victoria and Albert for Plymouth, where Her Majesty's ship Hero, Capt. Henry Seymour, is waiting to convey the Prince of Wales to Canada.

Her Majesty drove down to the Trinity-pier, East Cowes, with the Prince Consort and the Prince of Wales, accompanied by Princess Alice, Princess Louisa, Prince Arthur, and Prince Leopold, and attended by the Countess of Caledon and Major-Gen. the Hon. C. Grey.

The Prince Consort and the Prince of Wales embarked immediately, and the Royal yacht left Cowes Roads, for Plymouth.

The Prince Consort, attended by Colonel the Hon. A. Hardinge, is expected to return to Osborne to-morrow evening.

B

The suite which will accompany his Royal Highness the Prince of Wales to Canada, consists of the Duke of Newcastle, Secretary of State for the Colonies; Major-Gen. the Hon. R. Bruce, Governor to the Prince; Major Teesdale, R. A., and Captain George Grey, Equerries; Dr. Ackland and the Earl of St. Germains, Lord Steward of Her Majesty's household, who will join His Royal Highness at Plymouth.

Vice-Admiral Sir Charles Fremantle's Channel squadron, consisting of the flagship Royal Albert, 121, Capt. Henry T. Dacon; the Donegal, 101, Capt. Henry Broadhead; the Aboukir, 90, Capt. Douglas Curry; the Greyhound, 17, Capt. W. Sullivan; the Conqueror, 101, Capt. Edward S. Sotheby, C. B.; the Trafalgar, 90, Capt. Edward G. Fanshawe; the Centurion, 80, Capt. Henry G. Rogers, C. B.; the Edgar, 91, Capt. James E. Katon; the Algiers, 91, Capt. George W. D. O'Callaghan; the Mersey, 40, Capt. Henry Caldwell, C. B.; and the Diadem, 32, Capt. James H. Cockburn, under canvass only, with a smart breeze a little to the southward of east, hove in sight from Mount Wise at 8½ o'clock this morning in two lines. They then formed one line, and stood in for the port.

At half-past ten o'clock the ships were in succession, and away to the westward. Shortly after they came in sight more to the southward. Their funnels are ready for use. The only ship likely to enter the Sound is the Diadem, which is said to be short of fuel. The Earl of Mount Edgcumbe, in his steam-yacht, near the Royal William Victualling-yard, is waiting the approach of the Prince of Wales. The Hero continues inside the breakwater ready for sea, and arrangements are made for the expected departure of His Royal Highness to-morrow (Tuesday) morning. Her escort, the Ariadne, will probably take the Osborne in tow. The Flying Fish has gone on to Newfoundland.

Sir Charles Fremantle's squadron, which arrived off the port this morning, formed two lines, ranging about north and south, in the afternoon, to receive the Royal yacht, which hove in sight at 7 o'clock, and was saluted by the Impregnable and other ships in homage. On rounding the west end of the breakwater the yard-arms of the Hero, St. George, Emerald, and Ariadne, in the Sound, were manned, and the three last named and the Plymouth Citadal saluted. At 8½, when the Prince left the yacht to join the Hero, the Emerald and the Citadel repeated the compliment.

The weather is extremely fine, and thousands of the inhabitants were assembled on the heights.

The following account from an American paper may not be uninteresting as regards the titles of His Royal Highness, but as evincing that partiality of feeling afterwards shown him on his reception in the United States.

Albert Edward, heir apparent to the British Throne, was born at Buckingham Palace, on the 9th of November, 1841. He is, consequently, in his nineteenth year. His visit to this continent has naturally caused great interest, partly on account of its being the first visit ever paid by a Prince of Wales to the Great Republic, but more particularly by reason of the universal respect entertained by the American people for his mother, Queen Victoria. It has been the fate of few women placed in so elevated a position to receive so wide-spread a reputation for womanly virtues, and it would seem as though she had determined to train her children with as much care as she had been trained herself. The Prince of Wales, we understand, is every way worthy of his illustrious parent; of this we shall soon have an opportunity of judging for ourselves, since he will visit many of our large cities in the ensuing autumn. There can be no doubt of his receiving a reception due to his position and the great interests he represents.

The titles of the Prince of Wales are Duke of Saxony, Prince of Saxe-Coburg Gotha, Duke of Cornwall and Rothesay, Earl of Chester, Carrick, Dublin, Baron Renfrew and Lord of the Isles. These titles he derives partly by inheritance and partly from creation, from the circumstance of King Edward 1. having, in politic concession to the Welsh chieftains, created his heir " Prince of Wales," a few days after his birth, which took place in Caernarvon Castle. A few days afterwards he was created Earl of Chester, which title has been retained up to the present time. This was the unhappy Edward II. who was so barbarously murdered by Mortimer in Berkeley Castle. The Scottish titles of the Prince are derived from Robert III., in whose reign they were invested in the heir apparent of the Crown of Scotland. His Irish titles were conferred on the present Prince of Wales by Queen Victoria, on the 10th of September, 1849, in commemoration of her visit to Ireland. In the House of Lords he is known as the Duke of Cornwall.

Dod, the great authority on all these questions, thus defines the rank and position of the Prince of Wales. "The Prince of Wales has ever been regarded as the first subject in the realm, the nearest to the throne, the most dignified of the Peers of Parliament, and though not exercising any political power beyond his vote as a legislator, yet regarded by all men as the most eminent person in the State next after the sovereign." The Princes of Wales, previous to the present subject of this memoir, have, for more than a century, been all placed in false positions. Since the accession of the Georges they have invariably been in opposition to their father. The conduct of George IV. had sadly tarnished the high distinction; let us hope the present bearer of that title will redeem it.

The education of Albert Edward has been conducted under the immediate supervision of the Queen. In the languages, classics, natural philosophy, mathematics, jurisprudence and other branches, His Royal Highness has had the most eminent professors of the day, and it is stated that after his tour in America he will return to his studies at Oxford.

On the 9th of November, 1858, he was appointed Colonel, and a few days afterwards he was gazetted a Knight of the Garter.

He soon after went on a visit to Berlin, when, after remaining a few days with his sister, the Princess Frederick William of Prussia, he proceeded to Italy. Before he left England he took the first step in his official life, by presenting colours to the 100th Regiment, or Prince of Wales Royal Canadian Regiment of Foot, then stationed at Shorncliffe, near Folkestone.

Towards the end of January, 1859, the Prince of Wales arrived in Rome, and spent several weeks in exploring ancient and modern Rome. During his stay here he paid the Pope a visit, in company with Colonel Bruce, a circumstance which some of the Protestant divines, more especially the Scotch Presbyters, did not fail to animadvert upon it with considerable acerbity. The breaking out of the Italian war having changed the aspect of Europe, the Prince hastened his departure from the Eternal City, and he proceeded to Gibraltar, from thence to Spain and Portugal. He returned to England, June 25th, 1859. On his return he took up his residence in Oxford, to pursue his studies.

With that common sense which distinguishes the Queen, she has sent him to this continent, rightly judging that it is highly important for the future ruler of the British Empire to see with his own eyes the working of the great system on this side of the Atlantic.

On the 9th July, the Prince of Wales embarked at Davenport on board the Hero, ship of war, and sailed for America on the following morning.

St. John's, Newfoundland, July 17, 1860.

THE "OSPREY."

In order to secure an efficient communication with Newfoundland and a prompt delivery of the mails, matters have thus been arranged by the Imperial Government. The Cunard steamers, which each fortnight leave Boston, call at Halifax, where they connect with the *Osprey* for St. John's. The *Osprey* is a small screw steamer of about 150 tuns burthen ; built upon the model of the *Europa*—in fact a small edition of that noble vessel in all things save the paddle-wheels. She belongs to Messrs. Cunard, is well fitted up, and is a capital sea boat. On Thursday afternoon the sailing of the *Europa* from Boston was telegraphed, and about twelve o'clock, p.m., the gun from the citatdel announced that she had entered Halifax harbour. Upon the wharf a crowd of people were gathered awaiting her arrival ; gradually her huge form became more and more distinct, and soon she took her place near the little *Osprey*, which by the contrast appeared to lose half her size. The first thing accomplished was the landing of the mails. By a cart kept in readiness they were speedily conveyed to the post-office, the letters intended for Cape Breton and St. John's quickly sorted from the mass and brought down to the *Osprey*, which immediately proceeded on her voyage. The whole of the next day and night but little was seen of the land ; oftentimes it was completely out of sight, sometimes it was dimly visible, like a huge cloud upon the horizon.

It was not until Saturday morning, when Cape Breton was rounded and Sydney harbour made, that aught disctinctive of *terra firma* could be seen. Sydney is a small town situated on the eastern coast of Nova Scotia, on the eastern side of the south-west arm of the harbour. When Cape Breton was a separate colony, this was its capital, and the buildings in which the legislators of olden times used to make laws for the common welfare still stand. But with the annexation of Cape Breton to Nova Scotia, the glory of Sydney mainly departed. Some time ago there was an agitation for the repeal of the union ; and a strong feeling in favour of such a move still exists, but is not likely to be gratified.

The principal seat of trade is not Sydney itself, but North Sydney, five miles distant, and on the opposite side of the harbour, at which place all vessels desiring coal stop. At the very entrance to the harbour, on the north side, partially hidden by rising ground, are the mines. They are connected by a railway to the wharf for the convenience of loading. Being situated upon high ground, the road from the pits is a constant decline, so that there is no necessity for an engine to drag the waggons down. Once started, they run rapidly of themselves, their speed being checked by the application of large brakes, so constructed that a very great pressure can be immediately brought to bear upon them by the man in charge. The road is elevated about ten feet above the wharves for the convenience of loading vessels, an operation which is quickly effected. It is done in this way :—the ship having taken up a position indicated, a sort of drawbridge of immense strength is lowered from the track over her hold, but ten or twelve feet above. By the aid of boards a sort of huge tundish is constructed, tapering from underneath the bridge to the deck. A waggon load of coals, weighing three tons, is then brought down the track, and when opposite the end of the bridge, by the aid of a turn-table, turned round, run on to the bridge, and placed exactly above the vessel's hold. At a signal given, a trap door in the bottom of the waggon is opened, and the black mass tumbles into the cavity, raising a dust which flies high into the air, and blackens all within its reach. The process is repeated an indefinite number of times, until a sufficient cargo has been supplied. There were a large number of vessels in the harbour, almost all colliers. Lying in the bay, however, was a rakish-looking screw steamer, which turned out to be a French man-of-war. No one new her strength or her name, from whence she had come, or whither she was going. The Captain of the Osprey does not think much of her sailing qualities. He has passed her twice under easy steam, and would have done it on Friday a third time had she not altered her course for the north, for she steamed out of the harbour about an hour before the Osprey, but she was close on her heels, ere she had cleared the bay. Speed—eight knots an hour. But to return to the Sydney coal. The amount exported last year is estimated at about 100,000 tons, worth two dollars and a half per ton. There are three pits in operation, all belonging to the General Mining Association. They furnish employment to about eight hundred men, and confer great benefits upon the locality in which they are situated. Covering an area of 120 square miles, it will be some time before they are exhausted, while the position of Sydney is most advantageous for the trade.

But Cape Breton, though rich in minerals, by no means depends upon them alone for support. The country is well adapted for agriculture, and by means of the Bras d'or—so named, as by it admission is gained to a magnificent region—abundant water communication from the interior is supplied. A very large quantity of butter—several thousand pounds, and a considerable number of sheep, products of the neighboring farms, were shipped on board the Osprey for St. John's, Newfoundland. A great deal of fishing is carried on by the inhabitants.

In Cape Breton, it will be recollected, was once situated the celebrated fortress of Louisburg, founded by the French in 1720, taken from them—by John Bull,—in 1745, when it was blown to pieces—restored in 1749, and again taken in 1768. Haliburton says it was built at the cost of 30,000,000 livres, that when captured 220 pieces of cannon were found there, and that it cost $12,000 to destroy it. The remains indicate its circumference to have been about a mile and a quarter, instead of three miles, as is somewhere stated by a French writer, quoted by Mr. Justice Haliburton, and the harbour is not nearly so good as is generally believed. It is small and open to winds, which render it insecure. The British Government would appear to have done well in selecting Halifax in its stead as a *point d'appui*, a place more commandingly situated, and with a harbour capable of holding in perfect safety a larger fleet than has ever yet been got together.

And while upon this subject, it is as well to speak of St. Pierre, and Mr. Haliburton's elongated story about the French fortifications there. We are informed upon very good authority that the statements made by the parent of Samuel Slick, are as exaggerated as any ever emitted from the mouth of the celebrated clock-maker. The formidable fortifications resolve themselves into two earthwork batteries, containing eighty-six four pounders, and four guns of smaller calibre. When Lord John Russell was questioned upon this subject in the house, he stated that the French, in erecting those batteries, had not broken the treaty. The matter had been submitted to the Attorney-General, and, in his opinion, no solid ground for complaint existed. By what curious course of reasoning the learned gentleman arrived at such a conclusion, many were puzzled to think, as the treaty is very definite, and when Lord John Russell did not condescend to enlighten the house, he required that his *ipse dixit* should be accepted, and accepted it was. But the explanation, is this. The "enormous fortifications" were erected during the Russian war, with at least the tacit consent of the British Government, the French pleading that if they left St Pierre exposed, their men of war being employed in the Mediterranean, it was possible that either Russian ships, or enterprising Yankee privateers, would annoy fishermen and their miserable town. Surely in such a case as this, the British Government did well to allow the matter to pass over quietly. Our great ally has but few colonies to protect, but he does well jealously to guard those that he has—even St. Pierre, which the British in their magnanimity presented to France after having taken the whole of North America from her. The garrison of this redoubtable place consists of four *gens d' armes* who fire salutes. There is not even a ditch to render the batteries less easy of assault, and, besides, the guns are so placed that while they afford adequate protection to the ships in the harbour, the batteries might easily be shelled from an outside point upon which the cannon cannot, from their position, be brought to bear. Then again, there are no large depots of coal in the island. The place from which the French would lay in a supply of black diamonds is Sydney, but from the people there, they have only taken sufficient for current use, and visitors to the island have seen nothing at all confirmatory of Mr.

Haliburton's allegations. The naval force at present on the station consists of a ten-gun brig; but a forty-gun frigate is soon to be placed there instead, the reason for this addition being that the extent of present means does not permit the exercise of that hospitality the Emperor deems desirable, and accommodation is therefore to be increased. Of course we are bound to believe our honourable ally, but if any other than a Frenchman offered such an excuse, one might be tempted to imagine he was not telling the precise truth. St. Pierre itself is described as one of the most miserable, dirty places under the sun; owning between two hundred and fifty and three hundred fishing smacks, principally engaged in catching cod. Detailed and precise particulars upon these points will doubtless be in the possession of the British Government ere long, as H. M. S. Cossack returned to Halifax last week from the debatable island.

From Sidney to St. John's nothing was seen of the land, until on Monday evening the harbour was entered of the latter place; for a thick fog enveloped all things. During the night it was impossible to see the length of the vessel, and the utmost caution was needed in traversing so dangerous a coast. On Sunday morning Cape Race was rounded, the lead being constantly used, many stoppages of the vessel as a consequence taking place. During a great part of the voyage, a head wind considerably impeded progress, but the cape once turned the vessel went on quickly enough.

Few harbours have a more beautiful or grander entrance than St. John's. The coast is exceedingly bold, a succession of hills rising precipitously from the water, stretching away to the north and south, until they are lost in the far distance. The bay proceeds inwardly due west for a short distance, and then takes a sudden turn towards the south-west. Both sides of the harbour are hedged in by high hills, which thus form a natural wall of the most gigantic proportions. As they near the terminus of the south-western arm of the harbour, they gradually lessen in height, and approach each other until they form a *cul-de-sac*, which soon verges into the plain beyond. The height of the citadel of Quebec above the water, is estimated at three hundred and forty feet; the height of a small fort on the north side of St. John's harbour is about eight hundred feet.

C

The rock is perpendicular, and the fort, being placed at the bend of the bay, commands both the entrance to the harbour, the harbour itself, and the town upon its banks. Besides this, other batteries are placed among the rocks, from which a concentrated fire would issue if required. There are few guns mounted—but few are wanted. The channel is only about one-sixth of a mile across at the entrance. It widens a little towards the centre, and then decreases towards the Pancake Rock and Chain Rock; it measures but one hundred and ninety yards. In time of war a chain would connect these two points, in order to prevent the entrance of a hostile fleet into the harbour. The town of St. John's is situated on the west side of the south-western branch of the harbour. The hills upon which it is built are less steep than those on the opposite side, but, nevertheless, the streets which run up from the wharves, have only just sufficient of a decline to permit of them being scaled without the feat being boasted of as requiring much skill and firmness of nerve.

The principal thoroughfare is Water Street, which runs parallel to the shore, following its indentations, and, therefore, extremely irregular. It resembles, in some particulars, the Front Street of Toronto. It is a considerable height above the water, but between it and the wharves, on what was once an esplanade, numerous houses, stores, and extensive warehouses have been built, monopolising every inch of available ground. Most of the houses are of brick and stone. In this, the principal street, few of wood are seen, but higher up the hill they abound. One of the principal objects which strikes the eye when entering the bay, is the Roman Catholic Cathedral, an immense stone building. The Episcopal Cathedral, near by, is a less pretentious edifice. As yet it is only half finished; but when completed will be cruciform in shape, and Gothic in style. So far, $120,000 has been expended upon it. On the opposite side of the harbour to that upon which the main portion of St. John's stands, is a continuous row of houses built at the foot of the hill, and supplied with wharves. On the hills themselves not a tree is to be seen, the slate rock being too near the surface to permit of much cultivation.* Here and there, however, some industrious Newfoundlander has turned what soil there is to as profitable use as may be, and detached squares of a few acres each, carefully railed in, attest the fact that potatoes and grass may there be raised. The remaining and main portions of the hills show nothing except the hard rocks of which they are composed, or a carpet of stunted trees, so small, that from the opposite side of the harbour it is easy to mistake them for a coating of moss. Past the surrounding wall nothing can be seen. There is no opening by which a glimpse of the country beyond can be obtained; nothing but the hills, the harbour, and the town are visible. No better place for founding a Utopia could be selected. The harbour is, as it were, at the bottom of a huge dish; the town is on a narrow ledge running round the harbour, and those who wish to get out of it would have to climb the sides, did not the entrance from the sea furnish an easier method.

The wharves are crowded with the shipping of all nations. Many vessels come here from the Catholic countries of Europe to procure fish, and the Spaniards who visit Newfoundland for that purpose supply in exchange pure Oporto wine—or rather the purest Oporto wine to be met with on this side of the Atlantic.

In the town the smell of codfish prevails to a most disagreeable extent. It hangs alike upon the wings of the softest zephyr, and most blustering boreas. It haunts cool retreats and shaded nooks. It adds additional noisomeness to the smells of the streets, and occasionally bursts upon the olfactory nerves with an intensity which might give rise to the suspicion that the concentrated essence of the billions of codfish murdered by man was stinking in ghostly revenge. On both sides of the entrance to the harbour, on the side of the harbour itself, and by the sides of the "coves" —as the entrances to the wharves are called—acres of slaughtered cod lie drying. There they are, as Titus said of the marble palaces of Jerusalem—"terrace o'er terrace;" and the supply seems inexhaustible. In a small bay formed by the receding coast, at the outside entrance of the harbour, covering an area not larger, if as large, as Toronto bay, were counted one hundred and fifty fishing boats, their crews actively at work hauling up cod with astonishing rapidity. What can be done with them all, is almost as great a miracle as that so many should exist.

PREPARATIONS FOR THE RECEPTION.

Among the numerous wharves which line the shore, is one belonging to the Government, at which His Royal Highness the

Prince of Wales will land. Upon it seats, calculated to accommodate four hundred and fifty persons, have been erected. I say "calculated"—but if four hundred and fifty persons are to sit there, crinoline will have to be prohibited, with a certainty of rebellion among the female population. A fine sight that will be for the Prince. Passing through the iron gates into Water Street, His Royal Highness will proceed to the east road, and in due course find himself underneath a triumphal arch of lichens and spruce, surmounted by a monster plume nine feet in height. The arch springs from two large circular columns, composed of a number of round poles covered with moss. In various parts painted shields appear, bearing the Royal arms, the arms of Newfoundland, and the quarterings of the Prince. A short distance from this spot a large arcade is in course of erection. It consists of a number of flag-staffs, ranged at a distance of about fifteen feet from each other, in the form of an oblong square, connected together by arches of evergreens. From the top of the poles flags will float, and various bright coloured ornaments, such as wreaths and festoons of flowers, natural and artificial, will give their briliancy to the arrangements. Beyond the arcade is a second arch, at the head of Cockrane Street, near the entrance to Government House. It is forty-four feet high, and while built of similar materials to the one previously mentioned, is of a superior design. There is one large central Gothic arch, 44 feet high, and a small one on each side. The pillars are square, and rise above the other portions of the structure.

This passed, the Prince will enter Government House, the residence of Sir Alexander Bannerman, the present governor of Newfoundland. It is an oblong building, principally of a dark-coloured stone, upon a foundation of granite, very plain in appearance, and not unlike the old Parliament buildings in Toronto, but the wings less extended. The cost is said to have been $200,000,—about three times the value of such a building in Canada. The grounds around are nicely laid out, and planted with trees, among which are some lilacs in full bloom (we have not got past the lilacs yet here) which shine conspicuously. Circling the grounds is a sort of promenade—a wide foot-path, protected by white palisades, having a very neat appearance. One room alone in the Government House has been refitted for the Royal visitor'. The furniture was imported from New York, and cost $800. Close by are the provincial buildings, of a white stone found in the island. They are nearly square, with six large circular columns in front supporting the gable end of a slanting roof. The entrance door is gained by ascending a very handsome flight of steps, which lead into the grand atrium—as I suppose an architect would call it. From the hall rises a double staircase, terminating in a gallery, out of which the doors of the different Government offices open. Over the door is a niche for a statue, not yet occupied—doubtless an object of anxiety to the youth of the island. The chambers of the Assembly and Council are on opposite sides of the first floor. There is nothing particular in their appearance. The House of Assembly is at present denuded of its furniture, and is being fitted up as a refreshment room. The walls are stone-coloured, and the ceiling is almost without ornament. The chamber of the Upper House remains undisturbed. It is furnished with elegant walnut chairs covered with red satin, and presents a very respectable appearance. A portrait in oil of Governor Darling, during whose stay here responsible government was inaugurated, hangs from the wall. Over the Speaker's chair is a print of Her Majesty in her coronation robes. An active politician was asked how many members there were in the Legislative Council. He said fifteen was the right number, but the seats were never filled, as the Governor found it necessary to preserve a few vacancies, that he might, when occasion required, harmonise the Upper with the Lower House.—Not long ago, for this purpose, three members were added. Rather curious, but certainly an effectual mode of proceeding, and one which appears to be taken so much as a matter of course that I was afraid to express surprise, lest I should be accused of ignorance. On the outside of the building a wooden ball-room is in course of erection. It is to contain twelve hundred people. The inside is hung with calico of various colours; the roof is being covered with moss, and a large quantity of artificial flowers (the Receiver General's room full) will be arranged in divers patterns upon the walls and ceiling. The whole will be lighted with gas. The House of Assembly, as already mentioned, is to serve as a refreshment room—in other words, a supper is to be given, and champagne is to flow freely; but it is not to be called a supper, or a dinner, not even a luncheon, only a "refreshment," because it is thought if Victoria Regina should hear of her son dining out, she would discharge the Palmerston ministry, consequent upon the Colonial Secretary, the Duke of Newcastle, permitting such a breach of her orders.

St. John's is a happy city. Although possessing upwards of thirty thousand inhabitants, it is not yet incorporated, municipa affairs being managed by a committee under the control of the Board of Works. What a happy condition of society! No aldermen, no city councilmen, and, as a consequence, few police— only fourteen. But my reason for mentioning the fact, is to notice that there is no mayor here to show his self-denial—as all the Canadian mayors are going to do—by declining the honour of knighthood.

But though not possessed of a mayor and corporation, it has volunteer militia companies, three in number, and each sixty in strength. They have been raised for the occasion, and will be ready to perform the arduous duties that will devolve upon them —if their uniforms are ready. Two companies have been supplied, and the tailors are working hard at the clothes wanted by the third. Then there is the Royal Newfoundland Company, numbering two hundred and fifty men. This corps is composed of volunteers from the line; well conducted men, who have been quartered in Canada, and who are allowed to complete the term of service for which they have enlisted, here. It is not required of them that they should have served fourteen years before they can enter; a good character and a vacancy is all that is necessary. By this means younger men than those who serve in the Canadian Rifles are secured—better soldiers they cannot be. The militia and the volunteers together, then, will form a respectable force to receive His Royal Highness, and with the aid of national societies, add to a procession of considerable length.

July 19*th.*

A notice appears in the Royal *Gazette* announcing that the following gentlemen will be required to meet His Royal Highness at the wharf, namely:—The Right Reverend Edward Field, D.D., Lord Bishop of Newfoundland; the Right Reverend Thomas Mallock, D.D., Roman Catholic Bishop of St. John's;

Chief Justice the Hon. Sir Francis Brady; the members of the Executive Council; Hon. L. O'Brien, President; Hon. Geo. J. Hoghbett, Attorney-General; Hon. John Kent, Colonial Secretary; Hon. Thomas Glen, Receiver-General; Hon. Edmund Hanrahan, Surveyor General; Hon. J. J. Rogerson, Hon. Edward D. Shea, and the Hon. George H. Emerson, Master in Chancery, and holding by Her Majesty's patent the rank and precedence of an Executive Councillor; the Members of the Legislative Council; the Speaker of the House of Assembly, with such Members as may think proper to be present; Major J. J. Grant, Royal Newfoundland Company, and the Officers of the Garrison; the Garrison Chaplain, the Rev T. M. Wood; the Archdeacon, the Venerable Henry Martyn Lower, M.A.; the Foreign Consuls; the Clerk of the House of Assembly, Mr. John Stuart; and finally, the Stipendiary Magistrates of St. John's Messrs. A. Peter, W. Carter, and Thomas Bennett. Here then we have the names of the *elite* of the Island.

NEWFOUNDLAND MINERALS.

Among the more worthy objects of note which exist in St John's, is a cabinet of minerals, principally copper ores, collected in Newfoundalnd, by Mr. Frederick N. Gisborne, the well known electric telegraph engineer and pioneer. The richest of these copper specimens, consisting of gray sulphurets, peacock and yellow sulphurets, have been discovered in amygdaloidal trap. One mine, "Turk's Head," near Brigus Conception Bay, owned principally by Mr. Gisborne, and the Hon. Charles F. Bennett, an old established and enterprising merchant of St. John's, now yields fair returns. A newly discovered copper lode near Placentia, (grey sulphuret in calc, spar and slate), also looks promising. Another mine, (galina in calc, spar and metamorphic slate,) owned by the Newfoundland Telegraph Company, yielded $80,000 worth of lead in two years; but work there is now temporarily suspended, in consequence of some dispute about the property. The Terra Nova Mining Company are also working a large deposit of mundic, with some yellow copper intermingled, in Green Bay, the ore being there in any quantity, if the quality will answer.

Mr. Gisborne is now engaged in making a thorough exploration of the coast and interior, the many indications of copper, silver, and lead, being satisfactory evidence that a persevering search may eventually be well rewarded. The Colonial Government have had it in contemplation to assist Mr. Gisborne in these researches, and it is generally thought no wiser expenditure of the public money could be made, for Newfoundland requires something beyond the fisheries to ensure the future welfare of her increasing labouring population, while at the same time there appears to be but one opinion as to the most fitting person to perform the duty of exploration.

The interior of Newfoundland is exceedingly rugged for forty or fifty miles inland, and in general is covered with dense— almost impenetrable woods of small spruce, juniper, and birch. Countless lakes, ranging from a few hundred yards to fifty or sixty miles in length, are interspersed here and there, while deep gulches or ravines traverse the land. The rivers are mountain torrents; fierce and violent after long continued rains, but generally comparatively shallow in their beds, not only in consequence of the rocky nature of the country, but also from a deep covering of moss which everywhere clothes the land, which retains and but *gradually* parts with its moisture. Further inland vast barrens and marshes of brilliant hues dotted with clumps of trees like an English park, but upon a much grander scale, small lakes and picturesque waterfalls make up the scene, while further north dense spruce woods exist and almost defy progress. Large herds of migrating deer, (of the reindeer species,) wolves, bears, beaver, and other fur-bearing animals frequent the country; ptarmigan or Arctic grouse, hares of large size, salmon, and an endless variety of trout furnish good sport in their respective seasons and localities. Black flies and mosquitoes are also abundant. It was through four hundred miles of such wilderness as this that Mr. F. N. Gisborne undertook to plant the electric telegraph, which now connects Newfoundland with Canada and the United States. On the 2nd of September, 1851, he took his departure from St. John's, accompanied by six men, he and they each carrying from 60 to 70 lbs. weight of provisions, guns, &c. Quite a number of people assembled to witness the departure of the expedition, never expecting again to see the members thereof. On the 4th of December, after a desperate season of rain and snow, Mr. Gisborne accomplished the journey. He arrived at the western extremity of the island with two Indians in company. The white men he had started with had been replaced by six Indians before half the journey was accomplished; but of these, four deserted. Of the remaining two, one died from fatigue a few days afterwards; the other, though he survived for a time, gradually sunk. The people of Newfoundland, as a mark of their appreciation of Mr. Gisborne's service, presented him with a beautiful piece of plate which cost $1,200.

There are two peculiarities about St. John's especially deserving of remark. I suppose no man ever landed from a steamer on any wharf in Canada or the United States, or stepped from a railway car on to any platform who had not immediately made to him numerous offers of assistance from hotel runners and enterprising cab-drivers. They swarm about the traveller like a myriad of wasps. They carry off carpet bags and portmanteaus in as many different directions as there are carpet bags and portmanteaus to carry off. They proclaim in loud tones, or make known in whispers, scented with whiskey and tobacco, that the hotel to which they owe particular allegiance is the very best in the city, town or village, as the case may be. They bewilder and bully, flatter or swear, as suits their several tempers, and give cause for much thankfulness when escape from them is effected. At least, that is the feeling generally entertained. Here we have the opposite extreme. The steamers came up to the wharf—not a solitary jarvey is to be seen. Nothing is heard of the hotels—not a runner shows his nose. The men belonging to the vessel place your luggage on the quay, and you are assured that it will be sent for from the hotel. Not feeling satisfied, you leave a friend to guard his and yours, and go seek for a cab. But you seek in vain. If you want a vehicle, you must give notice of your want at the stable, and in due course a light waggon will be at your service. Unable to find a cab, you have recourse to a solitary dray seen passing along the street, the driver of which being induced to go to the wharf, conveys your luggage and that of your fellow passengers—for they are all happy to receive his assistance—safely, but slowly, to the hotel.

The second peculiarity of St. John's is the absence of boards giving the names of the streets, but they are not christened.

D

This is a characteristic belonging exclusively to Constantinople; but the reason given for the neglect, though it may be satisfactory to the residents here, is by no means so to strangers. It is, that all the St. Johns' folks know the streets well enough without names. Taking these two things together, you would be apt to form a far worse opinion of the city than it deserves; and when mention is made that it has scarcely any sidewalk, and these constructed by the people opposite whose premises they are made—in patches along the thoroughfares—people will certainly condemn it as a place unfit for civilized beings to live in. Still, as a whole, it is far better than could be expected. The roads, being on the rock, are good; the principal street (Water-street) has no wooden buildings, but many stores of large size and business-like appearance. There is plenty of paint upon the houses, and very few pigs in the streets. Cows, fowl, and horses, without their owners, are never seen in the King-street of St. John's. A few years since it was an offence for a man to repair a chimney or to build a house in the place. The imperial government did every thing they could to discourage settlement upon the shores of Newfoundland. But, by-and-bye, they were obliged to give way, and, in spite of the opposition which pressed so heavily upon it, St. John's has at length risen to riches and greatness. It is now a growing and exceedingly promising city.

Although there are many vessels lying in the harbour, there are but few compared with the number that will be here a few weeks hence. It is not until the middle of August that the fishermen upon distant parts of the coast bring in their fish for exportation. Then they flock by thousands to St. John's, and are met by numerous ships from the West Indies and the Mediterranean. The returns of last year's trade are not yet printed, so that those of 1858 are alone available. In that year the revenue raised from customs amounted to £88,935. The principal items were as follows:—Ale in casks, 104,938 gallons; duty, 9d. the gallon. Bread and biscuit, 66,550 cwt.; duty, 3d. Butter, 5,920 cwt.; duty 3s. Chocolate and cocoa, 16,128 lbs.; duty 1d. Coffee, 217,624 lbs.; duty 1d. Fruit, 189,203 lbs.; duty 10 per cent. *ad valorem;* duty raised, £738, giving a value of £7,880. Molasses, 719,637 gallons; duty 2½d. Salt, 49,808 tons; duty 6d. the ton. Brandy, gin and rum, 166,653 gallons;

duty 4s. Refined sugar, 1,466 cwt., duty 12s. Unrefined sugar, 13,307 cwt.; duty 7s. 6d. the cwt. Wine—port, 4,500 gallons; duty 5s.; sherry, 1,147 gallons; value, £419. Barley and oats, copper, copper sheeting, bars, bolts and nails, medicines, oakum, poultry and fresh meat. are subject to a duty of 10 per cent. *ad valorem;* and other wares not specially mentioned, to a duty of five per cent., under which latter head come cottons, cloths, and general hardware. Of the ten per cent. the value entered in 1858 was £93,431; of the five per cents., £299,163. The following table exhibits the value of the imports and exports for five years:—

	Imports.	Exports.
1854	£ 964,527	£1,019,572
1855	1,152,084	1,142,212
1856	1,271,604	1,338,797
1857	1,413,432	1,651,171
1858	1,172,862	1,318,836

The exports consist mainly of fish, forwarded principally to Catholic countries. Below is given a return of the number and tonnage of vessels entered from and cleared for each country, at ports in Newfoundland, in the year 1858:—

	ENTERED.		CLEARED.	
	No.	Tons.	No.	Tons.
United Kingdom	201	39,067	129	21,459
British Possessions	683	67,472	708	84,589
Denmark	3	538	1	198
Hamburg	32	5,305	...	......
Spain	147	20,937	72	8,850
Portugal	64	7,959	67	7,832
Italy	1	153	27	2,744
Sicily	...	......	1	75
Greece	...	......	1	105
Ionian Islands	...	......	1	131
United States	188	30,637	90	15,854
French Colonies	35	1,129	4	151
Spanish Colonies	30	3,713	32	4,980
Danish Colonies	1	286	...	......
Brazil	55	10,904	139	28,641
Total	1,440	188,100	1,266	175,699

The Spanish vessels coming here bring large supplies of fruit and vegetables. The hotels are supplied with potatoes grown in Spain; even the cabbage placed upon the table comes from the country of the Dons. And as the animal food is mainly imported, living, you may be sure, is rather expensive. Mutton fit for the table is worth from 9d. to 1s. per ℔.; beef 8d. to 10d.; flour, best quality, 45s. per brl; potatoes 25s. per barrel—as much as 40s. has been paid within the last four days; cabbage (Spanish) 1s. each; butter 1s. to 1s. 6d. per ℔.; eggs 1s. 3d. to 1s. 6d. per dozen.

St. John's, Newfoundland, Monday, July 23rd.

From papers brought by the *North Briton*, we learn that the Prince of Wales left for this place on the morning of the 10th, as the weather so far has been exceedingly favourable, we should no be at all surprised if the Royal fleet were signalled early to-morrow morning. Every body is in a state of suspense, and each time the flag announcing an arrival is hoisted, a rumour spreads through the town that the squadron is at length in sight. What remains of the preparations yet to be completed is hurried forward as rapidly as can possible be. Business—except in the coloured calico shops—is entirely suspended—the cod are left for a time to roam the seas in peace. The merchants instead of remaining behind the counters are busy fixing flag staffs and arranging bunting. The fishermen are all in town, the sailors belonging to the different vessels in the harbour, their preparations completed, are roaming about the streets. On Saturday there were fifteen meetings of societies to make final arrangements for the part they are to take in the procession, and this evening there are to be about fifteen more. The natural staid and sober character of British-blooded folk is quite lost—a French excitability of temperament has taken its place. Stages from which to view the procession are being erected in every available corner, and numerous placards announcing the accommodation to be had, are seen in every street.

The Attorney-General, the Hon. George Hoghbett, was seen the other day erecting his own flag staff by the aid of his own arms, and rumour has it that another high functionary was seen washing with soap and water a union jack which had done duty in former years, and which is now to do duty again. Nothing is thought of, nothing is talked of, nothing deemed worthy of note except those things which appertain to the reception of the Royal visitor.

What's that. The squadron in sight. Somebody has felt it necessary to fall down stairs—everybody is falling down stairs! "The Prince has come!" "Nonsense! It's the *Golden Fleece* from New York." No, it's the Prince, for from the flag staff on the high hill yonder wave the signals which denote the appearance of men-of-war. It must be a hoax. Surely it must be; and yet—why there's a policeman running! And there's—why there's not a man walking at an ordinary pace. But some are turning back. Why? Oh! it's another hoax. A French man-of-war and the *Golden Fleece* have been signalled. Indeed! But the *Flying Fish* would not run up her colours for that. It must be the Prince. "But," urges an obstinate one, "there's the Frenchman with the tricolour flying." "Well, he is *in* the harbour, so the signals cannot be up for him." Yes, it *must* be the Prince. No one doubts it now. The throng of people increases—the streets are "crammed." Everybody is treading upon everybody else's toes.

The Governor is at the Queen's wharf. He is bothered terribly. People make as free with him as they would were he an elected president. He has evidently been hurried like all the rest. He is a fine old man, nearly eighty years of age, still active, and "in the full enjoyment of all his faculties,"—a peculiarity to be noted in a Governor of the present day. But he is annoyed. The preparations are not all completed. Copious pinches of Scotch snuff he takes to himself while thinking; as a Yankee "whittles" a stick while talking. "But," says one, "the Governor migʰᵗ have written to the Duke to ask for delay. Of course the Prince won't land. Why our windows are not washed yet, and the arches are not completed—and the candles are not cut—and our flags are not up—and a thousand reasons of equal importance render it impossible that the Prince should land to-night! But still,—has the Prince come? Yes,—most decidedly:

There goes Capt. Orlebar and the little steamer to pilot in the Royal vessels, now seen in the distance opposite the entrance to the harbour.

The best view will be attained from the block-house, high on the hill above, where the cliff bends over the Narrows, from which a stone may be dropped on to the deck of a ship passing beneath. The summit is far away, and reached only by a precipitous road, but a good one of hard rock. By the aid of a reckless Irish driver, full of loyalty—and whiskey—the top is soon gained. A glorious scene is the reward. Down in the hollow lies the town and harbour, the house tops glittering with flags; the ships dressed out in their gayest colours; every yard manned with sailors; hundreds of little boats flitting about the harbour hoisting their flags too, while far away to the north stretches mile upon mile of undulating land, the white lines of the roads distinctly seen winding along the valleys, or here and there, crossing the very summits of the hills. Small lakes, too, dot the expanse, and neat country residences pop out from the midst of the trees with which, by much care and great patience, they have been surrounded. Eastward lies the mighty Atlantic, and overhead shines as bright a sun as ever adorned the vault of Heaven since the fiat which created it went forth. Right! A good view of the vessels is gained from the hill. They have furled all their sails, and lie nearly motionless waiting for the pilot who is rapidly approaching. The *Hero* is nearest the harbour, but both ships are close together, the bow of the *Ariadne*, as would appear from the land, nearly touching the port side of her companion. They are still too far off to enable us to see what is being done upon deck, but the pilot boat has neared the *Hero*, and they will soon make for the harbour. There they are under way,—the *Hero* leading; the *Ariadne* following in her wake.

Gradually their huge bulk grows more distinct; gradually the forms of moving things on deck become visible. And now by the aid of a glass an officer in uniform can be seen. A little later and a group in plain clothes is made out; still a little later and there, between two gentlemen, is a young man whom we take to be the Prince. We become sure of this in a few moments, and the people, they were not many, assembled upon the hill, lift their hats and give forth a vigorous hurrah, lost, alas! to Royalty, for it is unheard in the depths below. But a louder, if not a more beautiful token of welcome is in course of preparation. At the guns upon one of the batteries below stand the gunners, ready at the word of command to set match to powder. It is not long delayed.

The *Hero* has entered the Narrows and a Royal salute of twenty-one guns is thundered forth ; the sound rolling and tumbling, rattling and reverberating among the hills, until so much noise is made that even the "good Queen Bess" herself, fond of noise as she was, would have been amply satisfied. The sailors then man the yards, up they go, one after the other, the supply seemingly inexhaustible, until every spar has its compliments of blue jackets. A French man-of-war lying in the harbour, the *Sesostris*, H. M. B. screw the *Flying Fish* follow the example thus set, and all get ready for a "rousing" cheer. Meanwhile, those who know well the harbour, become nervous. Where is the *Hero* going ? Why right into the Merlin rock—where many a vessel has struck and sunk. But all is safe. Within the last few days that rock has been so blasted that there are now twenty-seven feet of water over it, and none need fear it longer. A little further on lies a raft which has been used by the workmen employed in reducing the rock. To a vessel of ordinary size it would be an obstacle ; but the *Hero* glides over it majestically ; and the broken, smashed, splintered timbers which rise from under her stern tell which of the two have had the worst in the encounter.

Down in the city the excitement increases : all St. John's is out of doors. But there is in reality little crowding. The streets running lengthways along the shore form a series of terraces, each one of which commands a view of the harbour, and there is scarcely a house roof or upper window from which the ships cannot be seen.

At ten minutes after seven the squadron dropped anchor in North American waters. The sailors sent up a cheer from the shrouds, enthusiastically answered by tens of thousands of voices, from vessels in the harbour, from the streets, from the houses, and from the hills. It commenced in the west and travelled east ; it was wafted through the air by the evening breeze, and was echoed loudly from the opposite shore. It was such a cheer as can only be given by a people who render a free and sincere homage to the son of a much-loved and venerated Queen. Money could not purchase it ; hypocrisy could not have uttered it. It was the heartfelt tribute of a grateful and a contented people. So ended the day which witnessed the entry of the Prince into Newfoundland waters.

But something more remains to be said. Rather a funny affair occurred when the pilot steamer set out from the wharf. Two pilots were on board, both of whom were desirous of proceeding to the *Hero* with Captain Orlebar, R. N., to bring in the Prince. While the back of that gentleman was turned, they commenced quarrelling, and from words soon came to blows, selecting as the scene of their operations upon one another a paddle-box of the steamer. One of the combatants was popped into a boat and sent ashore—the pair may fight out the quarrel at their leisure.

From enquiries made, I learn that the Prince has had a very rough voyage. The wind, which I noted above as favourable for crossing the Atlantic, proves to have been heavier than was to be desired, and the *Hero* has consequently been knocked about a good deal. But, as befits the future monarch of Great Britain, His Royal Highness is a capital sailor, and has suffered little annoyance from the waves. During the last three days of the journey, however, the vessels were enveloped in a thick fog, and this alone made those on board right glad to see the land.

The Prince repeatedly expressed his delight at the beauty of the harbour, which, to some extent indeed, seemed to take all by surprise. When the request of the Lieutenant-Governor was made known to him, that the landing should not take place until to-morrow, he immediately acceded to it. He was plainly dressed in a felt hat and black clothes, not the least attempt at display being manifest.* Soon after the anchor dropped, the sun set behind the hills, and naught was seen of the Royal vessels save the lights which shone from her masts and through her numerous port-holes.

But the people were not satisfied. If they could not see the Prince they were determined to see something else, and, instead of returning home to bed there to refresh themselves for the morrow, they hung about the streets and sang songs and fired crackers, and drank healths and gave themselves up to a general unmitigated "spree." The Colonial buildings were illuminated with numerous lanterns, and from the roof very many fire rockets were discharged. From the lofty towers of the Catholic Cathedral, on ropes reaching to the ground, descending at an angle of about forty-five degrees, coloured lamps were suspended, and a

---

*Note—Likeness in plain clothes in consequence.

magnificent peal of bells sounded forth the notes of welcome. Passage along the streets was by no means pleasant for nervous folk. Imagine the celebrating ten thousand Queen's birthdays concentrated into one, and you will have an idea of the amount of crackers, squibs, serpents, wheels, back-rapers, and rockets fired off. Until a late hour in the night, or rather until an early hour in the morning, the noise made furnished abundant evidence that St. John's had not, in its own opinion, fully celebrated the arrival of His Royal Highness.

Comment upon the disappointment which was felt by many whose arrangements were not complete is useless.

July 24.

During the night workmen were engaged all through the town, carrying out as rapidly as possible preconceived designs. For some hours they made fair progress, and hope was entertained that before the morning broke every arch would be adorned with its full compliment of boughs, flags, and garlands fittingly arranged.

But an unlooked-for calamity put an end to such pleasurable anticipations. The day had been fine. When the sun had set scarce a cloud was to be seen in the sky, and to those not of the prophet species, or who were unpossessed of barometrical corns, every thing betokened the continuance of fine weather. St. John's retired to rest, feeling assured that the next day would be as fine as the one which preceded it. Never was a greater mistake made. Scarcely had the twelve o'clock bells rung when the rain descended in torrents. It poured down with as little hesitation as it would have done had the Prince not been there. Ladies who had carefully laid out nice new bonnets and light summer robes, that they might be ready to slip on or jump into, in the shortest possible space of time, heard with disgust the pattering on the window panes, and sighed, as they thought of the opportunity lost for the exhibition of their charms. The triumphal arch manufacturers retired within doors, leaving behind them skeleton proofs of their good intentions, and all who were awake agreed that the best thing they could do was to go to sleep, hoping that before long the rain would cease, being per-

E

fectly convinced that it could not last for ever. The hour at which the disembarkation would take place had not been fixed. When, however, the morning sun did manage to penetrate the thick strata of cloud and fog which hung in dense masses upon the hills, hiding them from view, large placards were discovered announcing that His Royal Highness had been pleased to name ten o'clock as the time. About nine o'clock, the rain which had previously been continuous, abated somewhat, and by degrees ceased. Thousands upon thousands of loyal people of St. John's upon this hurried out to do homage to the son of their Sovereign. Scarcely, however, had they got into the streets when the rain again descended, wetting to the skin every one who did not seek shelter, or who had not attired himself in clothing through which the rain could not pass. It then became known that the landing had been postponed until twelve o'clock, and two more miserable hours, checkered by alternate hopes and fears, had to be passed.

In the rain the Royal Newfoundland Company of Rifles, under the command of Captain Bold, were marched down to the wharf, and took their stand in a double row along the eastern slip. By and bye, the ladies who had secured the necessary cards, took their seats in the places reserved for them, along the wharf on the western slip. And by degress the clergy also ventured out. The Right Rev. Dr. Field, Bishop of Newfoundland ; the Right Rev. Dr. Mallock, RomanCatholic Bishop of St. John's ; the Right Rev. Dr. Dalton, Roman Catholic Bishop of Harbour Grace ; the Rev. Henry Daniel, Chairman of the Wesleyan District ; the Ven. H. M. Lower, Archdeacon ; the Rev. Donald McRae, minister of the Church of Scotland ; the Rev. Moses Harvey, of the Presbyterian Church ; and the Rev. Charles Pedley, Independent minister—all stood quietly by the side of the wharf, in a crowd, almost undistinguishable from the lawyers who were mixed up with them. I say "almost"—because there was no mistaking the Roman Catholic Bishops, in their pink stockings, buckled shoes, knee-breeches, and canonical drapery, especially as round the neck of each was supended a massive gold chain, supporting large crosses of the same valuable metal. Shortly before twelve o'clock the rain ceased, and the clouds began to break. Then the Governor, dressed in a uniform of blue and silver came down, attended by his Secretary, Lieutenant Coen, the

Premier of the Government, Hon. John Kent, Colonial Secretary, and the rest of the ministers. The Spanish Consul, dressed in an excessively showey uniform, cream-coloured trousers, scarlet dress coat with buff facings, appeared in company with Brother Jonathan's representative in black coat and white shirt. Captain Clorie of the *Sesostris* also appeared. Meanwhile they had not been idle in the streets outside. The different companies and the various societies had formed all along the line of route from the wharf to Government House, numbering altogether about a thousand men. The Volunteer Rifles looked exceedingly well in their new uniforms, and executed the duties assigned them with promptitude and exactness. The Masons wearing the paraphernalia of their order were placed nearest the gate. Next to them were the members of the Benevolent Irish Society, with green scarfs, the harp of Erin and shamrock being embroidered thereon. Then came the Newfoundland British Society, St. Andrew's Society, the St. George's Society, the Newfoundland Native Society, the Phœnix Volunteer Fire Company, the Sons of Temperance, the Coopers' Society, and the [Total Abstinence Society. There was scarcely a single house which had not a banner hung from a widow or floating over the roof, while the greater part of them were furnished with enough bunting to dress out a first class man-of-war.

The scene from the wharf was striking. At one end lay the *Hero, Ariadne* and *Flying Fish* moored, in a semi-circle, a little distance off, dressed out in their colours from stem to stern. Near by was the French steamer *Sesostris*, also exhibiting her flags, while all the merchantmen on both sides of the harbour aided in the display. At the northern end of the wharf was a large arch of evergreens—upon the top the Royal Arms; underneath an inscription—"God save the Queen." A number of banners and garlands of artificial flowers upon it were tastefully adjusted. On the opposite side—that side of the arch facing the road—was an inscription—"Welcome Prince," with the monogram A. E. on both sides. In a space, unoccupied by houses, rising from the road to the street above, was a large gallery, exactly opposite the wharf, upon which were seated some hundreds of people, and above them again was the hill, swarming with a loyal multitude. The house tops were all crowded; from every window peered the merry faces of folk anxious to see the Prince, and the masts of the vessels from which a view of the landing could be obtained groaned under the weight of all the sailors in St. John's.

Exactly at twelve o'clock the Prince descended into the Royal barge, the *Ariadne* and *Flying Fish* manned their yards and thundered forth a salute of 21 guns each—compared to which the noise made from the batteries on the previous day, was a mere pop-gun affair. For a moment or two a breathless silence succeeded, during which the splashing of the oars as they dipped into and withdrew from the water could be distinctly heard, and then rose a mighty cheer, commencing on the wharf and continuing throughout the city, spreading far away along to the Government House, echoing and reverberating until it died in the distance, then as it were, returning to its source, and with renewed force, again and again sweeping through the air. In acknowledgment of these plaudits the Prince repeatedly bowed, evidently much pleased with the enthusiasm of the people. Quickly the barge was pulled to the wharf, and His Royal Highness ascended the stairs covered with scarlet which had been prepared for him. At the head stood the Governor, Sir Alexander Bannerman, who welcomed the Prince to the capital of Newfoundland. After His Royal Highness, there landed from the barge the gentlemen who accompanied him—the Duke of Newcastle, Earl St. Germains, Major General Bruce; Mr. Englehart, secretary to the Duke; Dr. Ackland, and the equeries, Major Teesdale and Captain Grant.

The band beloging to the Royal Newfoundland Company then struck up God save the Queen, and the Prince, bowing as he walked up the wharf, was conducted to the Governor's carriage. The Duke of Newcastle and Sir Alexander took their seats in the same vehicle, and proceeded onwards at a moderate pace. The procession was soon formed, as pre-arranged, the societies falling into marching order after the Prince had passed through their ranks. The progress of His Royal Highness was one continued ovation. There was little crowding; the people behaved themselves most admirably, and a clear course was kept the whole distance. As soon as the carriage containing the Royal visitor had passed particular spots, the occupants would suddenly vanish up the cross streets, and by taking short cuts, appear further along the line of route in time to gain a second view of the Prince. The arches served the purpose for which they were intended, and were right handsomely got up. Upon the lawn in front of the Government House were drawn out a large number of Sunday School children, who welcomed His Royal Highness with the National Anthem. Amid the enthusiastic cheers of the vast multitude he alighted from the carriage, entered the Government House, and was lost to view.

The next thing was the holding of the levee. The central hall of the Government House is nearly square and of ample dimensions. Right and left run the corridors, out of which open windows leading to a suite of rooms which have to be traversed before the Royal presence can be reached. In the hall was assembled a very promiscuous crowd. Lawyers, doctors, judges, soldiers, bishops, naval officers, editors, volunteers and civilians; long and short, stout and thin, of intelligent looks, of stupid looks, of humble bearing, or of manifestly quiet self-importance. There they were, all wedged together, anxious to render personal homage to the Prince. Each was provided with a large card of a specified size, upon which was legibly written his name, and if he chose, his profession. About two o'clock the doors were opened, and each gentleman present found himself in as bad, or rather as firm a fix as though he were seeking entrance into a theatre on boxing night, or was one of Her Majesty's faithful Commons struggling into the House of Lords to hear the Queen's speech. *Punch* once represented the struggle upon a like occurrence in Buckingham Palace, when dresses were torn, and shoes lost, and jewellery broken, over the title of "The real mob," and if the *leveeans* did not deserve that name in St. John's, the lords and ladies at home must indeed have behaved badly when they earned it. As the fourth room where the Prince was approached, however, the pressure moderated and breathing became easier. Let us take a look at the arrangements. The door way is in the centre. From the left hand side proceeded a brass rail extending across the room, behind which rail stood his Royal Highness the Prince of Wales, attired in the uniform of a colonel of the army—a scarlet tunic, black trousers and sash. On his left breast shone a large star worn only by the Heir Apparent to the British Crown.

To the right of the Prince in a line extending to the door stood the equerries in waiting, Major Teesdale and Captain Gray, the High Steward of Her Majesty's Household the Earl St. Germains, in a uniform of blue and gold, and the Hon. John Kent, the Premier of Newfoundland. To his left stood His Grace the Duke of Newcastle and Major General Bruce. The card of the person desirous of being presented, was first handed to the equerry nearest the door, and passed on to the Earl St. Germains, who bowing to the Prince read aloud the name, and then handed the said card to Mr. Kent. The Prince then bowed to each gentleman so presented who acknowledged the favour, and passed out through a door on the opposite side of the room. The number of persons presented was two hundred and eighty. Fifteen addresses were read. To them His Royal Highness gave a single reply—the more important being answered separately. He was exceedingly gracious in his demeanour, and had a pleasant smile for every one. The portraits which lately appeared of him in Toronto are good likenesses—a little too young perhaps, but the features are the same. All came away much pleased with the appearance of their future King.

The levee being over, His Royal Highness kindly consented to review the three companies of Volunteers lately raised under the command of Captains Tasker, Wallbank and Clift. He proceeded to the parade ground in company with his suite, and the men having executed a few manœuvres in a manner exceedingly creditable to themselves, His Royal Highness was pleased to express to the officers the pleasure he felt at witnessing their proficiency.

Still later in the day he rode rapidly through the town on horseback, to the Lunatic Asylum, where he was received by the Physician, Dr. Henry Stabb, and conducted through the building. While riding he was saluted with a running fire of cheers, for the streets were crowded with people, who as the Royal cortage dashed past lifted up their hats, waved their handkerchiefs, and vented forth many a stout hurrah.

In the evening the following besides the members of the suite had the honour of dining with His Royal Highness—Commodore Seymour, of the *Hero*, Capt. Oslebar, R. N., of the *Margaretha Stevenson*, Captain Vansittart of the *Ariadne*, Capt. Hope, of the

Flying Fish; Major Grant, Royal Newfoundland Rifles; Major Bailey, of the Engineers; Lieutenant Coen, the Governor's private Secretary; Capt. Clorie, of H. I. M. ship *Sesostris;* His Excellency Sir Alexander Bannerman, and Lady Bannerman.

Soon after dark the grand display of fireworks took place, the least successful part of the arrangements. It consisted of little else than the discharge of a larger number of fire rockets—very good in their way, but wearisome without variety. The *finale* was the exhibition in blazing gunpowder of the motto, "Long live the Prince of Wales." The Colonial Buldings, the Post-office, and the lodge of the Government House were all illuminated. The entrance arch to the first mentioned place was exceedingly handsome, lamps of variegated colours being placed among the foilage, and banners festooned arranged along the top. The Roman Catholic Cathedral was illuminated as on the previous evening. Very few houses were lighted up, in consequence of a protest of the Insurance Companies. But the people contented themselves with parading the streets, and with seeing what was to be seen. As on the previous evening, the juvenile portion of the population indulged themselves *ad libitum* in the use of crackers, back-rappers, serpents, and squibs. How so many got into Newfoundland is a problem no one I have questioned is able to solve.

St. John's, Newfoundland, July 25.

Yesterday addresses were presented to the Prince, to which he replied as follows:—I sincerely thank you for the addresses presented to me and for the hearty welcome received from all on my landing on the shores of this the earliest colonial possession of the British Crown. I trust you will not think me regardless of your zealous loyalty if I acknowledge these addresses collectively. It will afford me the greatest satisfaction to report to the Queen the devotion to her crown and person unmistakeably evinced by the reception of her son, eloquently expressed in the addresses from various bodies in this town and Harbour Grace. I am charged by the Queen to convey to you the assurance of the deep concern she has ever felt in this interesting portion of her dominions. I shall convey back a lively recollection of this day's proceedings, and of your kindness to myself personally, but above all of those hearty demonstrations of patriotism, which prove your deep rooted attachment to the great and free country of which we all glory to be called her sons.

Wednesday, July 25.

Early in the morning, St. John's was all alive, and soon rumours were afloat that His Royal Highness had been seen galloping hither and thither across the country. But it was all a mistake. The Prince did not stir out until twelve o'clock, when he visited the regatta.

Previous to that, however, the Premier and some of the members of the Government waited upon him and presented him with a Newfoundland dog in the name of the people of the Island. The gift proved acceptable as it was appropriate—His Royal Highness manifesting genuine pleasure when it was delivered to him. The dog is a beautiful, thorough-bred animal, of a jet but not a glossy black, and very strong. Round his neck was a massive silver collar, manufactured in New York expressly for the purpose to which it has been put. Cost $216. It has engraven upon it two shields, each of which bears the Royal Arms. Between them is a third and larger shield, inscribed with the words, "Presented to His Royal Highness, Albert Edward, Prince of Wales, by the inhabitants of Newfoundland, A. D. 1860." Hearing that there were many people desirous of seeing the collar, His Royal Highness took it from the dog's neck and sent it to the Colonial Buildings for exhibition. The dog was placed on board the *Hero*, and when last seen was in good health, but somewhat distressed in that he was unable to drag from its place an eighty-four pounder to which he was fastened. The Governor asked the Prince by what name he intended to call the animal, and suggested Avalon—the district of Newfoundland in which St. John's is situated. But Albert Edward replied that he thought Cabot, the name of the discoverer of Newfoundland, would be most appropriate, and "Cabot," accordingly, the dog is called.

Then the regatta. It was held on Quidi Vidi, or, as the people more commonly call it, Kitty Vitty Lake, a beautiful sheet of water about half the size of Toronto bay, surrounded by high hills, and owing to its great depth, blue as the ocean itself.

It is gained by a winding road which descends gradually into the valley, and from the higher portion of which a fine view of the country is gained. When it became known that the Prince would honour the regatta with his presence, an arch was erected, and the road for a considerable distance lined with branches of green spruce, which being planted close together, presented the appearance of a permanent hedge. Farther on, where the road narrowed to a lane scarcely wide enough for two carriages to pass, was a real hawthorn hedge, growing from grassy banks—a bit of scenery His Royal Highness will learn to appreciate before he has travelled far on the American continent. Not less than ten thousand people were congregated to witness the regatta. To accommodate the multitude very many booths were erected, inside of which were vended eatables and drinkables, and from which, later in the day, proceeded sounds of merriment which proved that His Royal Highness' health had been enthusiastically drunk. The following are the races rowed :—

	1st prize.	2nd prize.
1st race six-oared gigs (amateurs)	$45	$25
2nd " " whale boats (set crews)	30	20
3rd " " to be rowed by men from H. M. ships	30	20
4th race six-oared gigs (set crews)	30	20
5th " " (tradesmen)	30	20
6th four-oared gigs (amateurs)	30	20
7th " " (set crews)	20	10
8th race six-oared gigs (juveniles)	15	5
9th " four-oared whale-boats (set crews)	20	10

Leaving Quidi Vidi His Royal Highness proceeded to Portugal Cave, fourteen miles distant, and ascended a hill whereon a sort of terrace had been made, and from which a splended view of the surrounding country can be gained. The eminence is in future to be called the "Prince's Hill."

His Royal Highness returned to Government House, about 8 o'clock, and dined with the Governor and Cabinet. For the information of the curious in such matters it may be well to state that by the express command of Her Majesty no speechifying is tolerated. Any, therefore, who expect to "draw out" the Prince or the gentlemen who accompany him will be disappointed.

F

July, 26.

Last night the ball, the most important of the many events which have been crowded together within the last forty-eight hours, took place. The room in which it was held is built of wood, on the western side of the Colonial Buildings. Entrance to it was gained by what may be termed a broad vestibule, reaching from the stone steps in front of the buildings to the ball-room itself. Inside and outside the pavillion was covered with pink and white calico—the colours of Newfoundland—nothing of the wood-work could be seen. The bearers supporting the roof were decorated with evergreens; round the walls festoons and garlands of artificial flowers, gracefully arranged, were hung. At the upper end of the room was erected a dais, over the centre of which was a canopy surmounted with the Prince of Wales' plume, and a gilt cornice underneath supporting curtains of dark scarlet. Right and left of the canopy the banners of England appeared, arranged in the same way as upon the Royal Arms. The room was further decorated with numerous very excellant steel plate engravings lent for the occasion by various gentlemen, and from a large number of gas burners the whole was brilliantly lighted. Across the ceiling of the vestibule rows of small coloured lamps were hung, looking pretty enough. A recess on each side of the room, to which admittance was gained from the outside, was occupied—the one to the right of the dais by the band of Her Majesty's steamship Hero; the others by that of the Royal Newfoundland Rifle Company.

As the ladies had not enjoyed the privilege of being presented to the Prince—the Queen having, it is said, given orders that as the Prince is under age, no ladies should be presented at his levees—they had determined to make the most of the opportunity now offered. Accordingly—no doubt to spite Her Majesty—they one and all looked their prettiest. There was not an ugly woman in the room—not a single discontented face—all were joyous and happy. About eight hundred tickets were sold, and as it proved there was ample space for those who desired to dance. Among the company assembled were the officers of the different ships in port, dressed in full uniform; the officers of the Royal

Newfoundland corps, and of the French ship, the Sesostris, together with a plentiful sprinkling of gentlemen belonging to the militia—all contributing to lend additional *gaiety* and brilliancy to the scene.

It was understood the Prince would open the ball at ten o'clock, and as the hour approached intense anxiety was depicted upon many countenances, especially upon those of the ladies. They had one and all made up their minds not to refuse His Royal Highness, should he request the honour of dancing with them. But, how many would have the chance of showing their loyalty, was the question ? Would he dance with any one of them ? Would he dance with more than one ? If so, with whom ? If so, with how many ? It had been reported that the French Governor of St. Pierre, who is said to be a Count, would visit St. John's with his lady, and that if such was the case, the Prince would be obliged to confine his attentions to her. The Newfoundland ladies were indignant. If they were not as good as the parvenu nobles of the empire, they would like to know the reason. Of course they would, and so would many others besides. But the Count and his Countess did not come, so there was no necessity for pushing the enquiry. Sill, however, the question was an open one. With whom would the prince dance ? Competition would not solve the problem ; and so the anxiety to witness its practical solution increased as the time neared, when none would be long left in doubt. The occasional cheers which issued from the streets, when a larger rocket than usual was let off, or when some public man made his appearance on his way to the ball, caused many a heart to jump, many a stout heart to be shaken ; many a half suppressed whisper of—"He's coming," to pass round the room ! !

But a few minutes before ten o'clock, a loud hurrah sent up by the crowd surrounding the Government House, conveyed to the anxiously waiting people within the ball room knowledge of the fact that His Royal Highness had at length most certainly started. Then began the stewards to bustle about. "Ladies to the front, gentlemen behind," was the order they gave, and very quickly they succeeded in forming an avenue of fair ones, extending from the entrance to the dais. Scarcely were the arrangements completed, when in came His Royal Highness and suite, accompanied by the Committee deputed to conduct him to the ball room ; the Chief Justice, Sir Francis Brady ; the President of the Council, the Hon. Mr. O'Brien ; the Commandant of the Forces, Major Grant ; Major Bailey of the Engineers, and the Hon Charles Fox Bennett. The Prince immediately took his seat underneath the canopy ; the Duke of Newcastle, Earl St. Germains, and Major General Bruce standing beside him. Three genuine hurrahs were given, which His Royal Higness gracefully acknowledged. One of the stewards then called out, "choose your partners." But gentlemen were not inclined to obey. It would have been a dangerous thing just then to ask a lady to dance, with about the five hundredth fraction of a chance in her favour that the Prince would desire to be her partner. So Albert Edward had to lead off. "Who has he chosen ?" "What's her name ?" Every body was on tip-toe—every body risked the dislocation of his or her neck, anxious to catch a glance of the fortunate one.

She proved to be Lady Brady, the wife of the Chief Justice, and as the Prince led her to her place a murmer of approbation ran through the room. The opposite couple were His Grace the Duke of Newcastle and Miss Grant, sister of Major Grant. The side couples were the Hon. Mr. Kent and daughter, and Major Teesdale and another Miss Kent. As soon as the dancing commenced, it was perfectly evident His Royal Highness had determined to enjoy himself. He chatted away with Lady Brady in the intervals of the dance, looked exceedingly pleased, danced buoyantly and gracefully, and by his demeanour placed every body at their ease. He was dressed, as on landing, in a colonel's uniform ; and managed his spurs so well that no crinoline was torn.

The first quadrille over a second one was called. It seemed to be the general impression that His Royal Highness' performance was finished. Not so, however, Mrs. Bailey, wife of Major Bailey, was next favoured by him. It is useless to record the alternate hopes and fears that arose, and were expressed as each dance was finished—they were but repetitions of those which preceded. Suffice it to say, that when the third on the list was reached, curiosity seemed to have arrived at its culminating point. Would the Prince waltz ? Ladies and gentlemen crowded to the doors, and at that instant, and only that instant, was there the slightest approach at anything like rudeness.

The Prince would waltz. He selected for his partner Mrs. Ridly, wife of a merchant of Harbour Grace, and twisted her round vigorously and well. People were fully satisfied from the skill he manifested, that this was by no means the first occasion upon which he had placed his arm around a lady's waist.

Then arose another question,—would he not dance with any but married women? Number four settled the point. Miss McCarroll was chosen. Then No. 5, a quadrille, he danced with the Hon. Mrs. Kent. No. 6 he missed. No. 7, a galop, and Miss Carter—sister of the leader of the Opposition—was chosen. No. 8, 1 Lancers, Miss Grant; Nos. 9 and 10 missed. No. 11, a quadrille, Miss Robinson.

Then to supper, prepared in the Council Chamber. As the Prince left the room he was cheered vociferously, the delighted people again and again testifying the pleasure they felt at his condescension by repeated rounds of applause. How much his popularity was increased by the way he had mixed with his future subjects, we can scarcely venture to tell. His praise was in everybody's mouth—all agreed that he had left nothing undone to gain the goodwill of the people. Especially proud were the ladies of him; so much had they to say in his favour, that many of the opposite sex found consolation in calling to mind the fact, that His Royal Highness will not be allowed to marry a subject. Refreshments having been taken, the ball-room was a second time sought, and dancing recommenced. The names of those ladies whom His Royal Highness favoured were—No. 13, waltz and galop, Mrs. Young; No. 14, Lancers, Mrs. E. Shea; No. 15, Varsoviana, Miss Jarvis; and No. 16, Schottische, Miss Tobin, a daughter of an M.L.C. At a quarter to three o'clock, when only four more dances remained upon the programme, His Royal Highness left the room and repaired to Government House. And thus was closed the most eventful night St. John's has witnessed this many a long year.

It had been arranged that His Royal Highness should embark this morning at seven o'clock, but the Committee of Management petitioned that a later hour should be named, resting their request upon the ground, that, as the weather had been so unfavourable on the Tuesday morning, many people had been prevented from witnessing the landing, who would again be disappointed if the squadron departed at the time proposed—so much earlier than was anticipated. To this a favourable answer was returned, and eleven o'clock named. The arrangements in the streets were the same as when the landing was effected. His Royal Highness drove down to the wharf, bade adieu to the Governor, bowed repeatedly in acknowledgment of the hearty cheers with which he was saluted, and jumped into a barge in waiting. When he reached the *Hero* he leaped on board with an alacrity worthy of of his brother Alfred the sailor Prince, and once more lifting his hat disappeared behind the bulwarks. The men manned the rigging, and from the *Ariadne* and *Flying Fish*, the orthodox Royal salute was thundered forth. Another half hour was spent by the ships in weighing anchor and by the people cheering. At twelve o'clock a start was made, and under the pilotage of Captain Orlebar, the squadron steamed out of the harbour, each ship getting an extra cheer from the volunteers, who having chartered a tug for the purpose, accompanied the *Hero* until she had once more entered upon the waters of the broad Atlantic.

And just while starting, and have thus a moment's leisure, it may not be out of place to tell how His Royal Highness was cheated by a "middy." You are aware that in crossing the Atlantic it is not an uncommon thing for lotteries to be formed in this wise: pieces of paper are inscribed with figures, denoting the different hours of the day—ten o'clock, eight o'clock, or nine o'clock. A sum of money is paid by each who takes part in the affair, in exchange for which he is allowed, on arriving in port, to draw out of a bag one of the said tickets; and should the hour mentioned thereon be that in which the anchor is cast, he takes all the cash collected. The Prince had joined in one of these lotteries, but had lost. Desirous of trying his luck a second time, and having ascertained that the midshipmen had not drawn in a lottery of their own, he asked a little fellow about as high as his elbow for how much he would sell his ticket? "Ten shillings," replied the lad—and ten shillings the Prince immediately handed over. No sooner had he done so, than "middy" coolly informed His Royal Highness that the ticket originally cost one shilling and sixpence sterling. The affair created a laugh, in which the Prince heartily joined, though there is a very strong suspicion that after all those who were "taken in" were they who thought His Royal Highness had been duped.

A very pleasing remark made by the Prince to a lady is quoted. He was introduced to Mrs. Dr. Stabb, wife of the medical attendant of the Lunatic Asylum, and, finding she was a German, enquired in what part of the fatherland she was born. She replied, in Saxe-Gotha; upon which the Prince, in a tone of the utmost sincerity, said that he was always delighted to meet with a native of the principality from which his father came. Such a sentiment redounds much to his credit.

DESCRIPTION OF THE "HERO."

The *Hero*, in which His Royal Highness has made his passage across the Atlantic, is one of the finest vessels in the service of Great Britain. She is commanded by Commodore Seymour, a gentleman of great experience in naval matters; carries ninety guns, and has a complement of eight hundred men. Her engines are six hundred horse power, burthen 3,040 tons. Fitted up with every improvement which modern skill can devise, she is one of the most tremendous instruments of destruction ever made by man. The Prince occupied the captain's apartments. Very little alteration had been made for his accommodation, and all the furniture is of a very plain, but of a very substantial description. At the stern of the vessel is his sitting room, leading from it his bed-room. Passing from the sitting-room forward to the gun-room, a dining room is entered. The panelling is plain white, with gilded beadings. Two large common tables occupy a considerable portion of the space. Leading from this room is the steward's pantry, and state-rooms occupied by members of the suite. There is little ornament in any of the apartments. The furniture is of oak, stained to show the grain; the carpets are dark crimson; the chairs are covered with red morocco.

The cot in which His Royal Highness slept, and which was selected for him by his royal mother who visited the *Hero* for the purpose, is suspended from a couple of iron arms, and has no curtains. What is generally considered to be a "republican simplicity" marks the whole. The Heir Apparent to the throne of Great Britain—so far as the mere appearance of the furniture goes—is, when on board the *Hero*, not more comfortably lodged than the master of many a trading vessel, and any cabin passenger by a Cunard or Canadian ocean steamer enjoys conveniences to which the most favoured inmates of the *Hero* must be strangers. In the gun-room, hanging over a side table, are four silver candlesticks with glass funnels—once belonging to the immortal Nelson, and used by him on board the *Victory*. They are worthily placed and in good keeping.

The *Ariadne* is a frigate, but, though carrying only twenty-six guns, is larger than the *Hero*. Her burthen is one hundred tons greater, her engines are eight hundred horse power, and she has on board about four hundred and fifty men, some three hundred short of her full compliment. Of the two, she is perhaps the best vessel. Her guns throw an eight inch hollow shot, weighing sixty-eight pounds, and possess a three mile range. She towed the *Hero* a considerable distance across the Atlantic. Her commander is Captain Vansittart.

The third vessel of the squadron is the *Flying Fish*, under the command of Captain Hope, through whose kindness was obtained a passage from St. John's to Halifax. The boat is 237 feet long, with only a twenty-seven feet beam; has engines of 350 horse power, and 870 tuns burthen. Of guns she mounts but six, but two of them are capable of throwing a solid 68 lb shot a distance of three miles. The other four are thirty-two pounders. Number of men on board one hundred and nine. Like the others of the squadron, she is a splendid vessel. She saluted in company with the rest on leaving St. John's, but having only six guns, she had to re-load several times. The celerity with which this was done was perfectly marvellous. The officer in charge held in his hand a sand-glass, and at an interval of several seconds gave the word to fire, which was obeyed instantaneously. By the time he had gone the round, the first gun was ready. Not the slightest irregularity could be perceived. Time was as well kept by the gunners as a musician keeps it with the keys of a piano-forte.

Off Cape Sambro, Sunday, July 29th.

We lost the *Ariadne* and *Hero* in a fog the morning after starting, and have not seen them since. The *Flying Fish* is now waiting ten miles off Cape Sambro for their appearance. There was some talk before leaving St. John's that the Prince might take a look at St. Pierre, passing between that island and St. Miguelon, and afterwards proceed to Sydney, but the proposition was abandoned. It looks very much as though something of the sort had been done, or the squadron would be here.

July 30*th.*

This morning at four o'clock, the *Hero* and *Ariadne* hove in sight, and having got pretty close, stopped to admire the proportions of the *Flying Fish*—and they are at it yet. What time the Prince intends to go into Halifax we cannot tell. We learn by a boat which just now came from the *Hero*, that His Royal Highness passed between St. Pierre and Miguelon, visited the coal mines at Sydney, and took a peep at Louisburg, the site of the old French fortifications. He did not find much of them left.

HALIFAX.

Twelve months ago this visit could scarce have been hoped for by the loyal people of Nova Scotia, and that so great an honour was about to be conferred upon them, as that they should receive such a mark of consideration is notable from a member of the Royal family, the Heir Apparent to the throne. The circumstances which led to the visit were these: when the Victoria Bridge at Montreal, that magnificent monument of enterprise and architectural genius was completed, our fellow colonists in Canada, deeming that its inauguration was an event of such importance as to be not unworthy of being graced with the presence of royalty, sent a respectful memorial to the Throne, praying that our Sovereign would deign to honour that province with a visit, and preside at the important ceremony referred to. There were insuperable objections to the Sovereign of England making a voyage to Canada, and being absent from the seat of the Empire so long a time as would be consumed by such a visit, but, while setting forth this objection, the Imperial reply to the invitation of the Canadian Parliament signified Her Majesty's desire to gratify the North American Colonists as far as lay in her power, by sending as her representative, her eldest son, the Heir Apparent to the throne.

Immediately on it becoming known in this province that the Queen had responded favourably to the memorial of the Canadians, the two branches of the Legislature then in session, passed a joint address to Her Majesty, praying that the visit of His Royal Highness might be extended to Nova Scotia. This address was forwarded by His Excellency the Lieutenant-Governor, at the request of the Legislature, on the 22nd of March; and on the 3rd of May, the following despatch to Earl Mulgrave, returning a favourable reply to the prayer of the petition was, by His Excellency's command, laid on the table of the House of Assembly.

Downing Street, 19th April, 1860.

My Lord—

I have the honour to acknowledge the receipt of your Lordship's despatch, No. 34, of the 22nd of March, enclosing a joint address to the Queen, passed by both branches of the Legislature, praying that the approaching visit of His Royal Highness the Prince of Wales, to Canada, may be extended to Nova Scotia.

I have laid the address before the Queen; Her Majesty has been pleased to receive the same very graciously, and to command me to request your Lordship to convey to the Legislative Council and House of Assembly, the assurance that it will afford the Prince much gratification to respond to the sentiments of loyalty and attachment to Her Majesty's throne and person expressed in their address, by complying with the wishes of the Legislature of Nova Scotia. A visit to Nova Scotia has, from the first, formed part of His Royal Highness' projected tour.

I have, &c.

(Signed.) NEWCASTLE.

The Earl of Mulgrave, &c.

The gratifying intelligence thus conveyed, was hailed with sincere and universal delight, not only in the Legislature, but throughout the province. On the 4th of May, the House of Assembly, on motion of the Hon. the President of the Council, unanimously resolved to authorise His Excellency the Lieutenant-Governor to spend whatever sum might be "necessary for the suitable reception and accommodation of His Royal Highness the

Prince of Wales and suite." This liberality on the part of the Legislature was warmly approved of by the people, who were desirous that nothing might be left undone to give His Royal Highness such a reception as was due to his exalted position, and would prove the devotion and loyalty of the people of Nova Scotia.

After the prorogation of the Legislature, a public meeting of the citizens of Halifax was held on the 23rd of May, in Mason Hall, where resolutions were passed requesting the city authorities to make all suitable preparations in conjunction with the Executive Government, for the cordial reception of His Royal Highness the Prince of Wales; "that the citizens and people from all parts of the Province, might have an opportunity of evincing their fervent and loyal attachment to his illustrious mother, and to himself, as Heir Apparent to the British Throne." At this meeting, also, a numerous Committee of Arrangements were appointed, comprising the members of the Executive Government and of the City Council, several of the Judges, the Sheriff, the City Recorder, the members for the town and county, and other prominent and influential citizens. A few days subsequent to this meeting, the City Council resolved to appropriate the sum of £1,000 for the purpose of decorating the public buildings, and other expenses that might fall within the sphere of their authority. At a meeting of the General Committee, appointed at Mason Hall, an Executive Committee of nine gentlemen was appointed, representing equally the Executive Government, the citizens, and the City Council, as follows, viz.: Hon. Wm. Young, Hon. Joseph Howe, Hon. Benjamin Wier, His Worship the Mayor, and Charles Twining, John A. Bell, John Tobin, A. M. Uniacke, and W. Cunard, Esqrs.

This Committee was organised by appointing the Hon. Wm. Young, Chairman, and P. C. Hill, Esq., Secretary. From this time forth the preparations for the reception of the Royal visitor went on with a heartiness and enthusiasm never called forth by any previous event, however important, in the history of Nova Scotia. In all the arrangements a deep interest was taken by their Excellencies the Earl of Mulgrave, the Lieutenant-Governor, and Rear-Admiral Sir Alexander Milne, and by the Commander of the Forces, Major-General Trolloppe. Intelligence having been received that His Royal Highness would remain in Halifax during three days, arrangements were made for a series of festivities and loyal demonstrations, to occupy the whole time of his stay. The programme comprised an official reception by the authorities at the Naval Yard, the place selected for the landing of the royal party, a procession, a review of the troops and volunteers, a regatta, a ball, an illumination of the town, and a display of fireworks. As the time for the visit of His Royal Highness approached, the work of preparation went busily on, and before the day named for his arrival, the whole aspect of the town had changed; the city was gay with evergreens; splendid arches of various designs and tastefully embellished, were erected in all the principal streets, while all the public and many of the private buildings were decorated in a style appropriate to the great approaching event, the naval, military, executive and civic authorities, the various societies, and the citizens generally, vieing with each other in all those outward demonstrations of a heart-felt and devoted loyalty.

On the 10th of July His Royal Highness embarked at Ply_mouth on board H. M. S. *Hero*, 91, Captain H. Seymour, which ship was accompanied by the *Ariadne*, and the *Flying Fish*, The suite accompanying the Prince, comprised the the following distinguished persons:—the Duke of Newcastle, Secretary of State for the Colonies : the Earl of St. Germains, Lord Steward of Her Majesty's Household ; Major-General the Hon. R. Bruce, Governor to the Prince ; Major Teesdale, R. A., and Capt. George Gray, Equerries, and Dr. Ackland.

On Monday, the 22nd of July, the ships of the Royal squadron arrived at St. John's, Newfoundland, where His Royal Highness remained, enjoying the hospitalities of the people, until Thursday, the 26th, on which day he embarked for Nova Scotia at ten o'clock, A.M. On Saturday, the 28th, the fleet arrived at Sydney, C. B., where His Royal Highness and suite landed and remained a few hours. No intimation of their intention to land at this place had been received, but, although the people of the place were surprised by their unexpected arrival, and had, of course, made no preparation for a reception such as became the exalted rank of their visitors, yet they extended to him a hearty and loyal welcome. During the afternoon, His Royal Highness visited the mines and other places of interest, and inspected the

Volunteer Rifle Corps, who promptly turned out under Col. Brown, to form a guard of honour at his landing and re-embarkation.

On Saturday evening, 28th July, the Prince sailed from Sydney for Halifax. Early on the morning of Monday, the 30th, the *Hero* and accompanying ships were telegraphed from the outposts, and at 7 A. M., the promised signal,—the union jack flying on the flag staff, and three guns fired in quick succession from the Citadel,—told that the Royal squadron was near the harbour. The appearance of the noble ships, as they majestically neared the city, the *Hero* leading, was very fine, as battery after battery in regular succession—York Redoubt, Point Pleasant, Fort Clarence, George's Island, the Lumber Yard and the Citadel —saluted the Royal Standard of England with Royal salutes of twenty-one guns. The steamers *Eastern State* and *Neptune*, the *Daring*, and a number of yachts, gaily dressed for the occasion, and crowded with ladies and gentlemen, met the ships of the Royal fleet, and accompanied them up the harbour. For several days previous to the 30th, visitors from all parts of the province had been crowding into the city to witness the festivities, and these, with the citizens, to the number of many thousands, viewed the animated panorama which the harbour presented, from the glacis of the citadel, from the house tops and from the numerous wharves, from which enthusiastic cheers went up as the *Hero* passed by. At a few minutes past 9, A.M., the ships arrived at their moorings under a Royal salute from the flag ship *Nile*, the *Valorous*, and other ships of the station in port. His Excellency the Lieutenant-Governor immediately proceeded on board from the Dockyard, and His Excellency Rear-Admiral Milne from the *Nile*, to pay their respects to the distinguished stranger.

At 10 A.M., it was announced by a signal from the masthead of the *Nile*, that his His Royal Highness would land at 12, noon. In the mean time preparations were being made for the proper reception of the Prince on landing, and for the procession to escort him to the Government House. The streets through which His Royal Highness was to pass, on his way to Government House, the distance being about a mile and a quarter, were lined with the troops, and volunteers, and with the members of the various societies, in the following order. At the gate of the

Dockyard, extending southward, were the Firemen in their uniform, their engines beautifully decorated. Next to them, in succession, were the Caledonia Club, the North British and Highland Societies, Charitable Irish Society, St. George's Society, Carpenters' Society, Grand and Subordinate Divisions of Sons of Temperance, and the Catholic Benevolent Total Abstinence Society. Then came the Liverpool Brass Band, who volunteered their services for the occasion. Next to the Band were the various companies of the Batallion of Volunteer Rifles, the Halifax and Dartmouth Companies of Volunteer Engineers, extending south to Buckingham Street. The Royal Artillery and Royal Engineers filled the space thence to George Street, whence to the residence of the late Judge Robie was occupied by the 62nd Regiment, which formed the guard of honour at that place.

From the landing through the Dockyard to Water Street, the line was kept by the Marines from the *Nile*. Within the Dockyard the arrangements made by Admiral Milne were of the most perfect and satisfactory kind—the Judges, the Members of the Executive and City Councils, the Members of both branches of the Legislature, and other persons of note, being provided with suitable positions according to their rank; while the representatives of the press, and thousands of citizens occupied seats and stages prepared for their accommodation in various parts of the ample grounds. As the hour of noon drew nigh, eager expectation was depicted in every face, while the greatest quiet and order prevailed in the immense multitude. At length a barge, with the Royal Standard at the bow, was seen to leave the side of the *Hero*, and, in an instant, the scene was changed from the state of stillness that prevailed, to one of the greatest enthusiasm and excitement. The defeaning peals of cannon from the ships, the citadel, and the several forts around the harbour, the stirring cheers of the sailors of the *Nile*, the *Valorous*, the *Hero*, the *Ariadne*, and the *Flying Fish*, who, as if by magic, had manned yards of their several ships, where they were seen through the up curling wreaths of smoke, the electrical excitement and the irrepressible shouts of welcome, which burst from the thousands on shore, all formed a scene, which, to be once witnessed, can never be forgotten.

When the barge touched the landing, His Royal Highness was received and welcomed by His Excellency, Rear Admiral Sir Alexander Milne, and was by him conducted up the steps under an archway to where His Excellency the Lieutenant-Governor stood, by whom Major General Trolloppe, the Lord Bishop of Nova Scotia, the Members of the Executive Government, the Mayor and Corporation of Halifax, and other distinguished persons, were presented. At this point His Royal Highness was welcomed to the city by an address, read by the City Recorder, of which the following is a copy:

To His Royal Highness, Albert Edward, Prince of Wales, Prince of the United Kingdom, Duke of Saxony, Prince of Saxe-Coburg and Gotha, Duke of Cornwall and Rothsay, Earl of Dublin, Chester and Carrick, Baron of Renfrew, Lord of the Isles, Great Steward of Scotland, Knight of the Garter, &c. &c.

MAY IT PLEASE YOUR ROYAL HIGHNESS,

We, the Mayor and Aldermen of the City of Halifax, in Nova Scotia, in the name of the citizens, do most cordially welcome your Royal Highness to our shores.

We rejoice that our city should be thus highly honoured by the presence of the son of our revered and beloved Queen, the grandson of that illustrious Duke whose memory is gratefully cherished as the warm and constant friend of Nova Scotia, and the Heir Apparent to the powerful and glorious empire over which Her Majesty has, for so many years, so wisely and so beneficially ruled.

We venture to approach your Royal Highness with the expression of an earnest hope, that your sojourn in this city, and on this side the Atlantic, may be attended with much pleasure.

We are fondly persuaded that the reception which Your Royal Highness in every portion of Her Majesty's North American dominions, will not only impress you with the conviction that devotion to the British Throne and attachment to British institutions, form abiding elements in the minds of the inhabitants, but that the lustre which has been shed on the Crown by the christian and domestic virtues of our Most Gracious Sovereign, is justly and gratefully appreciated by all her subjects.

We earnestly implore the Giver of all good to guard and protect you, to restore you in safety to the parent land, and to that illustrious family circle of which we regard you as the ornament and the pride, and that He may be graciously pleased long to spare Your Royal Highness to fulfil those distinguished destinies to which your high position points.

SAMUEL R. CALDWELL, PHILIP THOMPSON.
Mayor. JAMES DUGGAN.
WILLIAM SUTHERLAND, W. C. MOIR.
Recorder. S. TRENAMAN.
JOHN L. GRAGG, *City Clerk.* WILLIAM EVANS.
HENRY E. PUGSLY. EDWARD LEAHY.
CHARLES GOGSWELL. JEREMIAH CONWAY.
JOHN DUGGAN. RICHARD T. ROOME.
MATHEW LOWNDS. JOHN A. BELL.
CHARLES BARNSTED. M. H. RICHEY.
JOHN D. NASH. J. JENNINGS.
CHARLES TWINING. L. HARTSHORNE, *City Treas.*

His Royal Highness was graciously pleased to reply to the address as follows:

GENTLEMEN,—

I have been led to expect that the loyalty and attachment to the British Crown which exist amongst the inhabitants of Halifax, would insure to me a kind reception in your city, but the scene which I have witnessed this morning proves that my expectations are more than realized.

For your welcome to myself I feel, I assure you, sincere gratitude,—but it is still more satisfactory to me, as a son and as an Englishman, to witness your affectionate attachment to the Queen, and to the laws and institutions of our common country.

Your allusion to my illustrious Grandfather is a most grateful to my feelings, and I rejoice to find that his memory is cherished amongst you.

In your noble harbour the navies of Britian can ride in safety, whilst you prosecute that commercial activity, which, under their protection, would seem destined to make Halifax one of the most important cities of the Western World, and to raise her inhabitants to a high position of wealth and prosperity. That such may be the fate reserved for it by Providence, is my very earnest hope.

I request you to convey to the citizens of whom you are the representatives, my cordial thanks for the greeting they have given me.

After reading the above reply, the Prince engaged for a few minutes in conversation with those about him, when horses being brought, he, with the members of his suite, mounted, and proceeded at once towards Government House. His Royal Highness was supported on his right by His Excellency the Earl of Mulgrave, and on his left by the Duke of Newcastle; he was preceded by Major General Trolloppe and Officers of his Staff, with various civic officials, and followed by General Bruce and Earl of St. Germains, and by the Judges, Members of Government, Legislative Councillors, Members of Assembly, the Sheriff, Customs, Heads of Departments, and others, the members of the different Societies filing into the procession from the rear as the Royal cortege passed between their ranks. The progress through Water Street, Granville, George and Barrington Streets, was a like continued triumph. The greatest enthusiasm and excitement, coupled with the greatest decorum and good order, prevailed. At one point of the procession, a scene presented itself by which His Royal Highness was visibly affected. On the Grand Parade, opposite the head of George Street, a stage was erected, on which were seated near four thousand children, in such a position, that, at a glance, every one of the four thousand little ones could see and be seen by their future Sovereign, as he ascended the hill; and when, on His Royal Highness coming in full view of the platform, the four thousand, at a signal from their leader, (Mr. Ackhurst,) rose simultaneously, and waving a welcome, sang the National Anthem, two verses of which, as given below, were written for the occasion, the scene was felt by all who witnessed it to be sublimely grand, beautiful, and affecting!!!

I.

God save our Gracious Queen!
Long live our noble Queen!
   God save the Queen!
Send her victorious, happy and glorious,
Long to reign over us,
   God save the Queen!

II.

Welcome! our Royal Guest;
Welcome! from every breast,
 From every tongue;
From hearts both warm and true,
Hearts that beat high for you,
Loudly our welcome due
 To thee be sung!

III.

Prince of a lofty line,
The virtues all be thine,
 Which grace our Queen!
To her we pay through thee,
Love, faith, and loyalty—
Homage which fits the free;
 God save the Queen!

At one p. m., the Royal party arrived at Government House, the Troops and Volunteers filed off to their respective quarters, the various Societies disbanded, and the first and grandest feature of the reception of the Prince of Wales in Nova Scotia was ended. Immediately on his arrival at Government House, the following address from the Executive Council of the Province was presented by the Hon. William Young, President of the Council.

To the Most High Puissant and Illustrious Prince Albert Edward Prince of the United Kingdom of Great Britain and Ireland, Prince of Wales, Duke of Saxony, Prince of Coburg and Gotha, Great Steward of Scotland, Duke of Cornwall and Rothsay, Earl of Chester, Carrick and Dublin, Baron of Renfrew, and Lord of the Isles, K. G.

The Members of the Executive Government, on behalf of the Legislature and people of Nova Scotia, tender to you, the son of their Sovereign, and Heir Apparent to her throne, the respectful homage of a loyal and united population, and cordially bid your Royal Highness welcome to this continent.

Founded by the British races, and for more than a century, amidst the vicissitudes and temptations of that period, preserving unsullied her attachment alike to the Throne, to the people, and to the institutions of the mother country, this Province has grown with a steady growth; and we trust that your Royal Highness will observe in it some evidences of public spirit and material prosperity, some faint traces of the civilization you have left at home, some indications of a desire to combine commercial activity and industrial development with the enjoyment of rational freedom.

To the members of your royal house who visited Nova Scotia in her infant state, our country was deeply indebted for the patronage which enabled many of her sons to distinguish themselves abroad, and during the reign of your illustrious mother, the blessings of self-government and of unrestricted intercourse with all the world have been graciously conferred upon this Province.

With pride we saw, during the Crimean and Indian wars, Nova Scotians winning laurals beneath the Imperial flag; and your Royal Highness has seen as you passed to your temporary residence, what honour we pay to the memory of our countrymen who fall in defence of the Empire.

We trust that your Royal Highness will also observe in the discipline of our volunteers a determination to foster the martial spirit inherited from our ancestors, and energetically to defend, if need be, this portion of Her Majesty's dominions.

To the loyal welcome which we tender to your Royal Highness, we beg to add our fervent prayer that the blessings of Divine Providence may be freely showered upon you, and that you may be long spared in the high sphere in which you are called to move, to illustrate the virtues which have enshrined your royal mother in the hearts of our people.

WILLIAM YOUNG.	JOHN H. ANDERSON.
JOSEPH HOWE.	WILLIAM ANNAND.
ADAMS G. ARCHIBALD.	JOHN LOCKE.
JONATHAN McCULLY.	BENJAMIN WIER.

To this address His Royal Highness replied in the following terms :

GENTLEMEN,—

I am deeply touched by the warmth and cordiality with which I have been welcomed to this colony, and I thank you most heartily for your address.

It will be my duty, and it certainly will be no less a pleasure to me, to inform Her Majesty of the proofs which you have given me of your feelings of loyalty and devotion to her Throne, and of your gratitude for those blessings, which it is her happiness to reflect, have, during her reign, been bestowed upon you, and so many others of her subjects in all parts of the world.

Most heartily do I sympathise in the pride with which you regard the laurels won by sons of Nova Scotia, and the affection with which you honour the memory of those who have fallen in the service of my country and yours.

The monument you refer to, will kindle the flame of patriotism in the breasts of those volunteers whom I have passed to-day, and, who in this, and the colony which I have lately quitted, are emulating the zeal and gallant spirit which have been exhibited throughout the mother country.

One hundred years have now elapsed since the international struggles which retarded the prosperity of this country were brought to a close.

May peace and harmony amongst yourselves complete the good work which then commenced, and increase the happiness and contentment of a loyal and *united people.*

In the afternoon, the Prince, accompanied by the Duke of Newcastle, the Earl of St. Germains, the Earl of Mulgrave, and several officers of the staff, rode out in the direction of Point Pleasant. A dinner at Government House, at which several distinguished citizens were present, occupied the evening. Arrangements had been made for an illumination of the city on this evening, but the rain which poured down in torrents prevented it from being as general as it would otherwise have been.

Early on the morning of Tuesday, July 31st, the second day of the Prince's sojourn in the city, the streets were filed with crowds of persons ready to enjoy any spectacle presented to them, and to prove by shouts of enthusiasm, whenever a sight of a Royal visitor gave them an opportunity, how joyful the visit of the Prince had made them. The Common was covered with thousands of loyal citizens awaiting the hour when the now very popular Son of a most beloved Sovereign should review the troops in the garrison and the volunteers. The ground appropriated on the Common for the Prince was kept by the Royal Marines, who held the space for the military manœuvres. At 11 o'clock precisely a salvo of military saluted the Prince of Wales'

Standard which was hoisted on the staff, and the Prince himself, who, with a brilliant suite, was approching the exercising ground. The combined bands having played the National Anthem, the Prince, preceded and followed by a staff of twenty mounted officers, rode up and down the lines, greeted as he passed each company with a flourish of trumpets. On the extreme right of the long double file were Royal Artillery, next were stationed the Royal Engineers, then the 62nd and 63rd Regiments. The Volunteer Artillery came first of the Volunteer forces, supported by the Volunteer Engineers, and next were drawn up the Halifax Battalion, headed by their Captain Commandant, which on the left was supported by the Victoria Rifles. The regular and volunteer troops then marched past His Royal Highness in slow and quick time, saluting and being saluted, and the brigade advanced in line saluting Royalty with colours and presented arms. The marching of both Regulars and volunteers elicited we believe the warmest commendation, and certainly their soldierlike bearing had a claim to the highest credit. The regular forces having retired from the ground, Capt. Chearnley put his efficient battalion through several manœuvres for the gratification of the Prince, and His Royal Highness expressed his approbation of their conduct. After many a hearty cheer from the assembled multitude, and a battalion shout from the volunteers, His Royal Highness visited the Citadel, and then returned through crowds of the populace to Government House, whence, after a short rest, he rode out without uniform, and attended by the Lieutenant-Governor and his own suite, to view the sports on the Common. Here the crowd was immense, and the Prince was fairly though not inconveniently thronged by admiring and loyal Haligonians, and acclaims of welcome passed from lip to lip wherever His Royal Highness moved. A ride into the beautiful suburbs, in the course of which he visited the grounds of Mr. Downs, of whom he was graciously pleased to accept a splendid moose head and antlers, occupied the afternoon; a state dinner at Government House in the evening, and a magnificent ball in the Province Building, at which His Royal Highness selected some twenty partners of the lady citizens, made the hours pass pleasantly until Wednesday morning.

In order to afford the necessary accommodation for the ball, spacious temporary wings had been erected at either end of the Province Building, that at the south end being appropriated for the dancers, and that at the north for the supper room. The decorations of the building were superb and tasteful, the assemblage brilliant, and the arrangements from the first quadrille to the last toast perfect. The ball room was a fairy scene—drapery, flowers, music, and company together, made up a dazzling tableau, while a military trophy burning in gas and a motto of bright fire *Motris Carissimæ fili care*, over the dais, aided appropriately to illuminate the gay picture. The hall of the building was beautifully ornamented, and opposite the main entrance a fountain with its sparkling waters and rippling music lent elegance to the scene.* The supper room had been draped with foreign ensigns by the sailors of the *Nile*, and also ornamented with numerous flags bearing the names of distinguished Nova Scotians, and the gay and variegated bunting above, with the well-filed tables beneath pleased at once eye and palate. At 9 p. m., His Royal Highness entered the Ball Room, and shortly afterwards opened the ball with lady Mulgrave. At 11 p. m., the Prince led Lady Mulgrave to the Refreshment Room, and at one he proceeded to the Supper Room, where a magnificent repast was provided. The health of the Royal Visitor's Mother and Father having been drunk with enthusiastic delight, and his own with an uproar of loyal shouts, the Prince retired from supper, and two hours more were spent in the Ball Room, when His Royal Highness departed amid the cheers of hundreds who had waited

---

* The ladies selected were principally the wives or daughters—much oftener the latter—of gentlemen connected with the staff or with the Government of the Province. About half-past one His Royal Highness adjourned to the supper room, begging, it is said, that the ball might not proceed in his absence, as he would not be long away, and his programme was full. He speedily returned and continued hard at work for two hours more. The news of his condescension to the ladies of St. John's, had speedily spread through Halifax, and you may be sure produced much joy among the female portion of the population. He last night more than sustained the reputation he earned in the sister Province. But I am afraid he will do a great deal of mischief. It is not only that he is a Prince—he is also an exceedingly handsome young man, and wins more hearts than he would know what to do with, did he desire to possess them all. I question if any colonist will ever dare to look again in the face—any lady with whom he has danced. They will all consider themselves fit mates for a Duke at the very least. Either their parents will have to export them to England, or the matter will have to be compromised by manufacturing a lot of provincial nobility out of the best materials we possess. However that may be, depend upon it, he has made the ladies more loyal to the throne than ever, if that is possible. The advantage of having their support is known to every man who has had aught to do with politics.

outside all night to see him drive off; and thus ended the second day of the visit of the Prince of Wales.

On Tuesday evening, also, the illumination took place. To describe it in detail is impossible, but we cannot refrain from noticing a few features of the display. The lighting up of Her Majesty's six ships was peculiarly beautiful. At some signal unseen by those on shore, every cross spar became a line of delicate light, revealing the tars, who, each with a blue light in his hand, had manned the yards, while from every ship a flight of rockets went up with a rush and discharged their fiery Prince's Feathers in the air. The brief but exquisite exhibition having died out, the squadron floated like sombre shadows on the water. This illumination at the far north was well matched by the unique display afforded at an arch erected by the Fire Company, in the extreme south of the city. There a resplendant Prince's Feather blazed steadily, supported by revolving gas lights and appropriate transparencies. From that point to Government House, the private residences displayed their well-furnished interiors and their lamp-lighted outsides ; the house of the Judge of the Admiralty being ornamented with an illuminated anchor, with the scroll of fire, "Welcome, Royal Rothsay, welcome." The lights burning on the substantial arch opposite Government House threw a bright gleam on the foliage which overshadowed the crowds beneath, bringing out in bold relief the colossal lion sculptured to the memory of Wellsford and Parker, and giving a park-like appearance to that portion of the street overhung with trees. The next illumination in that street was at the Glebe House, where the Archbishop had, on the splendid Gothic arch, erected by him, placed a motto, "Welcome, Prince of Wales, to the land of the Mayflower," in gas, behind coloured foil,—his residence being decorated with the sentence, *Procede, propere et regnabs.* The Masonic body had raised an elaborate arch opposite their hall, by daylight exhibiting numerous emblems of the craft, which, being transparent, at night were illuminated, and showed to better advantage than in the day. Conspicuous in this dazzling display, besides the places mentioned, were the Bank of Nova Scotia, the Market House, the City Court House, the Dockyard Gate, Dalhousie College, the Engine House, the Glebe House, the residence of Judge Stewart, the stores of J. B. Elliot & Co., E.

Billing, Jr., & Co., West & Knight, W. S. Symonds & Co., C. Phelan, R. McMurray & Co., E. W. Sutcliffe & Co., G. McKenzie, P. Doyle, Woodill, and a host of others. The Lunatic Asylum, on the other side of the harbour, was a grand sight also.

These few specimens of illuminations have only been taken to show on what a grand scale the city was lighted up in honour of the Royal Visitor, but the effect produced throughout defies description. No expense, no trouble was spared by the citizens, to show with what hearty welcome they rejoiced to celebrate the visit to the metropolis of a Prince, always respected for his mother's sake, and now loved for his own.

Wednesday, August 1st, the last day of the visit of His Royal Highness, was as pleasant as bright sunshine and refreshing breezes could make it. Shortly before 11 o'clock a crowd of visitors, who had come to be presented at the Levee to the Prince, entered Government House, and at 11 o'clock the doors were opened for their presentation. His Royal Highness took his position in the Drawing-Room, and his Suite, with the Staff of the Lieutenant-Governor, Major-General and Rear-Admiral, drawn up on either side, from the door to where the Prince was standing, formed a lane through which the persons to be presented passed. Their names were announced by the Earl of St. Germains, (Lord Steward to the Queen's Household,) and as each gentleman passed, His Royal Highness gracefully acknowledged his presence with a bow. It having been announced that it was his pleasure to receive all addresses prepared for presentation on this occasion, the following were presented without being read, and received by the Prince in person :

An address from the Lord Bishop, on behalf of the Clergy and Laity of the Church of England ; one from the Governor of King's College, Windsor,—both of these were presented by the Bishop.

An address from the Masonic body, presented by the Hon. A. Keith.

Addresses from the Wesleyan Conference, the Free Church of Scotland, the Kirk, the R. C. Church, the Presbyterian Church of Nova Scotia, and the Governors of Acadia College, were also presented.

The numerous visitors (upwards of 500) having recorded their names in an elegant book prepared in Halifax for the purpose, departed. And His Royal Highness and Suite having afforded Mr. Chase an opportunity of taking a photograph in memory of the visit, proceeded to H. M. S. Nile, to view the Regatta, from whence they steamed up the Basin in the *Valorous*, to the Prince's Lodge, where His Royal Highness landed, and walked through the ruined grounds which his grandfather had laid out. In association, this visit to the traces of royalty in the Colonies was, doubtless, one of the most interesting in his sojourn in Nova Scotia, and will form a topic of conversation when returned to the Palaces at home. A large dinner and reception at Government House, a torch-light procession of the Firemen, in which they made a magnificent display, and an exhibition of fire-works from the glacis of the Citadel, closed the entertainment of that day.

On Thursday morning, August 2nd, His Royal Highness left Halifax for St. John's, N. B., via Windsor. At half-past 6 a. m., he left Government House, a Guard of Honour composed of the Volunteer Engineers and Scottish Rifles saluting him as he departed. A little before seven, he arrived at the Richmond Railway Station, where a Guard of Honour composed of the Chebucto Grays and Mayflower Rifles, was in waiting, the ships and the Fort firing a salute. Here he was shown into the car prepared for his reception by the Hon. Mr. McCully, Chief of the railway department, Lady Mulgrave and Lady Trolloppe, the Duke of Newcastle, Earl St. Germains, General Bruce, Major Teesdale, the Governor, the Admiral, the General, the Aides, and others of the party followed. The members of the Legislature, to the number of fifty or sixty persons, including all the members of the Executive Government, the members of the Executive Committee of Preparations, and many other gentlemen, accompanied the royal party to Windsor at 8 a. m., an hour and a half after leaving Richmond, the train entered Windsor Station. Here the party were met by the local authorities, with the Hon. R. McHeffy, Custos of the County, at their head. A Guard of Honour formed of the Halifax Rifles and Irish Volunteers, was in attendance, and a salute was fired by the Halifax Volunteer Artillery, all of which Companies had gone up to Windsor on an early morning train. The party proceeded immediately to the Clifton House, where breakfast was prepared, to which the whole company present sat down with His Royal Highness. An address from the county, read by the Rev. Dr. McCrawley, President of the King's College was presented, and an answer returned, as follows :

To the Most High, Puissant and Illustrious Prince Albert Edward, Prince of the United Kingdom of Great Britain and Ireland, Prince of Wales, Duke of Saxony, Prince of Cobourg and Gotha, Great Steward of Scotland, Duke of Cornwall and Rothsay, Earl of Chester, Carrick and Dublin, Baron of Renfrew and Lord of the Isles, K. G.

MAY IT PLEASE YOUR ROYAL HIGHNESS,

We, the loyal inhabitants of the township of Windsor, of the county of Hants, in the Province of Nova Scotia, beg leave to approach your Royal Highness to offer the humble expression of a heartfelt welcome, and to thank your Royal Highness for the unprecedented honour of this opportunity condescendingly offered us, of avowing our devoted loyalty and unwavering attachment to the throne and person of our most gracious Queen, and to her illustrious house and family, our exalted admiration and respect for the eminent talents and virtues of her Royal Consort, and our fervent aspirations and hopes for a long career of happiness and glory to your Royal Highness. Representing on this happy occasion the loyal feelings of the oldest University town in her Majesty's widely extended colonial possessions, we view it as our highest privilege and singular honour to be permitted to greet your Royal Highness in the immediate neighbourhood of an institution founded by His Majesty King George the Third, the august and illustrious ancestor of your Royal Highness. Believing that the University of Windsor has continued during successive years to answer the wise and benevolent purpose of its founder, and knowing that in King's College, under the Royal Charter then granted, have been educated in religion, in literature and science, a great number of the clergy, many of the most distinguished members of the bench and bar in this and the neighbouring colonies, many military men whose heroic achievments have been widely celebrated, and several others, including members of the different religious denominations, equally conspicuous in the various walks of life, all of whom have ever manifested the firmest allegiance to the British throne and Government. But we are aware that your Royal Highness has only a few moments to bestow for this brief but ever memorable occasion. We are extremely grateful, and we hope that your Royal Highness' visit to Nova Scotia may be agreeable to your Royal Highness, as it is most welcome and most gratifying to us ; and that on your happy return to Windsor Castle and to the renowned University in which your Royal Highness is enrolled, your Royal Highness may convey to Her Gracious Majesty our beloved Queen, the assurance of the sentiments of inviolable loyalty to the throne and of affectionate veneration for the constitution which pervade all ranks and classes of Her Majesty's subjects in this portion of her dominions ; and not least the youth of our University, educated in a town whose ancient fortress was honoured by the presence and still bears the name of her Majesty's illustrious father.

   (Signed)   R. A. McHEFFEY,
            Custos. Co. Hants,
        On behalf of the inhabitants.

The Prince then read in his usual manner this brief reply :—

GENTLEMEN,—The address which you have presented to me demands my acknowledgments. It is a pleasure to me to visit, even though it be but in passing, this seat of learning in British North America ; to find that the sons of these Provinces are successfully pursuing, within the precincts of your town, the studies which I have myself abandoned only for a time, that I might come to these lands. I thank you for your kind recollection of my grandfather, and for your loyal sentiments.

His Royal Highness received and replied to the above address, standing in view of the assembled thousands, on a small platform on the balcony of the hotel, over which was an awning of festooned crimson damask, surmounted by a Prince's Feather and the motto, "Ich Dien." On the left of His Royal Highness, in front of the Depot, was erected a staging, upon which stood about 600 of the youth and beauty of the female population of Windsor and vicinity, gaily dressed in holiday attire. The depot was ornamented with flags, and upon it in evergreens were the words, "To our Prince, all hail." In front of the Prince on a staging sat the children of the Sabbath and Day Schools—a lively picture. On the Prince's right on Water Street was an arch 32 feet high and 23 feet wide, with wings or side arches 21 feet high and ten feet wide, in the Roman triumphal style, the whole being covered with evergreens. In the spring of each arch rested the Shield of the Union, with trophies of flags and pennons branching therefrom. The motto, "God Save the Queen," formed the cap of the central arch, while surmounting the whole glistened the Royal Crown, with gold, jewels, and ermine complete. Through this arch might be seen the fine natural arch formed by the elm trees in front of P. M. Cunningham's office. Beyond this was a very tastefully decorated arch, hung with wreaths of flowers and festoons of evergreens. Upon it was the motto, "Mœnia ipsa atquæ tecta exultant." Further along Water Street, in front of T. S. Harding's warehouse, a private arch was erected by M. Harding and others. It was surmounted by a model ship full rigged, and the motto, "Ships, Colonies, and Commerce,—Old England for ever." A close hedge of spruces extended from Water Street—a distance of over 200 yeards—to the Avon Bridge. At the gate of the bridge was a very tasteful Gothic arch, with the motto, "Welcome." The private buildings in Water Street were decorated with wreaths and festoons of flowers, bunting, &c., and here and there might be seen for mottoes, "Welcome to the Colonies," "May God give thee a safe return," &c.

At 10 a. m., the carriages in attendance drew up, and His Royal Highness and Suite, attended by a long procession, drove off amidst the roar of artillery, and the cheers of the populace, for Hantsport, at which place, after receiving an address from the inhabitants, they embarked on board H. M. S. *Styx*, at 11 a. m., and immediately sailed for St. John's, N. B.

The visit of His Royal Highness, thus far, was, in all respects, most gratifying. The frank, joyous, and kindly expression of his youthful countenance, his unaffected courtesy and urbanity of demeanor, combined with a manliness and dignity of bearing almost unlooked for in a youth of nineteen, completely won the hearts of all who approached him, until the abstract sentiment of loyalty which largely prompted the ovations with which he was greeted, was warmed and kindled into a universal sentiment of personal esteem and admiration. There is reason, also, to believe that the evidence of this sentiment which greeted him on every hand, were not unappreciated by the Prince and the noblemen who accompanied him. On Saturday, the 4th inst., a Royal Gazette Extraordinary was issued, containing the following documents:

Government House, Halifax,
3rd August, 1860.

GENTLEMEN—

I should neither be performing my duty, or consulting my own feelings, did I not embrace the earliest opportunity of informing you that His Royal Highness the Prince of Wales expressed to me, in the strongest terms, the pleasure which he felt at the reception given to him in this Province.

Where all have united with so much cordiality and good feeling to do honour to the son of our beloved Sovereign, I feel that it would be invidious to particularise any ; but, as all organizations and arrangements must fail unless under proper management, I feel that I am doing injustice to none when I express to you, the Executive Committee, and through you to the people of Nova Scotia, my sincere and hearty congratulations on the very satisfactory and pleasing manner in which every thing has been conducted during the stay of the Prince of Wales in this city, and I doubt not that His Royal Highness will long remember with pleasure the loyalty and affection evinced by all parties in this portion of Her Majesty's dominions.

To yourselves, Gentlemen, I feel that my especial thanks are due for the attention, time and energy which you have devoted to the arrangements committed to your charge, by which alone the perfect order, regularity and appropriate decorations, which have characterised the whole proceedings, could have been secured.

I have the honour to be,
Gentlemen,
Your most obedient servant,
MULGRAVE.

To the Chairman and members of the Committee of Management, for the reception of His Royal Highness the Prince of Wales.

MILITIA GENERAL ORDER,—HEAD QUARTERS, HALIFAX,

Adjutant General's Office, August 3rd, 1860.

"I am directed by His Excellency the Lieutenant-Governor and Commander-in-Chief, to express to the officers and men of the various Halifax and Dartmouth Volunteer Companies, the great satisfaction which he felt at their steadiness and soldier-like bearing, both on the occasion of the landing of His Royal Highness the Prince of Wales, and at the review which took place on the 31st ult.

"His Excellency is aware that it will be a source of the highest gratification to them to know that His Royal Highness expressed himself much pleased, not only with their appearance and the proficiency in drill at which they had arrived, but also with the loyal spirit which had induced them, at considerable sacrifice to themselves, to devote so much time and attention to their duties.

"His Excellency feels sure that the knowledge that their exertions have been fully appreciated by His Royal Highness, cannot fail to be most encouraging to the Volunteers, and he rejoices that he has had so favourable an opportunity of bringing their efficiency under the notice of His Royal Highness.

R. BLIGH SINCLAIR, *A. G. M.*

At 4 a. m., on Wednesday morning, 8th inst., H. M. S. *Styx* arrived at Hantsport from St. John's, N. B., with the Prince and Suite on board, and shortly afterwards His Royal Highness was again on Nova Scotia soil, and on the road to Windsor, where he arrived at 7 a. m. Having breakfasted, he left Windsor shortly before 9 o'clock, by rail for Truro, at which place he arrived at 11 a. m., the distance, 79 miles, having been traversed in two hours and sixteen minutes. The arrangements made for the conveyance of His Royal Highness over the railway, by the Honourable Mr. McCully, Chief of the Department, were of the most perfect and satisfactory character, and such as to ensure, as far as human prudence and foresight could accomplish it, the comfort and safety of the royal traveller. The car in which the Prince rode was, perhaps, less richly decorated than some which he will see in Canada, but it was no less comfortable, being carpeted with fine Brussels carpet, and furnished with neat table, chairs, mirrors, &c. This was the first experience of our distinguished visitors in railway travelling in America, and that the experience was not an unpleasant one, may be inferred from the fact that before leaving Truro, His Royal Highness left £20 sterling to be distributed among the subordinate employees on the train by which he had travelled.

Arrived at the depot at Truro, the Prince was received with a Royal Salute fired by the Halifax Volunteer Artillery. The Victoria Rifles formed a Guard of Honour on the occasion. He was met at the station by the Executive Committee, by whom he was conducted, amidst the cheers of the populace, to his carriage, in which, accompanied by the Duke of Newcastle, the Earl of Mulgrave, and the Earl St. Germains, he proceeded to the Court House, followed in procession by the other members of the suite, His Lordship the Bishop, General Trolloppe and suite in carriages ; and on foot by the Chief Justice, the Honourable Provincial Secretary, and other Members of the Executive Council, the Speaker and Members of the House of Assembly, Clergy, Magistrates, Sons of Temperance, and other organised bodies. In passing the Normal School grounds, His Royal Highness paused a few minutes, while the pupils of the Normal, Model, and other Schools there assembled, to the number of 400, sang the National Anthem. Arrived at the Court House, where the Dartmouth Volunteer Rifles and the Dartmouth Volunteer Engineers formed a Guard of Honour, an address from the inhabitants of Colchester County was read by the Hon. Attorney General, as follows:

To the Most High, Puissant and Illustrious Prince Albert Edward, Prince of the United Kingdom of Great Britain and Ireland, Prince of Wales, Duke of Saxony, Prince of Cobourg and Gotha, Great Steward of Scotland, Duke of Cornwall and Rothsay, Earl of Chester, Carrick, and Dublin, Baron of Renfrew, and Lord of the Isles, K. G.

We, the Sheriff, Clergy, Magistrates, and other inhabitants of Colchester, beg leave respectfully to welcome Your Royal Highness to this county. We are proud to be able to assure your Royal Highness that the people of Nova Scotia yield to no portion of the subjects of Her Majesty in loyalty and devoted attachment to her person and throne.

The visit of your Royal Highness will foster this feeling. It will unite still more closely the ties which bind us to the parent state, while gratifying the just pride we feel in being recognised as an integral portion of the mighty Empire over which your Royal Mother reigns. It will strengthen the surest foundation on which her throne reposes, the love and affection of her people in this province. The rewards of industry if never large, are always secure; our population, blest with the comforts of life in moderate profusion, are contented and happy—the free institutions which are the pride of Britain have been claimed and conceded as our birthright, while the spectacle your Royal Highness has just witnessed in passing the Provincial Normal School, will call your attention to the institutions we have founded for diffusing common school instruction among the masses of the people, and making widely disseminated education the basis of political privilege. The visit of your Royal Highness we shall long remember with pleasure and pride,—we are quite sure that the gratification it has enabled your Royal Highness to confer upon a large body of Her Majesty's subjects will be felt by you as some alleviation of the fatigues of the journey, and it is our earnest prayer, that, shielded and protected by Divine Providence, you may return in safety to the seat of the Empire,—and be able to assure our Gracious Sovereign that she has not over-estimated the affectionate loyalty of the *people* of Nova Scotia.

To which His Royal Highness was pleased to make the following reply :

GENTLEMEN,—Accept my thanks for this address, and for your welcome to the County of Colchester and town of Truro. I gladly pause for a moment, on my journey, to receive this additional proof of the loyalty of this Province, and of the hearty reception which they have prepared for the son of their Queen. I shall never forget the many interesting scenes which have passed in quick succession before me since I landed in these Colonies.

Descending from the platform at the Court House, His Royal Highness entered McKay's Hotel, where he appeared on the balcony and acknowledged in the most gracious manner the cheers, again and again repeated, by the crowds which entirely filled the parade ground.

Here, again, he was greeted with the National Anthem, sung by the pupils of the schools, who had marched down and taken up their position in front of the hotel.

His Royal Highness having expressed a wish to see a class of the Model School pupils go through their exercises in mental arithmetic, a dozen of the pupils, six of each sex, selected by a vote of the scholars themselves, with their teachers and Dr. Forrester, were in attendance. The exhibition by the pupils appeared to give His Royal Highness much satisfaction, and elicited the most gratifying remarks from some of the distinguished personages of his suite.

The decorations of the village were exceedingly beautiful, and did great credit to the gentlemen who designed them ; but it is unnecessary here to describe them in detail. With flags flying from every house top, with the dwellings of all, rich and poor, neatly decorated, with the rich green of the arches, the fields and gardens, contrasting with the pure white of the houses, fences, and pailings, and the village itself resting like a flower bed in the midst of the surrounding rich, alluvial country, Truro presented a picture of neatness and beauty perhaps not excelled by any other village in British America. His Royal Highness having partaken of luncheon at McKay's Hotel, started at one, p. m., in the carriage of the Chief Justice, and accompanied as before, for Pictou, the Halifax Volunteer Artillery firing a salute, and the assembled populace renewing their cheers as the carriage drove off. The Hon. Provincial Secretary and other Members of the Legislature accompanied the Royal party to Pictou.

The journey from Truro to the town of Pictou, 40 miles, was made in a little over four hours. At a distance of 12 miles from the town a magnificent arch was erected, and here the Prince was met by the High Sheriff, the Custos and magistrates, and about 4000 of the yeomanry and ladies of the county, who lined the road on each side, some distance from the arch, the ladies strewing the way with flowers as the royal cortege passed through. After passing this arch a procession was formed, the High Sheriff of the county preceding the carriage of His Royal Highness, and about 100 carriages and 200 horsemen following. At Durham village, seven miles from Pictou, another arch had been erected, and here also an immense number of persons were assembled, lining the road on either side, to catch a view of their future sovereign, and greeting him as he drove slowly through the lines with right loyal cheers. The procession, largely augmented in numbers at this point, proceeded towards Pictou. At the Three Mile House, another arch, of exceedingly beautiful design, was

K

erected; and here also vast crowds had assembled to testify their loyalty to their Sovereign, by welcoming with cordial cheers her son and representative. Before arriving in Pictou, the procession had increased so as to exceed in magnitude any similar demonstration ever witnessed in Nova Scotia. On arriving at the western entrance of the town, the Prince was welcomed by a Royal salute from the Pictou Volunteers, under Captain McKinlay, stationed near the residence of A. J. Patterson, Esq. Entering the town by Church Street, under a splendid arch, and through lines formed by the Masonic body, with the Hon. A. Keith, Grand Master, at their head; the Sons of Temperance, Odd Fellows, Fire Companies and other public bodies. His Royal Highness drove to the Court House, where he was received by a guard of honour,—composed of one company of the Albion Mines Volunteers, besides from 10,000 to 12,000 of the people of the surrounding country, who greeted him with heartfelt cheers of welcome. Here he was met by the Executive Committee and other gentlemen, by whom he was conducted to a platform erected in front of the building, where he received the following address:

To His Royal Highness, Albert Edward, Prince of Wales, Prince of the United Kingdom of Great Britain and Ireland, Duke of Saxony, Prince of Saxe Coburg and Gotha, Great Steward of Scotland, Duke of Cornwall and Rothsay, Earl of Chester, Carrick and Dublin, Baron of Renfrew and Lord of the Isles, Knight of the Garter.

MAY IT PLEASE YOUR ROYAL HIGHNESS—

The inhabitants of the county of Pictou beg leave to express their sincere gratitude for the distinguished honour conferred upon them by the visit of your Royal Highness, and they now greet you with a warm and cordial welcome.

They hail the visit of your Royal Highness to Her Majesty's North American colonies, as a pledge and assurance of the deep and lively interest which our most gracious Queen takes in the prosperity of her extended dominions; and they rejoice in this opportunity of being enabled so directly to manifest their devoted attachment and loyalty to the Crown and Sovereign of Great Britain.

Enjoying the great happiness of being British subjects, and the recipients of the blessings which that glorious privilege confers, their hearts are knit in indissoluble bonds of loyalty to the British throne.

The wisdom and justice which have distinguished the reign of our Most Gracious Sovereign, and the virtues which adorn Her Majesty's court and life, have secured from her subjects in Nova Scotia feelings of the most devoted attachment to Her Majesty's royal person and family.

Within a century past the primeval forest covered the soil, where, in the progress of Your Royal Highness this day, many happy homes and productive fields have presented themselves to the eye. These have been acquired under the fostering care of the state, and from the influence of the virtues and industry which have always characterised the inhabitants of the British Islands, whence this county was originally settled.

"The inhabitants of the County of Pictou offer their sincere prayers, that Your Royal Highness may have a prosperous and pleasant journey through the dominions of Her Majesty in North America; and that Your Royal Highness may return safe and gratified to that country, which even in this distant land, is designated by the endearing name of "home."

On behalf of the inhabitants,

WM. H. HARRIS, Sheriff.
ROBERT McKAY, Custos.
A. C. McDONALD, M. P. P.
R. P. GRANT, M. P. P.
JAS. McDONALD, M. P. P."

To which His Royal Highness was pleased to make the following reply :

GENTLEMEN,—In your town I close a visit to the Province of Nova Scotia, which has given me unmixed pleasure, and has brought forth proofs of devotion to the Queen and to your mother country, which must ever remain engraven on my memory.

I thank you for an address which, so short can be my stay in this place, is at once a welcome and a farewell.

My journey this day through your beautiful county has impressed me with an additional sense of the great destiny which awaits these lands.

I hereby wish success and happiness to the settlers whom I have passed, and a speedy and productive development of the vast mineral wealth which lies beneath and around you."

The platform on which His Royal Highness stood, with his suite, Earl of Mulgrave, Major-General Trolloppe, and other distinguished gentlemen, was elevated sufficiently to give the assembled thousands a full view of his person. After reading the reply to the address, the Prince was greeted with nine tremendous cheers, shortly after which he entered the building where a luncheon was prepared, and partook of some slight refreshment. He then returned to his carriage, and, followed by a procession formed by the leading officials, and the members of the various societies with which the streets were lined, filing in as the royal cortage passed through, procceded down College street and Water street, to the Market wharf, where he was to embark. The streets through which he passed were spanned by arches of various and beautiful designs, several of which were dedicated to different members of the Royal Family, and embellished with appropriate mottoes and devices. The houses also, were gaily decorated, the citizens of Pictou vieing with those of Halifax, in the profusion and beauty of their embellishments.

At the wharf, His Royal Highness was received by a guard of honour, composed of the second company of the Albion Mines Volunteer Rifles, under the command of Col. Scott, and here, a few minutes after six, p. m., he entered the royal barge, and finally bade good bye to Nova Scotia—the Pictou Volunteer Artillery under Captain McKinley, firing a royal salute from the Signal Hill, as he left the shores. He was soon on board the *Flying Fish*, and at 7. p. m., was under way to join the *Hero* outside, thousands of people on the wharves and on Battery and Signal Hills following him with farewell cheers, as the ships passed down the harbour.

His Royal Highness was accompanied on board by Lord and Lady Mulgrave, Major-General Trolloppe, His Lordship the Bishop of Nova Scotia, and the Rev. Charles Elliott, Rector of St. George's, Pictou. By the latter, he sent a message to the citizens of

Pictou, thanking them for the reception which they had extended to him, and expressing regret that arrangements had been made previous to his arrival, which prevented him remaining longer among them, to witness their festivities and partake of their hospitality. Notes were addressed by Major-General Bruce, at the request of the Prince, to Col. Brown, of the Sydney Volunteers, and Col. Scott, of the Albion Mines Volunteers, thanking these gentlemen for their attention to His Royal Highness on the occasion of his visits to Sydney, C. B., and Pictou. A similar compliment, doubtless, would have been extended to Capt. McKinlay and the Pictou Volunteer Artillery, had that corps not unfortunately been stationed in a position which deprived them of the privilege of being near the person of His Royal Highness.

The Prince was now gone, but the popular demonstrations of respect and loyalty were not yet ended. At half-past seven, a large party of gentlemen, among whom were the Hon. Provincial Secretary and several other members of the Legislature, sat down to a supper where patriotic and loyal sentiments were proposed, and speeches made. During the evening the town was brilliantly illuminated, and between nine and ten o'clock, there was a magnificent display of fireworks, while on many a hill-top within a region of twelve miles around, large bon-fires flamed far into the night.

One or two incidents connected with the Royal visit, and indicative of the generosity of the Prince, must be mentioned before closing this brief account of his visit. The spot where the feet of His Royal Highness first touched the soil of Nova Scotia, has been marked by a marble slab, in commemoration of the event, bearing the following inscription—"H. R. H. the Prince of Wales landed here, July 30, 1860." Besides the gift to the railway employees, already mentioned, His Royal Highness, before leaving the province, presented the sum of £100 sterling to the managers of the Asylum for the Deaf and Dumb. He also left £50 sterling for the Indians who were present at his reception in the dockyard, and a handsome sum was placed at the disposal of Lady Mulgrave for distribution among the poor of Halifax.

Thus ended the visit of the Prince of Wales to Nova Scotia; a visit which forms one of the most auspicious, and, to the people of the country, one of the most gratifying and felicitous events, which has ever occurred since this Province first became an appendage of the British Empire. Here is briefly sketched the leading features of that visit; and, while reflecting on the harmony which cemented all shades of religion and politics, the enthusiasm and honest loyalty which filled all hearts and gushed from every lip, the irrepressible evidences of respect and love which greeted His Royal Highness wherever he appeared, the propriety of conduct,—the order and respect for law which reigned every where,—in city, town and village, throughout the whole season of enthusiasm and excitement—honours Nova Scotia; and it is hoped that, while relating to His Royal Mother the history of what he saw and heard in British North America, the Prince will remember with gratification and tell with approval, with what eager, fervent, and united hearts the people of Nova Scotia greeted his landing, paid homage to him while present, and wished him God speed when he left the shores. That he has derived much gratification from his brief sojourn, while there, there is scarce room to doubt; that his visit has given a large amount of pleasure and happiness to the people of this Province, all know; and that it will result in great future good, all trust and believe. One result, at least, is certain : the sentiment of loyalty and devotion to the Throne of England, so warmly cherished by Nova Scotians, even while thousands of miles removed from all outward evidences and symbols of royalty, has been quickened and intensified by the Royal visit. The admirable and amicable qualities of heart and mind exhibited by the Prince, have every where called into existence a feeling of personal respect and love for Victoria's Son, which will excite a warmer love for his Royal Mother ; and henceforth Nova Scotians will be conscious of a deeper and more engrossing sentiment of devotion, as they join in the National Prayer—

"GOD SAVE THE QUEEN !"

(From an English view.)

THE PRINCE OF WALES AT HALIFAX.

The arrival of the Prince of Wales at Halifax, was one of the most memorable incidents of his visit to the North American provinces. Immediately the *Hero* and her escort came to their moorings a train of some ten or twelve Indian canoes paddled up under the stern of the *Hero*. The Indians in them were of the tribe of the Micmacs, who had come in from the woods especially to do honour to his Highness. Their light birch-bark canoes had little sprigs of fern in them at the bows, and looked characteristic enough. Not so did their occupants, who were dressed in blue frock coats and trousers, and had their swarthy, broad, Mongol features, and long black hair, almost concealed under common English beaver hats, about twice too large for their heads. By way of reconciling them to this most un-Indian costume, the cuffs and colars of the coats were ornamented with rough bead-work, making such a curious *mélange* of the whole dress that it was hard to say of the two whether civilization or barbarism was most travestied. The men themselves, though carefully selected from the best of the tribe, and in most cases tall, and in one or more instances athletic-looking, were on the whole immeasurably inferior in physical developement to the average of ordinary white men. On Lake Huron, real Indians,—Indians who would not know what to do with all the trousers in Bond street, if they were given them to wear for nothing,—were to meet the Prince, race in canoes, run, wrestle, swim, and shoot before him. But, alas for what the Micmacs could offer! In their long blue coats and ornamented cuffs and collars they looked like the mummies of beadledom. Their chief was a fine looking man, but he was an Englishman, who had "taken up" among the Indians as a "medicine-man," and to whose ministerings, by-the-way, the dilapidated appearance of his new associates might be, perhaps, ascribed. Lord Mulgrave, with the Admiral, at once went on board the *Hero*, and had an interview with His Royal Highness, who expressed to them his intention of landing at twelve o'clock. Precisely at that hour there was a little stir on board the *Hero*, and shaking hands as he left with the officers of the ship, the Prince of Wales came down the side, and followed by the Duke of Newcastle, the Earl of St. Germains, Major-General Bruce, and the other officers of his suite, took his seat in the Royal barge. As it pushed from the side the Prince's Royal Standard— the arms of England quartered according to the heraldic bearings of the next heir—was hoisted, amid a thundering roar of guns from the fleet and forts.

The Prince disembarked at a triumphal arch, which, to show the nautical character of the decorations, was moored by two small archors at each side, with a canoe on the top with the Prince of Wales' feathers springing out of the middle like three little masts. Under this the Prince landed, in the uniform of a colonel in the army, with the broad blue Ribbon of the Garter across his breast. Here he stood for some seconds motionless, for he had complied with a request of the city that a photograph might be taken of him as he first landed on Nova Scotia soil. It was rather a trying position for any young man, even though a Prince, to stand motionless, close to the eager, scrutinising, admiring gaze of thousands for nearly half a minute, without varying a feature or a muscle, and amid such silence that almost the breathing of the crowd was audible. But with his hat raised, and a kind smile on his face which reminded every one irresistibly of his Royal mother, the Prince bore the ordeal gracefully and well— so well that a tremendous cheer, with applause from the ladies, and cries of "How kind of him!" "How condescending!" "How affable!" rewarded him amply for his slight delay. Before he had well done acknowledging the salutes of the Governor, the Legislature, and the Judges, His Royal Highness was already more popular at Halifax, if possible, than he had even been at St. John's.

The Mayor and Corporation, having been formally introduced to His Royal Highness, read an address of congratulation on his arrival among them. Immediately after, and amid loud cheers, the Prince, mounted on horseback, and accompaned by the Lieutenant-Governor and all his suite, issued from the dockyard into the main street leading up towards the town. Here, indeed, all Halifax was out, shouting, cheering, waving handkerchiefs, and clapping hands, as if they were beside themselves. For the first part of the way the street was kept by the Fire Companies, then by corps of volunteers; among them was a strong company of negroes, and then came the regulars. But through all these barriers, save the last, the crowd went plunging on, quite irresistible, not only at times overwhelming the thin line of sentries, but sometime carrying them with them with a headlong rush that no obstacle could check, till they were abreast of the Prince, when they stopped, and with scrupulous reverence forebore to crowd on him, though they made up for their reserve by cheering, shouting, and throwing their caps into the air like madmen. The great street was soon entered,—one long vista of flags, arches, flowers, and wreaths, with the roadway densely crowded, and all the windows, roofs and balconies thronged with ladies waving handkerchiefs and throwing down bouquets till the whole place seemed fluttering in the wind. The whole scene was one of the most enthusiastic delight, the contagious spirit of which spread even to the coldest, till the people seemed actually as if they were taking leave of their senses. The Prince's horse started now and then at the cheers, but, as the Prince sits his horse beautifully, the fretfulness of the steed only showed off the rider to the best advantage; and the expressions of fervent admiration which were heard now and then from the ladies in the balconies as he rode by bowing to them, in spite of his unruly horse, with easy grace, were enough to turn the head of any Crown Prince in Christendom. At last the procession turned out of the street leading from the dockyard and wound up the hill to the Parade, where a beautiful scene presented itself. Over the whole Parade-ground had been erected an immense bench of seats, something like the orchestra of the Crystal Palace, which held nearly 3,000 children, the sons and daughters of the citizens. All were very nicely dressed, and looked at a distance, in the gay confusion of colours, like a huge flower-bed, framed in by the arches and flags and evergreen in the background, in a bright striking picture. At the foot of the gallery the Prince reined in his horse while the children sang "God Save the Queen," with all the strength and harmony of their little voices. The first verse was very well given; so well that the Prince made them a low bow as the second was proceeding, and this put an end to the music, for, carried away by enthusiasm at the graceful compliment, two or three rosy little girls and boys began to cheer, and in a second they all rose and shouted, clapped their hands, and waved bonnets, caps, and handkerchiefs in such a vivid and spontaneous burst of juvenile enthusiasm as was really touching.

Again the procession continued its course towards the Government House, all along meeting with the same enthusiasm, the same demonstrations of eager loyalty and respect.

At Lord Mulgrave's the Prince alighted, and proceeded at once to visit the Countess and Lady Milne. Here Lady Mulgrave gave him a present which had been left at the house for him by a young Indian girl that morning. It was a little cigar-case, beautifully worked in slips of different coloured woods, and further adorned with the little coloured bead ornaments in making which the Indians so excel. With the case was a small basket, similar in its make and decorations, which the girl begged the Prince would take to the Queen. Both were made by herself, she said. After a short interval the Prince received a deputation from the members of the Government and Legislative Assembly.

A banquet took place at the Government House the same night, and about thirty guests were invited to meet the Prince. In the evening fireworks and a general illumination were to amuse the town ; but before three in the day the hopelessness of expecting any display from this source was apparent to every one. The rain set in, not in showers, but with a massive, steady, down-pour like thunderstorm rain, with a certainty of its continuance for hours. Under such a waterfall, of course, the fireworks were a failure. The fleet had been ordered to illuminate, but, of course, counter-orders were sent.

The next day was religiously held as a holiday. Not only were the shops closed, but the telegraph stopped work, no mail went out, and there were no newspapers even. In fact, to use the favourite expression there, Halifax was in "a general bust," and nothing but holidays and fêtes were thought of. Even the special *Gazette* containing the addresses could not be brought out until, as it is said, some members of the government who were conversant with such matters went down to the office, and, with the assistance of a captured printer's apprentice, managed to set up the types for themselves.

This day the Prince went to the common near the Citadel, and reviewed the two regiments of the garrison with all the various corps of rifle volunteers. Of these there were about 1100 present, all composed of volunteers belonging to the town of Halifax, and divided into different companies, whereof one was entirely of negroes.

At the conclusion of the review, and after some stirring cheers from the troops and spectators, His Royal Highness and suite next visited the Citadel. It is a very strong fortress on the peak of a hill, which dominates the town and country for miles round.

In the afternoon military games, races in sacks, climbing the greasy pole, and other sports for the people, took place on the common; but at these His Royal Highness was not present, and he only left Government House at ten o'clock, with all his suite and staff, to honour the grand ball with his presence. This ball was the great feature of the Halifax entertainment, and it certainly was a most successful and a most brilliant affair. It was given in the Province House, where the members of the Nova Scotia Legislature hold their Parliament. This building, however, though a large and roomy one, was far too much broken up into apartments for the Cabinet, for the House, for the President of Council, &c., to afford any space in which some 1200 persons could promenade, dance, and flirt. The House of Commons room, therefore, was given up bodily to refreshments, and the little Speaker's chair and strangers' gallery were half concealed among the roses and evergreens which formed an ornamental background to the tables of confectionery. The supper was laid in a large wooden building specially erected for the purpose, and another to correspond was built for the ball-room. All the passages between these were handsomely decorated with mirrors, evergreens, banks of flowers, groups of weapons; and gas stars and chandeliers innumerable. The ball and supper rooms were draped in the style of tents, canopied with pink and white. On the whole, the entire aspect of all the rooms was tasteful and striking in the extreme; and the assembly would have done honour to any ball-room in Europe. The Prince arrived exactly at ten o'clock, and was welcomed with tremendous cheers by the crowd outside—by the visitors in the ball-room with bows and courtesies. As His Royal Highness was in high spirits, and seemed anxious that no time should be lost, the ball commenced at once, the Prince opening it in a quadrille with Lady Mulgrave. He next danced with Lady Milne, which duties discharged to the two chief ladies present, he sought partners for himself in every succeeding dance till he quitted the room, and led out some one or other of the distinguished young belles of Halifax. It need hardly be said how popular was this mode, even among the young officers and dandies whose "engagements" he must have broken through in the most ruthless manner, and whose fair partners he bore away in triumph. At about twelve o'clock His Royal Highness went to supper, which was laid out in the temporary building with great taste and splendour. Here, at the conclusion of the repast, the Mayor of Halifax gave "The health of Her Majesty, the Prince Consort, and the Prince of Wales," toasts, which were, of course, received with immense enthusiasm, and there was evidently a lingering expectation in the minds of the good citizens of Halifax that the Prince would favour the company with a speech in reply to each. His Highness, however, had more taste than to prefer speech-making to dancing, and, accordingly, as soon as the toasts had been duly honoured, he bowed his acknowledgments, and returned at once to the amusements of the ball-room. Here he again continued dancing till a little after two o'clock, when he took his departure. He was accompanied to his carriage by nearly all the visitors, who added their cheers to the enthusiastic shouts of the crowd as he drove off. Next day, and the last of the Prince's stay in Halifax, there was a regatta, after which the Prince took a ride into the country, resuming his progress to Windsor and St. John's on the following morning.

His Royal Highness's tour in the lower provinces of North America was concluded at Charlottetown, Prince Edward Island. Here on the 11th ult. he held a levée at the Government House, and received an address from the Legislature. On the same day the Prince and suite embarked for Gaspé, the forts firing salutes, and the ships manning their yards, as did also the French frigate *Pomone*. On Sunday afternoon (the 12th) the Prince arrived at Gaspé, and was met there by the Governor-General of Canada and his Cabinet. He remained for the night, and proceeded westward the next day.

In attempting to steam out of the harbour the *Hero* ran aground, and remained hard and fast upon the stony bottom. The *Ariadne* upon this endeavoured to tow her off, but it was not till she had broken three large hawsers, and the *Hero* had lost three anchors and some sheets of copper, that this was accomplished. The Prince, during the two hours aground, was on deck, interesting himself in the work of getting his ship off, which was at first feared would not be done till the next tide.

The Prince's squadron arrived at Quebec on the afternoon of the 18th ult., and was received with a salute from the men-of-war, the citadel, and the town. The shipping were dressed with flags, and their yards were manned. The fortifications and the roofs of the houses were covered with spectators. The scene was very animated. The city was crowded with visitors from all parts of the British possessions and the United States. Great enthusiasm prevailed.

Extensive preparations were being made at Montreal for the entertainment of the Prince, and at Bermuda. A meeting of the most prominent merchants, bankers, and others of the city of New York, was held on the 14th ult., to adopt measures for giving an appropriate reception on behalf of the people of New York to the Prince on the occasion of his visit to that city.

There is one manifestation of Canadian loyalty which deserves kindly notice. We refer to the resolution arrived at by a convention of coloured men to present an address to the Prince as an expression of their gratitude for the liberty which they enjoy under British rule.

The following beautiful verses were presented to His Royal Highness the Prince of Wales, by Lady Laura Phipps, on behalf of the ladies of Hants County :

TO THE QUEEN.

Queen of the thousand Isles! whose fragile form
  'Midst the proud structures of our Father Land,
Graces the throne, which each subsiding storm
  That shakes the earth, assures us yet shall stand;
  Thy gentle voice, of mild yet firm command,
Is heard in every clime, on every wave ;
  Thy dazzling sceptre, like a fairy wand,
Strikes off the shackles from the struggling slave,
And gathers 'neath its rule the great, the wise, the brave.

But yet, 'midst all the treasures that surround
  Thy royal halls, one bliss is still denied,—
To know the true hearts at thy name that bound,
  Which ocean from thy presence must divide,
  Whose voices never swell the boist'rous tide
Of hourly homage that salute thy ear;
  But yet who cherish with a Briton's pride,
And breath to infant lips from year to year
The name thy budding virtues taught them to revere.

How little deem'st thou of the scenes remote,
  In which one word, all other words above
Of earthly homage, seems to gaily float
  On every breeze, and sound through every grove—
  A spell to cheer, to animate, to move—
To bid old age throw off the weight of years,
  To cherish thoughts of loyalty and love,
To garner round the hearts those hopes and fears
Which, in our western homes, Victoria's name endears.

'Tis not that on our soil the measured tread
  Of armed legions speak thy sovereign sway,
'Tis not the huge leviathans that spread
  Thy meteor flag above each noble bay,
  That bids the soul a forced obedience pay!
(The despot's tribute from the trembling thrall.)
  No! At our altars sturdy freemen pray
That blessings on Victoria's head may fall,
And happy household groups each pleasing trait recall.

And gladly with our country's choicest flowers,
  Thy Son and Heir, Acadia's maidens greet,
Who shared thy roof, and deigns to honour ours
  For moments rapt'rous, but alas how fleet!
  And if in future times the thoughts be sweet
To him, of humble scenes beyond the sea,
  When, turning home his mother's smiles to meet,
And mingle with the high-born and the free—
We'll long remember him who best reflected thee!

After embarking on board the *Flying Fish* for the *Hero*, no incident of importance occurred until his arrival at half past ten at St. John's, New Brunswick. Then the Prince with his suite left the *Styx* in a boat for the shore amid the thunder of royal salutes. He was received by the Governor of New Brunswick, the Mayor and Corporation of the city, and by them conducted to his carriage. The guard of honor, the 63rd regiment, from Halifax, lined the way, and the cheering was enthusiastic. He then drove to the residence of the widow of the late Chief Justice, where his grandfather had once resided, between ranks of volunteers and trade societies. Thousands of school children sang the National Anthem and flung him bouquets as he passed under a triumphal archway, and through the grounds of the house.

At half past twelve he drove to the Court House and took his stand on a platform in front, while the volunteers and societies filed past, cheering him as they went. The following is the address of the Corporation of St. John's to His Royal Highness, and the Prince's reply :

N. B.—The compiler offers this as a perfect gem in his compilation.

To His Royal Highness, Albert Edward, Prince of Wales, Prince of the United Kingdom of Great Britain and Ireland, Duke of Saxony, Prince of Saxe Cobourg and Gotha, Great Steward of Scotland, Duke of Cornwall and Rothsay, Earl of Chester, Garrick and Dublin, Baron of Renfrew and Lord of the Isles, Knight of the Garter.

We, the Mayor, Aldermen and Commonalty of the City of St. John, hasten to approach your Royal Highness for the purpose of welcoming to New Brunswick the Heir Apparent to the throne and the future Sovereign of this Great Empire, of which it is our pride to form a portion, and over which the benificent sway of our benevolent Queen day by day strengthens those ties which happily unite us with the mother country.

Among us is still found a remnant of those who, in the last century, witnessed and partook of the joy and enthusiasm with which your Royal Highness' Grand-father, the Duke of Kent, was received on his visit to the infant city, upon the founder of which, in token of Royal approbation, great benefits have been recently conferred by the Royal Charter of his Majesty George III., and with just pride we declare to your Royal Highness that the feelings of loyalty and attachment which led to the shores the founders of this city, still eminently characterise the entire population of this colony.

It is our prayer that your Royal Highness will have a propitious termination to the tour through Her Majesty's North American dominions, in which you are now engaged; and we hope that you will vouchsafe to assure our Gracious Queen that peace and contentment are found among us under her rule, and that love and attachment to her person and crown is the common sentiment of her devoted subjects in this the commercial capital of her province in New Brunswick.

The Prince received the address personally from W. R. M. Burtis, to whom it was handed by the Recorder, and returned the answer direct instead of through the Duke :—

" GENTLEMEN,—I thank you with all sincerity for the address which you have just presented to me, and for the welcome which it conveys by the colony of New Brunswick and the important city of which you are the municipal representatives. When my

Grand-father, the Duke of Kent, paid to this place the visit to which you make so gratifying a reference, he found but little more than a village. It is my good fortune to receive on the same spot from a city—which affords a striking example of what may be effected under the influence of free institutions by the spirit and energy of the British race—these demonstrations of love and loyalty to the Queen, which are at this moment reflected before me. Your commercial enterprise has made this port the emporium of the trade of New Brunswick, and as the noble river which flows into it brings down for export the products of your soil, so I trust the vessels which crowd its piers will reward your successful industry with the wealth of other lands.

"I am not unmindful of the origin of this city, and it will be a subject of pride and pleasure to me to report to the Queen that the descendants of its founders have not departed from their first attachment to the Crown of England which brought them to these shores."

The city was illuminated and fireworks set off—there was a great crowd in the city, and triumphal arches and processions were the order of the day; His Royal Highness was much pleased with the reception and decoration.

On Saturday morning at 9 a.m., the Prince started for Frederickton, the capital of New Brunswick. In the river above St. John's is a rapid, which at low water is impassable for vessels, but, as the tide rises very high, it can be run in safety between the ebb and flood. As this arrangement of nature, however, is attended with many inconveniences in a commercial point of view, a railway has been constructed to Rothsay, about eight miles up the river, at which the boats stop. The St. John's railway station is a very nice wooden building of considerable size, and was ornamented extensively in honour of the royal traveller. The interior of the slanting roof was covered with bright coloured drapery—evergreens and banners were plentifully bestowed—and a large arch, very handsomely decorated, stood over the road which leads to the platform.

Several trains preceded His Royal Highness, containing some thousands of passengers. The cars commonly in use proved insufficient to accommodate all, and, as a consequence, trucks with temporary railing placed round them had to be provided. By these large numbers were enabled to reach home, who otherwise would have been under the necessity of staying another day or two in St. John's. The Prince was received at the railway station by two companies of volunteers, who formed a guard of honour, and the train immediately started. The road is very smooth, and exceedingly well built. The run to Rothsay was accomplished in a few minutes, and the Prince landed from the train under a cupola prepared for him.

So far so good—but it was too bad to make him and his suite walk a distance of two hundred yards upon yielding, drifting sand, to the wharf where lay the *Forest Queen*, ready to convey him up the St. John's river to Fredericton. A very high wind was blowing at the time, and there was no reason to believe that the dust it raised was more polite to His Royal Highness than to others. It got into the eyes, grated in the teeth, and choked up the nostrils. A guard of volunteers from St. John's, under the command of Capptain Armstrong, formed for a certain distance (as great as their numbers would permit) a line through which the Prince and his suite had to pass, but as soon as he had passed there was a rush of spectators down the bank, and during the rest of his progress towards the boat His Royal Highness found himself literally among the people. Fortunately there were not many of them, so that he was not actually crushed, but a considerable increase in dust was the consequence. The Prince, despite the deficiency in the arrangements, preserved his good-tempered look, and politely bowed in response to the cheers with which he was greeted. About ten o'clock he got under way for the capital. The *Forest Queen* is a small paddle steamer, newly painted for the occasion.

There were on board, besides the Prince and suite, many members of the New Brunswick Legislature, who had been in St. John's ; His Excellency Sir T. B. Manners Sutton, the Mayors of Boston, Halifax, and Montreal, and the members of the fourth estate. The Prince occupied the after deck, and the upper cabins of the steamer were reserved for himself and suite. The saloons had been freshly carpeted and draped, but there was nothing at all noticeable in the arrangements so far as splendour is concerned,— rather the opposite.

The scenery of the river is very grand near Rothsay, the land being high, the hills covered with dark woods, the shores bulwarks of rock. The same characteristics mark the course of the river for the next thirty miles northward. Comparatively little cultivation is seen, for the land is not so fertile as to hold out much encouragement to the farmer. But the remaining portion of the route is all that can be desired. The river is studded over with islands, formed by the gradual deposit of soil brought down by the stream in its course. They do not lie very high above the water, and some of them get occasionally overflowed, but the land is the most fertile in the province, never requires manure, and is easy of tillage. This "interval" land, as it is called, is not all surrounded by water. Along the shores, much of the same description occurs, and wherever seen there also is seen abundant evidence of its fertility. There is much still in process of formation; marsh land, where rushes grow, lines the river's bank so regularly that in many places it looks as though the shores had been cut to measure and trimmed by the square. Once passed the rocky portion of the river I have mentioned, the hills retire inland, and the country between them and the stream becomes flat. This is the general characteristic, though by no means always the case. In very many instances the hills come down to the river's bank, and a high, though not precipitous shore, is followed for miles. The scenery is very diverse—always beautiful. The white houses and out-buildings of the farmers line the stream, reminding one, to some extent, of the St. Lawrence; though here, the residences appear on a larger scale than the shanties of the French *habitants*. The cultivated land stretches away into the interior, or climbs the fertile hills, making large square patches of green fields to be seen among the surrounding woods, "amid the forest primeval." The forest primeval was swept away by fire from the borders of the St. John's river about eighty-five years ago, and that which now exists is a second growth—a juvenile race of pines, elms, ash, walnut, and maple. This is not the same fire mentioned as having ravaged that portion of the country, but a predecessor, which did nearly as much, if not more, damage. The consequence is, the timber bordering the river is not generally very large, and thus the farmers find it easy to extract the stumps after clearing. None of those ornamental adjuncts to a landscape are seen: His Royal Highness will have to get to Canada before a really good collection can be shown him. Very little wheat has, of late years, been cultivated along the St. John, the midge having destroyed so many successive harvests that the farmers have given their attention to the production of rye, oats and barley. For these they find a large market among the lumberers—by whom the Province gets its living. Flour is imported from Canada. Another verification of the old proverb—"It is an ill wind that blows nobody good."

As the *Forest Queen*, with the royal flag flying, passed up the river, people hurried down to the banks to catch a sight of their future monarch. Sometimes one man alone came; at others his wife and children came with him, and when the proximity of a few houses allowed it, a small crowd gathered and bade the Prince welcome. In several places companies of militia appeared, and fired salutes; arches were erected, church bells rung, flags hoisted, and every thing done to express the joy the people felt at the visit of the Heir Apparent. When there were no big guns available, the farmers frequently assembled, in knots of ten or twelve, and fired off their muskets, as the vessel got near them; but more frequently a military settler came running from his house, and made what noise he could with the aid of his rifle. Each salute was acknowledged by a shriek of the steam whistle, which, during the latter portion of the journey, was kept going nearly all the time. Very frequently the vessel was brought near the shore in her course; occasionally within a few yards of the small wharves which here and there occurred, and thus a good opportunity for seeing the Prince was gained by many. As he stood in the stern of the boat, and as there was a large number of persons in the bow, some difficulty was experienced by those ashore in discovering His Royal Highness. But as a general rule they found where he was, and he for his part seemed never tired of raising his hat as the cheers of the delighted rustics reached his ear.

It was with great concern that the travellers on board the *Forest Queen* heard that his Grace the Duke of Newcastle was indisposed. He unfortunately suffered somewhat, and had to retire to his room. The Prince seemed very anxious about him, and as he did not return as soon as was expected, went to the berth himself. He found the Duke asleep and would not disturb him. His grace appeared upon deck afterwards much refreshed, and apparently as vigorous as ever.

Fredericton was made about seven o'clock in the evening. The landing was effected at a new wharf, built by Mr. W. A. McClane and his partner. The bank of the river here rises to a height of thirty-five or forty feet, and the wharf is built immediately below it. Upon the bank, and almost overhanging the landing place, are some very beautiful willow trees, large in size and most luxuriant in foliage. Ropes from one to the other were placed to prevent the crowd, in their curiosity, tumbling headlong on to the Prince. To the right, stretching over the road above, was a large arch with a crown in the centre, and Prince of Wales plumes on the sides. Opposite to it was erected a gallery, on which a number of ladies were seated. As soon as the steamer was sighted from the city, two cannons were discharged; an ample notice was thus given of the approach of His Royal Highness. The populace dressed in gala attire, and the Prince, too, and his suite, who had made the voyage in plain clothes, adjourned to their cabins and shortly afterwards emerged in all the glories of cocked hats and gold lace. No sooner was this done than the Volunteer Artillery saluted, and as the vessel was moored to the wharf saluted again. A guard of honour, composed of members of the Volunteer Militia, who had been attending steadily to drill, presented arms as His Royal Highness landed, who, preceded by the Governor, walked to the head of the wharf, entered a carriage and was driven to the Government House.

There was very little attempt made at display. Some few arches were erected, but none worthy of any commendation for beauty of design. The telegraph posts, stretching a considerably distance along the road leading to the Government House, were ornamented with flags, and a great deal of bunting was displayed from the windows, roofs and chimneys of the houses. Ordinarily Fredericton contains about 5,000 inhabitants. Upon this occasion the population was doubled. The principal street is Queen-street, fronting the river. At right angles, proceeding from it to the left, is King Street, by which the Government House is reached. Neither the firemen nor any of the societies turned out as in other cities to line the streets, but for so small a place there was a large number of soldiers, and among them the first Volunteer Cavalry I have seen out of Canada. The order of procession was as follows :

The City Marshal, Mr. Charles Brannan.
Escort of Yeomanry Cavalry, Major Wilmot.
Field Officers of Militia, Colonel Hayne, Adjutant General George F. H. Mitchell, Deputy Adjutant General.
The Provincial Aides-de-camp, Lieut. Colonel Drury, and Lieut. Colonel Hayne.
Major Carter commanding H. M. Troops.
Lieut. Governor's second carriage (Earl St. Germains, General Bruce, His Royal Highness' Equerries.)
Lieut. Governor's third carriage—(The remainder of H. R. H's Suite.)
The Chief Justice, Sir James Carter.
The Judges—Hon. R. Parker, Hon. Newell Parker, Hon. W. J. Ritchey, and Hon. L. M. Wilmot.
President of Legislative Council, Hon. W. Black.
Speaker, Hon. J. M. Johnson.
High Sheriff, W. A. McClane, Esq.
Clerk of the Peace, G. I. Debille.
Provincial Secretary, Hon. Samuel L. Tilley.
Attorney-General, Hon. C. Fisher.
Solicitor-General, Hon. Mr. Waters.
Surveyor-General, Hon. J. R. Partlow ; Auditor-General, W. H. Steeves ; Chief Commissioner Board of Works.
James Stadman, Postmaster-General.
The Heads of Civil Departments.
Executive Committee.

The names of the officers commanding the Volunteers, were— Captain William S. Baird, Woodstock Rifles ; Captain McGiven, Douglas Rifles ; Fredericton Rifles, No. 1 Company, Captain Brannan ; No. 2 Company, Captain Macdonald. The artillery was from St. John's, under the command of Captain Wilmot. All the men looked well, but no opportunity was given of testing their discipline, as they merely fell into marching order, and followed His Royal Highness to the Government House, where he landed. On Saturday evening nothing further was done beyond the illumination of a considerable number of houses.

The Prince attended Divine Service in the Cathedral. It being expected he would make his appearance within the sacred fane, the grounds by nine o'clock had many occupants, and by the time appointed (eleven o'clock) a very great number had assembled. Something of the sort had been anticipated, and arrangements were made to meet the difficulty. The regular members of the congregation were first admitted through the vestry door, and seats thus provided for them. At half-past ten o'clock the main doors were thrown open, and every available inch of space, save that reserved for His Royal Highness and suite, was speedily occupied. A few minutes before eleven o'clock the Prince arrived. The Bishop, bearing the pastoral crook, met him at the door and conducted him to his pew, the organ meanwhile playing "God Save the Queen," and all the congregation rising to their feet—more out of curiosity than respect, as was evidenced by the fact that many of them stood upon the seats. The following was the programme:—

Venite, 98: Glorias to Psalms: Chant No. 76; Te Deum: Boyce in A; Jubilate, Service: Boyce in A; Anthem: God is Our Hope; Psalm, 100: Tune No. 17; Hymn: Tune No. 3: V. in Unison; Introit; Kyrie: Gloria No. 5.

The sermon was preached by the Right Rev. J. Mealey, D.D.

The Cathedral is a very beautiful Gothic edifice, built of dark freestone. Fourteen hexagonal pillars inside support the roof; the windows are all of stained glass; and the stalls for the clergy are handsomely carved. There are no galleries to disfigure the edifice, and the window-frames are of Caen stone. The spire is very high and contains a peal of fine-toned bells. The grounds which surround the cathedral are well laid out, and the situation in which it stands, close to the bank of the river, is delightful. The total cost was over $100,000, and the money was well laid out.

Fredericton itself is a beautiful little city.

The first thing done in the morning was the levee at the Government House. About two hundred gentlemen were presented.

The ceremony differed in no respect from that observed on previous occasions. The room in which the reception took place was handsomely covered with dark red drapery. The house, which, previous to the announcement of His Royal Highness' intention to visit Fredericton, had been in somewhat of an unfit condition for the residence of Royalty, had been fitted up, re-painted, and re-papered at considerable expense, and presented a very creditable appearance. The levee commenced at 12 o'clock, and was over before 1. Every thing passed over as well as could be desired.

Before proceeding further it may be well to say a little more about the City of Fredericton. It is a small place, with a population of about five thousand inhabitants, and is beautifully situated upon the St. John. Traversing nearly the whole length of the city, on the borders of the river is a beautiful esplanade—nearly as wide as that which Toronto would have possessed for pedestrian purposes had it not been covered with wharves, houses, warehouses and railway tracks. But Fredericton has few wharves, and those of small size. As the Legislature has not yet seen fit to build a railway to compete with the water communication of the river, no round-houses or steam-horses obstruct the river, or destroy the beauties which nature has most beautifully bestowed thereabouts. The esplanade is covered with green grass; adorned here and there with rows of gigantic willows. The street is plentifully supplied with trees, and nearly all the houses are situated in the centre of well-wooded grounds. The wealthier portion of the inhabitants reside there; the houses of the Provincial Secretary, the Attorny-General, the Bishop of Fredericton, the High Sheriff, and other gentlemen, together with the splendid cathedral and the buildings in which the Legislature holds its meetings, all fronting the river, and giving the street quite an aristocratic appearance. The river is about half a mile wide; so that the objects on the opposite bank can be distinctly seen. The shore rises gradually, but ascends to a considerable height.

White farm-houses stud the landscape, and the different gradations of colour, as the vegetation varies, from bright yellow to darkest green, with the blue, smoothly flowing at the foot, the dark pine on the summit, and the clear sky overhead, form a scene of striking beauty and grandeur. The high road which leads to Canada runs for many miles along the river's bank. Occasionally the hills approach near to the water's edge, so that if your horse choose to prove restive you may, after falling through the trees and shrubs which every where abound, find yourself floating down the stream towards the city of St. John. Frequently between the hills, the now almost dry channels of small streams have to be crossed; reminding one to a certain extent of the scenery met with in travelling through Western Canada near the shores of the lakes, with this exception, that the country is far more undulating, and the shore, generally speaking, rising to a greater height. Sometimes the road is arched with trees but to no very great length. The land is, generally speaking, well cleared, and much care seems to be taken to have ornamental trees in the fields, great taste being often manifested in this way by the proprietors of the larger houses upon the river's bank. The turnpike road is very good; well macadamized and kept in excellent repair. From the high ground in the rear a capital view of the city is obtained. Besides the cathedral there is no stone place of worship in Fredericton. The rest are built of wood. The Wesleyans have a very fine church of this material, with a lofty spire. The Church of Scotland has a less pretentious edifice, but of considerable size. The Presbyterian and Colonist Baptist churches, and the church of the Roman Catholics are also neat and commodious places of worship. The provincial buildings are of wood. As already mentioned, they stand in the centre of a plot of land facing the river, with many trees around. They are low, and have no pretensions to architectural beauty, but still are sufficient for the pupose to which they are put. Whether that were the case or not, however, there is little prospect of any better being erected, as a strong desire exists in certain portions of the Province to remove the Seat of Government to St. John's. The Legislative Halls are now in readiness for the ball which is to be held to-night· Both the Assembly and Council room have been called into requisition. To each side of the latter, which is in the upper story of the building, a wooden wing has been added, for the purpose of giving more accommodation to the dancers. These wings are not large, but, from appearances, the room provided will afford more space for the company in proportion to their numbers than any ball-room the Prince has yet visited on this side of the Atlantic. The decorations are not very extensive. In fact the rooms, with the exception of those temporarily erected, do not need it. The pillars of the gallery in the House of Assembly have been wreathed ; and a good many flags, coats of arms, and various matters of that description have been hung from the walls. Some very fine pictures, of bye-gone kings, judges, and governors are placed in both houses. The rooms, upon the whole, look decidedly respectable. One of the best buildings in Fredericton is the barracks, capable of holding a thousand troops. They are very substantially constructed of stone, in the centre of large grounds facing the river, with, as usual, some gigantic willows on their borders. Before the Eastern war broke out a whole regiment was quartered here ; but since then, to a company of the 63rdthe duty of supporting the honour and dignity of Great Britain has been confided. To them another company of the same regiment have, within the last few days, been added from Halifax. They encamp alternately near the gate in the grounds of the Governor for the purpose of protecting His Royal Highness the Prince of Wales.

Yesterday His Royal Highness, besides taking a drive to view the scenery of the surrounding country, paid a visit to Gabriel an Indian, and Governor of the Millicete tribe. This Chief is a very respectable man, and frequently accompanies the Governor upon his fishing excursions. There is an encampment of Indians upon the side of the river opposite Frederickton. The Prince visited Gabriel's tent, and was afterwards paddled upon the river by him in a canoe. Several Indians strut about the city with a great deal of fuss. They were presented to the Prince at the levee this morning.

The Attorney-General, the Hon. Charles Fisher, gave a lunch to the members of the Legislature assembled in Frederickton. It was an informal affair, but a very pleasant one. The opposition and the supporters of the ministry drank their wine together as though never upon the floor of the House of Assembly had hard words been interchanged or hard blows struck. Some few speeches were made; the first by the Attorney-General, in proposing the health of His Royal Highness. Mr. Fisher is a fluent speaker, and is a slashing debater, able to make his points tell

N

well. He concludes his sentences with great neatness, and appears never to be under the necessity of spinning them out in order to save an abrupt termination. One of the leaders of the opposition, the Hon. Mr. Hazen, proposed the health of the Governor, which was drunk with an enthusiam by all present, which speaks well for Mr. Sutton. Mr. Hazen is more delicate than the Attorney-General, the difference between their oratory being very much like that which exists between the charge of a judge and the speech of counsel. Mr. Fisher is fifty years of age, tall, with black hair and rather sallow complexion. The government he heads is liberal, and has been in possession of office for the past five years.

The lunch over, an adjournment was effected to a new park, to be opened by the Prince. It is sixteen acres in extent, and has been presented to the city by a gentleman named Odell, with certain conditions attached to it, among which is one, that an avenue passing one end of the park shall be kept in repair. The spot is not far from the Government House, and well situated for the convenience of the people. There are not many trees upon it; but in the course of a few years there will be if the promises of planting are carried out. A large canopy, placed upon a platform raised about two feet from the ground, was erected for the Prince and his suite. The chair placed for His Royal Highness was one used by the Duke of Kent many years ago—old and yet very handsome. Opposite to this sat about eight hundred school children. By the aid of a large body of volunteers, infantry and cavalry, a lane was formed between them and the place where stood His Royal Highness. In the centre was a pool of water, with a tap spouting forth a small stream, in due time to be elevated into the dignity of a fountain.

The crowd was immense, not less than eight thousand people being present. The trees were loaded with adventurous youngsters; every place from which a view of the Prince could be obtained was occupied; a general desire being manifested by each individual present to stand close beside him. It was with very great difficulty that the land spoken of as between His Royal Highness and the children could be kept. It was in vain that the yeomanry cavalry charged backwards, bumping their horses against the most advanced portions of the crowd—the human mass could not but press forward. The day was intensely hot, and made every body uncomfortable. But the loyal multitude stood its ground, not a man budged a single inch until the Prince left the place. And what was it all about? The people wanted to see the Prince—that is the sum and substance of the proceeding. Nominally his Royal Highness came to open the park, really he came to be looked at. He was accompanied by the Governor and his lady, and his suite. Upon alighting from his carriage he stepped on to the platform and remained standing until the proceedings were concluded.

The school children assembled, sung the National Anthem very prettily, and a few minutes afterwards a little girl stepped forward and presented the Prince with a boquet of flowers, for which he kindly thanked her.

By-and-by a man was discovered pointing a camera, for the Prince had been gracious enough to consent to allow his portrait to be taken by an artist of the city. But so soon as the man had got his tools in working order, somebody would run between the lines and the platform, and thus spoil the picture. The "special" constables were frantic in their efforts to prevent this, and spoilt more than any one else. Women crushed in the crowd were continually making their escape into the opening space; volunteers, on horses which would not be quiet, performed various *pas* in front; children who had lost their parents, and parents looking for their children, all were continually passing to and fro, spoiling the Prince's picture and irritating every body except His Royal Highness, who again and again consented to allow the disappointed artist to try once more. At last the task was accomplished, and the royal cortege drove off, amid the cheers of the assembled thousands.

The Prince starts for St. John at six o'clock in the morning, from whence he goes to Pictou and Prince Edward Island.

A state dinner, at which the members of the Executive were present, has been given at the Governor's this evening, and the Prince goes to the ball.

The opening of the ball in Fredericton was only delayed until His Royal Highness should arrive from the Government House. A loud cheer from the crowd outside told that the important event had transpired,—that our future monarch was again about to mix with his future subjects, and by his affability and his courteous demeanour, to rivet more strongly the bond which unites him with the people. Through a collection of hot-house plants placed in the corridor His Royal Highness passed to the ball-room, where, arrayed on either side, leaving a narrow lane in the centre leading to the dais usually occupied by the President of the Legislative Council, he found some hundreds of ladies, who gave to the Prince a most cordial welcome. What could Albert Edward do but look his best, and again and again thank them by most courtly bows. The Council Chamber, not being large enough to hold all who were expected to gather together, other rooms had to be called into requisition. But in the earlier part of the evening they proved comparatively useless. Of course the great object the ladies had in view in going to the ball was to see the Prince—it would be uncharitable to suggest that they all expected to dance with him. The room in which he was was thronged.

By great exertion two or three sets of quadrilles were formed, and His Royal Highness opened the ball with the wife of the Governor, Mrs. Manners Sutton, for his partner. But, of course, that dance would end, and another would begin, who could tell who next might be selected? Standing upon tiptoe, some leaning on the arms of the few gentlemen who had forced themselves into the room, the beauties of New Brunswick strained their necks and their eyes, to get a glimpse of the Prince, to watch his dancing, to wonder what he was saying to his partner, to admire his round face and graceful figure. Although he could not be otherwise than aware that he was the observed of all observers, His Royal Highness, as though perfectly unconscious of the fact, talked with the ladies with whom he danced; and the pleasant smiles which lit up the features of one and all, told plainly that he was making himself excessively agreeable. He has that faculty, belonging only to the true gentleman, of setting at ease those who may be in his presence. There is about him no affectation, no look or movement which can be pointed to as an assertion of superiority. The ladies who dance with him appear to forget in a moment the previous tremour with which they are seized when he requests the honour of their hand for the next quadrille. They make no more mistakes than usual,—perhaps it should be said less than usual, for be it known, that during the month preceding the visit of the Prince to each Province, the dancing masters have had full employment; and many a family party has been made up for practice, in order to ensure the greatest possible efficiency for the Royal ball.

The Prince is a great favourite with the ladies every where, and though by some a little disappointment was felt, that they had not had the honour of dancing with him, yet, as they are constitutionally bound to do, they lay the blame upon the heads of his advisers, the Duke of Newcastle, Earl St. Germains and General Bruce. The Duke comes in for the greatest share of the anathemas hurled at the head of the trio. His Grace, however, is not to blame. The selection of ladies is entrusted to the wife of each Governor, subject of course, as a matter of form, to superior approval. So far as I have been able to learn, much wise discrimination has been exercised, no favouritism shown, and great satisfaction as a general rule given.

The ladies with whom the Prince danced at Fredericton were Mrs. Manners Sutton, wife of the Governor; Miss Sutton, daughter of his Excellency; Miss Florence Parker, daughter of a Judge; Miss Fisher, sister of the Attorney-General; Miss Lizzy Hazen, daughter of one of the members of the opposition; Miss Medley, daughter of the Bishop; Mrs. Justice Ritchey; Mrs. Dr. Bayard, and Miss Robinson. The Prince danced almost without intermission, from the time he entered the ball-room until three o'clock in the morning, excepting a little time lost in taking supper. When it is remembered that the hour announced for the embarkation on the same morning was 6 o'clock, it is not to be expected hat His Royal Highness displayed no little devotion to the fair sex of Fredericton.

Before taking leave of Fredericton, it must be mentioned that the Provincial Buildings were illuminated very brilliantly, large Chinese lamps being suspended from the surrounding trees, and two letters, V. R., in coloured lamps ran from the roof to the ground of the house. In the city too, a great display was made. A company of volunteers bivouacked in the grounds. Those of the people who could not enjoy themselves at the ball resorted to other methods. During the whole night bursts of music and of songs issued from many different quarters. The good people of Fredericton, like all the rest of those visited by the Prince, celebrated his short sojourn enthusiastically and generally. There was no exception to the rule—no old curmudgeons objected to it. And when at last His Royal Highness emerged from the ballroom, there were still hundreds assembled, who gave him a hearty farewell.

As already noticed six o'clock was the time announced for the embarkation, but the previous day had been excessively hot, and when the morning broke, a thick fog overhung the river. "It would break as soon as the sun ascended in the sky," the Fredericton people all declared—they were indignant at the idea that they were ever subjected to a prolonged annoyance of the kind, by which the shores of the Bay of Fundy are so often made miserable; and they were right in their prognostications, for before seven o'clock had arrived, the fog began to rise. Shortly afterwards the Prince arrived, and immediately went on board the boat, two companies of Volunteer Artillery saluting, and several companies of Riflemen presenting arms, as he made his way down the wharf. A goodly number of people were present, who so far as loud hurrahs and raising of hats and handerchiefs could go, did their utmost to please His Royal Highness. He, to confess the truth, did not look so lively as upon previous occasions. Even our Prince cannot dance till three o'clock and get up at six, without feeling fatigued. The voyage down was almost a repetition of the voyage up. During the journey the members of parliament on board were introduced, and shook hands with the Prince, an honour they had not previously enjoyed. The people thronged the banks, with their bands of music, their riflemen, and their societies, and His Royal Highness, despite his fatigue, bowed for the nineteenth hundredth and ninety-ninth time, as the boat swiftly passed each little gathering.

The landing was effected at Indian Town, at half-past two o'clock. Indian Town is a suburb of St. John, above the Falls. No sooner had the *Forest Queen* touched the wharf, than she was visited by two officers of the Telegraph Company, with a message from Father Point, sent by order of Her Majesty, informing her august son that his sister, the Princess Frederick William of Prussia, was doing well after her late confinement. The Prince read the message, smiled, communicated its contents to one of the noblemen near him, and complacently put it in his pocket.

His Royal Highness had to walk some little distance before getting to his carriage. In doing so he passed under a very nice evergreen arch, Gothic in design, and very large, one of the best erected in New Brunswick. A little farther along the route, were a large number of children of the Methodist schools, on the steps of the meeting house, who, as the carriage passed them, sang the National Anthem, the Prince, as usual, and all present, remaining uncovered until it was over. It had been arranged that the embarkation on board the *Styx* should take place at Carleton, on the opposite side of the river to St. John. To reach this place it was necessary to traverse a suspension bridge, erected across the river. The route at both ends was one continued ovation.

But it was on the Carleton side that His Royal Highness met with perhaps the most enthusiastic reception that has yet been given to him. Carleton ordinarily contains about five thousand inhabitants; on this occasion there were thirty thousand people in it. St. John was emptied of all save a few who could not do otherwise than stop at home. Houses were locked up, hotels deserted, business received an additional suspension, Carleton was sought as though it were a city of refuge from St. John, over which some destroying angel was shortly to sweep. The people took with them their flags, their garlands of roses, indeed almost all that could be made available to add to the attractions of the little town. Their firemen, their volunteers, their societies went also, all did their utmost to bid, as befitted New Brunswick, an enthusiastic good-bye to the Prince.

When His Royal Highness crossed the limits, the firemen of Carleton, consisting of two companies, took the horses from his carriage, and attached to it a grappling hook and themselves drew it along. The scene at the pause caused by this operation forbids description. The thousands of people assembled cheered almost incessantly; true British cheers. No mincing matters. All roared out "hip, hip, hurrah," as loud as they could; as though their welfare, for ever after, depended upon rending their throats, and bursting the ear-drums of all present. To add to the excitement a number of those nearest the carriage, forcing their way still closer, extended their hands towards His Royal Highness.

The Prince seeing their desire, stood up in the carriage,

stretched out both his hands, and clasped the first of those who clasped his. One old lady cried out—"God bless you—God bless your mother!" Fervently the words were uttered ; fervently were they taken up by the crowd. "God bless you, God bless your mother," spread rapidly around ; and when the hook was at length attached, and the hand shaking necessarily stayed, the words were still heard among the *vivas* of the crowd. At the corner of one of the streets a stage was erected crowded with some hundreds of loyal folk ; many of them ladies, who rained down upon the carriage a shower of bouquets. One of these the Prince picked up, and raised it aloft so that it might be seen. Shortly afterwards an Indian squaw came forward, holding some beadwork in her hands which she offered to the Prince, and which he received. The Duke of Newcastle put his hand in his pocket for money, but found none. Another pocket was tried; but with no better success. The Earl of St. Germains was a richer man ; he had a sovereign half hidden somewhere in the corner of his pocket, which was rapidly transferred to the squaw's palm. This episode over, an arch was reached, upon the abutments of which were placed a number of little girls, dressed in white, who threw down bouquets as the carriage passed underneath—a hint which may be profitable to Canadians—and another large assembly of children raised their voices in prayer for a blessing upon the Queen. The streets here, for some distance above and down to the wharf, were lined with shipbuilders, fire companies, and militia. When the carriage stopped, after being drawn by the men for near a mile and a half, the Prince visited a large saw-mill belonging to the Hon. John Robinson. He had not time to stay long, little more than to walk through and take a rapid glance at the kind of machinery by which New Brunswick makes so much money.

Meanwhile the royal barge had been lowered, and was alongside the wharf. Previous to jumping on board the Prince sent for Captain Crookshank, the senior officer in command of the volunteer companies, and requested him to convey to the men his high sense of the admirable manner they had discharged their duties, and his pleasure at seeing them in so efficient a condition. The band then struck up "God save the Queen,"—two companies of artillery, commanded by Captains Durant and McLauchlin, fired the final salute, and amid the music, the thunder of the cannon, and the cheers of the thousands assembled, His Royal Highness was rowed to the ship. There was some little delay before the *Styx* moved towards the mouth of the harbour. This gave time for the volunteers and fire companies to embark on board three steam boats, each loaded with living cargo. Under their escort the *Styx* left the shores of New Brunswick.

The Prince took his stand on the hurricane deck; the sailors manned the yards, and, led by His Royal Highness, cheered and cheered again. A more enthusiastic, a more really genuine demonstration, was never made in favour of any Prince, in any age, or in any country. It was all genuine, the real feelings of the people were manifest. "God bless you—God bless your mother" —though uttered by comparatively few, was the sincere, heartfelt prayer of every man, woman, and child among the vast concourse who crowded every wharf, every street, and every house-top. Surely such a lesson of popular good-will ought to sink deep into the hearts of those monarchs who would treat the people as *canaille*, as animals out of whom no good is to be got save by blows.

Up again at seven o'clock the next morning, (Wednesday,) with the intention of proceeding to Shediac by the new line of railway, and thence per the *Arabian* to Charlottetown, again to meet the Prince, who, pursuing a different route via Truro and Pictou, in Nova Scotia, was expected to arrive about the same time. Upon reaching the railway station, the correspondents were presented with a free ticket, and ushered into a car prepared for the Prince of Wales, where were assembled many members of the legislature, and others connected with the road. The car itself was fitted up in excellent taste, but with little attempt at display. It was divided into two compartments, separated by crimson curtains. From the one-half the ordinary furniture had been taken, chairs, couches, and a large table of maple being substituted in its stead. The carpet was crimson interwoven with yellow stripes, arranged in diamond form. The other half of the car was in keeping with the whole.

The New Brunswick Railway was originally intended to form a link in a line of road connecting Halifax and Portland. Its total length is one hundred and eight miles, and the opening of the entire line took place but a few days ago. It was hoped that the Prince of Wales would make a trip over it, and for that purpose it was hurried forward to completion. But previous arrangements compelled His Royal Highness to abide by the course originally marked out. The road was commenced in 1853. In 1858 it was opened from St. John to Hampton, a distance of twenty-five miles, and with such success that in the first year, after paying all expenses, a margin of $12,000 was left. In 1859 it was opened for forty-four miles, and a surplus of $24,000 left at the expiration of the twelve months. The whole is expected to pay its running expenses and a portion of the interest. The cost has been $40,000 per mile. The issue of $4,000,000 worth of debentures, running for twenty years, and bearing an interest of six per cent, has been authorised. Those placed in the market have hitherto sold at a premium of from seven to ten *per cent.*; the profit thus made, being applied to a sinking fund for the redemption of the debt. The payment of the interest required has been ensured by an increase in the the tariff of two and a-half *per cent.* The road is beautifully built, and it is boasted by those connected with it, that it is the best in America. All agree that on a more smoothly running line they never travelled. Everything about it is finished with a neatness observable certainly upon no railway in Canada. Both the cars and engines have been built in the province; the former by Mr. F. K. James and the latter by Messrs. Fleming and Humbert—both of St. John. The engines are beautiful specimens of workmanship; constructed with all the latest improvements, having horizontal cylinders sixteen inches in diameter and giving a turn of twenty-six inches. The bridges are all of iron and stone, most of them having the Warren girder. The advantages possessed by this invention are many. Among them may be mentioned, is the facility they afford for rapid construction. One beautiful specimen of the engineering art passes over the Trout Creek, at a distance of forty-four miles from St. John. It has three spans eighty feet each in length, and was put together in a fortnight after the arrival of the parts from England. A great difficulty frequently met with in erecting iron bridges as generally used, arises from the fact that workmen have to be sent from England to rivet the different portions together, and they, feeling themselves to a great extent independent of their employers when they arrive, are apt to work only when they please. But the Warren girders can easily be united, without the assistance of individuals so difficult to deal with. In illustration of the rapidity with which some portions of the road were built, in anticipation of the Prince's visit, it may be mentioned that, in the short space of six weeks twenty-eight miles were laid and ballasted by Mr. Stevens, all the material being brought from one end. The line traverses a most beautiful and fertile section of country. Thousands of acres of interval land spread far away on either side; much of which is under cultivation. Occasionally the train dashes through forests of spruce, amid which, as yet, few settlements have been made. But there are few spots in which the handiwork of the farmer is not visible. Agriculture, however, is not yet resorted to by the people of New Brunswick to any thing like the same proportionate extent as in Canada. Wheat is little cultivated, as lumbering monopolises nearly the whole attention of the people. The railway, it is expected, will take from Shediac large quantities of Canadian produce for the supply of the lumberers, and find in the trade one of the principal sources of revenue. Those who do farm in New Brunswick are said to be getting rich very fast. It is a pity that the occupation is not more generally followed.

At Shediac, the *Arabian*, already crowded with people from the upper ports, from Richibucto, Miramichi, Dalhousie, and Bathurst, all anxious to proceed to Charlottetown, there to meet the Prince; to these were added nearly the whole of those who had arrived by the train from St. John. The consequence was between four and five hundred persons found themselves on board the steamer, wedged closely together. The day was very hot, and from the clouds was pouring a torrent of rain, which compelled the reeking mass of humanity to remain between decks. Every state-room, every berth, every sofa, every table, every plank, was occupied by pleasure excursionists in the recumbent posture, while others for want of space were compelled to stand, and so in compact masses, scarcely able to move from the spot where they had first got stuck. It was a terrible state of affairs. Something like the black-hole of Calcutta and all its horrors. Matters were somewhat mended, however, shortly after the start by the staying of the rain, so that many were able to go on deck. But the heat still continued, which, together with the damp thick atmosphere, altogether made the voyage nearly as unpleasant as it could possibly be made. To the relief of all, Charlottetown was reached at half-past eleven o'clock.

Soon after daylight in the morning, two guns from the blockhouse announced that the Royal squadron was in sight. All the people turned quickly out of their houses, and the streets were rapidly filled with an excitable, anxious, wondering, expectant crowd. Charlottetown did indeed present a contrast to that furnished by it on the occasion of the last visit. Then it looked like a quiet Canadian town. On Thursday every thing was reversed. For a week past the people had been pouring in from all parts of the island, until it is estimated not less than from fifteen to twenty thousand strangers, or one-fourth of the entire population, were present. The clouds hung thick and heavy in the sky; a strong wind sprung up, and about nine o'clock the rain once more commenced to descend. There was much discussion respecting the hour the Prince would land, but that at length was settled by the arrival of a messenger from the *Hero*, who named one o'clock as the time. Soon after twelve o'clock the Royal vessel entered the harbour, followed by the *Ariadne*, saluted by H. B. M. steamer *Valorous* and *Cossack*, and H. I. M. steamer *Pomone*, 36 guns. Then, together with H. B. M. surveying vessel the *Margaretha Stephenson*, sent their men to the masts, who cheered loudly as the Prince descended into the royal barge. His Excellency the Lieutenant-Governor, George Dundas, Esq., had proceeded on board the *Hero* previously, and left in company with the Prince.

The wharf at which the landing was effected is a very spacious one, extending far into the water, so that the upper end of it had alone to be guarded. Assembled upon it were Chief Justice Hodgson and Mr. Justice Peters; the Marquis de Montiguæ, Captain of the *Pomone*; Captain Vansittart, *Ariadne*; Captain Aldham, *Valorous*; and Captain Hancock, *Margaretha Stevenson*; the members of the Legislature, including the Premier, the Hon. Charles Palmer; the Sheriff of Queen's county, Mr. Duncan; the Mayor, the Hon. T. H. Howland, and Corporation; the Colonial Secretary, Hon. Mr. Pope; the Attorney-General, Hon. Mr. Hanraham; the Archdeacon, Dr. Reid, of St. Eleanor; the Roman Catholic Bishop, Dr. McIntyre, and the clergy of other denominations; the Provincial Treasurer, Mr. George Wright;

the Comptroller of Customs, Mr. Longworth; the Postmaster-General; the Registrar of Deeds, Mr. Crawford; the President of Legislative Council, Hon. Charles Young; the Speaker of the Legislative Assembly, Hon. Donald Mongomery; the Governor's Aide-de-camp, Hon. Colonel Gray and Colonel Swaby; the officer in command of the troops, Lieutenant Colonel Longworth. By the side of the wharf a company of the 62nd regiment was drawn up, and on Queen street Major Davies' troop of volunteer cavalry were posted, who, in company with the band of the 62nd, headed the procession. The guard of honour at the landing place was Captain Lea's volunteer company; at Government House, Captain Murphy's. Several other volunteer companies, with the assistance of St. Andrew's, St. Patrick's, Masonic, and Temperance Societies lined the streets. Before reaching his carriage His Royal Highness had to walk a considerable distance along the wharf to near the first arch at the foot of Queen Street. He was loudly cheered by the people in the streets, on the house-tops, on the decks and rigging of the numerous vessels which crowded the beautiful harbour of Charlottetown.

For a time it seemed that the weather was about to clear up. A solitary gleam of sunshine for a few moments managed to penetrate the dense canopy of clouds which dulled the brilliancy of all things; but in the struggle darkness got the better of the light, and shut off the hope-giving rays.

The arch placed at the street end of the wharf was built of evergreens, surmounted by a picture of Britannia sitting on a sea horse, in the act of ruling the waves, and by two large carved lions. The motto it bore was—"Welcome to Prince Edward Isle." On a second arch festoons of roses were suspended from the hands of lovely-looking ladies in wood, who were, from the trumpets at their mouths, supposed to proclaim the words written underneath—"Welcome our future King." Another arch still in Queen street, bore figures of two volunteers, with guns and knapsacks all complete, and it was upon this erection that the words—"May thy visit prove Great Britain's heir a closer bond with home." Opposite Queen's square, in which are the Provincial buildings, images of two Scotch grenadiers appeared, also surmounting an arch. The circular-pointed market house, an ugly building, had been planted round with spruce trees, and so hidden with bunting and flowers, that it was scarcely known. The post-office too had been decorated with equal success. In the square was the tent of an Indian chief, who with his warriors and squaws paddled out to meet the Prince, and joined their voices with that of the applauding throng. Soon after passing the square the procession moved down Kent street to the Government House. In Cochrane square a large number of Sunday school children, about a couple of thousand, were assembled, who sang the National Anthem and gave three cheers for the Prince, each waving a white handkerchief, as the hurrahs were uttered. The arch immediately opposite the Government House was the most beautiful of the whole. From the hands of two dancing girls flowers were suspended ; and stars formed of bayonets, pikes, and swords were inserted in the pillars. His Royal Highness upon alighting immediately entered the house, and was seen no more that day, save by the Governor and his immediate attendants.

The decorations, of Charlottetown showed a full complement of bunting, of floral crowns, of evergreen decorations, of spruce trees, of mottoes, and of those hundreds of little things which go towards making a great display. The Chief Justice had a very nice little mottoe—" In hoc signo spes mea," —the sign being the Prince's plume. The scene from the wharf was very grand. Union street is very wide, and rises gradually from the water, so that for upwards of a mile the mass of people could be seen, the narrow lane preserved by the militia being distinctly visible all the way up.

A large volunteer force was in Charlottetown. There were several companies, truly, from the interior turned out, and there were at least five hundred men upon the ground. The volunteer cavalry were excellent ; their horses equal to those of the regular troops, and ridden by men who knew well how to manage them. There was not much diversity in the uniform of the rifle companies, who kept the ground well, and displayed great steadiness in marching.

Great preparations had been made for an illumination in Charlottetown, and some hundreds of candles and gas devices were lighted and rockets fired off, but the torrents of rain which descended spoiled every thing except the grass and the foliage. A dinner, a ball and levee are to follow the reception described, and the Prince will leave to-morrow for Gaspé, where the *Arabian* will meet him, and where he will meet the Governor General.

Father Point, Tuesday Morning, August 14.

At Shediac the "surplus population"—the crowd of excited beings who had been to see the Prince in Charlottetown, and who had seen him, will henceforth keep his memory enshrined in their hearts, and the day on which they saw him marked in the calendar. The weather cleared up, and comfort once more began to be thought of by those on board the *Arabian.* The vessel pursued her way in peace over the smooth sea.

After getting out of Richebucto bay the *Arabian* steamed along the coast just far enough off not to be able to see any thing of it until the arrival on Sunday to within sixty or seventy miles of Gaspé Divine Service was conducted on board by the Rev. Mr. Alexander, a Presbyterian minister of Brantford, who preached a very excellent and appropriate sermon. Proceeding on deck, was seen far away in the horizon a streak of smoke; or rather what appeared to be three streaks of smoke, which all came to the conclusion were made by the vessels of the royal fleet. Glasses were brought out, eyes strained, men sent aloft, and after some hour or two of anxious examination it was positively affirmed that the *Lady Head* was near—and only the *Lady Head.*

All along the shore wherever a few habitations existed, groups of men and women were gathered together, all in a state of the highest excitement, and mightily disappointed that the steamer had not brought the Prince. One matter of surprise was the number of cannon the people seemed to have. They blazed away at the *Arabian* every few miles, as though there was a whole arsenal of guns behind them, ready to be worn out. They had their flags too hoisted, ready to be dipped when the royal fleet should pass, and by way of securing proficiency in this mode of salute, they dipped and dipped again at the *Arabian*, until it was not known whether they were getting sarcastic, or waxing Frenchifully polite. Their salutes, however, were returned by a "shriek" from the steam trumpet.

About five o'clock in the evening we steamed into Gaspé basin, and there found waiting the arrival the steamer *Victoria*, with his Excellency Sir Edmund Head and the Ministry on board. The Chief Commissioner of the Board of Works put off in a boat towards the vessel, and was told in reply to a question he asked, that the royal fleet was within two hours' sail of the port. He returned to the *Victoria* as swiftly as the arms of six strong men could take him. Over the stern of the celebrated craft to which he was making his way bent a figure in the attitude of expectancy. It was the Governor-General. Hon. John Rose, the aforesaid commissioner, hailed him from the boat, and afterwards immediately disappeared—whereto cannot be told—but a man on board the boat, with a telescope in his hand, declared that a few minutes afterwards he saw Sir Edmund walking upon the deck, in his official uniform of blue and silver, with his sword girded to his loins, his cocked hat, feathers and all, upon his head. His Excellency had not long to wait.

Soon after seven o'clock, *Hero*, *Ariadne*, and *Flying-Fish* entered Gaspé harbour, and after a little delay cast anchor at Douglastown, about ten miles from Gaspé basin. The *Victoria* immediately went alongside, and remained there all night.

On entering the harbour of Gaspé, it was fully expected His Royal Highness would land there. An arch of evergreens with the word "Welcome" upon it, and adorned with numerous signal flags, was erected upon the wharf. Every house was adorned with bunting—all had their share of flag. Embosomed among the hills rising on each side are many half hidden residences; and when night had closed in, from the windows of those shone forth the rays of many lights, for Gaspé illuminated on the arrival of the Prince as other places of greater size had already done.

When daylight broke, all hastened to see what had become of the royal fleet. After some trouble, some scrambling up the hills, some walking along roads overhung with trees, they were made out lying at the place already mentioned. There was little time for enquiry, for the *Arabian* sailed at seven o'clock. But it was found the Prince was not to land at Gaspè. The three vessels weighed anchor at eight o'clock, sailed round the outer harbour to get a good view of the shore, and then proceeded at once to the Saguenay. It may be recollected that Gaspé bay and Gaspé basin are two distinct places. The bay is by far the larger harbour of the two, and has many settlements upon its banks, among which is Douglastown, opposite which the *Hero* anchored. Gaspé basin is the inner harbour, a most beautiful spot, surrounded by high hills, with a great depth of water in the harbour, and affording as safe an anchorage as there is in the world. There is no place better fitted to give His Royal Highness and those who accompany him a favourable first impression of the great colony of Canada.

As the *Arabian* passed the royal vessels, the smoke issuing from their funnels told that preparations for further progress was being made. There was no excitement observable among them. Their tall taper masts stood motionless, the white cliff behind rendering them clearly visible. But a sign of excitement was not wanting. The little *Victoria* was "up and doing." Sir Edmund had been on board during the night, and at seven o'clock in the morning, thinking perhaps His Royal Highness was rather dilatory in sending an invitation to breakfast, determined to awaken him to a sense of duty by means of a royal salute. But the *Victoria* had only one gun; still, better one than none. With perseverance, twenty-one rounds might be fired; and, if there was a little irregularity in the time which elapsed between one shot and another, His Royal Highness would no doubt kindly excuse the want of skill manifest. So at it they went, making a great deal of smoke and some noise. After they had got about half way through, however, they stopped. Why, cannot be told. Perhaps the invitation to breakfast had arrived—perhaps the powder had fallen short—perhaps Commodore Seymour had threatened, if the folly were persisted in, to put the whole under hatches. At any rate, the royal salute was prematurely cut in two.

Sir Edmund Head and all his Ministers, except Vankoughnet, arrived in Gaspé on Friday. His Excellency was in a state of nervous excitability. He could not sleep, he could not eat, he could not think, he feared so much that the Prince might slip past unnoticed by him. On Sunday he went to church, he was scarcely able to sit the service through, although he did not enter until late.

Sir Edmund Head is not the only celebrated personage who

P

has been sunning himself here of late. The *Arabian* on her last trip down was startled by a most unexpected apparition. Early one fine morning, when about half a dozen miles from the land, opposite Fox River, north of Cap Rozier, a fishing boat was observed standing out to sea. Presently a small squat man was seen in the bow, dressed in a monkey-jacket and trowsers of freshwater sailor rig, waving his cap most frantically around his head. Captain Steen altered the course of the steamer and steered for the little craft, thinking doubtless that he was about to know something of momentous importance. Having got within hailing distance and stopped the engines, he asked "Whatever is the matter?" And the little man in the monkey-jacket responded by asking another question, " Have you got any letters for me?" Now, to say that Captain Steen didn't swear, is not very improbable. It is more likely that he asked, "And who the d—l are you"—than simply, "Who are you?" But whatever words he used the answer came back—"Robert Moodie," and something about Chief Inspector of Fisheries, and captain of the steamship *Fire Fly*, being lost in the distance. For a moment all on board held their breath, and the next the paddles were again revolving, and "Bob" was left alone upon the watery route. The next I hear of this worthy representative of your noble Province is in Gaspé, where the people appear to look upon him as a *lusus naturæ*,—neither fish nor flesh. It appears, according to his own account, delivered to an admiring crowd in the bar-room of the hotel, that somewhere upon the coast he was seized with the "gripes." Desirous of procuring brandy to alleviate his sufferings, he went to a shanty where it was sold ; but as the keeper of the place was a Frenchman, and all were French around, Bob, who does not understand a word of the language, found considerable difficulty in making himself understood. At length by rubbing his stomach with one hand, and by imitating the act of drinking with the other he managed to make his wishes known. Having taken his drink a second difficulty arose. How much was he to pay ? The Capting says the fellow asked for a "paster" (piastre)—but what a "paster" was how was he to tell ? He put down a dollar, and "didn't get no change ; not a red cent, Sir." After stalking about in Gaspé for a few days, and astonishing the fishermen with his knowledge of navigation, he hired a canoe and proceeded on his way towards Dalhousie, in the Bay of Chaleurs, intending to coast all round. Nothing more has been heard of him since. Among other things, he is collecting statistics respecting the fisheries, but it so happens that the cod fishery, especially upon the north coast, is nearly over, and a large number of vessels have left with cargoes for their customary markets, so that no account can be taken of them. It may be expected to hear of this watery gentleman somewhere off the coast of Newfoundland, stopping our Atlantic steamer to know if there are any letters "for me, Bob Moodie, &c., &c."

Yesterday about twelve o'clock the passengers on board the *Arabian* were delighted with the appearance of a *mirage*. The sun was shining very brightly, and the sky was clouded with light fleecy clouds, save between them and the horizon a space of blue sky was left. In the centre of this space was a narrow belt of somewhat darker clouds than those above, circling the entire horizon as far as the eye could reach, until intercepted by the land to the west. To the north-east were five large ships, directly north were two others loaded with canvass, their white sails reflected in the sun. Sitting on the deck admiring the beauty of the scene, suddenly in the narrow belt of vapour described, appeared inverted *mirages* of the two vessels to the north—every spar, every rope, every sail complete,—no photographs could be more distinct. The other vessels to the north-east were reflected in the same manner, but as they were further off the phenomenon could not be so well observed,— though plain enough by the aid of a glass. The aerial ships continued suspended for about half an hour, and then either gradually disappeared or became lost by a near approach to the reality. When first seen the vessels were about ten or twelve miles distant.

The Prince of Wales' squadron, consisting of the *Hero*, 91, Captain Barnard ; perhaps the finest line of battle ship of her class ; the *Ariadne*, 26, Captain Vansittart ; one of the fastest, most heavily armed, and altogether finest of British frigates ; and the *Flying Fish*, 6, screw steam sloop, Captain Hope, left Charlottetown, Prince Edward's Island, last Saturday afternoon passing cautiously through the Straits of Northumberland during the night, and steaming at full speed across a portion of the Gulf of the St. Lawrence the next morning, keeping in line the whole distance. The fleet sighted the shores of Canada on Sunday, the 12th of August, at noon. It was drawing towards evening as the vessels passed between Bonaventure Island and the Cape, and the magnificent scenery showed on that account to perhaps greater advantage. The day was fine and the sea so calm that the surf could hardly be heard gently sighing its life out either upon the above-named precipitous island, which lay within rifle shot on the right, or upon Percé Island, situated at about the same distance on the left, and well so named from the caverns, sea tunnelled completely through it, or upon the mainland, which the ship's course was skirting. The features of the continent there are very remarkable. In some places the green fields, studded with white cottages, reach a considerable distance from the beach towards a mountain, which rises to the altitude of 1,200 feet and more, while in others, instead of gentle slopes, jagged picturesque cliffs present their bold front directly to the waves; nor did the inhabitants of the coast forget their duty, but every now and then a flash and a spirt of white smoke were distinctly visible from the ships, while in a few seconds the boom would be heard which made one certain that cannon of greater or less size were being fired as a salute. After passing this Gibraltar-like scene, and crossing Mal Baie, the squadron entered Gaspé bay, at sunset, the reds and yellows of the sky contrasting beautifully with the indistinct greens of the shore, and the hazy blues of the distant hills. Here the *Lady Head* and *Victoria*, Canadian Government steamers, the latter with the Governor-General of British North America on board, met and dipped their ensigns to the Prince's fleet, after which the whole five vessels dropped their anchors for the night in the land-locked harbour. "Is the Governor-General on board! sang out the *Hero*." "He's on board," was the answer from the *Victoria*. But no further intercourse took place that evening. It is understood that the Governor-General chose Gaspé basin in which to meet the Prince as being surrounded by natural beauties, and that His Royal Highness' first impression of Canada should not but be favourable.

Monday, the 13th, at half-past eight o'clock, the Governor-General and one of his Aides left the *Victoria,* under a Royal salute from that vessel, went on board the *Hero,* and the five steamers then proceeded to Gaspé Basin. As they were opposite the south-west arm where are the fishing village and the house of Mr. Le Boutillier, from whose grounds a salute was being fired, a rather untoward accident occurred. A spit runs out there some distance from the shore, and on the end of it the *Hero* grounded. The *Lady Head* dashed across to see what assistance could be rendered, but the line-of-battle ship preferred receiving help from her consort only. So the *Flying Fish* was summoned to carry out an anchor into deep water, and after some delay a hawser was sent on board the *Ariadne.* The latter vessel then shot ahead and the jerk, though it broke the cable, luckily got the *Hero* off. Several boats had meanwhile put out from shore with the sheriff and other officials, bringing an address to His Royal Highness, and a request that the free port there to be established might be called Port Albert.

The Prince stated, in reply, that he felt grateful for their kind wishes, and that the change of name depended on the local authorities. It is understood, however, that it will be made under the authority of Government.

The Canadian Ministers then went on board the Prince's ship, and were presented. By this time it was one o'clock, and the squadron then steamed slowly towards the open gulf again. On the way out, the Governor and his Ministers returned to the *Victoria,* and the *Hero* lost a man overboard, who was, however, speedily picked up by the Prince's life-boat. Cape Gaspé was reached at at a quarter to four by the whole of the fleet, the Canada steamers leading the way. Shortly after Cape Rosier light-house was seen, but then a thick fog came on, and the vessels lost sight of each other and the land. When it lifted in a couple of hours, no ship was visible from the *Ariadne,* and as it was supposed the *Hero* had gone ahead, full steam was put on and guns were fired every half hour. At ten o'clock some rockets were sent up and blue lights burned on the topmast yard arm, which were answered from the *Hero* in the position anticipated, and the ships again joined company.

The next morning the vessels crept along the coast under the Saint Anne's mountains, near enough to perceive distinctly their features, and to see the long street of houses which stretches along the south shore continually. The *Hero* was of course leading. The *Ariadne* was next, and the *Flying Fish* third. At noon the *Ariadne* was just about taking the *Flying Fish* in tow when one of her bearings heated and the white metal melted, so she had to make a new one. It was nearly ten o'clock at night before she again got under steam, having meanwhile tacked once or twice across the Estuary, only just holding her own against wind and current. She passed Father Point at full speed at two o'clock in the morning, which is the reason why the telegraph boat was not sent out, and found the rest of the fleet at half-past eight o'clock waiting off the mouth of the Saguenay. As soon as she was observed by them, the *Hero* made for the entrance to that river. In a few moments, however, she was seen to strike sharply on Bar Reef, and as the tide had not quite run out, her bows were soon so much out of water as to make her cant over slightly. The *Ariadne* at once went to her assistance, but before it could be rendered, she had moved her guns aft and the rising tide floated her off very little damaged. The Prince then went on board the *Victoria*, which had joined company during the night, and, preceded by Mr. Price's little steamer *Tadousack*, went up the Saguenay. The fleet, discouraged by the *Hero's* grounding, remained outside. The day was very showery and cold, and the tourists suited themselves to the exigencies of the weather,—the Prince wearing a pot hat and the roughest of clothes ; the Governor-General, the Ministers, and the rest of the party, wearing water-proofs of some kind. The *Victoria* went forty-five miles up the river past Cape Eternity, and as the weather was unpropitious, her passengers sought consolation in cigars or refreshments. They all admired the scenery exceedingly, and perhaps the rain and clouds added much to its usual wildness and grandeur. Coming down they put on full speed and reached the *Hero* again at about nightfall. Among other things to wonder at they saw the *Magnet*, one of the lake steamers, whose two tiers of cabins above deck were a novel sight to the greater part of them.

The next day was cold but sunny, and the Prince again went up the river in the *Victoria*, and was landed about fifteen miles from its mouth on the St. Marguerite. There tents had been built by Mr. Blackwell, the lessee of the river, and fishing tackle provided. The party, consisting of the same persons as were on the steamer the day before, engaged in fishing and shooting. The Prince had no luck. Lord Mulgrave and some others caught a few trout. All enjoyed themselves. In the afternoon, after lunch, the whole party ascended the St. Marguerite with the tide in birch canoes—the Prince paddled by two French Canadians leading the van.

The *Flying-Fish*, with the greater part of the officers of the squadron, also went up the Saguenay a long distance, and as they passed the tents were the royal standard was flying, they fired a royal salute of 21 guns. The echoes among the precipitous rocks close at hand, and the echoes from the more distant hills, were strikingly sublime, and much delighted the royal party. Among the incidents of this day were the introduction by his Excellency to the Duke of Newcastle and the presentation to the Prince by him of George Macbeth, who had come down to urge the acceptance by His Royal Highness of an invitation to a ball in London. Mr. Macbeth was most courteously received by the whole party, and His Royal Highness was at once pleased to signify his acceptance. The Prince enjoys dancing much. An invitation to a ball is, therefore, perhaps, the most acceptable compliment of the kind that can be paid him. The Prince is expected to appear with his squadron before Quebec to-morrow (Saturday,) at two o'clock, to land at four o'clock the same day. With his own squadron will be Admiral Milne's flag ship *Nile*, 91 guns, and the paddle-wheel steamer *Valorous*, 26 guns.

This may be the proper place to state that the Prince appears on all state occasions in the full uniform of a colonel in the army, but not as colonel of the 100th or Canadian Regiment, as is generally imagined,—wearing the orders of the Garter and the Bath. His complete suite consists of the Duke of Newcastle, Colonial Secretary; the Earl of St. Germains, Lord Steward of the Household; Major-General Bruce, Governor to His Royal Highness; Major Teesdale, R. A., and Captain Grey, Grenadier Guards, Equerries, and Dr. Ackland, Regis Professor of Medicine, for medical attendant. With the Duke travel Mr. Engelhart, his private secretary. Accompanying the Prince are also his Excellency the Earl of Mulgrave, Lieutenant-Governor of Nova Scotia, his aide,

Captain Stapleton, of the Grenadier Guards ; several other gentlemen accompanying the party, but not in any official capacity. Besides there are six or seven servants and a courier. The Prince has frequently expressed himself delighted not merely with the heartiness of the reception he had met with from the inhabitants of the Lower Provinces, but with the good taste displayed in most of their arrangements. Chiefly, however, he has been surprised by the evidences of civilization and material prosperity. In Canada, it is to be hoped, he will be still more delighted and surprised. His Royal Highness by no means confines his observations to the ceremonials laid down in the official programmes, or his physical exercise to the prescribed plans. He took frequent opportunities of conversing with those who had the honour of being presented, and proceeded into the country in plain clothes on a tour of inspection. He has invariably charmed those with whom he has conversed, and has shewn himself possessed of discrimination and an excellent education. While, although the mere state progresses, levees, and balls which have been indispensible, have much fatigued his suite, he has in addition found time for and pleasure in riding on horseback, fishing, shooting, canoeing, and even bathing. Sometimes almost all of these in a single day. He rides well, dances gracefully, and seems passionately fond of music. His manner in public is singularly courteous ; in private, exceedingly animated.

Quebec was not only handsomely decorated but crowded with strangers, who had come from the east and west literally by the thousands, over-loading the steamers and the trains of the Grand Trunk Railway.

Most of the members of parliament were among the visitors, who will not present their addresses until next week, as also numbers of official personages.

The triumphal arches were not so numerous, but more massive than those that were exhibited at Halifax, and many of the streets were converted into avenues of spruce. There were arches even on the road to Montmorenci Falls, which the Prince is expected to visit.

At the market wharf, where His Royal Highness landed, a cupola had been erected, under which the corporation presented him with an address. Opposite to this a platform of seats had been erected, as also under Mountain Hill, and in several other places.

The preparations for illumination were extensive, and the programme for the display of fire-works promised great things.

A fleet of river steamers were out hovering around the Prince's ships before and at the time of his leaving the *Hero*.

After receiving the addresses, the Prince passed through various streets in a procession, headed by the Chief of Police, whose deputy brought up the rear ; between which two dignitaries were officials and members of societies of all kinds. The Prince then took up his quarters at the Parliament House, which was also tenanted by the British ambassador to Washington, Colonel Irvine, and Sir Allan McNab, Her Majesty's Aide-de-Camp.

Admiral Milne issued from the *Nile* a general memorandum respecting the fleet, as follows :—"On H. M. S. *Hero*, with standard of His Royal Highness Prince of Wales nearing anchorage, H. M. ships will be dressed, and a royal salute of 21 guns will be fired ; and before the *Hero* comes to an anchor, the yards of H. M. ships present will be manned, and His Royal Highness cheered. On Saturday, 18th, H. M. ships will be dressed at eight a. m., and on His Royal Highness leaving the *Hero* for the shore, the yards will be manned, a royal salute fired, and His Royal Highness cheered. A further royal salute will be fired on the arrival of His Royal Highness at the Parliament House, when His Royal Highness' standard will be hoisted there. H.M. ships present will follow the motions of the flag ship, commencing in each case to salute when she fires her second gun."

All Her Majesty's ships in port shall be illuminated on some early day next week.

The following is the military programme. Before the ship in which His Royal Highness is on board comes to anchor, a Royal salute will be fired by the Royal Artillery from the Citadel, and likewise by the Volunteer Field Battery from the Durham Terrace. The same will again take place on the landing of His Royal Highness.

The Quebec Cavalry, under Lieutenant-Colonel Bell, will furnish an escort from the wharf to the Governor-General's residence. A guard of honour of the Royal Canadian Rifles, under a field-officer, will receive His Royal Highness on landing.

Heads of departments to be in full dress.

A guard of honour of the 17th Regiment, with Queen's colours and band, will be sent to the Governor's residence to pay the usual compliment upon the arrival of His Royal Highness there. A subaltern's guard of the Royal Canadian Rifles will mount at the Governor-General's residence on the morning of the day His Royal Highness will land.

Double sentries will invariably be posted at the principal entrances to the several residences of His Royal Highness.

Upon His Royal Highness landing, the Royal standard will be hoisted at the Citadel, at the landing place, and at the Governor-General's residence. The 17th Regiment to furnish a guard of honour at the wharf on the embarkation of His Royal Highness for Montreal.

The effect of all the salutes combined is expected to be unusually grand. The Governor-General has appointed to-morrow as a general holiday in the City of Quebec.

Quebec, August 18th.

This Saturday morning broke very inauspiciously, the skies were lowering, and ere long it began to rain heavily. The streets became muddy, and the spruce trees, planted all along the sidewalks, becoming wet, walking was disagreeable, nay, almost impossible.

Just as at St. John's and at Halifax, so there in Quebec, the weather seemed made on purpose to vex the would-be-sight-seers; but with the same good luck with which his Royal mother invariably meets, the Prince was favoured in the afternoon, the time fixed for his actual landing, as the clouds rose higher the breeze freshened, and the sun almost shone out.

At three o'clock, the *Hero*, *Ariadne*, and *Flying Fish* came round Point Levi, and their appearance was the signal for a general salute from the *Nile* and *Valorous* in the harbour, and from the Citadel and other batteries of artillery on the shore.

The scene then presented was very magnificent. Three fine ships of war were steaming up, under the most picturesque, and almost the strongest fortress in the world. Clouds of smoke were not only half enveloping the men of war, but capping the lofty steeps which frown down upon the water, and almost mingling with the scud which was drifting overhead.

The Citadel, the Cavalier, and Grand Batteries, Durham Terrace, the roofs of all the houses facing the St. Lawrence, were black with the multitudes of people. The yards of all the ships were manned by tars, to be numbered by the thousand, and the wharves were covered with crowds. The river was alive with steamboats of various sizes, which, as well as the men of war and every prominent point on shore, were gaily decked with many coloured flags. A balloon or two were floating in the air,—and when an hour afterwards His Royal Highness landed, a similar scene was visible.

On the Champlain Market wharf, and immediately opposite the fine new market building, a grand stand had been erected capable of accommodating over a thousand people. This was filled chiefly by ladies. In front of this and immediately opposite the landing stairs, from which a crimson carpet led to it, was a pavilion under which, perhaps, fifty people could conveniently stand. Its floor was slightly raised, its pillars draped with flags, its roof composed of green spruce boughs, and surmounted with various coloured gonfalons and the royal standard.

This was the central point of the whole display. To this pavilion, just before the landing of the Prince, came the Mayor of Quebec, attired in silken robes, leading his Council in full evening dress, and attended by his clerk and other civic officers. Then came the Cabinet Ministers of Canada in their new uniform. Next came the Anglican Bishop of Quebec, Right Rev. Dr. Mountain, with his chaplain, secretary, and some of his other clergy with their gowns. Then the Roman Catholic Hierarchy appeared in their robes. The Archbishop being unwell, the Administrator of the Diocese, Mgr. Baillargeon, Bishop of Tloa, came in front, and with him Mgrs. Bourget of Montreal, Gargnes of Ottawa, Larocque of St. Hyacinthe, Horan of Kingston, Pinsonneault of Sandwich, Farrel of Hamilton, Lynch of Toronto, Cook of Three Rivers. They were all dressed in episcopal purple soutans and cloaks, and wore heavy gold crucifixes and other symbols of their position, and then came the Superiors of the Seminaries of Montreal and Quebec, and several of their clergy.

Then the Governor-General, Sir Edmund Walker Head, and a brilliant staff.

Next came the Adjutant-General, De Salaberry, General Williams, commander of the forces in Canada, the Earl of Mulgrave, Lieut. Governor of Nova Scotia, each with several officers about them.

Last almost of all came Lord Lyons, British Ambassador at Washington, in the same costume as the Canadian Ministers, and two of his secretaries somewhat similarly dressed.

A number of members of Parliament, and some private citizens as well as members of the press, completed the list.

Precisely at four o'clock, the Prince's standard being lowered from the mast head of the *Hero*, told the multitude His Royal Highness was leaving for the shore, and presently his barge was seen cleaving the waters and impelled vigorously towards the land, while the salutes from all the ships and land batteries were again renewed, and all the church bells were set violently ringing

His Excellency, the Ministers and the Coporation went to meet His Royal Highness, and he soon stepped lightly ashore and advanced to the appointed place under the cupola. There the Mayor stood in front of him, Sir Edmund Head at his right, his equerries, with their hats on, immediately behind, and right and left from them, the Earl of St. Germains, the Duke of Newcastle, Col. Bruce, Admiral Milne and the Ministers of the Crown in this colony, as well as Sir E. P. Tache, and Sir Allan McNab, Aid-de-camps to the Queen, specially ordered to receive His Royal Highness, as her representatives.

A small circle then formed itself round, while the Mayor read the addresses to the Prince first in French and then in English, the English version being as follows :—

MAY IT PLEASE YOUR ROYAL HIGHNESS,—

The Mayor, Councillors, and Citizens of Quebec are happy on being the first among the Canadian subjects of her most gracious Majesty the Queen to present their respectful homage to your Royal Highness.

They will long continue to regard as a memorable epoch the day on which they have been permitted to receive within the walls of their city this visit from the eldest son of their beloved Sovereign, the Heir Apparent to the British Crown.

When we became aware that Her Majesty, finding it inconvenient or impracticable to proceed to so great a distance from the central seat of Government, had deigned to testify the regard which her Majesty entertains towards her Canadian subjects by sending our future sovereign in her stead, we felt grateful and proud in receiving such a mark of distinction from one whose public and private virtues command the admiration of the whole world.

We feel assured that our most gracious Queen was desirous to show that by that act of condescension that she knows how to appreciate and honour, in an especial manner, the most important of her Colonial possessions.

In this Province your Royal Highness will find a free people, faithful and loyal, attached to their sovereign and their country. In this the most ancient city of Canada, your Royal Highness will be in the midst of a population devoted to your interests, testifying by the heartiness of their acclamations and good wishes that though they derive their origin from various races, and may differ in language and religious denominations, yet they have but one voice and one heart in expressing loyalty to their Sovereign, and in welcoming him who represents her on this occasion, and who is one day destined, according to the natural order of events, to become her successor.

The people of Quebec rejoice in beholding your Royal Highness in the midst of them; they are happy because they have the opportunity of expressing in a direct manner their respect and attachment. Happy, because he who will hereafter, in all human probability, wear the crown of this great empire, will be enabled, during his brief sojourn in Canada, to judge for himself of the loyalty of the whole Canadian people in general, and of the citizens of Quebec in particular.

Your Royal Highness will also enjoy the opportunity of forming an adequate opinion of the extent of the country, its productions, its resources, its progress, and the great future reserved for it, and will be enabled to perceive that Canada, with a population of three millions of inhabitants, though only an appendage of the United Kingdom, possesses institutions as free, and a territory three times as extensive.

In conclusion we entreat your Royal Highness favourably to

accept for our most gracious Sovereign and yourself, along with our loyal and respectful homage, the assurance of our sincere attachment, with the most fervent wish that this visit to Canada may prove as gratifying and agreeable to yourself as it is to the citizens of Quebec.

(Signed) HECTOR L. LANGEVIN,
Mayor

This finished, the Prince received the parchment originals, and handed them to the Duke of Newcastle, from whom he received the reply, which he read in his usual clear and deliberate manner, emphasizing all the leading words :—

GENTLEMEN,—It is with no ordinary feelings of gratification and interest in all around me that I find myself for the first time on the shores of Canada, and within the precincts of this its most ancient city. I am deeply touched by the cordiality with which I have been welcomed by the inhabitants. For the address which you have just presented to me, I beg you to accept the hearty thanks, which, in the name of the Queen, I offer to you. Be assured that Her Majesty will receive with no little satisfaction the account of my reception amongst you, proving, as it does, that her feelings towards the people are met on their part in the most devoted and loyal attachment to herself, her throne, and her family. Still more will she rejoice to hear from your own lips that all differences of origin, language, and religion are lost in one universal spirit of patriotism, and that all classes are knit to each other and to the mother country by the common ties of equal liberty and free institutions. For myself, I will only add that I shall ever take a deep concern in all that tends to promote the prosperity of this beautiful and interesting city.

The Mayor then called for three cheers for His Royal Highness the Prince of Wales, and they were lustily given, at least by those in the vicinity of the Prince.

In a few moments more the Prince took his seat in the Governor-General's carriage, with the Duke of Newcastle, General Bruce, and Earl St. Germains, the other official personages occupying carriages behind them, and after some delay in organising the procession the cortege started slowly.

To move fast would have been out of the question, in the narrow crowded streets of Quebec, and as it was the crush was indeed awful, especially near Prescott gate.

The Indians from Lorette came out in force, handsomely dressed, and the various societies mustered their bands.

The Bishop was almost the only representative of the Anglican clergy, which is perhaps due to the fact that, although the Roman Catholic Church dignitaries allowed him to take the precedence, they would not allow any of his clergy to go with him and before them.

Of course in all this the chief attraction was the Prince himself. To see him pass, seats in platforms by the street side, and windows in houses on the line of march, had been let at considerable prices, and all these were filled with anxious gazers.

Among the features on the route may be mentioned a large number of children posted on the vacant space near Prescott gate singing "God save the Queen," and a number of sewing and other machines set in motion on the top of the mechanics' arch in John Street.

The Prince went through St. John's toll-gate towards the Governor's residence, and the procession returned citywards.

The quantity of transparencies that were put up was really extraordinary. There were scores of Queens, Prince Consorts by the dozen, and of Prince of Wales no end. Then there were crowns and stars, and V. Rs. and V. As. without number. In the gasfit line too, the preparations were extensive, and the display correspondingly effective. Japanese lanterns were numerous, but not special favourites, wax candles in the window panes being preferred.

Then the mottoes which were brought out on the windows were various. The Prince was bid welcome a thousand times, and he was oftener called Prince de Galles than designated by his English title.

The public offices were perhaps the most brilliantly lit up of any. In front of the Finance Minister's residence was a ship. In front of the Board of Works office some brilliant stars were conspicuous. The old Chateau, St. Louis, was radiant. The Attorney-General's offices were covered with lamps and transparencies. But the finest display of any was made before the Receiver-General's. A huge inscription in the front told that it was the residence of His

Royal Highness the late Duke of Kent, in 1793, and the space between the building and the street was made a fairy bower of by means of coloured lamps and evergreens.

Next the public offices the Roman Catholic edifices deserved notice. The Cathedral windows were illuminated by lamps arranged in the form of crosses. The Archbishop's palace and the Convents all announce "Honneur au Prince," in flaming characters.

But the display was not confined to these stately buildings. In Grey Street, the houses were lit up though if only by sticking a bill on a window pane with a lamp behind it.

The French population as well as the Irish seemed to desire to testify their content with the constitutions they possess.

The illumination exceeded that of any place the Prince had yet visited.

The Prince and the Duke stayed at the Governor-General's.

The salutes from Durham Terrace were fired by a battery of Volunteer Artillery, who possess eight guns and very excellently horsed. A great portion of the route, as far as the toll-gate on the St. Louis Road, was guarded by about seven hundred Volunteer Rifles, under the command of Colonel Sewell. The men were placed about six feet apart, but as that would have been at too great a distance to enable them to keep back the crowd, the members of the different societies were placed in the spaces between. They mustered very strong, and looked exceedingly well with their banners, emblems, and paraphernalia. The St. Andrew's Society, headed by their piper, a very portly gentleman of immense importance, made a great show. Many of the youthful members carried painted sticks, upon the ends of which were placed tartan streamers. The members of the St. Patrick's Society wore green velvet scarfs; the members of the St. George's Society had roses in their button holes. The young St. Jean Baptistes mustered very strong, and had many fine banners of white silk. The Indians and Firemen followed. The former were from Lorette, and dressed out very fantastically with feathers, velvets, bead-work, and apparel of various colours.

The illuminations in the evening were on a large scale, but very little show was made save by the Government Departments. All these were lighted up.

The Board of Works exhibited a large Prince's plume, composed of illuminated lamps. It very rarely happens that portraits or figures of animals look well in an illumination. It is far better that illustrations should be confined to representations of fruits and flowers, banners, and emblematical devices, than to those things wherein discrepancies are sure to be most glaringly noticed. Some of the most beautiful, it may be said the most beautiful, effects were produced by stars, plumes, and crosses of glass lighted behind with gas. Over Russell's Hotel one of the best of this description of ornaments was erected. Chinese lamps hung in the trees, before the doors of the houses all along Durham Terrace, across the Governor's gardens to the citadel, had a pretty appearance. Very little gas was used; the light given was that of oil lamps and candles. The best part of the show was Point Levi as seen from Durham Terrace. The night was dark, nothing of the houses could be seen, but the lighted windows shone brightly in the distance, and were reflected upon the waters of the river, in ever-recurring, dancing gleams of light. In Quebec itself some of the people had followed the example mentioned as having been set by those of Halifax and St. John. They had displayed their goods in the windows to the best advantage, and brilliantly lighted up the whole shops. So with some of the private residences,—the best furniture was placed in the room fronting the street, the walls decorated with wreaths and festoons of drapery. Away from the Government offices, the principal seat of the illuminations was St. John Street and the Market Square. In the latter place the Cathedral is situated, in the windows of which three large crosses were placed. The Jesuit Barrack, fitted up with transparencies, lent its share of attractions, and from a number of small arches erected all along the sidewalks numerous lamps were suspended. In John Street the Corporation arch looked well, and Mr. David Bansley, late of Toronto, shed a flood of light over the street opposite his house. Of course the whole people were out of doors, thronging the streets and getting delighted with the exhibition. Frequently was heard the exclamation, "Magnifique;" and when the candles were out, the oil consumed, and the ladies taken home, a general glorification was indulged in. The whole night long the city was in a continual roar of "God save the Queen," "Marsellaise," "Partant pour la Syrie," and "Yankee Doodle." It was no use trying to sleep until daylight broke, and so sensible folk resigned themselves to their fate, and indulged in as few expletives as under the circumstances were at all possible.

On Sunday His Royal Highness drove to the Protestant Cathedral in company with his suite, and listened to an excellent sermon delivered by the Rev. Dr. Horseman, who chose for his text the third verse of the second chapter of Romans. The allusion made to the Prince was very slight. The church was very full, and the congregation conducted themselves in the most becoming manner. During the progress of His Royal Highness from Cataraqui to the Cathedral, he passed by many knots of people who had assembled at various points from which a good view of him could be obtained; but they sensibly refrained on the Sabbath day from any thing more than a quiet demonstration of respect.

This "Cataraqui" bothered many sadly. Where was it? The name was mentioned to many persons; they would turn it over on their tongues, but could make nothing of it. They would first try it as *Catara*-qui, laying stress upon the first three syllables; then upon the *qui*, but in vain. At last it leaked out that it was no other than the house occupied by the Governor, and rented from Mr. Burstall—had been so christened in honour of the Prince's visit, commanding a good view of the St. Lawrence, and is situated in well wooded grounds, laid out very tastily. There is a conservatory attached to the house; it had been fitted up with some extra furniture for the royal visitor.

While the Prince was fishing upon the Saguenay, he found the spot he had chosen surrounded by water, consequent upon the rising of the tide. A fisherman named Price went by, and offered to carry His Royal Highness across. But the Prince objected. "I may as well get wet as you," said he. But the boatman assured the Prince that he was wet already. "Well, if that's it," said the future monarch of the British empire, "I will accept your offer;" and he was forthwith carried in safety to the shore.

Among the strangers then present in Quebec was Mayor Wood's

Secretary, Mr. Thomson—who was here for the purpose of making arrangements relative to the visit of the Prince of Wales to New York. He had an interview with Lord Lyons to-day.

The following members of Parliament were in the city :—

Messrs. Abbot, Aikins, Bell, Benjamin, Bourassa, Brown, Buchanan, Bureau, Burton, Burwell, Carling, Chapais, Cimon, Connor, Cook, Coutlee, Daoust, Dorion, Dorland, Drummond, Dufresne, Dunkin, Ferguson, Ferres, Foley, Fortier, Foster, Fournier, Gill, Gowan, Harwood, Hebert, Huot, Jobin, Labelle, Lacoste, LeBoutillier, Loux, Macbeth, D. A. McDonald, MacLeod, McCann, McDougall, McKellar, McMicken, Meagher, Merritt, Morrison, Papineau, Patrick, Piche, W. F. Powell, Roblin, Rose, Rymal, W. R. Scott, Short, Sicotte, Simpson, Starnes, Thibaudeau, Webb, Wallbridge, White, Whitney, Wilson and Wright.

His Excellency Sir Edmund Head had fixed that His Royal Highness the Prince of Wales should visit the Chaudiere Falls. Early in the morning the sky was bright, and fair weather for the next twenty-four hours was confidently predicted. But before nine o'clock was reached the sky became rapidly over-cast, and torrents of rain extinguished all hope. Those who have the management of affairs, whoever they be, had taken good care the multitude should not know where the Prince was to be found. Few therefore were disappointed at the unfavourable state of the weather. They who did know of the proposed arrangement scarcely imagined that it would be carried out. It was such a horrible day—a day without one redeeming feature in it.

The village of St. Nicholas is built upon a hill, which rises precipitously from the shore, consists of about a couple of dozen of whitewashed wooden houses, and an equal number of pig-sties. The road leading to it was never made for the purpose of facilitating traffic. Always bad ; this day it was—ask the Prince, he can tell all about it. After much exertion to reach the top of the hill, in the stables of a tavern kept by Mr. Bazil Demers, more than thirteen horses were waiting for His Royal Highness and suite. This was about 12 o'clock. Shortly afterwards arrived a little steamer, the *Point Levi*, bringing Mr. Sanderson and the material for a lunch. So the Prince was really coming; the rain would not deter him ; it was set down in the programme that he should see the Chaudiere Falls, and see them he would. But there was one intention that could not be carried out. His Royal Highness might cross the river in the rain; he might ride to the Falls in the rain, but it could not be expected of him that he should dine in the open air, upon wet grass,—gipsey fashion. That item in the programme had to be "scratched," and accordingly preparations were made for lunch in Monsier Bazil Demer's hotel. Meanwhile intelligence arrived that the Prince had actually started. Away on the opposite side of the river, scarcely discernible amid the rain and mist, the royal standard was discovered. The Prince of Wales was seated in an open man-of-war's boat, with nothing to protect him from the pouring rain. St. Nicholas would soon have been reached, had not the proper landing place been mistaken and the boat steered half a mile above it, necessitating a heavy pull against an always swift current, then increased by the receding tide. After about an hour's rowing the right wharf was made, and the Prince leapt ashore. The horses kept in readiness were quickly mounted, and His Royal Highness leading, the party dashed up the road leading to the Falls, scattering the mud in all directions, and giving the astonished villagers but a single moment to familiarise themselves with the Royal looks. Of course they were much disappointed, but made up for it afterwards by mistaking Mr. Englehart for the Prince, and by staring at him with the greatest vigour.

The country round about the falls, through which the Prince passed, is a fair sample of Lower Canada. The falls themselves are exceedingly grand, well worthy a royal visit—in fine weather. The rains for a few preceding days had added very considerably to the volume of water, which, dashing down its deeply worn and narrow channel, is lashed into snow-white foam, rendered doubly beautiful by the contrast it affords to the dark rock of the banks, and of the green trees with which they are covered to the very edge of the cataract. Despite the unfavourable condition under which they were visited, many expressions of delight escaped His Royal Highness and the noblemen accompanying him. Not content with the view obtainable from horseback, he dismounted and walked about. Dr. Ackland endeavoured to take a sketch, but was obliged to desist, the rain rendering success impossible. The royal party reached the tavern about three o'clock covered with mud. Never were ten men in a dirtier plight. The pace at which the Prince rode was not less than ten miles an hour, and though some of his suite had considerable difficulty in keeping up with him, they all managed to be in time for lunch.

Lunch?—yes lunch! By the time the Prince had returned, every thing had been prepared, and despite his wet clothes, His Royal Highness set to work and made a hearty meal. A neatly printed bill of fare was placed before each guest, of which the following is a copy. By it you will see the Prince was well taken care of :—

GOUTER

POUR SON ALTESSE ROYAL LA PRINCE DE GALLES,

Aux Chutes de la Chaudiere.

Lundi, le 20 d'Aout, 1860.

La Ronde de Bœuf, salée.

Le Jambon froid, décoré a la galée.

La Mayonnaise de blanc de volaille, garnie.

Les Poulets nouveaux, rôtis.

Les Langues de Renne, décorées.

Le Paté de foies de canards de Toulouse, truffée.

Le Pâté de Becossines, truffée.

La Galantine de perdreax, truffée.

La Pâté de foies d'oies, de Strasbourg.

Les Pieds de cochon, truffes.

Les Saucissons de Lyon.

Les Sardines á l'huile.

Le Gingembre des Indes, au sucre.

Les Prunes, Reine Claude, á l'eau-de-vie.

La Marmelade d'Oranges.

Les fruits en candis.

Les Pèches, les Poires, les Raisins, les Prunes.

Le Vin de Champagne,

Le Vin de Xèrès,

Le Grand Vin de Château-Lafite, 1851.

L'Eau-de-vie de Cognac, 1834.

La Bière amèie,

L'Eau de Seltz.

The lunch dispatched, the horses were again brought to the door, and the wharf speedily reached. His Royal Highness crossed in the *Point Levi* to Cape Rouge, and from thence rode to Cataraqui, a distance of four miles, in the Governor-General's carriage, no doubt heartily glad that the trip was over.

Of course the people of the village were highly delighted with the visit. As for Mr. Bazil Demers, the man in whose house the Prince lunched, he will henceforth be the very largest man in the place. The chair in which His Royal Highnes sat will be held sacred; no one will be allowed again to use it. The room he occupied will be set apart, and a sight of it permitted only to Mr. Bazil Demers' very particular friends. Shouldn't wonder if he even went so far as to re-christen the whole house by the name of the Prince de Galles. The favoured chamber itself is not one of great pretensions ; it has an old wooden clock, a few rush-bottomed chairs, and some of those coloured prints intended to represent scenes in scriptural history.

The lunch, as already mentioned, was supplied under the supervision of Mr. Sanderson, who, by the way, denies your allegations that he is a cook. *The* cook is Monsieur Hardy, an *artiste*, who was once *chef de cuisine* in the establishment of the Comte de Baritenski.

The horses used by the royal party were supplied by Dr. William Kerwin, who will be employed during the Prince's visit. His Royal Highness rode a brown mare named "Lady Franklin." He was dressed in a white hat, long waterproof coat, and grey unmentionables.

The following is a list of the gentlemen who accompanied the Prince:—Earl st. Germains, Duke of Newcastle, Major-General Bruce, Sir Edmund Head, Commodore Seymour, of the *Hero*; Dr. Ackland, Captain Gray, Major Teesdale, and Captain Retallick.

Tuesday, August 21.

The most interesting ceremonial that has occurred since His Royal Highness landed on this continent, took place in the Parliament House, Quebec, on the 21st of August.

At about eleven o'clock the booming of heavy guns from the

whole of the batteries of the fortress and from all the ships in the harbour, gave signal that the Prince was leaving the Governor-General's, and was coming to take up his quarters in the Palace prepared for him, and he shortly afterwards made his appearance coming down between the files of soldiers who lined the streets.

It rained heavily all the time, but as His Royal Highness and suite were in a covered carriage, the brilliancy of their uniforms was by no means tarnished.

Having taken their apartments, all of which are beautifully furnished, and divested themselves of their over coats, &c., the Royal party entered the reception room, late the Legislative Council Chambers, and arranged themselves in front of the crimson drapery of the Throne.

The Prince was of course in front the central figure in the group, attired in the regulation dress of a colonel, with all his ribbons and orders around his person.

On his right hand was the Governor-General, in his blue and silver Windsor uniform, also the Earl of St. Germains, Colonel Irvine, Admiral Sir Alexander Milne, Major Teesdale, Captain Vansittart, Commodore Seymour, and a host of other naval officers. On his left was the Duke of Newcastle, brilliant in scarlet and silver lace, General Sir Fenwick Williams, with his stars and medals, Colonels Sir Allan MacNab and Sir E. B. Tache, aides-de-camp to the Queen, Lord Mulgrave, Lieutenant-Governor of Nova Scotia, in the same dress as Sir Edmund Head : Lord Lyons and his two attaches ; the Anglican Bishop of Quebec, and a large concourse of military officers.

The first presentations were those of the Roman Catholic Hierarchy, the whole of the Bishops in the province belonging to that church being separately introduced by one of their number.

No sooner had these dignitaries disappeared with their purple robes and their golden crucifixes, then the Judges of the Superior Court of Lower Canada came upon the stage in their silken gowns and linen bands; they, too, had the honour of separate and personal presentation, each advancing in turn from the semi-circle in which they had arranged themselves, bowing and retiring.

Next came the members of the House of Assembly and Legislative Council, who had previously gathered themselves together under the wings of their respective Speakers.

The members of the Upper House were all in costume, wearing coats, similar to those of the Queen's Counsel, on most of which were the polished steel buttons.

The Speaker wore, of course, his usual robe.

The Gentleman-Usher of the Black Rod, with his three bows, first entered the reception room, and after him the Sergeant-at-Arms, with his golden mace.

Next came Hon. Mr. Speaker, and then the whole of the honourables, who, it is right to say, were the best dressed and finest looking body of civilians that have yet greeted the Prince in any of the colonies. Having formed themselves into a crescent with regularity, the Speaker advanced, and first in English and then in French, read the following address:—

To the Most High, Puissant and Illustrious Prince Albert Edward, Prince of the United Kingdom of Great Britain and Ireland, Prince of Wales, Duke of Saxony, Prince of Cobourg and Gotha, Great Steward of Scotland, Duke of Cornwall and Rothsay, Earl of Chester, Carrick, and Dublin, Baron of Renfrew, and Lord of the Isles, K. G.

MAY IT PLEASE YOUR ROYAL HIGHNESS,—

We the Legislative Council of Canada, in Parliament assembled, approach your Royal Highness with renewed assurances of our attachment and devotion to the person and Crown of your Royal Mother, our beloved Queen. While we regret that the duties of state should have prevented our Sovereign from visiting this extensive portion of her vast dominions, we loyally and warmly appreciate the interest which Her Majesty manifests in it by deputing to us your Royal Highness as her representative; and we rejoice in common with all her subjects in this province at the appearance among us of him who at some future, but we hope distant, day will reign over the realm, wearing with undiminished lustre the Crown which will descend to him. Though the formal opening of that great work, the Victoria Bridge, known throughout the world as the most gigantic effort in modern times of engineering skill, has been made a special occasion of your Royal Highness' visit, and proud as are Canadians of it, we yet venture to hope that you will find in Canada many other evidences of greatness and progress to interest you in the welfare and advancement of your future subjects. Enjoying under the institutions guaranteed to us all freedom in the management of our own affairs, and as British subjects having a common feeling and interest in the fortunes of the empire, its glories and successes, we trust, as we believe, that the visit of your Royal Highness will strengthen the ties which bind together the Sovereign and the Canadian people.

The Prince received the beautifully engrossed parchment from M. Belleau's hand and gave them to the Duke, who delivered him the reply, which he read first in English and then in French, deliberately and distinctly. His pronunciation of the French language is as perfect as that of the English, a fact which surprised many of the members, although from one with a court education it was to be expected. The reply was as follows :—

GENTLEMEN,—From my heart I thank you for this address, breathing a spirit of love and devotion to your Queen, and of kindly interest in me as her representative on this occasion. At every step of my progress through the British Colonies, and now more forcibly in Canada, I am impressed with the conviction that I owe the overpowering cordiality of my reception to my connection with her to whom, under Providence, I owe every thing, my sovereign and parent. To her I shall with pride convey the expressions of your loyal sentiments, and if at some future period, so remote, I trust, that I may allude to it with less pain, it shall please God to place me in that closer relation to you which you contemplate, I cannot hope for any more honourable distinction than to earn for myself such expressions of generous attachment as I now owe to your appreciation of the virtues of the Queen. Few as yet have been the days which I have spent in this country, I have seen much to indicate the rapid progress and future greatness of United Canada. The infancy of this Province has resembled, in some respects, that of my native island ; and, as in centuries gone by, the mother country combined the several virtues of Norman and Anglo-Saxon races, so I may venture to anticipate in the matured character of Canada the united excellencies of her double ancestry. Most heartily I respond to your desire, that the ties which bind together the Sovereign and the Canadian people may be strong and enduring.

Address and reply over, the levee commenced. The reply
S

finished, there was little delay. By royal letters patent since the Prince arrived here, he has been made Viceroy of all the North American colonies, and so has power to confer the honour of knighthood. A moment of breathless suspense followed. The Duke of Newcastle handed his sword to the Prince ; Mr. Belleau bended the knee, and was told to rise up again as Sir Narcisse Belleau. Of course he obeyed, bowed, and retired.

Then came in her Majesty's faithful Commons, the ponderous mace glittering as brilliantly as it could of gold.

The Ministers being duly arranged Mr. Smith read the address as follows :—

To the Most High, Puissant and Illustrious Prince Albert Edward, Prince of the United Kingdom of Great Britain and Ireland, Prince of Wales, Duke of Saxony, Prince of Cobourg and Gotha, Great Steward of Scotland, Duke of Cornwall and Rothsay, Earl of Chester, Carrick and Dublin, Baron of Renfrew and Lord of the Isles, K. G.

MAY IT PLEASE YOUR ROYAL HIGHNESS,—

We the Legislative Assembly of Canada in Parliament assembled, approach your Royal Highness with assurances of loyalty to our most gracious Sovereign. The Queen's loyal subjects in this Province would have rejoiced had the duties of state permitted their august Sovereign to have herself visited this country, and to have received in person the expression of their devotion to her, and of the admiration with which they regard the manner in which she administers the affairs of the vast Empire over which it has pleased Divine Providence to place her; but while we cannot refrain from expressing our unfeigned regret that it has proved impossible for our Queen to visit her possessions in Canada, we are deeply sensible of her gracious desire to meet the wishes of her subjects by having permitted the opportunity of welcoming, in this part of her dominions, the Heir Apparent of the Throne, our future Sovereign. We desire to congratulate your Royal Highness on your arrival in Canada, an event to be long remembered, as manifesting the deep interest felt by the Queen in the welfare of her colonial subjects. On this auspicious occasion, when, for the first time, the colonies have been honoured by the Heir Apparent, we receive an earnest of the determination of our most gracious Sovereign to knit yet more closely the ties of affection and fidelity which unite us to the British Empire, and enable us to share in its liberties, its glories, and its great historical associations. The approaching opening of the Victoria Bridge by your Royal Highness has been the more immediate cause of your present visit to Canada. We trust you will find in that stupendous work the most striking evidence in which the capital and skill of the Mother Country have united with the energy and enterprise of this Province in overcoming natural obstacles of the most formidable character ; but we trust that in your further progress your Royal Highness will find in the peace and prosperity of the people, and in their attachment to the Sovereign, the best proof of the strength of the ties which unite Canada to the Mother Country, and of the mutual advantages to the empire and to the colony from the perpetuation of a connexion which has been fraught with such great and beneficial results. We pray that your Royal Highness may be pleased to convey to our most gracious Queen the feelings of love and gratitude with which we regard her rule, and especially of her condescension in affording us the occasion of welcoming your Royal Highness to the Province of Canada.

The Prince then made the following reply to the address of the Legislative Assembly :—

GENTLEMEN,—No answer that I can return to your address will sufficiently convey my thanks to you or express the pleasure which I have derived from the manifestations of loyalty and affection to the Queen, my mother, by which I have been met upon my arrival in this Province. As an Englishman, I recognise with pride in those manifestations your sympathy with the great nation from which so many of you trace your origin, and with which you share the honours of a glorious history. In addressing you, however, as an Englishman, I do not forget that some of my fellow subjects here are not of my own blood ; to them, also, an especial acknowledgment is due, and I receive with gratification the proofs of their attachment to the Crown of England. They are evidences of their satisfaction with the equal laws under which they live, and of their just confidence that whatever be their origin, all Canadians are alike objects of interest to their Sovereign and her people. Canada may be proud that within her limits two races of different language and habits are united in the same

Legislature by a common loyalty, and are bound to the same constitution by a common patriotism. But to all of you, and to three millions of British subjects, of whom you are the representatives, I am heartily thankful for your demonstration of goodwill. I shall not readily forget the mode in which I have been received while amongst you. I regret that the Queen has been unable to comply with your anxious desire that she would visit this portion of her empire. Already I have had proofs of the affectionate devotion which would have attended her progress; but I shall make it my first, as it will be my most pleasing duty, upon my return to England, to convey to her the feelings of love and gratitude to her person and her rule, which you have expressed on this occasion, and the sentiments of hearty welcome you have offered to me, her son.

Sir Henry Smith was then knighted as Speaker of the House, and retired.

A number of the officers of the garrison followed, after whom, came in the Synod of the Anglican Church, diocese of Quebec, Bishop Mountain, delegates and Clergy.

THE CLERICAL ADDRESS.

The venerable Bishop, his voice feeble with age, read the address from this body, to which all the Synod audibly said Amen, as follows :—

MAY IT PLEASE YOUR ROYAL HIGHNESS,—

We, the Bishop, Clergy, and Laity of the United Church of England and Ireland, in the Diocese of Quebec, in Synod assembled, gladly avail ourselves of the arrival of your Royal Highness on our shores, to testify our deep and fervent loyalty towards that sceptre which, in good time we trust, you are destined to succeed to, and also to express our heartfelt gratification that the Heir Apparent to the British Throne has, for the first time in its history, visited that great and important province in which our 'lot is cast. We believe that in this auspicious event is implied much more than the mere graceful recognition of the request made by our Canadian Legislature, for the presence and sanction of the greatest work of engineering skill the world has ever seen. We view it rather as an evidence of the more intimate union which is growing between the Mother Country and her Canadian offshoot, and as a pledge that that union will be developed into an enduring and indissoluble unity; and, moreover, we prize the more highly the presence of your Royal Highness amongst us, as we shall be enabled thereby to add the feeling of personal acquaintance and attachment to that abstract loyalty which we have always cherished. In the course of your progress, your Royal Highness will be in a position to judge of the rapid advance in material prosperity which the country has made in the last few years. Amidst the busy scene the Church of England may seem to have been remiss in her work, and to have done little to keep pace with the rapid motion of the world around. We have, it is true, comparatively few marks of outward prosperity; we have no state privileges; no great cathedral; no opulent endowments, and in this part of the Province we are scattered and few in number. Yet we are endeavouring as best we may, and, by God's blessing, we trust with some measure of success, to reproduce in the new land all that is essential and important in the doctrine and discipline of that pure and reformed branch of Christ's Holy Catholic Church, which in England are entwined so closely with the very foundations of the throne; and we pray you to remember that the petitions for the welfare and prosperity of Your Royal Highness will continue to be offered, and with not less fervency from our humble fanes as from those splendid fabrics which the wealth and piety of our ancestors have reared at home for the worship of the Almighty. That God may have you in his holy keeping,—that He may conduct you on your way and restore you to your native land in health and safety, is our sincere and earnest prayer. To His care we recommend you. May He ever bless, preserve, and keep you; may He fill you with the richest gifts of His Holy Spirit, and finally bring you to everlasting life, through Jesus Christ our Lord.

His Royal Highness was pleased to make the following reply:—

GENTLEMEN,—It is a source of no little pleasure to me to receive from you these words of welcome, and to hear from the lips of your Bishop the assurance that your prayers are offered for my future usefulness and happiness. Within the walls of your cathedral I have joined in the petitions offered for the Queen, and I am convinced that the ministers of the church from which this address emanates, do not fail to inculcate those principles of loyalty which are so characteristic of this Province. I trust that it may be my lot, whatever may be the future lot reserved for me, to realize the hopes which you have expressed, and to secure the beneficial results of this my first acquaintance with the Canadian people.

They then retired, and the general levee at 12 o'clock commenced. At the levee about a thousand gentlemen were presented, and a number of addresses from national societies and other confederated bodies, read. These were, however, delivered without receiving any replies. After the levee upwards of 50 gentlemen, members of the Legislative Council and Assembly and others, partook of a *dejeuner* with his Royal Highness.

The number of those to be invited to a repast with the Prince was about 180, and were divided into parts according to alphabetical precedents.

While the remaining portion of the very many desirous of paying their respects to his Royal Highness were being presented, Sir Henry Smith and the members of the House adjourned to the rooms provided for their accommodation, over Benjamin's store; and no expense was spared to make every thing as agreeable as possible.

At three o'clock the Prince lunched in the dining-room with the House of Assembly. About eighty sat down with him to the table. All the members of the Upper House present in Quebec were there, together with those of the Lower House, whose names do not commence with any letter lower down in the alphabet than I.

As all could not be accommodated at once, this plan of dividing them had been pursued to avoid jealousy. The room looked exceedingly well, and the table was nicely laid out, being ornamented, among other things, with vases of choice flowers. The dinner service was of excellent white china, with a border of green and gold, a Prince's plume occupying the centre. All the knives, forks, spoons, glasses and napkins had likewise the crest of the Prince de Galles. The healths of the Queen, the Prince Consort, and Prince AlbertEdward, were drunk, but no speeches were allowed. His Royal Highness proposed the Governor-General.

This part of the proceedings did not last very long. At a

quarter after four, his Royal Highness, accompanied by the Governor-General and suite, rode out to Montmorenci Falls. The scenery along the Beauport road is scarcely excelled in the province; and everything looked its best. The heavy rains of the past week had laid most effectually the dust; the highway was in good condition, and the rays of the sun, though warm, were not so as to render riding unpleasant. The long, straggling village of Beauport, had been highly decorated for the occasion. Many arches had been erected, and though there was nothing particularly beautiful about them, still they served the purpose for which they were built. The few square-yard fields of the French Canadians looked unusually green; the fences unusually white. All the people had dressed themselves in the clothes specially reserved for "highdays and holidays." Men, women, and children alike, had ceased work and all thought of it. They were seated at the window, on the balconies in or before the windows, on the balconies in or before the doorways of the houses, or had taken their stand in rows along the fences. From many of the houses tri-colored flags waved. Union Jacks were quite in the minority.

When his Royal Highness crossed from St. Nicholas, he sailed under a French flag. The Prince reached the falls a little after five o'clock, and first drove over the suspension bridge by which they are spanned. After looking about him for a while there, he re-crossed. He then entered the little lodge at the gate, and inscribed his name upon the visitor's book. Seeing the notice up, "Admission twenty-five cents," he pulled out his quarter and paid it; which honourable example was followed by the gentlemen accompanying him. His Royal Highness stayed a considerable period examining the falls, and derived great pleasure from them. They are higher than those of the Niagara, the distance the water descends being two hundred and forty feet; but they are only sixty feet in width. Professor Silliman's description of them is very accurate, and given in admirable language. He says:—"The river, at some distance, seems suspended in the air, in a sheet of billowy foam, and, contrasted as it is, with the black frowning abyss into which it falls, it is an object of the highest interest. The sheet of foam which first breaks over the ridge is more and more divided as it plunges and is dashed against the successive layers of rock, which it almost completely veils from view; the spray becomes very delicate and abundant from top to bottom, hanging over and revolving around the torrent till it becomes lighter and more evanescent than the whitest fleecy clouds of summer, than the finest attenuated web, than the lightest gossamer, constituting the most airy and sumptuous drapery that can be imagined." The return of the royal party was effected by eight o'clock. It must not be omitted to mention that the patients in the Lunatic Asylum on the Beauport road, were allowed to come to the front, and cheered the Prince as loudly as any others. The "jarvey" who drove us down remarked, "That's the place where *all* the mad folks are, sir." But he was not believed.

In the evening Admiral Milne illuminated his ships. The *Nile, Hero, Valorous, Flying Fish, Ariadne,* and *Styx.* The effect was very beautiful. The night was dark; from Durham Terrace the huge hulls of the men-of-war could be but indistinctly seen, until at the signal given, the whole lighted up with pits of blue flame—spars and port-holes at once. A more beautiful sight could not be conceived. The display was better than at Halifax, the blue lights being larger. Point Levi, too, illuminated grandly as seen from Quebec. Large rockets were discharged, cannon fire lighting up the river and allowing a momentary glimpse of the shipping lying so many feet below.

Among the gentlemen from the Lower Provinces in Quebec were Mr. Attorney-General Fisher, of New Brunswick; Hon. Mr. ›Tilley, Provincial Secretary; Hon. Mr. Steeves, Commissioner of the Board of Works, New Brunswick; and Hon. Mr. Pope, of Prince Edward's Island.

Wednesday, August 22.

The Music Hall here is the handsomest public room in Canada—it needed no additional decorations save the tasteful wreaths of white and red roses and pine leaves. The figure of Cupid hovering over each garland suspended from the gasaliers, and the beautiful bouquets of flowers profusely placed wherever there was room, made the locale of the Mayor and Citizens' Ball, last evening, the most attractive the Prince had yet visited. The decorations of the Halifax ball rooms were superb, and the other arrangements there exquisite; they were, however, so different from those at Quebec, that the latter, in addition to many other attractions, had the change of novelty too.

Punctual to the hour fixed for his arrival, His Royal Highness came and proceeded to the little side apartment fitted up for him, which was indeed a gem among dressing-rooms, so chaste were its floral ornaments, so sufficient, yet not obtrusive, were the handsome mirrors and other pieces of furniture.

Emerging thence into the corridors and the ball-room itself, he occupied, though but for an instant, the recess partitioned off, arranging the sets for the first quadrille, and then he opened the ball with the lady of the Mayor, Mrs. Langevin, Mrs. Caron being his vis-a-vis.

The view from the galleries at the moment and throughout the whole of the night was superb. The handsome uniforms of the military men were dimmed in brilliancy by the handsomer dress of the many naval officers present, and the scarlet, blue, gold and silver of the martial votaries of Terpsichore served to render civilians black and white by contrast, and made the ladies' various coloured robes more attractive as a setting of precious metals does jewels.

The bands of the 17th Regiment and of the Royal Canadian Rifles played alternately the following selection of dance music:— Quadrille and Bonnie Dundee polka, Tupid galop, the Reception quadrille, Queen's Canadian valze, Dinorah polka, Mazourka, Fairy Queen, Lancers, Original galop, Pellisier schotische, Deonorah quadrille, Palermo polka, "Ariadne" galop, "Hero" quadrille, Berimer couplet valze, Il Trovatore polka, Mazourka, Rigolettella, Lancers, Oival galop, Charivari polka, Selined quadrille, Don Pasquale valze, Dream of the roses galop, Stiopfiedee lancers, English valze, Sybil galop, Night Bell, Sir Roger de Coverley.

A slight accident occurred in one of the polkas. A little middy who whirled his partner into too close proximity to the Prince, tripped His Royal Highness up, who fell on one knee. The lady did not fall; and it is only to contradict the exaggerated rumours of the incident the fact is mentioned here.

T

The supper was admirably got up, and ample justice done by the Prince as by others to the fare. About 1,000 guests were present in all, among them a large number of naval and military officers; and, as usual, when the sister services meet on these occasions, the military generally go to the wall. There is an impetuosity about the gallantry of naval officers which carries all before it with the fair sex, and against which the conventional beau of a garrison town seems to stand no chance. Thus the Commanders and Lieutenants whirled off the prettiest partners in triumph, and were deeply engaged all through the evening, while Ensigns and Subalterns could scarcely find partners at all. The Prince arrived at 10 o'clock, and immediately betook himself to the festivities of the evening with that gallantry and keen relish of the scene which always distinguish the Heir Apparent at these balls. Except during a short interval, when he partook of some refreshment, he danced every dance that was danced between 10 at night and 4 next morning. Immense numbers were at the same time dancing, or rather trying to dance, and knocking against each other with an energy that was worthy a better cause. None can well avoid collision when limited to a spot not larger than a pocket handkerchief, and the Prince and his fair partners had to run the gauntlet of polkas and waltzes like the rest. It was in one of these Terpsichorean struggles that the *contretemps* already alluded to occurred, and the Prince, catching his spurs in a lady's dress, tripped and fell. He was up again in an instant, laughing and dancing away again more vigorously than ever. The supper preparations were for a time involved in a state of perilous uncertainty, for when the hour came for the banquet to be laid, it was found with dismay that the waiters were not in a condition to be trusted safely with glass or china. Eventually, by all sorts of aids and contrivances in the way of amateur assistants, this difficulty, which had been calmly expected and clearly foreseen by many, was overcome, and the curtain of the pretty little theatre at the end of the hall rose at last on the supper. Like most theatrical suppers, however, it had a bright unreal character, for the tables would not accommodate a tithe of the guests, and a very numerous majority therefore, could only feast their eyes,—the most unsatisfactory medium possible through which to enjoy a banquet; I will let the curtain fall again, therefore, over this delusive portion of the entertainment, and return to the hall, where dancing was kept up by almost undiminished numbers, and certainly with undiminished spirit, till the lights began to "pale their ineffectual fires" before the rising sun. The Prince was only highly popular when the fete began,—he seemed idolized when it was over.

At noon on the 22nd the Prince visited the Laval University, and in the reception-room he received and replied to addresses from the Hierarchy of the Roman Catholic Church, and the members of the University. Few persons are aware how large and beautiful a room the University possesses, and on this occasion, with its floor magnificently carpeted with costly Brussels, a throne encircled with gold damask curtains and surmounted with a crown and a Prince of Wales plume, from which drooped festoons of artificial grape vine, with sofas and chairs orderly arranged around and occupied by Priests, Bishops, and members of the Legislature, &c., with its galleries crowded with the beauty and fashion of Quebec and its visitors, the hall showed to great advantage.

His Royal Highness passed along the Grand Battery, which had been converted into a shrubbery of spruce, and amidst the cheers of those assembled he entered the main portals of Laval building, the band playing God save the Queen. He and his suite, in morning dress, walked the whole length of the reception-hall to the raised dais in front of the throne, preceded by the Vicars of the University in robes, with gold and silver wands of office. The first address was read by M. Baillarge, Bishop of Iloa, administrator of the diocese of Quebec, who advanced to the front of the throne, and was the central figure in a group of nine prelates, all attired in official purple, wearing the gold band. When the Administrator had read the address in French, he asked the Prince to allow Bishop Horan of Kingston, as representing the English speaking portion of Roman Catholics, to read the translation, to which His Royal Highness assented.

The next address was that from the Faculty of the University, who advanced in order, clad in their black gowns, relieved by scarlet edgings, and fastened by scarlet tassels; it, too, was read in French and English. His Royal Highness replied to both of them collectively in English only. [The proper authorities were applied to for copies of the documents, but, after waiting nearly half an hour, a reply came that they could not be given.] After the above ceremony, the Prince was conducted through the various rooms of the building to see the library, museum, and cabinets of various kinds—almost all of which are as yet in a very incomplete state.

After leaving the Laval University, the Prince went to the Ursuline Convent, in which was very prettily decorated a complete arcade of evergreens leading to its entrance, and flags with mottoes testifying respect and affection, hanging from every part of the building. An address was here presented to the Prince by one of the young lady pupils of the Nuns, who was very prettily dressed in white, and garlanded with flowers. To this address, with which his Royal Highness seemed particularly pleased, he returned a gracious reply, and in this building the Vicar-General Cassault, learning the incivility of his inferiors in position, at once ordered the address of the Bishop and the reply to be placed at the disposal of the press. The following is the address :—

To His Royal Highness the Prince of Wales, &c., &c.. &c.
MAY IT PLEASE YOUR ROYAL HIGHNESS,—

We, the Catholic Bishops of the province of Canada, assembled in Quebec, to take part in the universal joy caused by the visit of Your Royal Highness to this portion of the British Empire, hasten to express in our own names, and in behalf of our clergy, the feelings of happiness we experience in seeing in our midst the Heir Apparent to the Crown of England, the son of our august and dearly beloved Queen, who, by her virtues, adds a fresh lustre to the throne of one of the most powerful monarchies in the world. Charged with the sacred mission of preaching to the people confided to our care, the duties as well as the dogmas of Christianity, we are ever careful to teach them that it is "by God Kings reign," and that, therefore, entire submission is due to the authority that they have from high for the happiness of their subjects. We feel convinced it is to this traditional respect for the high moral principle of legitimate authority which constitutes the strength of all society, that Canada has long enjoyed in peace and tranquility, which promise to be of uninterrupted duration. We are happy in giving Your Royal Highness the assurance that the Catholics of this colony partake in our sentiments of gratitude to Divine Providence for the many advantages which they possess under the protection of the British Government, especially as regards the free exercise of their religion. We have a firm conviction that the presence of Your Royal Highness amongst us will tend to develop and to strengthen still more those feelings of attachment and loyal devotion which bind them to the mother country. In conclusion, we pray Your Royal Highness to accept our warmest and most ardent wishes for the prosperity of the vast empire, the destinies of which you will be called one day to rule. Happy in forming a part of an empire, under which this our own beloved country has made such rapid progress, we shall not cease to offer up our prayers to Almighty God to beg of him that those who wield authority may ever be guided by the unvarying laws of justice and equity, that they may labour with constantly increasing success for the happiness of the people subjected to their rule, and that they may thus perpetuate before the eyes of other nations the glory of the British Crown.

The address of the Laval University is as follows:—
MAY IT PLEASE YOUR ROYAL HIGHNESS,—
It is with feelings of the greatest respect that the members of the Laval University beg leave to lay at the feet of your Royal Highness their homage and the expressions of their liveliest gratitude. They are happy to see within these walls the Heir Apparent of a vast empire, the eldest son of a noble Queen, whose domestic and public virtues the world acknowledges and loudly proclaims. The worthy representative of that gracious Queen, to whom this University is indebted for the charter of its erection, is charged with the mission of receiving in the name of our august Sovereign the homage of her faithful subjects. Your Royal Highness will, we fondly hope, deign to accept the expression of the deep gratitude with which we are filled towards Her Majesty. Actuated by this feeling, we pray Your Royal Highness to believe that the professors and alumni of this institution will make it their constant endeavour to prove themselves worthy of the royal favor. This, the first and only French Canadian

University which has been honoured by the royal protection, will be a lasting monument of the desire of Her Majesty to provide for the happiness of all her subjects, while it will form a new tie between their fellow subjects of French origin and the mother country, to whose care we have been committed by Divine Providence. It is true that unlike the Alma Mater Oxford, where your Royal Highness has been pleased to martriculate, our existence cannot be counted by centuries. Our alumni are but few, our libraries, our museum, and our collections offer nothing to excite the curiosity of Your Royal Highness, accustomed to visit the antique institutions of Europe. Our beginning is but humble, our hopes are in the future. We trust in the future destinies of the colony, which, under the protection of England, is in the enjoyment of peace and abundance, whilst other countries are distracted by violent convulsions. We trust in the future of that glorious metropolis whose influence is so weighty in controlling the destinies of the civilized world. We place our trust in the protection and justice of that august Queen, to whom we are indebted for so signal a mark of benevolence. We also place our trust in the young Prince whom Providence will call one day to give on the throne the examples of all those royal virtues he has inherited from the most gracious of sovereigns, and the noblest of mothers.

The Prince replied to both of these addresses as follows:—

GENTLEMEN,—I accept, with the greatest satisfaction the welcome which you offer, and I assure you that I feel deeply the expression of your loyalty and affection to the Queen. I rejoice to think that obedience to the laws and submission to authority, which form the bond of all society, and the condition of all the civilised world, are supported and enforced by your teaching and example. The assurance that you enjoy the free exercise of your religion, and that you partake in the benefits of the British Constitution, is a pledge that your hearts and those of your fellow subjects, of whatever origin they may be, will ever be united in the feelings you have now expressed of attachment to the Crown of Great Britain. I acknowledge with gratitude the earnest prayer which you offer to Almighty God in my behalf, and I trust that my future course may be such as will best promote the welfare of this great province, and of its inhabitants.

To you, gentlemen, who are engaged within the walls of this building in the education of the youth of the country I also tender my thanks. I trust that your university may continue to prosper, and that in future years its sons may look upon the days they have spent under your instruction with the same gratitude and sense of the benefit they have enjoyed, as I and others feel towards the more ancient institutions of my own land.

The following is the address of the Ursuline Nuns, as translated:—

MAY IT PLEASE YOUR ROYAL HIGHNESS,—

The Ursuline Nuns will always regard as a signal honour the visit of Your Royal Highness to their ancient convent, and thus humbly ask that they may be allowed to lay at your feet in solemn manner the homage of respect and devotion. Although they live in the cloisters, they are indifferent to nothing which is of interest to their country. They have always been among the most thankful and faithful of Her Majesty's subjects in British America; how, then, should they not partake of the public joy on the occasion of the felicitous arrival of Your Royal Highness in this province? Twice already have princes of the glorious house of Brunswick visited this country; and when this most ancient educational establishment in British America and the annals of the convent mention events with happiness as being of good omen, with what enthusiasm shall we then not add to these illustrious names that of Albert Edward, Prince of Wales. It would be useless to try to repeat now what rumour says of the goodness of your Royal Highness and of all other qualities which will entitle you one day to sit upon one of the grandest thrones of the universe; but the Ursuline Nuns will endeavour to preserve intact and to transmit to their successors the remembrance and the impressions of their gracious visit. May heaven continue to shower favours on your august Sovereign, and may the ever-increasing prosperity of her reign be a happy presage of the glory which the future is preparing for the heir apparent to her brilliant crown!

At every paragraph of this address, the young ladies who surrounded the Prince courtsied together; it was spoken without any hesitation, and in the clearest of voices.

The reply read thus:—

MESDAMES,—I thank you for these expressions of kindly interest in my visit to the city of Quebec and the personal good wishes which this address manifests. Your exertions in the cause of education are well known, and I trust they may long continue to exert a beneficial influence upon the population of this interesting country.

One of the pupils of the convent then sang, accompanying herself on the harp, a "Song of Welcome" to the Prince. Returning to his palace, His Royal Highness entertained at lunch the remainder of the Legislative Assembly and Council.

The Prince, after lunch, went to visit the citadel, and walked round it, enjoying the beautiful views. He did not go to the races nor Lorette, as had been thought probable. In the evening he was expected to visit the esplanade to see the fireworks there: whether he did or not is not known; but this is certain, that a frightful accident occurred. The Corporation had built a platform from which to view the display, and, as soon as it was full, the ill-constructed seats gave way and hundreds of people fell, fortunately, not with a great crash, but with a gentle subsidence. Had the fall been sudden, there is no telling how awful the results would have been. As it was, it was very shocking; many ladies were injured and several gentlemen hurt—one, it was feared, fatally. A party of sailors from the fleet, who happened to be on shore, were of very great service in removing the sufferers from underneath the boards. At this hour it was impossible to know who was hurt. The only names known were Mr. Robert Shaw, whose leg was fractured and amputation necessary; and Rev. Mr. Plees injured seriously but not fatally. A child had its arm broken.

The Prince's departure on Thursday, Aug. 23, was very prettily arranged.

He left Parliament House at half-past ten with his suite in carriages. On the Champlain Market wharf was a guard of honour forming a hollow square, in which were the Corporation of the city in full dress and several members of the Government.

Preceded by the National Societies with banners, he entered the square at a quarter to eleven, and immediately went on board the

Kingston. The Quebec volunteer cavalry were drawn up in the court yard, and a guard of Canadian rifles marched down to the river. The volunteer artillery were placed upon Durham Terrace. Most of the flags, which after the reception had been carefully withdrawn from exposure to the air, were again hoisted; some of the fallen spruce branches were set up on end, and a general attempt at gaiety made. But, for all that, Quebec looked much like an exhausted beauty after a ball—the starch out of her dress—her hair somewhat dishevelled, her gloves and satin shoes considerably the worse for wear, and her whole motions exhibiting decided symptons of fatigue. The distance from the Palace to the wharf is short, but there was little crowding in the narrow streets as the Prince was driven down. Of course, all salient points were occupied. The steps opposite, the roof of the Laval University behind, and the windows all along the line of route, all had their quota of fair faces—albeit somewhat tanned by much exposure to sun and wind during the stay of His Royal Highness in the city.

The steamer had been specially fitted for his accommodation. The berths had been taken out of the state-rooms, and a comfortable bed placed in each. She had been thoroughly overhauled, and in addition to other ornaments a beautiful Prince of Wales had been painted on each paddle box, fresh carpets and furniture of all kinds had been supplied, and the sailors were all dressed in uniforms similar to that of the royal navy.

As soon as the Prince went on board his standard was hoisted at the fore, and saluted by all men-of-war in port, as well as by the citadel. The yards of the ships were manned, and their crews, as also the soldiers and the crowd assembled, cheered lustily.

The royal party, who were the only passengers, after going to see their rooms, went on the hurricane deck to enjoy the beautiful scene around. They remained close by the walking beam while the steamer moved away, which it did a few minutes before eleven o'clock.

The steamer *Kingston* returned half an hour after her departure, having left the provisions behind. Having got them on board she again started.

Among the last persons who saw the royal party was Mr

Thomson, secretary to Mayor Wood of New York. Mr. Thomson was much pleased with the courtesy of all the high personages of the suite.

The members of Parliament left in the afternoon at four, by the steamer *Quebec*, for Three Rivers and Montreal.

August 23rd.

His Royal Highness and suite reached the city of Three Rivers at 6.30, p.m., in the steamer *Kingston*.

On landing at the wharf His Royal Highness was saluted by a corps of royal artillery and a company of Montreal Light Infantry, commanded by Capt. Hunt. He was then received on a raised platform by his Worship the Mayor, Jos. E. Turcotte, Esq., the Corporation, the clergy, public officers and citizens, who presented him with an address, to which he made a short and suitable reply, after which three hearty cheers were given for the Prince, when he withdrew to the steamer.

The crowd, numbering about 25,000, then dispersed. The wharf was beautifully decorated with evergreens, &c. The centre was a large arch covered with paintings, suitable devices, flags, &c. The Boulevard Turcotte was also beautifully decorated, and the streets of the city had been ornamented with trees and arches.

There was a grand illumination in the evening.

August 24th.

Three Rivers was magnificently illuminated last night, rows of coloured lamps were stretched across the foot of the wharves, and chandeliers brilliantly lighting up the arch, under which the Prince received the addresses. The members of the Legislature, on the *Quebec*, arrived there while the Prince's boat, the *Kingston*, was at anchor. After a meeting had been held, Hon. Messrs. DeBlaquiere and Drummond were appointed a deputation to wait upon His Royal Highness, and request permission to be allowed to attend him as far as Montreal. The Prince assented. During the night, therefore, the steamers were ornamented with spruce trees, and in the morning early left in the wake of the Prince. At various points along the river groups of people were assembled cheering and waving their hats. In Lake St. Peter the very buoys were decorated, and here the Trinity Board on the *St. Lawrence* met the Prince and fell into line behind the *Quebec*. At ten o'clock it began to rain heavily and continued until Montreal was sighted. Another contretemps, too, was, that whereas it had been understood the Prince would leave by the south channel past Vercheres, where the whaives were crowded with people and decorated, and a fleet of river steamers had been assembled, he took the north channel, where no preparations had been made. He thus gave the steamboats the complete go-by. As soon as they perceived this, they put on steam and most of them managed to overtake him where the two channels meet at Bout De Lisle. While the *Kingston* passed them, there were numerous passengers cheering as heartily as if the weather had not obliged them to wear water-proofs and shelter themselves under umbrellas, when the whole of them fell into line, or at least followed in some way, and the sight of so many white floating houses, covered with boughs and flags, crowded with passengers, needed only sunshine to make it the most perfectly picturesque sight that could be conceived. As the fleet came up the rest of the way, some twenty miles, the church bells of the different villages on shore were all ringing, while the people in the steamers and on the land reciprocated repeated cheers. As before mentioned, the sun shone out when Montreal was sighted, so that His Royal Highness' first glimpse of its towers and spires, and of the Victoria Bridge, was not obtained under unfavourable circumstances. Below St. Helen's Island the *Kingston* anchored, and there the vessels, which had been distanced in the long and rather exciting race, came up. It seemed as if there was to be fine weather for a time, but it soon again began to rain. In consequence of the weather, the city authorities had not been able to complete their arrangements, and information was sent to His Royal Highness with a request that he would not land that afternoon. The landing, therefore, did not take place until the morning at 10 o'clock. The *Kingston* remained anchored below St. Helen's Island. The illumination was deferred until some future evening. There must have been forty thousand people gathered together on the quays there to witness the expected arrival of His Royal Highness, who were, of course, disappointed and soaked into the bargain.

The names of the steamers which went to meet the Prince were the *Caledonia, Terrebonne, Passport, Hochelaga, McKenzie, Mayflower, Salaberry, L'Aigle, John Redpath, Topsey, Bonaventure, St. Marie, St. Helena,* and *Bowmanville.*

The number of people assembled in front of Montreal was exceedingly large; the quays, streets, &c., being covered with not less than between 40,000 and 50,000.

The determination to request the Prince not to land was come to by the committee while it was still raining, but before the Prince arrived at St. Helen's the storm ceased. Ample time had elapsed, ere the rain again fell, for the Prince to effect a landing—at any rate it would have been better, even though the rain had continued, for His Royal Highness to have entered the city after the salutes had been fired and the whole of Montreal had gone down to the wharves to meet him. The greater portion stood for two hours in the rain and were extremely disappointed.

Mr. Cartier came along side in a steamer and started from the deck, to the assembled officials, that he would not land until to-morrow at nine.

So many people could not again be assembled. It was impossible for them to do so at so early an hour, as thousands had come from the country, and had been waiting all day.

The reception of His Royal Highness surpassed any thing ever before witnessed in British North America.

The Hon. Wm. Young, Chief Justice of Nova Scotia, had arrived.

The city was illuminated in many places, but the general. illumination was postponed until the following night. The Montreal Bank was lighted up most brilliantly. It had six very tall pillars in front, all of which were wreathed with flame. A Prince of Wales' crest was in the centre of the facade. On each side were large circular rings, with monograms of His Royal Highness. They occupied each window. There was an immense crowd in front, and as the rain held off the streets were thronged. Many of the windows were dressed out and figures placed in each. In nearly every house preparations for an illumination had been made, and the folks with great difficulty restrained themselves from following the example of some of their neighbours.

In saluting in the afternoon two men were killed. The *Flying Fish* having only six guns, had to re-load to complete a royal salute. One of her cannon had not been sufficiently sponged out and a premature discharge took place, blowing a man to pieces. A similar accident took place on the *Valorous*, also resulting in loss of life for same reason.

There were fifty thousand strangers in the city among them a company of Boston Militia, who took part in the procession.

It has been definitely settled that His Royal Highness is to stay in Hamilton, and occupy the houses of R. Junson, and W. P. McLaren, Esquires. He will inaugurate the water-works there.

The proceedings throughout Saturday, August 25th, were of the most interesting character.

It rained very heavily all night and all the morning until half-past nine o'clock, the hour fixed for the Prince's landing, but just at that time the rain ceased and the sun shone out.

Notwithstanding the condition of the streets, which were perfect pools of mud, immense crowds were assembled on the quays and steamboats, while the whole of the windows from which a view of the landing could be had were black with human heads.

Punctual to the hour the Prince's boat, the *Kingston*—the Prince and his suite conspicuous on deck—approached, and was saluted as it passed by the batteries on St. Helen's Island, while, as it neared the wharf, the crews of the men-of-war in port, the *Valorous*, *Styx*, and *Flying Fish* manned the yards. Repeated cheers from the multitude on shore were heard, and the city bells commenced to ring.

The scene from the Prince's boat was said, by members of the suite, to have been most striking.

There was some delay in mooring the steamer at the wharf, during which ample time was afforded for surveying the fine proportions of the lofty pavilion, brightly painted, under which a throne for His Royal Highness had been placed, and where he was to receive the address of the Corporation. Under this were gathered together the Municipal authorities, the members of the

Executive Council, the members of both Houses of Parliament, and a brilliant array of military and naval officers—all in uniform or full dress.

By Mayor Rodier the Prince was received as he stepped on shore, amid a thundering salute, and was conducted up the scarlet carpet leading to the scarlet dais; there, surrounded by his suite, His Royal Highness stood while first in English, then in French, His Worship, standing on the lowest step of four, read a long address. These, beautifully engrossed on parchment, he then enclosed in a crimson velvet case ornamented with gold and handed to the Prince, who read his reply in English only. The following are copies of the documents:—

CORPORATION ADDRESS.

MAY IT PLEASE YOUR ROYAL HIGHNESS,—

We, the Mayor, Alderman, and Citizens of the City of Montreal, most respectfully beg leave to approach your Royal Highness to felicitate you on behalf of the citizens of Montreal, on your safe arrival in this Province, and to offer to your Royal Highness our most cordial and hearty welcome to this city. We avail ourselves of this propitious occasion of a visit from the Heir Apparent to the British Throne to express to your Royal Highness our devoted loyalty and attachment to the person and government of our most gracious Sovereign, your illustrious mother, to declare our humble but fervent admiration of her wisdom, moderation and justice as our Sovereign, and our love and veneration of the virtues and graces which adorn her private life. As circumstances did not permit our beloved Queen to honour this distant but important section of her Empire with a personal visit, Her Majesty had been graciously pleased to confer on her faithful Canadian subjects the next dearest boon it was in her power to bestow, by authorising this most welcome visit of your Royal Highness; this gracious manifestation of Her Majesty's consideration and regard is hailed with thankfulness and joy by all her loyal and devoted subjects in these provinces. But we beg most respectfully to assure your Royal Highness that by none amongst the millions who compose their number, is it more highly esteemed, more fully appreciated, or more enthusiastically felt and acknow-.

ledged than by Her Majesty's devoted and loyal subjects, the citizens of Montreal. The immediate object of your Royal Highness' most gratifying visit to Canada is to open the Victoria Bridge, that magnificent monument of enterprise and skill with which the fame and prosperity of this city will evermore be most intimately connected, most permanently identified. In this stupendous work your Royal Highness will not fail to observe how natural obstacles, almost insurmountable in their ponderous strength and complicated capital and of Canadian energy and skill—and we beg to assure your Royal Highness that this wonderful achievement of engineering and mechanical perfection will henceforth possess a new claim on our interests and regards, associated as it must evermore be in our memories and affections with this auspicious visit of your Royal Highness and the interesting ceremony of its perfect consummation by your Royal Highness' hands. We earnestly hope your Royal Highness' visit to this city will be one of unmixed satisfaction and delight, and we pledge ourselves for the citizens of Montreal that they will, one and all, esteem it the highest gratification and honour to use every means in their power to render your too short stay amongst them agreeable, happy, and comfortable. We pray that your Royal Highness will be pleased to communicate to our most gracious Queen—your royal and beloved mother—our feelings of ardent loyalty and devotion to her royal person and crown, and our lively gratitude and acknowledgments for this last gracious evidence of her royal condescension and favour—our Royal Highness' most grateful and welcome visit to the city and Province.

His Highness was pleased to reply as follows :—

GENTLEMEN,—The address you have just presented to me, in which you proclaim your loyalty to the Queen and attachment to the British Crown demands my warmest acknowledgments. The impression made upon me by the kind and cordial reception which has been accorded to me on this first visit to Canada can never fade from my mind, and deeply will the Queen be gratified by the proof which it affords, that the interest which she takes in the welfare of this portion of her empire, and which she has been anxious to mark by my presence amongst you is met on their part by feelings of affectionate devotion to herself and her family. For myself, I rejoice at the opportunity which has been afforded me of visiting this city, a great emporium of the trade of Canada, and whose growing prosperity offers so striking an example of what may be effected by energy and enterprise under the influence of free institutions. That this prosperity may be still further enlarged is my earnest hope, and there can be little doubt that by the completion of that stupendous monument of engineering skill and labour which I have come in the name of the Queen to inaugurate, new sources of wealth will be opened to your citizens. and to the country new elements of power developed, and new links forged to bind together, in peaceful coöperation, the exertions of a wide-spread and rapidly-increasing population.

This ceremoney over, the party took carriages and drove towards the Exhibition Building. The progress thither was a most complete ovation.

In the Bonaventure Market, between whose lofty domes, lined with flags, every foothold had its row of tenants. The street was nevertheless well kept by lines of Militia, and the National and other Societies, who afterwards doubled in, and formed the procession under the direction of their mounted Marshals. All along Rue Main, Rue Notre Dame, Great St. James Street, and the other streets through which the Prince passed, there were similar crowds, while each of them were roofed in by flags, hung from lines stretching across from some of these ropes two crowns, and huge bouquets were pendant just above the head of His Royal Highness as he passed.

There were only three arches besides the one under which the landing took place, but these—one of Corinthian, one of Elizabethan, and one of nondescript design—assumed the proportions and had the effect of permanent structures. These as well as many houses along the route, were covered with loyal mottoes and words of welcome.

At the place d'Armes and Commissioners' Square, fountains were playing, that in the latter forming a beautiful Prince of Wales' plume.

There was one other feature particularly observable. The few scaffolds put up for people to sit or stand upon were the only vacant spaces. The people, warned by the accident at Quebec, were evidently disinclined to trust these frail structures with their persons.

Arrived at the Exhibition Building, a royal salute was fired, and His Royal Highness and suite entered the retiring-room especially prepared for them.

While he was there a large party of ladies and gentlemen, in official, and private stations too, occupied the seats assigned them on the floor and in the galleries, and prepared themselves to witness the inauguration of the building.

When all was ready, His Royal Highness entered the main building, and took his place upon the central dias—the organ pealing forth the National Anthem.

This finished, His Excellency and the members of the Government took a position in front of the throne, and presented the following address, His Excellency reading the inauguration address :—

MAY IT PLEASE YOUR ROYAL HIGHNESS,—

The people of this province are aware of the interest with which Her Most Gracious Majesty and the Prince Consort honoured the Exhibitions of 1851 and 1855. They know that among the objects which excited attention on those occasions, the productions of Canada held an important place, and they venture to hope that Your Royal Highness will, on the present occasion, condescend to meet their wishes by opening the Exhibition which is to take place in this building. They believe you may find that the objects submitted to your notice afford some evidence of the industry and progress of Canada, and some promise of her future success.

On the part, therefore, of the Provincial Government, I pray your Royal Highness to do us the honour of opening in the city of Montreal this Exhibition, and we trust that such condescension on your part, may stimulate our people to greater exertions, and may be long remembered among the gracious acts which are destined to mark the visit of the Heir Apparent of the Throne of Great Britain.

To this His Royal Highness replied as follows :—

GENTLEMEN,—Most readily I consent to the request you have made. A request the more agreeable because it is conveyed to me by my kind friend your Excellency, the Governor-General.

x

I am not ignorant of the high position obtained by Canada in the Great Exhibition of 1851, which was opened under the happy auspices of the Queen and the Prince Consort, and carrying out the design of the memorable undertaking this smaller, but to Canada most interesting collection, of the products of your land, and of works of art and industry, has my entire sympathy and claims my best wishes for its success. I hope and believe it will realize all the objects for which it has been designed.

The Governor then again took his place at the right hand of His Royal Highness, and Bishop Fulford offered up the following prayer:—Let us pray—Almighty God, the Creator and Governor of the Universe, we, thy creatures, desire humbly to approach the throne of thy Grace, confessing thee as the Author of our being, and the Giver of all good gifts, by whose mercy alone it is that we are enabled to think or to do any thing that is acceptable to Thee. We acknowledge with grateful hearts all Thy past mercies to us, and especially Thy goodness manifested in the abundance of the fruits of the earth, now awaiting the ingathering of the harvest. We also bless Thee, O Lord, for that continued public tranquility in the land which has given us the opportunity of pursuing with any measure of success those enterprises that belong to peace and promote the prosperity of Thy people. We beseech Thee now to look favourably upon this work of our hands, and while we give Thee hearty thanks that we have been allowed thus far to carry forward the execution of our designs, we beg Thy blessing on the undertaking which we are this day assembled to inaugurate. Let us not rest with pride or self-complacency upon the results of human intellect and human ingenuity, but make us always to remember that whatever is of the earth is earthly and perishable, and that all flesh is as grass, and the glory of man as the flower of grass, which withereth and falleth away. And enable us also to exercise our several talents as shall best promote Thy glory and edification and well-being of Thy creatures, that we may give account of the trust committed to us with joy, and not with sorrow. And we beseech Thee, O Lord, so to guide and direct our hearts and to over-rule our purposes, that while endeavouring to make known Thy power and wisdom in the works of creation, and to develop all our gifts as thy creatures in the advancement of science and art, we may allow no strife or vain glory to disturb our unity or action or hinder our success, and in order thereto may we be brought by the Spirit not to think too highly of ourselves, but in lowliness of means each to esteem others better than themselves. Grant that this mind may be in us which was also in Christ Jesus, for which we pray in His name, who died for us, that we might live unto Him, and and who now liveth and reigneth with Thee and the Holy Ghost in the Unity of the Godhead, Thy only Son our Lord. Amen. The grace of our Lord Jesus Christ, the love of God, and the fellowship of the Holy Ghost be with us all evermore. Amen.

A royal procession was then formed, consisting of His Royal Highness and suite, and their Excellencies and suite, preceded by Mr. Chamberlin, the secretary and members of the sub-committee of the Board of Arts and Manufactures, which went to the north-west end of the building, thence to the south-east end, along the south-west side, thence having crossed the south-east end ascended the staircase in the east corner, proceeded along the gallery of the north-east side, passed through the Fine Arts Court, and, descending by the staircase in the west corner, returned to the platform.

On his return His Royal Highness, at the request of Mr. Chamberlin, declared the Exhibition opened.

The Oratorio Society sang the "Hallelujah Chorus," and upon its conclusion His Royal Highness retired by the entrance by which he entered, and the whole party drove to the Point St. Charles station to witness the laying, by His Royal Highness, of the corner stone of the Victoria Bridge.

At this station none were allowed to enter excepting those who had received tickets of invitation, and these were assigned places in a long train of cars which shortly proceeded to the bridge.

All along the route by the side of the track were seats which were occupied by numbers of well dressed gentlemen, and elegantly attired ladies.

Near the portals of the bridge the train passed between trophies of locomotive wheels and mechanical devices, and it paused just before entering the tube—within the massive walls which there enclosed considerable space. Here the passengers, chiefly members of parliament and friends, disembarked, and took their assigned places—some below od a level with the track —some above on the top of the walls—some again near the platform to which His Royal Highness was to mount and lay the stone. This was in the centre of the masonry at the entrance to the tube at the top, just over the inscription which tells who built it.

This arranged, the Prince in a carriage drove to the spot —entered the space above mentioned, and ascended the steps of the platform—Hon. John Ross leading the way.

On the platform, which was covered with scarlet cloth, he was received by Mr. Hodges, the Builder of the Bridge, who, as soon as the Royal party were grouped around, handed him a silver trowel wherewith to spread the mortar. His Royal Highness did this in a workman-like manner, and then the stone, which hung suspended from a derrick, and measured ten and a-half feet by two feet, by three feet four inches, was gently lowered to its resting place—the Prince then gave it three raps with a mallet, and this part of the ceremony was complete.

Looking over the lowered stone the enormous length of the bridge was visible shining in the sunlight, and above it was a richly draped golden fringed arch, with the appropriate inscription, —"*Finis coronat opus.*"

The Prince then descended and took his seat along with a numerous body of officials in a beautiful car built specially for the purpose, open all around its roof, supported simply by wooden pillars. The engine screamed and the party were driven to the centre of the two mile tube, where they got out, and the Prince placed the last rivet of the Bridge in its place, which was at once hammered in by a chosen body of mechanics. Then they got on board again and went completely through the tube and returned to luncheon in the great car shed at Point St. Charles.

The luncheon was a remarkable one in every way. The immense room was tastefully adorned with evergreens, and from every festoon a medal drooped inscribed with the name of some eminent civil engineer. When the Prince and suite entered and took their seats at the raised table at the end, the thousand places at the four long tables were already occupied. "God save the Queen" was played as His Royal Highness entered; and when he was seated, the whole company then sat down.

Appetite satisfied, the three standard toasts were given by the Governor-General—"The Queen," "The Prince Consort," and the "Prince of Wales." The cheers at each were vociferous—at the last, specially so—the whole of the convives springing to their feet, and even standing on their seats.

The prince bowed his acknowledgments; and, almost as soon as the cheering had subsided, he himself rose to give a toast, and the deepest silence of course prevailed. "I propose," he said, and his clear voice was distinctly audible to the furthest corner of the great room, "the health of the Governor-General—success to Canada and prosperity to the Grand Trunk Railway."

At this the cheering was renewed with the most wonderful vigour, while the band struck up the beautiful melody which has become national in Lower Canada, "A la claire Fountaine."

The Prince then left, the company left too, and the scene was brought to a conclusion.

His Royal Highness then went to take up his abode in Mr. Rose's house on the Mountain, where he resided the remainder of his stay in Montreal.

There was but one opinion as to the excellent management of this portion of the proceedings, and but one general regret, that it was not as fine under foot as over head.

In the car in which the Prince was carried through the Victoria Bridge, the Directors of the Grand Trunk Railway who were in attendance, viz.: Messrs. Ross, Blackwell, Ferrie, Campbell, Cayley, and Beaty, presented an address to His Royal Highness, who in his reply alluded to the regret he felt that Stephenson had not lived to see the completion of the work, and that Mr. A. M. Ross, who is in an asylum, was not able to be present at its inauguration.

The workmen of the railroad also presented an address to His Royal Highness as he was going in to lunch. It was the most beautifully engrossed and encased of any yet read.

The officers of the Boston Fusiliers were presented, and Colonel William T. McLay, of the 97th Highlanders, New York, was attached in an honorary capacity to His Excellency's staff.

It was the *Valorous* which lost one man, killed in firing the salute; at the same time the *Flying Fish* lost two—completely blown away; and the man at the vent had his thumb torn off.

One person was trampled to death in the crush during the procession.

There was a fracas in Griffintown in the afternoon, about a flag which was in reality that of some German society, but which some said was Orange, while others denied it. Several persons were hurt, one, a policeman, dangerously.

The illumination was probably spoiled by the rain, which re-commenced; nevertheless it was very general and finer than at any time previously, many of the principal buildings being covered with devices in gas jets and lamps, as well as allegorical and emblematic transparencies and mottoes.

The main streets were kept clear of carriages and were crowded by persons, male and female, gazing at the sights, regardless of the mud.

Most of the vessels in harbour were also illuminated, noticeably were the *North American* and *United Kingdom* steamships.

Private individuals too, throughout the city, sent up a number of fireworks, but the display at the Victoria Bridge did not equal general expectation. There were a number of boquets of rockets fired and a quantity of fire bombs, but nothing was shown to accomplish that which pyrotechnic artists could not have been found to do here without bringing them from England.

On Sunday morning His Royal Highness attended divine service in the Anglican Cathedral. The arrangements were perfect, admission being by tickets, which had to be shown at the outer gates as well as at the doors. The whole of the seats were filled when His Royal Highness drove up. The Churchwardens, the Rector, several clergy attached to the Cathedral, and the Bishop, went to the door to meet him and conducted him to his place; with the Prince were the whole of his suite and most of the General's staff. The opening portion of the service was read by the Venerable Archdeacon Gilson; the first lesson by the Rev. Mr. Townsend; the second lesson by the Rev. Mr. Wood; the litany by the Rev. the Dean. The Bishop of Rupert's Land read the epistle: and Bishop McCrosky, of Michigan, the gospel. The Bishop of Montreal preached from I. Corinthians ix. 25, "And every man that striveth for the mastery is temperate in all things; now they do it, to obtain a corruptible crown, but we are incorruptible." Throughout the sermon there was not the slightest allusion to the presence of His Royal Highness.

The musical service was very beautiful, and admirably directed by Mr. Barnaby, the organist to the Cathedral. There was a large crowd outside the gates when His Royal Highness left, and some attempt was made to raise a cheer, but it was speedily hushed, and the Prince drove quietly to his residence.

This (Monday) morning the first item on the programme was a visit to the great crikct ground, where a game at Lacrosse and other Indian sports were to be held at 10 o'clock. The Prince and suite arrived there and took their stand on the platforms, from which they could overlook the extensive field. There were several thousand spectators around, many of whom had suffered considerably in the crush at the entrance. Lacrosse is a game very similar to the Irish hocky or shindy, but the clubs have the curved end filled with network, with which the ball may be carried as well as struck. The object of each party is to send the ball through the goal of the other, and swiftness of running is indispensable for this purpose. There was first a game between two parties of Indians, about a score on each side; then one between the Indians and an equal number of white players belonging to Montreal. This the Indians won.

The Prince was a very attentive observer of the fortune of the contest, laughing heartily at the loser, and applauding the winner in the separate encounters which occurred during its progress. The players were dressed in uniform, the Indians having red shirts, blue or white tights, and plenty of feathers and war paint on their faces and calves.

After the games at Lacrosse, a party of Indians with tomahawks, tom toms, rattle and horns, danced a war dance and shouted their war hoop. These performances were far more fantastic than terrible.

During the games the Boston Fusiliers marched into the ground, preceded by their band. They took up a position at the right of the Prince's platform. Their band first played "God save the Queen," the men uncovering, and the American flag being drooped. Next they struck up "Yankle Doodle," and the Prince returned the compliment just paid by taking off his hat and remaining barcheaded until the strains were over.

When the amusements had contined for about half an hour it suddenly began to rain heavily, and the Prince's carriage being sent for, His Royal Highness left, as did also most of the other spectators. The morning having been very fine but few had brought umbrellas, and many ladies' silks and laces must have suffered considerably.

The levee in the morning held in the Court House was very numerously attended. Upwards of 2,000 gentlemen paid their respects to the Prince and inscribed their names in the visiting books of himself and suite. A number of addresses were presented, to which His Royal Highness made one general reply. It may be possible to obtain the list of these documents hereafter, but it was difficult to procure official information, as the reporters for the New York journals sent so much false information to their papers that difficulties rather than facilities were necessarily thrown in the way of the press. It was definitely settled that the Prince would be at Hamilton, C. W., at noon on the 18th Sept., and that the public entry into the Exhibition there would take place between 11 and 12 on Wednesday. His Royal Highness had to leave for Chicago that evening, so that he would only occupy the house offered him at Hamilton for one night. Hamilton would be the last place in Canada at which he would stay. It was also definitely settled that the Prince would spend one day at Chicago; proceed to the prairies to shoot some prairie hens; go to St. Louis, Cincinnati, Washington, Baltimore, Philadelphia, New York, Boston, and Portland. It had been thought better to accept a ball than a dinner at New York, which would be on Friday, 12th October—the day of his arrival. The Prince would embark from Portland.

A royal salute was fired at noon by the ships of war in port, in honour of the birthday of His Royal Highness the Prince Consort, which fell on Sunday. At night, in spite of the rain, the vessels were illuminated. Many of the buildings in the city were also again lit up.

The *Gazette* and *Herald* published illustrated editions, containing cuts of the arches and other decorations.

The Prince expressed himself delighted with the beauty of the scenery, and the view from his residence.

The following addresses were presented immediatly before the levee:—The Anglican Synods by the Lord Bishop; the McGill College, by Hon. Mr. Ferrie, the Senior Governor; the College of Physicians and Surgeons, by Dr. Hall, President; the Natural

History Society, and the Fine Arts Society, both by the Lord Bishop, President of each.

The following is the address presented at the levee by the Synod of the Church of England in the Diocese :—

MAY IT PLEASE YOUR ROYAL HIGHNESS,—

We, the Bishop, Clergy and Laity of the United Church of England and Ireland in the Diocese of Montreal in Synod assembled, beg respectfully to assure your Royal Highness of our sincere attachment to the person, respect for the character, and devotion to the crown and authority of your Royal Mother our beloved Sovereign. As Her Majesty's representative and Heir Apparent to the Throne, we feel it a high privilege to welcome your arrival amongst us, but at the same time we wish to testify our respect for your Royal Highness' own character and person, and to express our confidence that the anxious care of your royal parents in preparing you for that exalted station which you yourself hereafter, we trust at some very distant day, may expect to be called on to fill, has not been without the most satisfactory results, and in that course of preparation to have seen with your own eyes those magnificent transatlantic possessions of the Crown of England, and to have become personally acquainted in their own countries with many of their inhabitants, will have been no unimportant event for ourselves as a Church. We neither occupy the same position as our brethren at home in relation to the State, nor can we be named in comparison with them for our numbers or our wealth, but we still feel we are members of the same body, we teach the same truths, we offer up the same petitions in behalf of the Queen and all that are in authority under Her, and ever pray for your Royal Highness that Almighty God will be pleased to endue you with His Holy Spirit, enrich you with His heavenly grace, prosper you with all happiness, and bring you to His everlasting kingdom for Jesus Christ's sake.

The reply was as follows :—

GENTLEMEN,—I thank you from my heart for this address, presented by your Bishop on behalf of the Synod of the Diocese of Montreal, which has been so lately constituted the Metropolitan

See of the Province of Canada. It is most agreeable to my feelings to receive such proofs of welcome to myself, and of loyalty to the Queen, from members of a Church to which it is my happiness to belong; but it would be most unjust if I were to forget, that since my arrival in this country the professors of every creed have given ample assurance that all join in one common sentiment of devotion to the Crown of England, and that all co-operate in the one great duty of enforcing obedience not only to heavenly laws but to those of earthly origin. I shall never cease to rejoice that I have been enabled to visit this distant portion of the empire, and to become acquainted with a people of which I shall carry back with me most pleasing recollections. I trust that on your part the prayers of which you remind me will henceforth be offered up in the churches of this land with even an increased earnestness.

His Royal Highness did, as already remarked, reply to the address of the workmen of the Grand Trunk Railway. The following is the address and answer :—

MAY IT PLEASE YOUR ROYAL HIGHNESS,—

It is with feelings of unmingled gratification and pleasure that we, the working men and artisans of the Grand Trunk Railway Company, cordially welcome to this portion of Her Majesty's transatlantic dominions one so nearly connected with our gracious Sovereign as yourself. Although separated by the wide ocean from the land which gave birth to the most of us, we yet bear in our hearts the warmest love towards it and the deepest reverence and loyalty towards their beloved Monarch, whose presence here to-day your Royal Highness represents. The noble structure which your Royal Highness has inaugurated, has been to many of us the scene of our daily toil, and whilst carrying out the gigantic conception of the designer we have been able fully to estimate the difficulties which he had to contend with and overcome. And now that he has passed away from the sphere of existence, we feel proud that we possess, in these Her Majesty's Canadian dominions, so magnificent a funeral monument of one who rose from our own class, and who shared with us the privilege of being a British subject. Before your Royal Highness departs from these shores, there will no doubt be many opportunities afforded you of judging of the loyal and devoted feelings of attachment general in these Provinces towards your Royal Mother, and we are sure that whatever spot you may visit, you will find one feeling common, we are proud to say, in every land where the English tongue is spoken, and in which we heartily join our love and attachment towards that lady whose virtues are known and acknowledged in every land and every home— your Royal Mother and our Queen. Wishing your Royal Highness every pleasure and benefit from your sojourn amongst us and a safe return to the parent land. Signed in behalf of the workmen of the Grand Trunk Railway.

J. CURTIS CLARK.

GENTLEMEN,—I accept with pleasure an address of artizans and working men, who have by the sweat of their brow and the skilled labour of many a hard day's toil, contributed to erect this monument to the greatness of their country—a structure scarcely less honourable to hands which executed than to the minds which conceived it. I mourn with you the loss of Robert Stephenson. You bring to mind that it was from your class that his eminent father sprung. Let me further remind you that England opens to all her sons the same prospect of success to genius, combined with honest industry. All cannot attain the prize, but all may strive for it, and in this race victory is not to the wealthy or the powerful, but to him to whom God has given intellect and has implanted in the heart the moral qualities which are required to constitute true greatness. I congratulate you upon the completion of your work. I earnestly hope that it may prosper, and to you who have raised it to its present grandeur, and to your families I heartily wish every happiness.

On Saturday night, the 25th, it ceased raining, and the illuminations were very fine ; it was the opinion of all that the display in Great St. James street, where the principal banks are, surpassed any thing ever seen on this continent, and was even finer than that at Berlin when the Princess Royal went thither after her marriage. The Prince drove into town to see it, *incog.*, but was stopped by a policeman, as no carriages were allowed on the principal streets. General Williams, who accompanied him, had to mention his name before the carriage was allowed to proceed; and the *incog.*, being thus destroyed, a vast concourse of people began to cheer.

It is universally admitted that the grand ball in Montreal transcended any of the other festivities of the jubilee; and that never, either on this continent or elsewhere, has there been an affair of the kind at all equalling it in any way.

Eight short weeks ago the cattle were grazing; in a fortnight more, they will again be ruminating where now there is a wonderful circular room, nearly 300 feet in diameter, with 32,000 square feet of flooring, in which about 6,000 people were enjoying the pleasures of the dance. Just as in the case of Sir Joseph Paxton and the great Exhibition of 1851, or that of Roebling and the Niagara Bridge, so here, too, a man came forward just when he was wanted with a thoroughly original idea; strange to say he was but a builder, not a regular architect at all, named Tafts; and, stranger still, liberal and energetic citizens were found to shoulder the pecuniary responsibility of having the idea realized. They called for no tenders; let out no contracts, but had the work commenced and finished under their own immediate supervision.

It literally rose by magic, with its artificial streets of water and plantations of trees, among which at night were hundreds of lanterns shining. It was lighted by nearly two thousand gas lamps arranged in concentric circles around its centre, where the orchestra was situated. Galleries ran all around, and under these were the refreshment tables stretching half way round the vast circumference, while hat and dressing rooms completed the circle. The decorations were not elaborate, but very effective, and all the arrangements were perfection itself. The music was good. The floor was well chalked and had just sufficient spring to be pleasant. The refreshment tables were profusely supplied with eatables, whilst a dozen fountains of choice champagne and copious claret cups, taps whence lemonade, &c., ran in plenty—supplied the wherewithal to assuage one's thirst. "Beats our Academy of Music, hollow," said the New-Yorkers. "You might put all Astley's in the middle ring of it," said the Englishmen.

The whole of the company were amazed and bewildered at the grandeur and novelty of all the details of the marvelous scene. In the interior you might look around for half an hour without being able to find your friend, so large was the building, so great the concourse; and, forseeing this, the Executive Committee had actually caused the twenty four interior pillars to be numbered for facility of rendezvous. You engaged a lady for a dance and agreed to meet her at pillar number so-and-so.

Around the orchestra were some half dozen jets of various perfumes—eau-de-cologne, lavender, &c., in which the fairer half of the brilliant assemblage could dip their tiny handkerchiefs.

Among the guests present were the Prince, the Governor-General, the Earl of Mulgrave, the Duke of Newcastle, Earl St. Germains, Lord Lyons, Sir F. W. Williams, Admiral Sir Alexander Milne, General Bruce, the Marquis of Chandos, Lord Hichinbrooke, Major Teesdale, Captain Gray, Hon. Mr. Ellis, Sir Allan McNab, Sir E. P. Taché, and a number of military and naval officers.

Among the ladies were the Marchioness of Chandos, Lady Georgiana Fane, Lady Milne, and Lady Franklin.

The Prince arrived at about ten o'clock, and soon after the first quadrille was formed as follows:—The Prince and Mrs. John Young at the head; Hon Mr. Cartier and Mrs. Dumas on his right; Major Teesdale and Miss J. Rogers on his left; the Duke of Newcastle and Madame Perrault *vis-a-vis;* General Bruce and Mrs. Colonel Denny; Captain Connolly and Miss Penn; Lord Mulgrave and Mrs. Delisle; Captain Denniston and Miss Tyre, and two other couples making up the set. In the next dance, a polka, the Prince led out Miss Delisle; 3. Waltz, Mrs. Cerventes; 4. Lancers, Miss Sewell, of Quebec.

At about one His Royal Highness went to supper. A private room had been set apart, but he preferred taking refreshments at the general table. He danced every dance but one, and only left at about 3 o'clock. The list of dances and music were as follows:—
1, quadrille, the Queen's Canadian; 2, polka, Minnehaha; 3, waltz, Sultana; 4, lancers, original; 5, mazurka, *billet doux;* 6, gallop, Reception; 7, quadrille, Palermo; 8, waltz, Trovatore; 9, polka, Ariadne; 10, lancers, English; 11, gallop, the Prince of Wales'; 12, mazurka, Sweet Thought; 13, quadrille, Lucia; 14, waltz,

Satanella; 15, polka, Sleeping Beauty; 16, lancers, original 17, gallop, Laughing; 18, mazurka, Sarline; 19, lancers, Queen; 20, waltz, Bertha; 21, gallop, Charivari.

Having danced all night until four o'clock in the morning, he was up again at eleven to visit Dickinson's Landing, seventy-seven miles from this city.

Thither he went by the aid of the Grand Trunk Railway. His reception was most enthusiastic. All along the line of route numbers of people were gathered together in the hope of catching a glimpse of the Princely visitor as he passed. At the landing he was greeted by all the farmers of the country thereabout, many of whom had ridden long distances on horseback, while acres of ground were covered with women and children, equally anxious with the ladies of the city to see, if it were but for a single moment, their future ruler.

The royal party went down the Long Sault rapids in the *Kingston*. It had been originally intended that at Lachine carriages should be taken and the residence of General Williams at once sought. But by the desire of the Prince, the Lachine rapids were at once run, and the steamer returned to Montreal about seven o'clock. As he drove rapidly to his temporary house, His Royal Highness was recognised by the people, and a continued series of cheers marked his progress towards the Mountain.

At dinner, so fatigued was he, that he fell asleep in his chair, and was allowed to take a nap undisturbed, the gentlemen with him no doubt being glad of the opportunity thus afforded to get a little rest too.

On the afternoon of the 29th there was a great gathering of firemen in Commissioners' square. Prizes to the value of $1,000 had been offered, and though the number of contestants was not so great as had been expected, yet the competition between those who were there was very keen. About three thousand persons were present, cheering on the men, and very great interest was taken by all. People who had never before looked at a fire-engine got excited, and discoursed learnedly upon the merits of the competitors— each one maintaining his opinion with the characteristic obstinacy of folks who know nothing of what they are talking. The first prize offered was a silver trumpet, valued at $225. The conditions were that the engine should be worked by not more than 44

men, that they should draught their own water, and play
through 200 feet of hose with a one-inch nozzle. Brockville sent
a "Button" machine and eighty men; "Horicon" Company of
Plattsburg, N. Y., a "Hunniman" machine; and Perry of
Montreal one of his own make. Brockville threw 170 feet;
Plattsburg, 165; and Perry, 150 feet. Of course Brockville was
the winner, a result which was received with much cheering.
For the second prize, a trumpet worth $175; the "Horicon" and
Perry contended. The former threw 165 feet; the latter 150
feet. In the third and fourth contests, Perry had it all his own
way; receiving a silver trumpet, value $125, and a Union Jack
worth $50. The fifth prize, a silver trumpet, value $200, the
gift of Mr. Thos. E. Blackwell, contested for by first-class engines
the property of Canada—was won by the Brockville men against
the Perry's. Montreal has no corporation engines, their splendid water works having entirely superseded them.

In the evening the firemen had a ball in the City Hall, where
they danced away in good stile until four o'clock in the morning.
Very good order was preserved, and the strangers were exceedingly
pleased with the treatment they received.

It was almost impossible to keep pace with the Prince; but, to
keep pace with Montreal, was still more difficult. The Boston
Fusiliers had a banquet; they were entertained at the theatre.
A review, a cricket-match between Canada and America, a
boat race at Longueuil, a visit of the Prince to Lachine, a torchlight procession, and a dozen other things came off. The shops
were for the most part open, but very little work done. The
cab-men had more than they could do, and consequently were
most extortionate. Each night some of the arches, and many
of the windows, were brilliantly lighted up, and bursts of music
and song issuing from private houses the night through, proclaimed that, independently of the public provision made for
pleasure, other sources of enjoyment had been sought. In fact,
Montreal used itself up.

Next, the concert was given in the ball-room. The entertainment of the previous evening was a magnificent affair;
the concert almost equalled it. Some say it was superior; but
they are the sentimental people who don't see that it possesses
any "soul-refining" influence. But music—with the emotions

which the works of the best masters raise in our breasts in earthly dress, is mingled; all is pure; the animal is forgotten; we live in spirit, we are elevated above "the smoke and stir of this dull spot, which men call earth," into an atmosphere clear as the sun-beam which first fell on the newly born world. It was left to His Royal Highness to say which' he prefered; a waltz with a pretty girl, or a cantata in his honour. Had he to choose, he would select the former. Not that there is a desire one moment to hint that the concert was out of place. The concert was *almost* equal to the ball. The entertainment was on a most magnificent scale. The vast edifice was occupied by not less than eight thousand people, for the most part ranged in a semicircle around a central platform, whereon were placed the performers, numbering two hundred and fifty. Many officers of the army and navy were present, attired in their showy uniforms; all the ladies were in full-dress. But the audience was not confined to those who sat on the floor. The gallery which circles the entire place was filled with an equally brilliant assembly. Here, too, the Royal box was placed; cushioned chairs, scarlet drapery, and a gilded coat of arms distinguishing it from the seats to be occupied by less distinguished personages. The concert was divided into three parts; the first consisting of selections from Hayden's Creation, performed by the Choral society. The second a grand Cantata, composed in honour of the visit of His Royal Highness to this Province, by Mr. Edward Temps, the music by Mr. C. W. Sabatier, the conductor. The third part, of selections from favourite operas, in which Madle. Adelina Patti, Madame Amelia Strakosch, Signor Brignoli, Amodio, Barili, and Susini, appeared. Truth to tell, but comparatively little attention was paid to the selections from the oratorios, though they were very beautiful, rendering the performers well worthy of all that can be said in their praise. But the Prince did not come—how could it be expected that while he was absent the people would be able to think of any thing else. It was him they had paid to see—the music was a bonus thrown in. He was thoroughly fatigued with the exertion of the last two days, and was taking a short rest— rest which he must very much have needed, and which none would begrudge him. But of this many were ignorant, and much anxiety was manifested that he should quickly appear. The first part of the Oratorio was got through with, and the Cantata was about to be commenced. In vain was it delayed, put off for one quarter of an hour, and then for another. No Prince came. At last, when hope had almost fled, the Cantata was about to be commenced, when shortly afterwards His Royal Highness appeared. He was loudly welcomed, and before taking his seat bowed to the audience repeatedly in acknowledgment of the applause rendered him. He stayed but for three quarters of an hour, leaving when the Cantata was concluded. The Strakosch Opera troupe rather felt this ; and it was a great pity that His Royal Highness did not stop longer to listen to the sweet voice of the justly renowned Patti. They must lay the fault, if blame there be, upon the Duke of Newcastle ; his shoulders are broad enough to bear it ; but he was right in using what influence he had with his Royal charge to prevent him, so far as possible, from over-working himself to a still greater extent than he had already done. The concert was not concluded until a late hour; and the famous singers who came last were occasionally heard but indistinctly by those on the outside of the semi-circle, on account of the continual walking in which a great number of the eye-glass and finger-ling fraternity indulged. They appeared to think, because it was called a "promenade" concert, that it was their duty to trot round and round all night. A great mistake, as those who are accustomed to such entertainments know.

At twelve o'clock in the morning the Prince went on horseback to Logan's farm, attended by the Governor-General and all the suite, excepting Lord St. Germains. There a review of the militia of the city was held. There were about 60 Cavalry under the command of Col. David; 60 Light Infantry under Major Dyde; 350 Rifles under Col Wiley; 120 Foot Artillery under Capt. R. S. Evans, and 60 men of the Field Battery under Capt. Stevenson. The whole force was under the command of Col. Dyde, to whom Capt. Pean acted as aide-de-camp.

When His Royal Highness came upon the field the artillery fired a salute, and the troops were then inspected, the royal party passing down the front, and up the rear.

The militia then marched past in open and close column, and performed several movements, throwing out skirmishers, &c., &c.

Finally, the Prince summoned their officers, complimented them upon their soldier-like appearance and withdrew, the corps all firing a *feu-de-joie*.

The Prince then proceeded to Isle Dorval and lunched there with General Williams, who occupied the house of Sir George Simpson, Governor of the Hudson Bay Company.

The trip was in every way a delightful one.

The Prince and his party went up to a point opposite the Island in carriages, and crossed in the *Valorous*.

Half way across the channel he was met by a dozen great Hudson's Bay canoes, manned by a score of men a piece, brought down by Sir George Simpson. They were in a double line of battle, and accompanied him to the island.

There no one was allowed who could not meet His Royal Highness' suite on terms of social equality, and there were no ladies except a niece of Sir George Simpson's, and the lady of Mr. Hopkins, Sir George's Secretary, with her sister.

Arrived at the island, lunch was had, and afterwards, with the Duke of Newcastle and General Williams, the Prince paddled about in a canoe and enjoyed himself much.

The Prince, accompanied by the Duke of Newcastle and General Williams, afterwards took seats in a large bark canoe, and made a tour of the Island. They then came by the north channel down the stream, direct for the wharf, which was crowded with people. The appearance presented was very beautiful. The sun rapidly setting in the west, tinged the fleecy clouds which hung over head with his golden hues, and shed his beams upon the mighty river, marking out his glorious pathway on the blue waves for the Royal Prince. The paddles of the Indians glistened at each of the quick strokes which they gave, as aided by the rapid currents they strained every nerve to propel their canoes swiftly along the stream. The dark foliage upon the surrounding banks, the glittering white houses peeping out from among the trees, the shining spires of the village churches all combined, produced a scene of exceeding splendour. The canoe containing the Prince was kept a little in advance, the rest were formed in a line behind. As they neared the wharf, the rapid action of the paddles became more distinct, the spray as it fell from the paddles glittered in the sunlight like showers of sparkling pearls. The Indians themselves were all dressed in red flannel shirts. Their canoes were also painted of the same colour; in fact, what with their red faces, red clothes, and red boots, they were one mass of red; varied only by their feathery head dresses of various colours, and by a broad streak of white which ran around their frail crafts. On they went, chanting their boat song, and occasionally sending up a shriek, which resounded far and wide. It was thought by all upon the wharf that His Royal Highness would immediately embark on board the *Kingston*, which lay waiting to receive him. But when within a few yards, at a signal given, the whole fleet suddenly turned. There was no apparent diminution in speed; with one stroke of the paddles each canoe was brought round. So close were they together that had any one of them failed, the whole line would have been thrown into confusion, and some by no means light collisions have taken place. But Indians make no such mistakes. They stretched in complete order across the river to Caughnawagha, and were paddled along the whole extent of that village, so that His Royal Highness might gain a just idea of the colossal proportions of the residencies of the two thousand Indians who dwell there. About half-past seven o'clock the party returned to the *Kingston*, and immediately returned to town. The Prince very kindly took his stand at the bow of the boat, thus giving to the people assembled a capital opportunity of seeing him. Some amusement was caused by a stalwart red man, who appeared to have been drinking freely of whisky. He loudly proclaimed his intention of looking upon the face of his "great father," and when he did get a sight of the little Prince, set up three or four lusty cheers upon his own account, waved his hat in the air, and declared that he could now die in peace.

He returned from Isle Dorval, at 7 p.m.

At the cricket match, Canada made—first innings 42; United States, 165. Canada, second innings, three wickets twenty-one runs. Canada, first innings—Fourdrinier scored nothing; Daily, 3; Chapman, nothing; Wester, 6; Patterson, nothing; Captain Leigh, 17; Napier, 1; Fisher, nothing; Morgan, 3; leg byes, 1; wide, 3—total 42. Second innings—Fourdrinier, nothing; Leigh, 4; Wiser, 5; Wester, 11. New York first innings—Waller, 6; Wright, 21; Vernon, 3; Gibbs, 37; Barclay, 7; Newhall, 3; Brett, 59; Walker, 18; Stevens, nothing; Davis, 2; Burnett, 4; byes, 2; leg byes, 1; wides, 4—total, 165.

The Duke of Newcastle intimated to the cricket club his regret that owing to late information, His Royal Highness could not attend the match.

The Prince left Montreal on 30th August, by special train, at ten o'clock, crossing the Victoria Bridge, and being rapidly driven past the intermediate stations, most of which, especially St. Hilaire, where Major Campbell had erected an arch, were decorated with spruce trees, arrived at St. Hyacinthe. Here he was driven in a carriage through the streets of the town, and under several handsome arches, to the college building, where three addresses were presented, from the town, country, and college.

He afterwards went to the roof of the building and surveyed the surrounding country.

Leaving St. Hyacinthe, he arrived at Sherbrooke at two o'clock, p.m. Fir boughs, flowers, flags, &c., had been erected, and under these he received the following address :—

To the Most High, Puissant and Illustrious Prince Albert Edward, Prince of the United Kingdom of Great Britain and Ireland, Prince of Wales, Duke of Saxony, Prince of Cobourg and Gotha, Great Steward of Scotland, Duke of Cornwall and Rothsay, Earl of Chester, Carrick and Dublin, Baron of Renfrew and Lord of the Isles, K. G.

MAY IT PLEASE YOUR ROYAL HIGHNESS,—

It is with feelings of peculiar satisfaction that, on behalf of the Corporation and citizens of the town of Sherbrooke, and on the part of the Eastern townships, we have the honour of addressing your Royal Highness, the representative of our gracious Sovereign Queen Victoria, and of assuring you of our hearty and cordial welcome to the Eastern Townships of Canada. Loyalty to the Crown, and attachment to the person of, your illustrious Mother, are as lively and ardent in these townships as in any portion of Her Majesty's dominions, and on your return to England you can assure Her Majesty of our attachment to the British Crown and to British institutions, and that we feel proud of our connexion therewith and of our relation to our gracious Sovereign, distinguished alike as a Queen and as a woman for those estimable qualities which have won for her the confidence and love of her people. Your Royal Highness can also assure Her Majesty that although situated on the borders of the neighbouring Republic, and intimately acquainted with the working of its institutions, yet, under our own constitution, connected with and protected by the British Government, we have no desire for any change in the relations existing between us and the Mother Country. We sincerely pray these may continue for ages to come. In visiting a new country, like the townships, your Royal Highness will not expect such progress in agriculture and manufactures, or such marks of competence and wealth as in the older settled portions of the country; still, we hope that what you may see, will impress you favourably with the natural beauties and the varied resources of the townships, and enable you to form an opinion of what they are destined to become through the industry and enterprise of the inhabitants. We sincerely and respectfully thank your Royal Highness for the visit, and would gladly hope that it may afford your Royal Highness as much gratification as it confers honour upon us. Permit us to hope that the Queen, Prince Consort, and their beloved family may long be spared to fill and adorn their high positions, and that when it shall please Almighty God in His wisdom to call upon you to assume and exercise the duties and responsibilites devolving upon you as reigning Monarch, your career may, like that of your Royal Mother, be prosperous and happy, benefitting the millions governed, and year by year reflecting additional lustre on your Royal Highness' person.

    (Signed).   J. G. ROBERTSON,
                    Mayor.

He replied as follows :—

GENTLEMEN,—I thank you warmly for your address welcoming me to this part of Canada, and expressing your loyalty to the Queen. I could not pass on, in my rapid journey through the Canadian provinces, without a visit to the Eastern Townships, and I only regret that the shortness of time in which so much has to be seen does not permit of a longer stay amongst you. Even in this hurried view of your country, I see much to indicate the future destiny which awaits a land to which so great energy and industry are devoted, and whose inhabitants are influenced by such attachment to the institutions in which they have been educated, as is evinced by your address. Accept my thanks for your kind wishes for my future happiness. In return, I wish you every prosperity.

He also read an address from Bishop's College, Lennoxville, an institution which has its seat within a few miles.

Then, while the bells were ringing, the people shouting, the band playing, and the artillery saluting, he drove up the street, exposed to a perfect shower of bouquets, to the residence of Hon. Mr. Galt.

Mr. Galt's house is on the summit of a hill, from which there is a pleasant prospect of the St. Francis river below, and of the undulating, fertile country beyond. It was prettily adorned with wreaths, garlands, and boquets of flowers. Here there were a number of well-dressed ladies upon the well-trimmed grounds, and the scene looked like a brilliant *fete champetre*.

As soon as His Royal Highness entered, a very singular but very pleasant levee commenced—singular in that, full dress was not required of those who wished to be presented. His Royal Highness was in undress himself, and could require nothing more of those who came to tender their respects. Several hundreds did so.

At the close of this levee the voice of Colonel or Captain Moore was heard. Colonel, by reason of his militia rank; Captain, because he is a retired naval officer. "Cheer," he loudly cried, "for justice has at last been done to as brave an officer as ever stepped the quarter deck." He said a few words more, but they were unintelligible, being either choked by emotion or drowned in the cheers that immediately burst forth. The cause of the commotion was from the following circumstance: John Felton, commonly called old Squire Felton in his own district, was signal midshipman on Nelson's flag ship the *Victory*, at the battle of Trafalgar. He was also at the battle of Copenhagen, and wears medals for bravery at both those actions. At the blockade of Guadaloupe, West Indies, in 1826, he was the officer of the watch on board the *Curieux*, sloop-of-war, when she struck on a rock and was wrecked. On the court martial, which was of course subsequently held, there were some enemies of young Felton's, and, perhaps to their personal hostility—perhaps to the fact that court martials were not held in those days with so much care for the ends of justice as now, he owed it that, although the wreck was caused by circumstances beyond his control, he was dismissed the service. His prospects were thus at once destroyed, and he finally emigrated to this country, where for four and thirty years he has lived-respected. His Royal Highness having been been made aware of the hardships of Mr. Felton's case—not by him—for he suffered uncomplainingly, chose this day as the occasion for exercising the prerogative delegated by Her Majesty to him, and when the old man presented himself at the reception, not only received him with the greatest cordiality, speaking to him kindly words, but intimated that from that moment he was restored to the position he had lost. This it was which caused the ebullition of feeling on the part of his brother sailor, Captain Moore, and the cheering on that of the crowd. The act was in itself graceful, it was gracefully performed, and it was highly appreciated. Every one looked delighted. Mr. Felton could not conceal his pleasure, though he tried to look unmoved, and Mrs. Felton looked at her husband with more than usual pride as he and she were receiving the congratulations of the people.

His Royal Highness and suite then commenced to vigorously attack the lunch at which they were entertained by Mr. Galt. This finished, His Royal Highness left, and returning to his train closely surrounded by a host of delighted township men, cheering frantically, was almost overwhelmed by flowers with which the township ladies were pelting him. The cars left under a salute from the artillery, which was, however, almost drowned by the shouts of the vigorous populace. The Prince's train consisted of an engine and tender, a baggage car, the director's car, and the Prince's gorgeous car. It ran at the rate of thirty-three miles an hour, including stoppages, and arrived at Montreal at 6.30.

His Royal Highness left Montreal on 31st August, at half-past seven o'clock. He journeyed from thence to St. Anne's by rail, where the Prince of Wales' steamboat was found. At the next portage he took the *Phœnix*, in which boat, at seven o'clock, he arrived in Ottawa, the *bond fide* capital of Canada.

The arrangements for and the reception at the landing place

of His Royal Highness, were on far too large a scale to be spoken of, after a cursory survey of them. The time at which it was expected the Prince would land was five o'clock ; at that time Ottawa stood in an attitude of expectation. All Ottawa tried to get good places from which to view the Prince as he passed. And not all Ottawa merely,.but the population of the regions round about. In came the stalwart lumber-men by the thousand ; and very few farm houses were there within a compass of ten or fifteen miles, which were not left to "take care of themselves." The landing place itself was mainly occupied by ladies, who sat upon a platform formed by nature when she scooped out the valley of the Ottawa, and it was free to the ticketless multitude.

When the *Phœnix* was within two miles of the city, she was met by a fleet of one hundred and fifty canoes, manned by near a thousand lumber-men. These were all dressed in white trousers and red shirts faced with blue. As they floated down the river they presented a most remarkable and exceedingly attractive appearance. To the measured cadence of their boating song all the paddles bent. There was no confusion among them ; all was order and precision, manifesting a skill which long practice alone can give. The banners on their boats floated freely, the sound of their voices reached the ears of the crowd on shore in wave after wave of wild, exciting melody. And when they gained the vessel containing the Royal guest, the hurrah they gave echoed far and wide ; it was a glorious hurrah, a real welcome ; an hurrah which came from the hearts as well as the throats of a thousand as stalwart men as the world may find. They say the Prince was a trifle excited ; and well he may have been. It is not often that he has had the chance of seeing so strange a sight. Their hurrahs finished, the canoe-men wheeled round and accompaned the Prince to the landing. It was hard work to keep near to hand, pulling against the heavy stream, racing with a swift river steamer. It was exciting too. Now the canoes got together in one or two sections, like fleet race horses, when the proper phrase to use in speaking of them is—"you could cover them with a pocket handkerchief." And then they would separate for a time as one or the other got ahead, only to close again in a still tougher combat. About twenty-five or thirty of them were around the *Phœnix* when she made the wharf, the rest came rowing in like bees to the spot whither their queen leads them.

Owing to the lateness of the hour, it was seven o'clock, the face of the young Prince could be but dimly seen in the rapidly declining light, by thousands who otherwise would have had an excellent view of him. He was received by a salute from the volunteer battery. The guard of honour consisted of Captain Abbott's company of rifles, Ottawa, and the other from Prescott. The salute was fired by Major Turner's Ottawa field battery, and the Port Hope volunteer cavalry formed the escort. The Mayor, Mr. Workman, attired in his robes of office—which he wore with much ease and grace, advanced to read the address. The day had previously been fine. Scarce a cloud was to be seen, those that were above only giving additional grandeur to the celestial vault, by the beauty of the colours thus reflected.

But the Prince was not destined for fair weather—that is plain. And this was also plain, that though the weather was foul, he bore himself most bravely. Scarce had the Mayor opened his parchment, scarce was the first word of the loyal congratulation fallen from his lips, when the rain poured down suddenly in perfect torrents. He cared no more, to judge from his outward appearance, about the huge drops which fell, than Nelson's men cared for French shot bounding about. But if he did not, the people did. Away the crowd rushed like a flock of wild geese hurriedly changing quarters. Naturalists say that these sagacious birds, when about to commence a journey, first elect the wisest and strongest of their number, and always hit upon the wisest and strongest—proving truly their superiority over man—to be their leader. He, they say, places himself at the head, the rest then form themselves wedge-shape behind, making him the apex of an immense triangle. When crowds rush forward some one always gets the lead without election, but by reason of his superior "wind and limb"—the weaker ones naturally fall behind.

They sought cover where they best could, and His Royal Highness, accompanied by the troops, the corporation, and civic officers, and those gentlemen whose immediate duties required them closely to attend him, sought his hotel, (the Victoria,) vigorously cheered through by the thousands who stood in the doorways, under each projecting piece of timber, which could afford protection from the rain; who thrust their heads out of the windows, and waved hats and handkerchiefs as he passed.

A2

The city corporation dealt liberally with the members of the Provincial Parliament, and members of the provincial press. Into the hands of each one a card was put, inscribed as follows :— "The Corporation of Ottawa request Mr.——, (M. or N., as they say in the cathechism,) to accept the hospitality of their city, during the celebration in honour of the visit of His Royal Highness the Prince of Wales. Alexander Workman, Mayor." Billets were also furnished for the hotels and boarding houses, upon handing which to the proprietor, comfortable quarters were immediately provided. Proceeding West in Canada, the attention paid to the Press became more marked; evidencing beyond all question the superior enlightenment of the people.

A very pleasant incident occurred in Montreal, in which His Royal Highness figured. A very fine company of Boston Fusiliers, who went to that city to pay their respects to the son of our Queen, on Thursday night, about ten o'clock, accompanied by their splendid band, proceeded to the house of General Williams, and serenaded the Prince. They played "God save the Queen" in capital style, and brought Albert Edward out to the balcony. He thanked them for their kindness, hoped to meet them again in Boston, complimented them upon their soldier-like appearance, (compliments as well deserved as ever man received,) and concluded by asking as a personal favour, that they would play "Yankee Doodle." Of course they obliged His Royal Highness, and were exceedingly pleased with the request. They now swear by the Heir Apparent to the British Throne, and are ready to defend him against all comers, at the risk of their lives. They have conceived a deadly hatred to all the breed of Frenchmen, and will help John Bull against Louis Napoleon, when the last mentioned personage commences operations. On our side we cannot but feel pleased at the compliment they have paid the whole of Canada, in visiting Montreal to do honour to the Prince.

Ottawa, Sept. 1.

At eleven o'clock this day His Royal Highness left the new hotel where he is staying, and which, in honour of Her Majesty's choice of Ottawa for the seat of government, is called the Victoria House, and proceeded to lay the foundation stone of the Parliament Buildings.

A great and handsome gothic arch had been built at the entrance to the grounds, and inside, at the spot where the ceremony was to take place, there was a Gothic canopy, immediately in front of which and over the stone was a gigantic crown.

Around the stone was a railing painted white. Outside this was an open space for the press and a few priviliged individuals, while surrounding this central space, canopy and all, was tier upon tier of seats, capable of accommodating several thousand people, all filled with ladies and gentlemen. On each side of the road leading to this amphitheatre were platforms for children and for those who could not be accommodated within it, while bands of music, companies of volunteers, hosts of lumberers in scarlet shirts, Orange Societies from the townships, mounted, and clad in orange frocks, parties of Roman Catholic clergy, &c. &c., were in their assigned positions in the line of march.

The day was fine, and the scene, consequently, magnificent.

Punctual to the hour, His Royal Highness arrived, followed by the Governor-General. Soon afterwards came the Duke of Newcastle, Earl St. Germains, General Bruce, General Williams, Lord Mulgrave, Sir Allan MacNab, Col. E. P. Tache, (Aid-de-camps to the Queen,) Major Teesdale and Capt. Grey, (the Prince's equerries,) and while all these took up their positions in a semi-circle, in which the Prince was the principal figure, the aides prolonging the line on one side, and the Canadian Ministers in blue and gold on the other.

On the lower side of the stone were Mr. Samuel Keefer, Assistant Commissioner of Public Works; Messrs. Stent & Laver, and Fuller & Jones, architects; Mr. Haycock and Mr. McGreevy, contractors; Mr. Morris and Mr. Grest, clerk and assistant-clerk of the works.

The actual ceremony was commenced by the reading, by the Rev. Dr. Adamson, chaplain to the Legislative Council, of the following prayer:

"Protect us, O Lord, in all our doings with Thy most gracious favour, and further us with Thy continual help, that in all our works begun, continued and ended in Thee, we may glorify Thy holy name, and finally by Thy mercy obtain everlasting life, through Jesus Christ our Lord. Amen. Our Father which art, &c.

Then the Prince and chief members of the suite advanced to the stone. It was of beautiful white Canadian marble, or crystalized limestone, brought from Portage Du Fort, and on it was the simple inscription:—"This corner stone of the building intended to receive the Legislature of Canada, was laid by Albert Edward, Prince of Wales, on the 1st day of September, 1860."

It was suspended from the centre of the great crown, previously mentioned, by a pully running round a gilded block; under it was a similar cube of the white Nepean limestone, with which the future building is to be faced, within a cavity in which was placed a glass bottle. In the bottle was a parchment scroll inscribed thus:—" The foundation stone of the Houses of Parliament in the Province of Canada, was laid on the 1st day of September, in the year of our Lord, 1860, in the 24th year of Her Majesty's reign, at the city of Ottawa, by His Royal Highness the Prince of Wales." Upon the scroll also were inscribed the names of all the members of the Legislative Council, the names of all the members of the Legislative Assembly, the names of all the members of the Government of Canada, the names of the architects, contractors, &c.

There was also placed in the bottle a collection of coins of Great Britain and of Canada, gold, silver, and copper.

The clerk of works, Mr. Morris, now superintended the spreading of the mortar, which Mr. McLauchlin performed, and to which His Royal Highness gave the finishing touch with a silver trowel, on the back of which was engraved a view of the future building, and on the front, a suitable historical inscription.

Then the stone was slowly lowered—the Prince gave it three raps with a mallet, and the Rev. Dr. Adamson read a prayer: " This corner stone we lay in the name of the Father and of the Son and of the Holy Ghost; and may God Almighty grant that the building thus begun in His name, may be happily carried on to its complete termination without injury or accident; and that, when completed, it may be used for the good of the Province, the glory of our Queen, the happiness of our Prince, and the good government of the people. Amen."

Mr. Morris then applied the plumb, which was in the shape of a harp; Mr. Keefer tested the work with the level, which was supported by lion and unicorn, and then removed the *debris;*

after which His Royal Highness, having been informed that the work was well performed, pronounced the stone laid—a fact which the Governor proclaimed aloud to the surrounding people.

Three cheers were immediately given for the Queen ; three for the Prince of Wales ; and three for the Governor-General. The band played the National Anthem, and the artillery fired a royal salute.

The architects and contractors were now presented to His Royal Highness, and while Mr. Rose was giving him the trowel as a memento of the day, these gentlemen removed the portrait of the Queen which hung behind the throne, and a doorway was disclosed through which the royal party passed and strolled along the brink of the cliffs, which hem the river in, towards a platform which they ascended, and for several minutes surveyed the glorious prospect there afforded of the brown Ottawa river, tumbling towards and over the Chaudiere Falls, and expanding into a blue bay below them—of the city itself, of Hull village, of the lumber yards and saw mills, of the fields and forests and mountains in the distance beyond. Then they left the ground, returning to hold a levee at their residence. There a larger number of gentlemen were presented, but no addresses.

Immediately after the Prince and his suite drove to Major's Hill, on which the Governor's residence is being built, where a number of tents belonging to the militia from a distance were pitched on the green sward under the trees. A beautiful view is obtained from this point also.

The next item in the programme was the lunch given by the Legislature in a wooden shed on the Parliament grounds. It was a most successful affair. The members stood around four long tables covered with delicacies, and at the head on a large platform was a cross table, at the middle of which the Prince sat ; at the ends the newly knighted Speakers, and between them the whole of the Royal party. After a reasonable time the Governor gave "The Queen ;" Sir N. Belleau, "The Prince Consort," and Sir Henry Smith, calling for a bumper, "His Royal Highness the Prince of Wales." The cheering at each of these was really extraordinary, for its heartiness and vigour. Next His Royal Highness rose and said, "I propose the health of the Governor-General, and the House of the Legislature." With one accord the company sprang up and a cheer burst forth which must have rung in the Prince's ears for an hour after. Bowing, he then left.

In a couple of hours the Royal Party took horse and rode, in plain clothes, to the Chaudiere, where they admired the Suspension Bridge and the beautiful arch of the lumberers, containing no less than 19,000 feet of deal boards, which formed a portal to it.

A novel and exciting incident now occurred. Dismounting, the whole of the party, including Earl St. Germains, walked along a boom to a crib which was moored at the entrance of the timber slide. A slide, every body should know, is an inclined plane, with several feet of water rushing over it, forming a water-way down which the crib can pass without damage, thus avoiding water-falls like the Chaudiere, where they would be broken and the timber injured. A crib consists of sticks of timber of any length, forming a small raft twenty-five feet wide, the longitudinal sticks have pieces across them to tie them, as it were, together. The crib, when fairly launched, goes down the slide with great velocity, the water rushing over the forward part and sometimes dashing over the men upon it. On each side of the slide on this occasion were thousands of people, and the numerous bridges which crossed it were alive with human beings. When the Royal crib got under way and shot down past or below them, these people cheered and waved their handkerchiefs, and the most intense excitement prevailed. For, although there is really little danger, yet accidents sometimes happen, and in every case the passengers who try this mode of locomotion for the first time have to brace their nerves and clench their lips and stand firm, lest the vibration and the shocks which the crib always receives should make them lose their footing. And when Albert Edward, Prince of Wales, was to undergo this experience, how much greater than usual was the interest taken in the running of the crib. Everything luckily went well, both with the Prince's raft and with that which was carrying the leading members of the press immediately following. The whole of both parties were delighted with the rapid descent; the cribs floated into the centre of the bay at the foot of the Chaudiere, and there they found themselves surrounded by a hundred birch canoes, manned by lumberers in scarlet shirts and white trousers. The Prince got into one alone—the rest of his suite and the newspaper writers into others, and all were paddled to a beautiful island in the centre of the lake-like expanse. There they sat on the grass, or strolled about or busied themselves with sketching the lovely scenery. The Prince's physician and the Duke's secretary, are both accomplished artists.

After a short but agreeable interval of repose, a barge with a blue silk canopy appeared, manned by half a dozen gentlemen of the city, in blue silk blouses and white trousers. The Prince, stepping into this, was rowed to a large scow, whence the canoes which intended racing were to start. Clambering to its deck, by the assistance of the boat's crew, who had to lift him shoulder high, he had a good view of the course. Nor were the arrangements at all exclusive, but all who chose went on board too, and it is very creditable to the people that the license was not abused, and that not the slightest inconvenience resulted. Six canoes started for the first race; ten for the second, and nine for the third. The course was probably a mile each way. The lumberers paddled well, magnificently even.

There must have been two thousand people in small boats on the water, 2,000 more in the half dozen steamers which were playing about. 20,000 on the heights on either side of the shore, and when the runners in each race came in, and the Prince clapped his hands, applauding, they all participated in his evident delight, and took up the applause in one tremendous chorous. Neither the Prince nor any other person that was privileged to see the sight can ever forget it.

Not before half-past seven did the Prince return to his place in the barge, which bore a beautiful silk Prince's standard at the stern, glowing in the red light of the setting sun. Not until then did any of the delighted spectators leave.

In the evening there were huge bonfires which reddened the sky and all the hills, and a fine illumination lit up all the streets.

There was also a procession of the physiocarnivalogicalist society, but after the splendid incidents of the day, it had comparatively small effect.

September 2.

The Prince attended divine service this morning in the Church of England, a small, plain stone edifice. Mr. Barnaby, from

Montreal, played the organ, and the following were the selection of music:—Introductory voluntary; Coronation anthem, "*Venite,*" M. Russell; "*Te Deum,*" Jackson; "*Jubilate,*" Humphreys; Psalm 119, Messiah anthem, "*I'll wash my hands in innocence.*"

The Rev. gentlemen who officiated were the Incumbent, Mr. Landor, who preached from the first epistle of Peter, second chapter and ninth verse, " Ye are a chosen people," &c. Also, Rev. Dr. Adamson, Rev. Mr. Lockhart, and Rev. Mr. Loucks. There was no allusion in the sermon to His Royal Highness' presence.

In the afternoon the Prince took a quiet drive round the city, passing through the beautiful grounds of Rideau Hall, the residence of —— McKay, Esq.

He leaves at eight o'clock to-morrow for Alymer, the Chats, Arnprior, Almonte, and Brockville, and expects to reach the latter place at dusk.

September 3.

His Royal Highness left Ottawa this morning at eight o'clock, a large concourse being gathered together to witness his departure.

On the road to Aylmer there were several arches, and at the village itself there were five or six with appropriate inscriptions.

Before leaving Ottawa it is right to mention that a meeting of members of Parliament was held, which was numerously attended. The Hon. George Brown was voted into the chair, and Mr. Tasse acted as secretary. It was there moved by Mr. Donald McDonald and seconded by Mr. Daost, and unanimously resolved—" That the thanks of the members of the Legislature be given to the Mayor and Corporation of the city of Ottawa, for their courteous attention during the visit of the Prince of Wales to the future capital of Canada."

'Brockville, September 3.

The Prince arrived at Brockville on September 3rd, at eight o'clock in the evening. He had been expected for several hours, a message had been received to the effect that he had left Ottawa at five o'clock, a.m.

The Mayor and Corporation, the Warden and County Council, as also other functionaries, a number of fire companies with their engines, and a crowd of some ten thousand people out of doors, besides those in the houses, had consequently been waiting, and with the most exemplary patience.

In front of the station a platform covered with a tapestry carpet had been built, and roofed in with cambric, in alternate stripes of pink and blue. The sides of the pavilion thus formed were ornamented with rosettes and with crimson, and with white lace curtains. There were six triumphal arches, chiefly of green spruce trees, in various parts of the town. The first being just below the platform, the last just above the steamboat wharf.

It was fortunate that preparations had also been made for an illumination, for it was dark when the train which bore the Prince came into the station. Lanterns and locomotive lights were placed all around the tent. The firemen set fire to their torches, of which there were at least three hundred. The inhabitants of the town lit up their windows, and night was thus almost turned to day.

On the arrival of the Prince the Mayor and Corporation of the town presented their address, as also the County Council. But what the ceremony was nobody could possibly divine. The noisy and disorderly pushed past the constables, mounted the platform steps, pressed in upon the Council and upon the Royal party themselves, and it was only after some trouble and no little difficulty that the Prince and suite were safely ushered into their carriages.

When, however, this was done, a very beautiful sight was presented. The firemen walked on each side of His Royal Highness, carrying not torches but an infinite quantity of Roman candles, and the various coloured fire and smoke of all these produced an effect much to be enjoyed, if not by the Prince, who was close by, at least by the spectators at a distance.

The Prince went through the principal streets, which, as well as the arches, were well illuminated, towards his boat the *Kingston*, where he slept, and in which he passed through the Thousand Islands for Kingston towards morning.

The following is the address of the Town Council, and his Royal Highness' reply :—

A 3

To the Most High, Puissant and Illustrious Prince Albert Edward, Prince of the United Kingdom of Great Britain and Ireland, Prince of Wales, Duke of Saxony, Prince of Cobourg and Gotha, Great Steward of Scotland, Duke of Cornwall and Rothsay, Earl of Chester, Carrick, and Dublin, Baron of Renfrew, and Lord of the Isles, K. G.

MAY IT PLEASE YOUR ROYAL HIGHNESS,—

We, the Mayor, Town Councillors, and inhabitants of the Town of Brockville, respectfully approach Your Royal Highness to tender our grateful acknowledgment of the kindness and condescension which have induced you to accept the invitation of the Canadian people to visit this country, and thus witness the universal joy which the presence of the Heir to the Crown was sure to evoke. As citizens of Brockville, a town which has shown its loyal attachment to the Crown, by perpetuating the name of the gallant general who fell fighting to maintain the integrity of the empire, we now beg to offer Your Royal Highness a heartfelt welcome to this portion of the wide spread dominion of our Sovereign, and to assure you that the same sentiments of attachment to the British soil which prompted the first settlers in this place to seek here an asylum from a hostile country, at the sacrifice of all they possessed, still animate their descendants. We beg Your Royal Highness to believe that the enthusiasm which renders your tour through this province one triumphant progress, does not wholly arise from laudable gratification, that the vast resources of the most important colony of the empire are seen by our future monarch, nor yet by temporary excitement caused by an unprecedented event. It is the expression of the deep-seated affection for the Crown and constitution of the United Kingdom which constrains us still to call the old country our home. It shall be our earnest prayer that your Royal Highness may long live to adorn the lofty position which you so worthily fill, and that the colonists of the empire may be enabled hereafter to feel towards their King the same emotions of loyalty and affection with which the virtuous and wise government of your royal mother is spoken of throughout that great kingdom over which she providentially reigns.

(Signed) WM. FITZSIMMONS, Mayor.

The Prince delivered the following reply:

GENTLEMEN,—I thank you sincerely for the address which you have presented to me. In the Queen's name I acknowledge the expressions of your loyalty to her crown and person, and for myself I am grateful to you for the welcome to your neighbourhood.

No reply was given to the County Council's address.

September 4.

The Prince was so much pleased with his reception in Brockville that he withdrew the short and merely formal reply returned on the previous evening, and, through the Duke of Newcastle, replaced it with the following, the Duke stating that the short reply was insufficient to express His Royal Highness' satisfaction at the reception accorded him by the people of Brockville:

GENTLEMEN,—I am deeply touched by the cordiality and warmth of feeling with which I have been welcomed to the town. For your address I thank you, and heartily appreciate the sentiments of attachment to your Sovereign and her empire which you have expressed. The name of your town recalls the memory of a brave man, and of brave deeds in times now happily past; may such men never be wanting to you, but may their services long remain uncalled for. I never doubted that the well known loyalty of this people would ensure to me a kind reception amongst you; but day after day convinces me that I have not fully estimated the strength and ardour of Canadian patriotism. Be assured I shall not soon forget the scene of this evening.

The Prince of Wales left Brockville on Tuesday morning, September the 4th. He was attended for some distance up the river by a fleet of small yachts, and arrived off Kingston shortly after three o'clock.

Five or six river and lake steamers with crowds of passengers and bands of music had gone off to meet and come back with him.

The Volunteer Rifles of Kingston were drawn up in line to receive him, also a battery of Volunteer Artillery.

A number of ladies and gentlemen having paid their half-dollars, were gathered together on the market battery platform, where the ornamental cupola was erected, under which the city address was to be presented.

As the *Kingston* came into the harbour the batteries saluted, and the Prince disappointed those who expected to see him, for he did not land, although it was difficult to narrate the exact facts which led to such an untoward event without making some errors.

The following information was given with a desire to be scrupulously exact. Some time since when it became known that the Orange Society intended turning out on the arrival of the Prince, a number of Roman Catholics met together in the College Building, and passed a series of resolutions containing remonstrances against the proposed course of the Orangemen, which were forwarded to the Duke of Newcastle. Letters were received from the Governor-General and from the Duke. The latter stated that the Prince would not land in any place where there were party demonstrations.

In the morning the Mayor of Kingston, Mr. Strange, went down the river several miles to meet the royal party, and further confer upon the subject. He had, of course, to tell them the facts, which were that two orange arches were erected on Princess street, the chief thoroughfare of Kingston, the principal of which was covered with Orange calico bearing the inscriptions : " Our God, our Country and our Queen, 1860," "The Gloriou Revolution of 1688,"—" Walker, Murray, Mitchell, Burns and Baker." On the reverse were the medallions of Garibaldi and the Prince of Wales; the former having the circumscription, "Garibaldi, 1860," the latter, " The Faith of my Forefathers and Mine." Above the arch were two flags, one with "1688—No Surrender—1690." The other with a burning bush upon it, and the words—" Ever burning but never consumed." The whole was surmounted with the Ark, a Cherubim, a Crown, a Bible, &c.

In addition to this his Worship had to say that a procession of Orangemen, half a mile long, with robes or badges, were awaiting His Royal Highness at the landing place.

The Duke of Newcastle hereupon told the Mayor that His Royal Highness could not land at present, but that he would give the people until nine o'clock on the following morning to know whether their partisan display could not be done away with. He also informed his Worship that if the Corporation should feel disposed to present their address on board the boat, the Prince would be happy to receive it.

The Mayor came ashore at 4 o'clock, and at once proceeded to the Council Chamber, where he laid before the Corporation the sentiments expressed by the Duke.

A debate at once arose which will appear hereafter.

While this debate was proceeding the *Kingston* steamer was cruising up and down the beautiful bay, and afterwards the winds increasing so that the motion of the waves was decidedly uncomfortable, she dropped down under the lee of one of the islands and lay there sheltered.

Another steamer was chartered, and proceeding to Alwington House and Morton Wood, took on board the dinners which had there been prepared and carried every thing on board the *Kingston*

The Prince left for Belleville at three o'clock.

Belleville, September 5.

The town of Belleville was very prettily decorated indeed, and several handsome arches were erected. That put up by the Orangemen had no orange colours upon it, and no orange flags or emblems. Mayor said he felt sure there would be no party demonstration made. There was a meeting of the Orange Lodges, to determine what course should be pursued. The most influential ladies of the town who had been getting up the decorations, petitioned the County Master to prevent steps being taken to hinder the Prince from landing, another petition for the same purpose was also circulated. The people said that but for outside influence from Kingston, every thing would have been harmonious.

The *Bowmanville* did not start from Kingston for Belleville, but pursued her way from Prescott.

The Prince was expected at Belleville the following afternoon. The Orange excitement abated since morning. They erected an arch; but no party decorations were yet on it. It was uncertain whether they would give up the right to walk in procession; probably they might adopt the action of the Orangemen in Toronto. The town was finely decorated, and otherwise the greatest enthusiasm prevailed.

Orders were issued all over the country to bring Orangemen together. The difficulties with the Belleville Orangemen would have been easily settled if the interference of outsiders had not prevented it. A lodge meeting was held. The question was what to do with the Orangemen who would come there. The requisition to the Orange Society was not largely signed, people disdaining to ask any thing of them.

The Prince arrived shortly afterwards The *Kingston* anchored one hundred yards off the wharf. Bonfires were lighted, church bells were ringing, and numbers in boats cheered His Royal Highness. It took people rather by surprise, and they were not quite prepared. It was rumoured he would land at ten o'clock, a.m. There was nothing further about the Orange Society.

September 6.

As no steamer save the *Kingston* came up the bay the previous night, it was hoped that the Orangemen did not intend to carry out the threat made in Kingston. The whole people of Belleville, save those in connexion with the Order, and a few supporters of Benjamin, were sincerely opposed to these demonstrations.

They wished the Prince to land upon even terms, and all the influence at command was brought to bear upon the address. It was therefore with the greatest satisfaction, that late at night they heard the announcement that the Orangemen had agreed so far to compromise matters, that they consented to stand by the arch they erected, and that they would not stir from it. The Prince might go another road if he so elected.

Still the fear subsisted that the outsiders who were expected to arrive would reverse this decision, and it was therefore with by no means a large amount of confidence that the people of Belleville sought their beds that night. Early in the morning their dearly cherished hopes were crushed by the appearance of the Kingston Lodge, with the man Anderson at their head, parading the streets with fife and drum, flying colours and dusty scarfs.

Shortly after other lodges arrived, and were also in the streets. Still the arch remained minus any particularly obnoxious matter until about half an hour afterwards, when it became apparent that outsiders had carried the day, and Orange colours, bearing Orange mottoes, were elevated.

It was really pitiable to see the disappointment of the people of Belleville. In no place which the Prince had yet visited, of equal size to this, had decorations been so numerous or in such excellent taste. Ten arches were erected, all of a very large size, richly ornamented with garlands of flowers and banners, contributed principally by the ladies of the town, who had been working night and day together. There was scarcely a house which was not ornamented.

The windows had been taken out and the frames covered with flowers, evergreens and ribbons. Every verandah was decorated, and the view along the streets was hidden by the flags which were hung from roof to roof. Thousands of farmers poured into town, some of them having come from a great distance, necessitating travel all night long. Many were on horseback, but the greater number in the largest waggons they possessed, having brought their wives and daughters, and large piles of provisions with them.

They, for the most part, arrived in ignorance of the state of affairs, but bad news soon spread, and though the sun was bright, though the gilded crowns, many-coloured flowers and flags, gave an air of gaity to the place, yet such a quantity of sullen, discontented faces never before was witnessed.

Meanwhile the Orange bands played, and each succesive arrival was hailed by the men with shouts and a more vigorous application of the drum-sticks. The people of Belleville were chafing with suppressed rage.

They knew that the Prince would not land. They counted the hours and the money they spent in making preparations. They looked down their streets, saw their arches and flags, and, if they knew how, would have speedily altered the condition of things. But what were they to do?

9.30 A.M.—The game was over. The Mayor had made a proposition to the Duke of Newcastle that the Prince should land on the wharf and receive addresses from such of the citizens as chose to appear there without party decorations, and His Worship would have issued a proclamation calling upon all loyal citizens to wait upon His Royal Highness, but the compromise was refused.

His Worship then returned, and the *Kingston* left the harbour about half-past nine o'clock.

In the telegraphic reports forwarded from Belleville mention was made of the extensive and beautiful decorations of the town. The limited time at disposal did not allow a note of the many details, but there were a few objects so striking that they deserve particular mention. The first was the arch of Mr. Lewis Wallbridge, M. P. P., of a very large size and very excellent design, bearing the motto—"To Virtue's dynasty a country grateful." Messrs. R. and R. S. Patterson had erected an arch most novel in design, but one which looked very well. Of its size some idea may be formed when stated that it was surmounted by a huge threshing machine, to the left of which stood a fanning mill. Hanging immediately below was a reaping machine and two cultivators. The pillars of the arch were all hung with smaller agricultural instruments; and further decorated with evergreens intermixed with which were sheaves of wheat and other grain. At the corner of Front and Main streets was the store of Mr. G. J. Brown, the roof of which was ornamented also with agricultural implements. In the centre was a large crown, surmounted by a Prince of Wales feather, skilfully made out of different kinds of grain. On either side were reaping machines, straw cutters, Scotch ploughs, jags, harrows, &c. In front of the foundry, belonging to the same manufacturer, was a large pair of scales; a Scotch plough on one side being balanced by grain on the other. Pillars made of potash kettles, piled one above another, all decorated with spruce, completed the arrangements. By this street the beautiful little river Moira flows. Many of the trees along its banks were hung with banners; and all the houses on the opposite side had their quantum of blue ribbons, flags and garlands. The Prince was expected to have passed this way to the Grand Trunk station. But, as all know, he did not. Had he done so, what a fair escort he would have had! For the past three or four months the ladies in and around the town had been learning to ride. Side-saddles, flowing robes, gay housings had been purchased, and it was the intention of their owners to accompany his Royal Highness to the station. Nothing was wanting to enable them to carry their determination into effect but the presence of the Prince. How bitterly they were disappointed none can understand save those who saw them after an hour's exposure to a hot sun and suffocating dust, riding dejectedly homewards.

September 7th.

What would be the result of the visit to Cobourg could not be told. It was sadly feared that a repetition of the scenes of Kingston and Belleville would be enacted, but expectations were happily disappointed. The station was richly decorated, as it was believed that the Prince would come by rail, not by water. A number of children were assembled, and "God save the Queen" was sung, under the impression that the Prince had arrived. It was a great pity that he did not travel so far by rail. On both sides of the line, all the way from Belleville to Cobourg, far as the eye could see, were fields glorious in golden grain. The reaping machines were at work; the labourers were all engaged in gathering up the fruits of the earth. Not since he had left England had he seen an agricultural country which could at all approach it in fertility, or excellent cultivation. Here and there truly were fields of wheat half cut, with the grain lying upon the earth; but asking for what reason, were told that the farmer and his men had thus left their crops while they went to Belleville, hoping that they might there see the Prince.

Once in Cobourg town, could be studied the programme with some idea that it would be carried out. Upon the walls were placards running thus:—"By telegraph to Sheriff Fortune. Your telegraph has given me the greatest satisfaction. H. R. H. will get to Cobourg as early as possible. Go on with your arrangements for the reception and ball most enthusiastically. Sidney Smith." The request was obeyed. The preparations for the reception and ball were proceeded with enthusiastically. Never did people work harder or better. Flags were hung out of windows; additional garlands placed over doorways. The final spruce boughs were nailed up; the ball dress was looked at with confidence; the kid gloves with hope. Cabs were engaged to take the ladies to the ball, "for certain," and the jarveys got proportionately saucey and extortionate. News was brought that a steamer was coming, and all rushed down to the wharf, although the said steamer was going towards the east instead of the west. In short, all Cobourg was in a state of most intense, joyous excitement. The spirits of the people had been depressed; and they then experienced a revulsion. The Prince was coming, every thing was going right, the ball would be honoured by H. R. H.'s presence, and all the enthusiastic anticipations of the last few months amply verified.

When darkness closed in, the town was illuminated; an attribute to royalty in which almost every one joined. The principal streets, King and Division streets, looked exceedingly well. The magnificent Town Hall was one blaze of light. No breath of wind was stirring, and as the moon was but dimly visible in the clouded vault above, the gas burned brilliantly and looked well too. Prince's plumes, stars, crowns and coronets, of every possible and impossible shapes, glittered every where. All the public buildings were illuminated—the Court House, Post Office, and the banks. Awnings in front of the shops were still allowed by the municipal authorities, and the pillars supporting these, besides being richly decorated with flowers, were hung with thousands of·Chinese lamps, producing an admirable effect. But the Prince had not come, and these things were but little noticed. The people gathered together to the east of the city upon the beach, or at any spots from which an extensive view of the lake could be obtained. These stood, gazing into the far distance, striving to penetrate the darkness beyond. At last the lights of a steamer were seen coming up to the port. The news spread as by lightning through the city, all hastened to gather themselves together in the streets through which His Royal Highness would pass. The artillery hurried down to the wharf, the Cobourg cavalry followed suit, and in a few moments the steady tread of the Volunteer Rifles was heard, making their way through the loyal throng. Then came the St. Andrew's Society, numbering two hundred men. The Native Canadians also were there; and they bore, as will shortly be seen, an important part in the evening's proceedings. In a very few moments every thing was ready to receive the Prince.

But he did not land so soon as was expected. The *Kingston* was moored to the wharf amid the enthusiastic shouts of the thousands present. In fact it was an exceedingly difficult matter to get an answer from any one in Cobourg in the morning, the folks were all so hoarse with hurrahing, they could not speak. The first important personage seen was Sidney Smith. He came forward and made a speech to the people to this effect—that a scientific man had pronounced the floor of the ball-room unsafe, and two gentlemen had been dispatched to examine it before the Prince went there. The real state of the case, was this. The Cobourg Town Hall was only completed a few days before, and the ball-room had consequently never been used. Other places in which His Royal Highness had danced had been tried by experience, except in the case of the Montreal ball-room, which was specially examined and reported upon. It was, therefore, considered advisable that before the Prince landed the Cobourg ball-room should also be examined, and Col. Eardley Wilmot with Mr. Trebenski, of the Grand Trunk, were despatched for that purpose. Their report was adverse. They did not think the floor—forty-five feet square, was strong enough to support the number of dancers expected. A number of cedar posts were accordingly placed underneath, and the room was thus beyond doubt made secure. Mr. Kivas Tully, of Toronto, was the architect of the building, and will, doubtless, have a word to say upon the subject. Folks there think that the floor was enough for anybody but the Prince. But, of course, they know nothing about the matter.

Every thing being ready, His Royal Highness was permitted to land. His carriage was brought up to the wharf drawn by horses; it was taken from them and drawn by men. A mistake was made in saying the St. Andrew's Society was the only society present. The Native Canadians were there, each one with a silver maple leaf upon his left breast. They took the horses from the carriage, and by means of ropes they had brought with them, drew it to the Town Hall. The scene was one of intense enthusiasm. The crowd was very large, and as the Prince was drawn through their midst they did their utmost by loudest shouts to testify their joy at his presence. The scene was very remarkable. The torches and the Chinese lamps were numerous, and for the most part concentrated within a limited space. But yet upon the edge of the crowd, far away, other lights glimmered; moving to and fro as the people themselves wavered, and giving an idea of vastness which might otherwise have been wanting. The wharf at which the *Kingston* lay is at the foot of Division street. Across it runs King street, and this junction had been selected as the spot whereon to erect one of the most tasteful ornaments the Prince had met with in his peregrinations. From a tall pillar, reaching as high as the house tops in the centre of the square, were suspended festoons of coloured drapery, attached to posts at each corner of the streets, so that a sort of open pavilion was formed, which being hung with different coloured lamps, and set off with transparencies, was the feature in the illuminations. Turning to the left His Royal Highness soon found himself on the elevated platform in front of the Town Hall. The finest of the buildings blazed with gas; the houses facing it were one mass of light. Here were also seats capable of holding comfortably twelve hundred persons. But on occasions like this —like the omnibuses and the cabs—about twice as many as was legitimate managed to crush in. Between this platform and that upon which the Prince stood, were people who chose to stand and take their squeeze free of charge; so that there was a sort of amphitheatre, near the centre of which stood His Royal Highness and attendant gentlemen. In the day time, many people were afraid to cheer lustily, lest they should attract the attention of their matter-of-fact neighbours, and be laughed at for too great enthusiam. The Cobourg folks, when countenances could be less easily discerned, had no fear of this. They rang out their huzzas loudly and freely, and kept up the amusement until sheer exhaustion compelled them to desist. Then the addresses were presented. There were a great lot of them—more, than can be enumerated. However, here are some. The address of the Mayor and Corporation of Cobourg; of the County council of Northumberland; of the Magistrates; of Victoria College; of Brighton Township Council; of Brighton Village Council, and of St. Andrew's Society, were all responded to by His Royal Highness, who went to the labour of listening and replying with characteristic good grace. Very nearly an hour was occupied with these formalities; at the end of which the Prince made his final bow to the outsiders, and retired within the building. As he went, three cheers were given for the Queen; three for His Royal Highness and for the Governor-General. In a telegraph forwarded you previously, the Prince intimated a wish that the

President of the St. Andrew's Society should be presented to him before the ball commenced. When the presentation was made his Royal Highness said:—"I thank you very much, President Morgan." General Bruce afterwads speaking to the President, said,—"I am very proud of the appearance my countrymen made upon the wharf to-day." The Duke of Newcastle also paid the St. Andrew's Society a similar compliment—at all of which the Scotchmen of Cobourg were highly proud.

The interior of the ball-room presented by no means a dangerous appearance, except to bachelors. How that came about, all who have seen the ladies of Cobourg may easily guess. The walls were white; the ceiling was coloured very brilliantly, but not in good taste—green and yellow being the most prominent hues. The room was nicely lighted, however, and the blue and scarlet drapery hung against the walls, together with the royal chairs with the red seats provided for the use of the company, gave a handsome appearance to the whole. Placed at the doors were members of the Cobourg Cavalry, dressed in their scarlet coats and bright brass hemlets, holding drawn swords ready to "do to the death" any intruder. Under these circumstances the ball began.

Cobourg is not a big place, that all know; but there are some big people in it, and proportionately large, therefore, were discussions on the relative merits of the ladies with whom the Prince was to dance. Many names were guessed at, and the good and bad qualities of the fair owners so far as known canvassed. But as all the guesses were wrong, it was by no means necessary that the said names of the confident and disappointed expectants should be published. Rather let a veil be thrown over their disappointment, and the following list of those who did dance with the Prince carefully scanned. Here it is—No. 1, Miss Beatty; No. 2, Miss Ewart; No. 3, Mrs. Reid; No. 4, Miss Fortune; No. 5, Miss Pringle; No. 6, Mrs. S. Smith; No. 7, Miss J. Daintry; No. 8, Miss Powell, of Niagara; No. 9, Miss Burnham; No. 10, Miss Bennett, No. 11, Mrs. Cubitt; No. 12, Miss Hall; No. 13, Miss M. Boswell; No. 14, Miss Gaer; No. 15, Miss Barron. Through these dances, with the supper in the middle, His Royal Highness did not get away until three o'clock in the morning, when he drove off to the Hon. Sidney Smith's, and there slept.

The dressing rooms set apart for His Royal Highness and the Duke of Newcastle, in the Town Hall, were most beautifully fitted up by Mrs. Wheeler, with fine furniture belonging to her own house. A large quantity of flowers for the occasion were supplied by Mr. Bernard and Mrs. Cockburn.

The Prince expressed himself highly delighted with the whole of the arrangements, which, for so small a place as Cobourg, were pronounced superb by His Royal Highness and suite.

The Prince was in plain citizen's dress, and was much pleased at being able to move about freely without being stared at or inconvenienced.

He opened the ball with the Mayor's daughter, Miss Beatty, as already mentioned.

Several retiring-rooms were arranged for His Royal Highness' suite, and for the general public.

The Prince left Cobourg in the morning at half-past nine, being accompanied from Mr. Smith's house to the railway station by an immense assemblage of people. As the special train started the Volunteer Artillery fired a salute, and the cheers from the people were very enthusiastic.

Arrived at Rice Lake, the Royal party embarked on the little steamer *Otonabee*, and, standing under the awning made of spruce and cedar boughs, crossed it. The train went over the bridge, which is three miles long.

The reason of the Prince going by steamer was not that the bridge was unsafe, for it had been much strengthened of late; but, that he might have a good view of the fir-covered islands, which picturesquely dot the lake, and also of the beds of wild rice in blossom, from which it derives its name. On the north side of the lake a sort of an arch had been erected by the Mississaga tribe of Indians, who stood by the landing place, fired guns as the Prince approached, and endeavoured to play "God Save the Queen," with their brass band, and their chief, Paudosh, who is 100 years old, presented an address to His Royal Highness signed with both his English name and Indian, "Totem;" then a number of birch bark baskets filled with Indian work, and having labels with the names of the squaws who had made them, were given to the Prince, and in the midst of a parting volley the royal train moved away.

The reception at Peterboro' was a very fine one in almost every way. The train drew up, so that from the Prince's car there was a fine view of the street along which the procession was arranged, and up which the party passed, as soon as they had taken their seats on the carriages set apart for that purpose. They went through the principal streets of the town, every one of which was handsomely decorated with arches, flags, and evergreens, to a platform below the court house. There the City and County Councils presented their addresses, to which gracious replies were returned. The place was well chosen, for the green sward, shaded by fine trees, sloped upwards from it, so that the six or seven thousand people who were assembled had a good view of His Royal Highness.

Leaving this, the party went to the Port Hope Railway station, passing under a lumber arch on the way made of rough boards only, on the crest of which a hundred red-shirted lumbermen were standing, and shouting welcome to the Prince.

Some of the carriage horses took fright at the unusual display, and some confusion and a little injury to a few of the carriages resulted.

A curious incident occurred on the way. Some ultra-enthusiastic man who was running at the side of the Prince's carriage put out his hand to His Royal Highness, which the Prince, in the fulness of his good nature, took without reflection and shook heartily. The man, elated by the honour, told his comrades of his good fortune. They at once rushed forward, and for several minutes the Prince was busily engaged in shaking hands with all who came. Soon, however, whether the court doctor told him his shoulder was in danger of dislocation or not, he turned towards the other side, and this demonstration closed. Not so, however, the cheers of the crowd, the throwing of boquets by the ladies at the windows, and other loyal displays of enthusiasm. The whole party were much pleased with Peterboro'.

The train in which the Prince was carried to Port Hope consisted of three cars, the first of which was ventilated on the system of Mr. Ruttan, who, in his uniform of Military Colonel, had accompanied the party from Cobourg.

Shortly after the start, Lord Lyons entered the car, and finding the atmosphere pleasant, requested Sheriff Ruttan to explain its *modus operandi*. This done, he constituted himself ambassador extraordinary to H. R. H., who examined the system with great attention.

Particular mention must be made of two arches in Cobourg. One was erected by the Grammar School boys and their head master, Mr. Barron, with whose daughter—as may be seen by referring to the list—His Royal Highness danced. It was of a very handsome design, and bore the following mottoes:— "Hoc olim meminesse juvabid." "Sensere quid meus, rite quid indoles, Nutrita faustis sub Penetralibus posset." "Juque dum procedis, Io triumphe." The other arch was erected by Mr. Highet. It was ornamented with ploughs, rakes, hoes, and spades, and trimmed off with wheat, pumpkins, squashes, and other fruits of the soil, making altogether a creditable appearance. Other decorations in the loyal town of Cobourg, equally as worthy of note must, from the little time available for their examination, be passed by. Every man did his best to add to the joyfulness of the occasion, and their efforts were crowned with the most complete success as it was possible to desire.

Friday, the 7th day of September, in the year of our Lord, one thousand eight hundred and sixty, will be a day long remembered by the inhabitants of Port Hope. On that day His Royal Highness the Prince of Wales, the Heir Apparent to the British Crown, visited the town, and partook of its hospitality. Before giving an account of his reception, we will glance briefly at the preparations that were made, the decorations, arches, &c.

Of all the towns in Canada which the Prince has visited, less time was spent in Port Hope than in any other. It was not definitely known until the afternoon of Saturday, the 1st inst., that His Royal Highness would honour Port Hope with his presence. When this point became settled the various committees at once commenced to work in good earnest. Not a blow, however, was struck on any af the arches until Monday afternoon, the 2nd inst., the decoration of the town was thus all accomplished in the incredibly short space of less than four days.

The decoration Committee decided that four triumphal arches should be erected on a scale in keeping with the occasion. Every man in town who could handle a saw, or drive a nail, or wield a "pick," was at once pressed into service, and from Monday afternoon until Friday at ten o'clock the work went rapidly and noisily on. Carts were hurrying hither and thither, hauling boards, scantling, poles, nails, &c.; and trains on the Port Hope, Lindsay, and Beaverton Railway came in at frequent intervals, bringing whole forests of evergreens—hemlock, spruce, cedar and pine trees of small growth, for planting along the streets, and around the market square. The ladies worked day and night in the market buildings, making wreaths of evergreens and festoons of flowers, and to their industry and skill the fine appearance of the decorations was in a great measure attributable.

The dais on which his Royal Highness received and replied to the address presented by the Mayor on behalf of the inhabitants of the town, was erected in the market square, in rear of the Town Hall. It was covered with crimson cloth, and otherwise tastefully decorated. From the dais to the track of the Lindsay Railway ran a platform about eight feet wide, which was handsomely carpeted, and fringed with rows of evergreen. Along the platform, which is now known as the Prince's Walk, His Royal Highness passed to his car when taking his departure.

The Town Hall, which was converted into a dining-room. was beautifully decorated. Against the centre of the east wall was a crown of crimson, green, and gold, in which glistened jewels in the shape of snow-drops and berries of the mountain ash. It was an exquisite ornament. The walls were hung with wreaths of evergreen and festoons of flowers, and so gay and brilliant did the room appear that the citizens hardly recognised the Hall in which they had so often met to listen to eloquence and song.

The Mayor's office was furnished as a dressing-room for the Prince, and fit for any Prince it was. The carpet and toilet set were supplied by Mr. Ralph Jones; the chairs by Mr. Faser; a magnificent consol etagierre, and tables by Mr. W. Russell. Mr. Russell's furniture was for sale, and any gentleman desirous of placing in his house what was a few hours at the disposal of His Royal Highness had an opportunity of doing so.

The Bank of Upper Canada was handsomely decorated. Wreaths of evergreen and festoons of flowers were arranged with admirable taste on the balconies; over the principal entrance the Prince's plume stood out in bold relief; and the British coat of arms appeared on the top of the cornice; while from a flagstaff in

A 5

the centre of the roof a Royal Ensign fell in many a graceful fold. The fronts of the buildings on each side of Walton street were decorated with evergreens, streamers of every colour, and the royal arms. Even as far up as Pino street the enthusiastic inhabitants beautified their houses.

Early on Friday morning, the 7th September, 1860, the inhabitants of the townships north, east, and west of Port Hope began to pour into town. The farmer left his field, wherein the harvest was ready even unto the sickle, and, harnessing up Dobbin, brought wife, sons and daughters to see a scion of royalty—a Prince who in the order of events will, in all probability, rule over an empire on which it is alleged, and with truth, that the sun never sets. By ten o'clock the streets were thronged—and still they came. At twelve o'clock the sidewalks from Queen street to the Walton street railway crossing were densely packed; and the roofs of the houses, and every fence from which a view of where the Prince was expected to alight from the cars could be obtained by the adventurous climber were taken possession of. There was great scrambling for "good places." The crowd generally "went in on muscle," and the best man or the most stalwart woman had of course the best of it. Between the market building and the railway track a space had been enclosed by a fence. Inside this enclosure the public were informed they could stand at a quarter of a dollar a head; while for an extra twenty-five cents a comfortable seat, commanding a good view of the dais on which His Royal Highness was to figure, could be obtained. The fifty cent seats, as well as a number of dollar chairs on a platform still nigher the dais, were soon filled; but the twenty-five cent *standing* places were a drug in the market. They wouldn't sell nohow. Somehow or other the people were foolish enough to believe that it was just as easy to stand outside the fence as inside. And they were right. So several thousand persons of all ages, classes, creeds and nations anxiously stood and waited, broiling in the hot sun, for the coming of the Prince.

About 11 o'clock Col. Jackson's field battery arrived in town. This is a Kingston Volunteer Artillery Company. Every inch the soldier looked Col. Jackson. And a fine looking, well-drilled, able-bodied, lot of men he commands. At twelve o'clock Col.

Jackson got his company into marching order on the market square. The word was given "to mount," and instantaneously, like "Clan Alpine warriors true," every man was in the saddle or on the guns. At the word "forward," the company dashed off up Queen street, at a rapid pace; the officers and soldiers in their uniforms of blue, red and gold, and the rumbling of the 9 and 24 pounders, reminded one very forcibly that swords were not beaten into ploughshares, or spears into pruning hooks. There was something in the military line entirely new to Port Hope, and of course attracted great attention. Boys and young men fired with a sudden ardour to become heroes, charged after the flying brigade, until between horses, guns, boys, and ardent young men, a cloud of dust was raised that choked those who stood open-mouthed gazing at the unwonted sight, and played sad havoc with the ribbons and curls of many a rustic damsel.

The Royal visitor was then conducted up-stairs to the Town Hall, where he and suite, the members of the Counties Council, Col. Jackson and officers, the representatives of the press, Mr. Sheriff Fortune, and a number of Cobourg gentlemen, and nearly two hundred gentlemen of Port Hope and vicinity, partook of a luncheon that had been provided for the occasion. The Prince occupied a seat at an elevated table, and under the crown alluded to in another place. On either side of him were the Duke of Newcastle, Earl St. Germains, the Governor-General, Lord Lyons, James Scott, Esq., Mayor of Port Hope, &c., &c. The lunch was an excellent one, got up in the best style, and the distinguished visitors evidently relished it amazingly. They were pleased to express their satisfaction in flattering terms. The toasts proposed and drank with deafening cheers were, "The Queen" and "His Royal Highness the Prince of Wales."

There was of course a great curiosity manifested to see the Prince. The crowd followed his carriage from the mechanics' arch, under which he left the train, to the Town Hall. Many people were sadly disappointed in his appearance. They expected to see a tall, straight, handsome and brilliantly-dressed young man, and not the modest, unassuming, and plainly-clad youth, who moved in their presence as the Prince of Wales. One elderly dame from one of the back townships gave vent to her disappointment by exclaiming, "Why he's only like other boys, after all." His Royal Highness wore a suit of grey cloth, and white hat, very like the hat which a well-known J. P. of Port Hope wears. Had he appeared dressed as a colonel of the army, or something of the sort, the people would have been more deeply impressed with the exalted position of princes.

The arrival and departure from Whitby was marked by the same domonstrations of ovation, but admitted of no delay, as the Prince and suite passed quickly from the well appointed barouche which had been previously provided for his especial use by the Corporation of Whitby.

His progress to Toronto outstripped his escort of lake steamers.

The Prince among us.

The seventh day of September, 1860, will long be cherished as the brightest day in the annals of Upper Canada. Many a year hence it will be told that on that day the Heir Apparent to the British throne made his public entry into the chief city of the Western Province, and received a welcome surpassing in magnificence and enthusiasm all the public ovations ever before witnessed in the New World. Elsewhere a full description will be given of the proceedings of the day; but no pen could adequately describe the unbounded enthusiasm of the joyous multitudes assembled to greet their future Sovereign on the banks of Lake Ontario. Nor will any one who witnessed it ever recall without thrilling delight the magnificent spectacle presented, when the Prince stepped from his vessel and took his seat on the throne, amid the thundering cheers of the vast concourse piled up in the noble amphitheatre around him.

The illumination of the city at night was a very grand sight—far surpassing, it is believed, any similar demonstration ever witnessed on this continent. Particular buildings may have been illuminated elsewhere on a grander scale, but as a whole it is doubted if the display of that night was ever excelled in America in extent, variety, and brilliancy of decoration. The Normal School, Osgood Hall, and the Romain buildings were magnificently decorated; and the *Globe* buildings, the St. Lawrence Hall, the Edinburgh Assurance Company, the St. Nicholas Restaurant, and scores of other buildings were illuminated in splendid style.

Many of the arches erected at the prominent points of the city were noble designs, and executed with a degree of artistic taste which must have astonished the illustrious guests who passed under them. The arch erected on the crest of the amphitheatre, at the landing, will be a lasting monument to the fame of its designer, Mr. Storm. Fine as were the arches in Quebec, Ottawa, and Montreal, the finest of them could not for a moment enter into competition with it.

As a whole, the pageant was a magnificent triumph. Toronto nobly maintained the credit of Upper Canada.

The great event is over. The prince arrived and received a welcome which in spirit and enthusiasm had not been equalled in any place which His Royal Highness had hitherto visited. The fears of the timid were set at rest; the Prince slept soundly in his bed at the Government House, uninjured by arch or ribbon. Not a word, not a sound, marred the harmony of the time. The people of Toronto of all classes knew how to discriminate between their duty to their princely guest and the assertion of their political rights as Canadians, and have suffered no word of complaint to reach his ears. They thought of nothing but their eagerness to show their devotion to their Sovereign, and her representative.

The reception of the Prince in the amphitheatre after his landing was as grand a sight as ever met human eyes or gladdened a feeling heart. The decorations of the buildings were described before, but must be done again in order to do justice to the occasion. Our readers who know Toronto are aware that what is called the esplanade is a flat piece of land lying between the edge of the bay and the high bank along which Front-street runs. A little wharf was run out in the front of the esplanade for the *Kingston* to touch at. The railway track lies behind, and then comes a platform with a canopy, many-coloured and tasteful in design, on which stood three chairs, one in the centre, of crimson and gold, for the Prince, the others for the Duke of Newcastle and Sir Edmund Head. Let us take our stand, before the Prince comes, under the canopy and look about us. Immediately in front, on the level ground, stood Colonel Denison's troop of Volunteer Cavalry, and very soldier-like they looked in their uniforms of blue and silver. A few yards behind them the amphitheatre of seats began.

At the base were the children of the Common and Sabbath Schools, marshalled by the teachers, dressed in their best, and well-dressed too. They had been trained in the hand-clapping exercise, and every now and again burst forth with a noise which startled the ear, the tiny hands keeping time with the shrill yet musical voices. Above them, tier beyond tier, rose the seats of the amphitheatre, filled with the citizens and their families, gaily dressed—a large majority of them ladies. If this were all it would have been a grand sight, but at the upper end of the amphitheatre a broad road led up the esplanade, and there were tiers of seats on each side, while at the top rose the superb arch which excited so much admiration. On each side of it, along the line of Front street, stretched streams of people, every corner from which a view could be obtained being occupied. Never before, in Canada at least, had so many people been grouped together in so favourable a position for seeing and being seen.

The hour of arrival was supposed to be five o'clock, but long before that time the greater part of the amphitheatre was filled. He left Port Hope at a little after three o'clock, in a special train for Whitby. The clouds which had been lowering all the afternoon began to shed some gentle drops of rain. The scene was magnificent; there was much to please the eye and ear, and even the ladies bore with patience the partial wetting. By and by the rain ceased; the clouds with their dull gray served to bring out in strong relief the gay colours of the amphitheatre and arch.

At six o'clock the *Kingston* was seen from the platform outside the island, and at half-past six approached the landing-place, accompanied by the *New York*, the *Cataract*, the *Zimmerman*, and the *Peerless*, all crowded with excursionists, who had gone down the lake to meet the approaching visitor. The *Fire-Fly* came through the eastern channel, and was soon close to the landing place. The other island steamer was near, and a number of yachts with flags displayed lay at their moorings, while numerous row-boats darted about the neighbourhood of the wharf. The water as well as the land was gay.

As the *Kingston* approached the Royal party were visible on the fore promenade deck, the Prince, a conspicuous object, with the Duke of Newcastle and Sir Edmund Head by his side, and a gay group of red and blue coats around him. Many of the gentlemen admitted to the platform, the Judges, Clergy of all denominations, Members of Parliament, the Mayor and Council with their officers, approached the landing cheering and waving their hats. It was the signal for an outburst of applause from the great multitude behind, such as was never heard before. Words cannot describe that vast volume of sound, thrilling, soul-stirring, heart-heaving. It carried everybody before it in a tempest of enthusiasm. A sailor dressed in the naval style threw the landing rope, the gangway was pushed out, the Prince stepped quickly ashore, and, surrounded by his staff, accompanied by the Mayor, walked rapidly up the wharf. Again the shout of applause rang out, and was taken up again and again as the Prince appeared on the platform. The vast multitude rose from their seats, the ladies waving their handkerchiefs and the gentlemen their hats, in uncontrolled enthusiasm. The light began to wane, and few save those in the immediate neighbourhood could distinguish the Prince's features. It was necessary to make speed. The Mayor and Councillors advanced, the Mayor read the address in his usual composed style, the reply was graciously given, and the Prince stood confessed the welcome guest of Toronto.

The address was as follows:

MAY IT PLEASE YOUR ROYAL HIGHNESS:

We, the Mayor, Aldermen, and Councilmen, on behalf of the citizens of Toronto, respectfully offer to your Royal Highness a most cordial welcome on your arrival in the capital of Upper Canada, and gratefully express our high appreciation of the distinguished honour which you have conferred upon us by your visit.

The annals of our youthful city present but little more than the record of improvement, steadily advancing in almost unbroken tranquillity; and the brief interruptions of its peaceful progress are now chiefly worthy of notice, as evincing an early attachment to British connexion so strong as to stand the severe tests of fire and sword, and so illustrating the happy influences of commercial and social intercourse in uniting the combatants in by-gone feuds as good neighbours and valued friends.

The generation which saw the settler's log house succeeding to the red man's wigwam on the site of Little York has not yet wholly passed away, and yet we venture to hope that your Royal Highness will look with satisfaction on the evidence which our city presents in our streets, our railways, our private buildings, and our public institutions, of the successful results of industry and interprise, fostered by constitutional liberty, and that you will regard our provision for the relief of misery, for the diffusion of education, for the administration of justice, and for the worship of God, as manifestations of that spirit which has been mainly instrumental, under providence, in placing our Mother Country in the glorious position which she occupies amongst the nations of the earth.

We desire again most respectfully to offer our grateful thanks for the honour which your Royal Highness has been pleased to confer upon us, and happily avail ourselves of the opportunity to renew the assurance of our devoted loyalty to the Queen, under whose benignant rule we enjoy the inestimable blessings of civil and religious liberty, and to express our undoubting confidence that our rights as freemen and our interests as subjects will continue to be faithfully maintained by Her Majesty's hereditary successor, whom we now rejoice to honour as our future Sovereign.

GENTLEMEN,—I receive this address with the most lively satisfaction; and I request you to convey to the citzens whom you represent, the expressions of my gratitude for the more than hearty welcome which I have just experienced.

You will not doubt the readiness with which I undertook the duty entrusted to me by the Queen of visiting for her the British North American dominions, and now that I have arrived at this distant point of my journey, I can say with truth, that the expectations which I had formed of the pleasure and instruction to be derived from it, have been more than realized. My only regret is that the Queen has been unable herself to receive the manifestations of the generous loyalty with which you have met her representative,—a loyalty tempered and yet strengthened by the intelligent independence of the Canadian character.

You allude to the marvellous progress which a generation has witnessed on this spot. I have already been struck throughout my rapid journey by the promise of greatness and the results of energy and industry which are every where perceptible, and I feel the pride of an Englishman in the masculine qualities of my countrymen,—in the sanguine and hardy enterprise—in the fertility of conception and boldness of execution which have enabled a youthful country to outstrip many of the ancient nations of the world.

I shall rejoice to see the public institutions of which you speak with a natural satisfaction, and I doubt not that I shall perceive in them a proof, in addition to the many which have been brought under my notice, of the value of equal laws and the working of a free constitution.

Then was produced a very pretty effect. Mr. Carter, the conductor, sprang to his stand in front of the children, and forthwith rose the strains of the national anthem, given by five thousand little voices. The time was admirably kept, the sound was full and clear, and the effect thrilling in the extreme.

Gentlemen who attended the Prince from the day he landed in Newfoundland, were unanimous in their opinion that the reception was the finest thing they had yet witnessed. The Prince himself expressed his pleasure to Dr. McCaul, the Chairman of the Committee of Programme. The children having finished, the almost complete darkness which had come on showed the necessity for haste. The side gates of the amphitheatre were thrown open, and the procession, which had been grouped outside, marched in. First came the coloured men, and then the Odd Fellows, who dipped their flags in honour of the Prince as they passed him and marched up to Front street under the arch. Then came the Firemen, marching well together and cheering with a will as they came on. Next walked the Canadians, some with silver maple leaves, and others with those supplied by nature. St. George's Society came next, followed by the St. Patrick's and St. Andrew's, the last being the most numerous of the whole. These came from the east side. Then marched from the west the pupils of Upper Canada College, and after them the Professors, Graduates, and Students of the University, the dons of the College waving their caps and shouting as enthusiastically as the under-graduates, who are rather famed for their power of making a noise. The magistrates, the town council of Yorkville, and the county council followed.

The Prince's carriage with four bay horses drew up to the platform, His Royal Highness stepped in, followed by the Duke of Newcastle, the Governor, and Earl St. Germains, the cavalry escort took their places in good style, and the cortege moved slowly up the ascent.

His arrival at that time was unexpected, and no preparations had been made. The time fixed for the illumination was eight o'clock, which had not arrived. And great were the exertions to hasten the lighting up. Enough was done, however, to show the Prince the extent of the preparations made, and to give him a favourable view of King street, with its arches, gas lights, transparencies, windows filled with ladies and children, waving handkerchiefs and cheering the Prince, gentlemen vociferating, setting off rockets and Roman candles, and making as great a commotion as their means allowed. Every window was occupied, every foot of standing ground was covered with pedestrians. Men rushed beneath the feet of the horses of the escort to get a glimpse of the Prince. The people, unfortunately, could not see His Royal Highness on this his first passage through the city. On the arrival of His Royal Highness at Government House he called for Colonel Geo. Denison, commandant of the active force, who was the first person presented, and thanked him for the services of the volunteer force, especially that of the cavalry escort, who, His Royal Highness stated, discharged their duty in a very praiseworthy manner.

The night finished what the evening had so auspiciously begun. The illuminations in Toronto were more general and profuse than they were in any other place. In Montreal, on the Place d' Armes, where the banks are situated, the show was possibly finer than in any like quantity of space in Toronto, but the display throughout the city was far better there than any where else. The arches were highly praised by visitors. They were higher, and consequently more imposing, than were those of Montreal and Quebec, and of more artistic design. Comparisons are said to be odious, but it is, after all, only by comparison that a correct standard of excellence can be arrived at.

The triple arch, the most beautiful erected in Toronto, or in fact in Canada or in the Lower Provinces, according to the opinion of gentlemen well able to judge, and who have visited every city through which the Prince passed, was designed by W. G. Storm,

Esq. It was of a mixed style of architecture and beautifully proportioned. It was sixty-five feet in height from the base of the apex, and, being situated at the top of the amphitheatre and fronting the reception platform, the effect produced was brilliant in the extreme. The arch had a span of 27 feet, and rose from piers 30 feet in height. At the angles of each pier, and supporting them, were four massive columns entwined with evergreens, and with handsomely decorated foliated capitals composed of lotus leaves tastefully gilt. These columns formed the side arches, under which were festoons of evergreens with pendant boquets of flowers. In the intercolumniations were enriched archivolts surmounted by Prince of Wales' plumes in beautiful fresco work. The cornices at the springs were highly ornamented with Roman mouldings and decorated in fresco. On the summit of the piers were four handsome large vases containing beautiful bouquets of flowers. Between the vases and projecting from the piers were trophies of red, white, and blue ensigns. On the south frieze, at the top of each pier, were the words "Albert Edward," and on the reverse, the words "Victoria" and "Albert," all beautifully gilt on a rich ground. The soffit of the arch was divided into three panels containing cartoons, and was most beautifully frescoed. In the centre panel the principal figure was a portrait of His Royal Highness. At each side were two female figures holding a pennon, on which was inscribed the word "Welcome." The portrait of the Prince was surrounded with figures emblematical of the arts, sciences, literature and commerce; a shield with the date of the Prince's birth, and and on the margin "7th Sept.," the date of His Royal Highness' arrival. Within each of the side panels were beautifully-executed Prince of Wales' plumes. On the south face of the arch and fronting the reception platform was the motto in a semi-circle, "Welcome to Toronto," in gilt letters, enclosed within handsome frescoed borders. On the reverse or north side was the motto, composed also of large gilt lettering, "Hail! Royal Prince." The outer or upper rim was composed of cups, from which sprang petit flags with gilt staffs. The arch was surrounded by the arms of the Prince of Wales, ten feet in height, handsomely executed, and enclosed within a trophy of large British Ensigns partially unfolded, and presenting to the eye of the spectator a brilliant appearance. From this handsome trophy rose a large flagstaff, floating a broad pennon, on which was emblazoned the plume of His Royal Highness the Prince of Wales.

This structure, viewed either from the north, the south, the east, or the west, presented a magnificent appearance. The longer it was examined, more beauties seemed to arise out of it. All seeing something to praise in its colossal proportions, its massive columns and piers—its elegant devices, its beautifully frescoed shields and plumes, in turn called forth admiration. The only regret expressed was that in a few short weeks the beautiful pile would be among the things that were; and every one be sorry that it would not be allowed to rear its proud head to the sky, a lasting and pleasing memento of the visit of the Prince. This arch, taken as a whole, was most creditable to the architect who designed it, and to the contractors, Messrs. Worthington & Mason, who so faithfully carried out the instructions and ideas of the designer and artist. The city of Toronto might well be proud of it.

That evening the arch was tastefully and brilliantly illuminated. Two rows of variegated lamps encircled the side arches. Two rows of a similar description were placed on the entablature, and on the faces of the arch and on the main corners was a row of lamps, red, white, and blue, while the outer rim and cups were decorated and illuminated in a similar manner. The illumination was introduced in such a manner as to bring out the mouldings and other prominent parts of this fine piece of architecture.

The fireman's arch was designed by Mr. J. H. Pattison, of the city Board of Works. It was very massive, measuring nine feet by six, and covered with evergreens. It was in the Italian style of architecture, with main cornice and floral consols. On the centre was placed "No. 4 Engine," flanked on each side with a large flag. The spandrills of the facade over the central arch were covered with brilliant crimson cloth, on which the letters "A. E." were emblazoned. The key of the arch was formed by the banner presented to the Fire Brigade by the ladies of Toronto, and by the banner belonging to No. 6 Fire Engine Company, with a number of emblems on each side belonging to the brigade. On each side of the main arch smaller arches were constructed. The general decorations were evergreens, and the arch constructed in the most substantial manner.

The Orange arch at the corner of Church and King streets was said to be a correct representation of the celebrated Bishop's Gate of Derry. The structure was covered with paper of stone colour about sixty feet in height. On the face of the arch were medallions on each side of "Victoria and Albert," and "William and Mary." In the centre was a shield with the Prince of Wales' arms. On the lower rim of the arch were the words, "Our glorious constitution," supported right and left by large portraits of Her Majesty and Prince Albert. In the evening the whole was brilliantly illuminated and had a fine effect.

The Masonic arch, erected at the foot of Toronto street on King street, by the free and accepted Masons of Toronto was a floral structure, and presented a very fine appearance. The arch rose from two massive piers covered entirely with evergreens. On each side of the piers were shields with the compass and square, the level, the cornucopia, the mallet and trowels, and other Masonic emblems. The shields were surrounded with tastefully-grouped trophies of British ensigns, and on the summit of each pier were beautifully decorated columns, supporting celestial and terrestrial globes. The arch was of the Gothic style of architecture, and sprang from the top of the piers to a height of fifty feet from the ground. In the faces of the arch, on crimson grounds, were the mottoes, "Hail! Grandson of a Grand-master," referring to his Royal Highness' grandfather, the late Duke of Kent, who was for many years the Grand-master of the craft in England. Rising from the summit of the arch was a "Jacob's ladder," the emblematic meaning of which is only known to the initiated "brethren of the mystic tie." Placed on it was the emblem of Hope, the anchor. The ladder enclosed a lofty flag-staff, from which proudly floated the banner of the Royal-Arch Chapter with a circle, inside of which was a triangle, beautifully executed in gold, on a white field. Immediately below the banner, and resting on the ladder, a blazing star, encircling "the all-seeing eye," while at the base was placed a hand with the index-finger pointing upwards. Pendant from the key-stone of the arch was a large compass and square, enclosing the letter "G." Round the outer rim of the arch were the handsome and tastefully-executed banners of the Royal-Arch Chapter and the Encampment, the centre being decorated with a trophy of British ensigns, while pending from the angles of each pier were clusters of banners belonging to the Knights Templar Order of Masonry. The whole tastefully festooned and decorated with flowers, a beautiful bouquet being pendant from the centre of the arch. The designers of this handsome structure were Messrs. Cumberland & Storm. It was tastefully illuminated by rows of coloured lamps round the summit of each pier.

The floral arch belonging to the citizens was erected at the intersection of Yonge and King-streets, and was amongst the most beautiful which had been erected. The great height to the summit, 64 feet from the ground, attracted the attention of the passers by. The arch proper, semi-circle in form, sprang from hansomely decorated oval piers 48 feet high, and standing 30 feet apart. Above the arch was a tympanum, the apex of which, 64 feet from the street, embraced on its faces the letters "A." and "E.," enamelled in floral wreaths, the whole being surmounted by a broad pennon flag flying from a lofty flag-staff which crowned the whole, and gave a most striking appearance to the arch. The centre had emblazoned on it the arms of His Royal Highness, with the arms of Canada, England, Scotland, and Ireland on each. On the top of each pier was a plume cut out of wood, and from this rose flag-staffs surmounted with red and blue ensigns. The springs were decorated with trophies of ensigns artistically grouped. The two side arches spanning the side walks were twenty-eight feet in height, and near the summit of each were beautifully executed shields, having the crest of His Royal Highness, with the motto "Ich dien." The columns were covered with evergreens, from which depended wreaths tastefully looped up, with spruce and cedar of a beautiful dark green. On the faces of the arch were the words, "Welcome" and "Albert."

While single and triple arches were being erected in various parts of the city, the quadruple arch spanned the streets from north to south, and from east to west, diagonally, entirely of rustic work. The *tout ensemble* produced a most pleasing effect, and the substantial cedar supporters with the bark on, the evergreens and cedar branches with which every portion of the arch was decorated, and the beautiful festoons of flowers, combined to form a spectacle which challenged the admiration of all. Mottoes stretched from every point of the compass. On the east was "Welcome our Royal Prince;" on the west, "God save the Queen;" on the north, "Long live the Prince;" and on the south, "Albert

Edward." Those mottoes, by the spectator moving to different points, produced cross-readings, which in this instance proved to be most appropriate.

An evergreen structure was erected at the corner of Temperance and Yonge Streets, heavily festooned with evergreens, ornamented with shields, having flags floating from the tops.

The members of the St. George's Society had erected a triple arch on Yonge Street, a very pretty and substantial structure, the design from the pencil of Mr. F. W. Cumberland, belonging to the Gothic order. The centre of the arch represented a large and well painted transparency of St. George and the Dragon, surrounded by a trophy of the red ensigns of old England. The two side arches were covered with evergreens and flowers, and on their faces the words "Albert Edward." From the embattlements of these arches rose a number of flags, which presented a fine appearance. On the piers of the centre arch were shields, with Prince of Wales' plumes and arms of England emblazoned on them. This structure was much admired by visitors, and highly creditable to the "Sons of St. George," who so proudly marched under it to welcome their future King on his arrival in Toronto, and assisted so ably in giving him a true British cheer.

The Church Street arch, erected by Mr. Angus Morrison, M.P.P., Mr. I. C. Gilmour, Mr. McCutcheon, Dr. Herrick and a number of the inhabitants of Church Street, in honour of the Prince's visit, was covered with evergreens. On the top of the piers were placed vases containing verbenas in flower, having on each side tasteful streamers. On the apex of the arch, forty feet from the street, was a Prince's plume cut in wood, surmounted by a flag-staff with the Union-jack floating at the top. On the face of the arch the words "Welcome to Church Street," and near the summit of the piers appeared the words "Albert" "Edward" on each side. The structure was tastefully got up, and erected at the junction of Church and Queen Streets. Mr. Morrison was entitled to much credit for his exertions.

In the whole history of Toronto, during the sixty or seventy years which have rolled on their course since the first log house was built by the hands of white men on the shore of Toronto bay, never before was she dressed in such a profusion of decorations as in every street, almost on every house, she exhibited on the 7th September, 1860. All the citizens vied with each other who should do the most to indicate the joyous enthusiasm with which all classes were eager to greet the advent of the Prince of Wales ; and the result was a display of evergreens and flowers, banners and bannerets, shields, drapery, and georgeous illuminations, such as never before had been equalled in Upper Canada.

It had been anticipated that the Prince would arrive by daylight, and the citizens, in planning how to show their loyalty, had two objects to keep in view, to make their stores and residences show well during the procession in the afternoon, and then to have a separate design to form part of the illuminations on that evening. The Prince landed when it was almost dusk, and as the procession passed through the streets most of the illuminations were lit up. In giving details of the decorations, it may be well to unite the descriptions applicable to both day and night.

As it would be invidious, and at the same time swell out to too great a length the compilation of these decorations, if it were entered upon—although the citizens would merit no more than their due if individually named—a short summary of the public institutions is necessarily selected.

The *Leader* office's transparency represented a lion apparently on the point of springing upon a beaver, from the other side of a separating stream.

The Bank of Upper Canada was gaily illuminated, and the old building put on as it were a new face to welcome the visitors who crowded on the streets to witness the effect of the illumination. Variegated lamps were on the balcony over the main entrance. A row ran up each column, connecting at the top with the shields of Scotland, England, Ireland and Canada; which were surrounded by a brilliant row of gas jets. The flag of each nation surmounted its own shield. Over the balcony a plume flanked by the letters "A. E.," and a handsome assortment of transparencies completed the whole.

The Bank of Montreal, a handsome star was placed in the centre with the letters "V. A." on each side. Below the Prince of Wales' plume "A. E." The whole in gas jets, looked very pretty.

The City Bank was decorated and illuminated with much taste. About the centre of the building was a plume of white lamps with coloured ones forming the base, and the letters "A. E." on each side. The cornice ornamented with white globes giving an excellent light and showing off a pretty moss shield at the top. Festoons, flowers and evergreens pending from all the windows and cornices.

The Post Office on Toronto street distinguished itself in the way of illuminations. It was most brilliantly lighted up, and the design was admirably adapted to the style of the building. Variegated lamps under which was a bright cluster of lights, including the Royal arms, shewed immediately below the cornice, and a crown in jets with monograms V. A. and A. V. on each side. At the base of the crown a handsome semi-circular arch with the word "Welcome" shewed in gas; also, a Prince of Wales' plume with two pretty stars, while along the first cornice were the words "Prince of Wales" in large letters.

The ample proportions of the Rossin House adapted it peculiarly well for taking on decorations. They were of a chaste and simple character. Garlands of evergreens were hung along the whole length of King and York Streets.

The Romain buildings were illuminated in a style that was scarcely surpassed by any other edifice in the city. The illuminations were on so magnificent a scale, covering the whole front of the building, that opinion was divided as to whether this pile of buildings or Osgoode Hall presented the finest illumination. Each was a credit to those who had the work in charge.

Mr. Stovel displayed a transparency worthy of especial notice. The design comprehended several figures; a young lion having the inscription *Ich Dien*, to indicate that he represented the Prince of Wales, was approaching a beaver with a maple leaf in his mouth, and was in the attitude of welcoming the noble visitor; while an eagle, soaring above Niagara Falls, with an olive branch in his mouth, looks with expectancy at the young lion, and an old crowned lion away beyond the dividing waters looks upon the scene with complacency.

The *Globe* office was decorated with a large number of national flags, and a variety of banners having inscribed on them mottoes, such as "Long Live the Prince," "Upper Canada welcomes her future King," "Cead mille failtha," "We welcome the Prince who has endeared himself to the people of British America,"

"Loyal to the Sovereign, faithful to the people," "Nemo me impune lacessit;" &c. The whole of the front of the *Globe* buildings were illuminated in a most pleasing and loyal manner.

The illumination in front of Osgoode Hall, a most beautiful edifice, was finer than any thing ever before attempted in Toronto, and Messrs Thompson, Keith & Co. seemed to have brought all the resources at their command to bear in producing something that would startle the public, and succeeded. One of the principal features was the excellent arrangements to show the more prominent portions of the building, and bring out the handsome capitals and mouldings of the columns and ornamental work. On the upper cornice of the centre building was a row of variegated cremorne lamps, and also running along the pediment. On the apex of the pediment was a crown of parti-coloured lamps nine feet in height with the letters "V. R." on each side. A row of lamps of various colours ran along the balustrading; and below the centre pediment was another row of bright coloured glasses. Encircling the volutes of each capital of the columns a cluster of green and ruby lamps showed the architectural work to good advantage. All the windows in this section of the building were inclosed with fire jets, while in the centre window was a most beautiful Brunswick star with very large letters, "A. E.," between the columns. A row of lamps ran along the cornice over the main entrance, which was ornamented and encrusted with lamps, as were also the lower portions of the main building. On the pediment of the west wing was a massive Prince of Wales' plume ten feet in height, composed of white lamps with red, blue, and green boards flanked with the letters "A. E.," while the windows were decorated with lamps. The east wing was similarly decorated and illuminated, and the effect produced when the whole was lighted up was such as has never been seen before in Toronto Crowds were assembled in front of the building until the gas was turned off, and every one who witnessed the grand spectacle expressed themselves as highly delighted.

The Court House on Adelaide street was tastefully illuminated, and claimed and received a good deal of attention.

The illumination of St. Lawrence Hall shone out brightly a second time, and several improvements had been made in the design. On the cornice over the front story was a row of handsome variegated lamps. Springing from this a row ran up each second pilaster, and the columns, in spiral form. These connected with the upper cornice, which was decorated in a similar manner to the lower. Running along the pediment were a row of cremorne lamps, while the dome at the base of the pillars and below the clock, was encircled with rows of white globes. On the apex of the pediment was placed a crown composed of white lamps, underneath which was an arch of lights enclosing the city arms. In the centre of the building was a massive Prince's plume in white, with "A. E." in purple and green letters on each side. A short distance above the main cornice were the letters "V. A." in claret and white glasses, the *tout ensemble* producing a magnificent effect. At the St. Lawrence Hall, while the illumination lasted, each successive crowd of gazors lingered for a longer period than almost any where else, blocking up the streets at that point. This was a sufficient evidence of the success of the illuminations put upon this beautiful building.

The Normal School, when lighted up, had the appearance of a magnificent triumphal arch, most brilliantly illuminated. In front of the tower surmounting the main entrance was a row of globes, with a small statue of the Queen in a niche, with reflectors on each side. Below the pediment was a beautifully executed crown, with the letters "V. R." in variegated lamps. There was a beautiful shield immediately below surmounted by a beaver, and bearing the crown, hatchet, anchor and sword, with the motto, "*Religio, Scientia, Libertas*," flanked on each side by transparencies, on which was emblazoned the Royal arms. Coloured lamps ran from base to top of the buildings, and gave a brilliant light. At each side of the main buildings were erected three tasteful arches in flowers and evergreens, and when beautifully illuminated the effect was magnificent. On the top of each were the shields of England, Scotland, and Ireland, with the rose, the thistle, and the shamrock. Handsomely painted transparencies, containing such mottoes as "Welcome to Canada," "Long live our Prince," were placed in various parts of the buildings. The wings had each a handsome crown on the top cornice, with the letters "A. E." on each side. The effect was most striking, and a perfect flood of light was thrown on the beautiful grounds.

Among the illuminations and decorations worthy of very

special notice, were those of the Northern Railway offices on York street, the Commercial Bank, the offices of the Edinburgh Assurance Company, and all the wholesale warehouses on Wellington street, some of whom made a very fine display.

The agent of the Prince, who is a cousin to him on Albert's side, arranged all his travelling matters, and stipulated in the bargain with the railroad companies, that, on no consideration, should any person be allowed on board the train, except those necessary to manage it; and those were prohibited from entering the royal car, but rode by themselves in a forward car.

It may not be uninteresting to know, that irrespective of the Prince being heir to the throne of Great Britain, he is also one of the richest gentlemen of the age, and has property at this time of over £700,000, irrespective of this accumulating estate.

This vast sum has arisen from the surplus revenues from the estate of the Duchy of Cornwall, to which he became entitled immediately after he was born, and which has been accumulating with interest from that time, and this fund will still go on increasing, until he, as other subjects of the Queen, attain the age of twenty-one, so that by that time the amount of money he will stand possessed of will be nearly £1,000,000 sterling.

It has been usual to consider the Princes of the Royal Family at age at eighteen, but the Queen, in this instance, as she has in all other matters, as a good mother, not allowed her children any more privileges than are enjoyed by others of her subjects.

Toronto, Oct. 2nd, 1860.

The Bishop of Toronto presents his compliments to the Editor of *The Leader* and requests him to insert the inclosed communication at his early convenience in his journal:—

Toronto, Sept., 1860.

MY DEAR SIR,—You mentioned to me some days ago, that you and many other friends were surprised that His Royal Highness the Prince of Wales did not visit Trinity College.

The members of Trinity College were indeed very anxious that His Royal Highness the Prince of Wales should visit their flourishing institution and receive their address within its humble walls, because they felt that such an honour conferred upon their infant seminary would prove beneficial to its future progress.

An application was accordingly made by me on the 4th of September, through his Excellency the Governor-General—from whom I received on the 5th an encouraging reply.

On Saturday morning, 8th September, it became a question whether it might not be better to present the address at the Levee, as the badness of the weather and the numerous claims on the time of his Royal Highness, might render it inconsistent to proceed to the College.

The wish to present an address at the Levee prevailed, and more especially as the members in attendance were more numerous than could again be easily assembled. Accordingly on application the address was received, and a very gracious written reply returned.

It was afterwards communicated to me by the Duke of Newcastle, as well as the Governor-General, that if we still wished for a personal visit from His Royal Highness the Prince of Wales it should take place. But as Monday was occupied by the excursion to Collingwood, and on Tuesday many of the College members had gone home, it was thought better not to press the wish, having received authority to state publicly that it would have been made with pleasure, had we concluded to desire it.

I trust that after reading this statement you will think with me that we have no reason to complain.

I remain, my dear Sir,
Yours faithfully,
JOHN TORONTO.

The Hon. James Gordon.

THE LEVEE IN TORONTO.

In consequence of the very disagreeable state of the weather on Saturday morning, and during the greater part of the day, the most important part of the programme was postponed to Tuesday. This, of course, mainly included the outside proceedings, such as the inauguration of the University Park, the laying of the corner stone to the statute of the Queen, and the review of the militia. The only thing that came off was the reception at Osgoode Hall.

At the hour appointed for holding the levee, eleven o'clock a.m., it was pouring down in torrents, greatly to the dismay of the good people who imagined that Toronto was going to excel her sister cities in every thing—even in the weather. Those who wished to pay their respects to the Prince had to enter by the gate on King street, and make their exit by that in Simcoe street. True, as the arrangement was not generally understood, many mistakes were made; there was much turning round, and considerable anathematizing by the drivers. But those who wished it, managed to get to Government House in time, notwithstanding the numerous fears for such cases made and provided. The attendance was very large : the ante-rooms were filled with a numerous body of gentlemen, all eager to find their way into the presence of the Prince.

The formalities of the Levee were the same as those observed heretofore. The Prince stood in the centre of a semicircle formed by the members of his suite, consisting of His Grace the Duke of Newcastle; Earl St. Germains; Sir Allan McNab; His Excellency the Earl of Mulgrave, Governor of Nova Scotia; Lord Lyons, British Ambassador at Washington; Commodore Seymour, of the *Hero ;* General Sir W. Fenwick Williams; Sir Edmund Head; the Bishop of Toronto and Bishop Lynch. Before entering, the card was presented to the first equerry, passed by him to the second, who read the name to the Chief Steward, who in his turn read it to His Royal Highness. Both Prince and subject then bowed, indulged in a little mutual admiration— and the ordeal passed.

A considerable number of addresses were presented. Replies were given to but four. The Lord Bishop of Toronto was allowed the precedence, and after reading the address of the Synod, took his place together with his Archdeacons along with the suite. The Rev. Mr. Clarke, who in the absence of the Moderator, presented the address from the Free Presbyterian Synod, was informed that had the Moderator been there he would have been treated as a Bishop, and allowed to take his place with the other two. There was some misunderstanding respecting the course pursued towards Dr. Stinson, the Chairman of the Methodist Conference, which has since been cleared up. The only address read previous to the general levee was that of the Anglican clergy, the others were read afterwards, and as it appeared in the order the various bodies chose to make their way through. The following is a correct list :—address of the

Anglican Synod; of the Free Church; of the Temperance Society; of the Canadian Institute; of the Trinity College Authorities; of University College; of the Bible Society.

After the Levee, His Royal Highness went with Captain Retallack and some gentlemen of the suite to the old Racket Court in rear of Lamb's Hotel, where they enjoyed themselves in a game of rackets; a few heard of it and went to the place—a number of young gentlemen procured ladders and mounted to the roof, and looking through the glass informed those on the ground that certainly the Heir Apparent to the British Throne was earnestly engaged at a game of rackets with his coat off. This was the signal for others to mount the ladders, for by this time another had been brought from one of the adjacent houses. In their anxiety to see the Prince several of the small squares of glass were broken, and the debris falling on the floor of the court, made it dangerous to continue the game. The Prince and the gentlemen who had been engaged in the game then retired to the wardrobing room and assumed their coats. Several in the crowd were ill-bred enough to stare in at the window while this was going on, but desisted on being remonstrated with by one of the suite stationed outside. Conjectures were made by the fifty persons who then assembled, as to the manner in which the Prince would reach the Government House. The difficulty was soon settled, for the gentlemen in attendance went to the gate and hailed a two-horse hackney coach which was standing opposite the Romain buldings. It was one of the nicest cabs in town; was drawn by two handsome grey horses, and owned by Louis Walker, and was entered in the License Inspector's books as No. 31. The persons in front of the Racket Court then formed a lane, and the Prince stopped and was received with a cheer. He was dressed in a suit of grey tweed, with a round hat of the same material. He marched briskly through the wet grass, the persons assembled standing uncovered, and cheering lustily as he jumped into the carriage, followed by the other gentlemen, and was driven rapidly to the Government House. The pedestrians on King street near the place were startled with the cheer, and made enquiries as to what it was all about. When informed that it was the Prince many of them ran after the cab, no doubt vainly expecting to get a glimpse at His Royal Highness before he got within the precints of his temporary residence.

All the afternoon and evening crowds were assembled in front of the Government House, anxiously expecting that His Royal Highness would again come out, but they were disappointed until the evening. They gazed anxiously in at the gate and saw the sentinel march his lonely rounds What they could see of Government House, the country folks made a note of, and will be able to give their friends a brief description of the dwelling in which the Prince sojourned.

As nine o'clock, the hour at which the Prince was expected to leave for the Osgoode Hall reception, advanced, the crowd in front of Government House began to increase. Every one was on tip-toe to get a good view as he passed, and large numbers of ladies lined the sidewalk. A number of men in front of the gate, which was shut, "took notes" of what was going on inside through the bars, and "reported" from time to time. About a quarter past nine the gates were opened, and a cab approached the gate. A slight cheer was raised, but it was soon discovered to be a "one horse affair," and the cheer died away, as no one could imagine that the future King of England would ride in a one-horse cab. A two-horse carriage came next, and up went another cheer, but some one got a good look in at the windows and declared that all in it had "grey-beards." A laugh followed this announcement, and every one was aware that His Royal Highness was not one of the occupants. Other carriages followed, and at length the band of the Royal Canadian Rifles, which had been playing during dinner on the lawn, struck up "God save the Queen." The favoured cab No. 31 came out. A cheer arose, and the Prince was driven rapidly to the reception. As all the carriages were close ones, it was not known to the greater portion of the crowd in which one he went, and they took the precaution to cheer all, so as not to make a mistake. Of course, the vast crowd assembled in front of Osgoode Hall did not expect His Royal Highness to arrive in a cab, and were not aware that he had passed through, until they heard the cheers from those standing to receive him on the steps in front of the Hall, and when the band of the Royal Canadian Rifles struck up the National Anthem.

All the afternoon the streets, especially King street, presented a busy appearance, being thronged with people and carriages, and vehicles of every description.

A large number of persons illuminated their dwellings in the evening, and the display was very fine, although not equal to that of the former evening. The beautiful triumphal arch at the foot of John street was illuminated with rows of lamps, and presented a most brilliant appearance, and attracted general admiration. The Masonic arch was lighted up with rows of white and coloured globes running all along the top, while the blazing star on the flag-staff was a blazing star in reality as well as name. The cornice on top of the piers had also rows of lamps upon them, and the effect produced was very fine. The Orange arch was also lighted up, as already described. Among other places were illuminated,—The Bank of Upper Canada, Post Office, Bank of British North America, Commercial Bank, City Bank, Terrapin Restaurant, Northern Railway Company's office, Messrs. Jacques & Hay's, Betley & Kay's, Levey Brothers', and Geo. Bostwick's store. The crowd was immense about nine o'clock.

THE BALL AT OSGOODE HALL.

Whatever may be said about the circumstances under which the ball that was given at Osgoode Hall, that it was a great success none can deny. There is not in America a more magnificent building devoted to law than Osgoode Hall. All that architecture can do to charm the eye or impress the mind with a sense of splendour is there. Your Montreal ball rooms, your large exhibition buildings, were excellent in their way. The brilliant display, the tastefully arranged flags and flowers, and the artistic combinations of colours were beautiful truly; but they are to the exquisitely wrought architecture of Osgoode Hall, as the theatre drop scene is to the work of Turner or a Claude. For a while the stern duties of the law were forgotten. In those courts where one was wont to hear naught beside the earnest voice of the barrister pleading, or the solemn tones of the judges, laughter and merriment reigned unchecked by any threat—of heavy fine or committal for contempt. Places reserved for learned counsellors were occupied by the fairest ladies Canada can boast of. Crinoline made itself comfortable in the capacious seats of their Lordships. Considering all things, the Judges bore it well. Imagine what Sir J. B. Robinson must have felt, at seeing a scarlet cloak in his chair, or Chief Justice Draper at finding his desk covered with ladies' shawls; their retiring-rooms filled with

A 8

looking-glasses, their consulting-chambers bedecked with confused heaps of female frippery. It was enough to try their inmost souls, but as already said, they bore it well.

Before the Prince came, dancing did not commence. But time dragged along very slowly; the lawyers were attired in their long gowns, and when His Royal Highness made his appearance, about half-past nine o'clock, the faces of all assumed a gayer aspect, and it became evident work would soon commence in earnest. The Prince was conducted directly from his carriage, through the beautiful corridor of white Caen stone, to the central atrium, and took his place on the slightly elevated dais prepared for him. He and the members of the suite, with the exception of General Williams, were dressed in plain clothes. Upon his right were the judges of the Queen's Bench; on his left were those of the Common Pleas. The cheers with which His Royal Highness was saluted having to some extent subsided, the band of the Royal Canadian Rifles struck up "God Save the Queen,"—a tune they are very fond of playing, at least it would so appear, for long after the Hon. John Hillyard Cameron, Treasurer of the Law Society, and Sir Allan MacNab, and the Hon. Henry John Boulton, two of the Benchers appointed to receive the Prince, had taken their places opposite, the first gentleman with an extended roll of parchment in his hand, ready to commence reading the address—the band continued hard at work, making the building re-echo with their musical strains. The Prince smiled; evidently enjoyed the joke; the more so as it gave him an opportunity of looking at the beautiful hall in which he stood—the tessellated pavement, the rich stone work, the arcaded gallery above, from which hundreds of bright eyes rained down upon the young Prince a flood of light. Of course he cared not for them. It was the domed ceiling of coloured glass through which the subdued light of numerous gas-jets shone, bringing to view each sculptured ornament on the walls, that most attracted his attention. It was to these works of art, not to the works of nature, he lifted his eyes, even when after active signaling from General Bruce the band ceased playing, and the sonorous voice of the treasurer pronounced the address.

Mr. Cameron then asked the Prince to proceed to the library, and consenting, he was conducted thither by the Law Society and the Judges, ascending the right hand flight of the broad stone stair-case, and passing through the central vestibule to a dais in the library, opposite the door-way. The gentlemen sought their wives, daughters, and sweethearts in the gallery, and squeezed their way in. There was much crushing of crinoline, and doubtless the personage who observed that "a good many hoops would be smashed," was right, but there is little use generally in proclaiming self-evident truths. The library was soon full, the centre of attraction being of course the dais round which a compact mass assembled. Those who have visited this really beautiful hall, will recollect that along both sides of it run tall fluted columns reaching to the richly decorated ceiling, between which columns the book-shelves are placed, leaving a square in the centre, over which is the large dome. The book-cases, of which there are four sets, being very large, served as galleries. Three of them were occupied by ladies, the remaining one was set apart for Poppenberg's band. The Prince having reached the dais, Mr. Cameron told him that it would give the Law Society boundless joy if His Royal Highness would graciously condescend to become a member thereof. His Royal Highness consented, of which important fact Mr. Cameron duly notified his brother Benchers. The roll was then brought, and the Prince signed his name, in which he was followed by the Duke of Newcastle and Lord St. Germains, also admitted members of the society. According to the programme His Royal Highness then declared "the Hall opened." Room for dancing was as soon as practicable secured, and the process of taking the polish off the library floor commenced. At the end of the third dance, the Prince proceeded down stairs, and there remained for the rest of the evening, excepting only a small portion of the time occupied in the supper room. The following are the names of the ladies he honoured with his hand : Mrs. J. H. Cameron, Miss Boulton, Miss MacNab, Miss Widder, Miss Robinson, Miss Powell, Miss McCaul, and Miss Draper.

The short evening passed pleasantly away, and the dancers were in active motion when the approach of Sunday gave the signal to stop. They had just reached the point in the Lancers where the gentlemen separate from the ladies and bow as gracefully as they know how, when the clock struck twelve, the music ceased, the bend was left unfinished, the band struck up "God save the Queen," and the company separated.

The room in which supper was provided was in the west wing of the building. Two tables were laid by Mr. Webb, in his usual excellent style, but beyond that there was nothing noticeable in the arrangements. The Prince stayed but a few minutes, because he very wisely prefers the company of the ladies to that of the gentlemen.

The Prince and suite attended morning service at St. James's Cathedral on Sunday. A large number of persons collected in front of Government House and on King street. A few minutes before eleven o'clock the carriage drawn by four bay horses, containing His Royal Highness, the Governor-General, the Duke of Newcastle, and the Earl of St. Germains, passed out at the gate, when a number of those present cheered the Prince. The coachman and footman wore plain black clothes, and no state was observed. While the carriage was passing along the various streets, the Prince bowed gracefully to a number of gentlemen who lifted their hats. He also bowed to the assemblage as he walked along the matting which had been laid down for the sidewalk to the door of the Cathedral.

The people of Toronto showed much greater inclination to early church-going than usual. As early as half-past nine o'clock crowds were proceeding to St. James's Cathedral, anxious to get good places to see the Prince. The admission was by ticket, but though the tickets were numbered, no attempt was made to identify the holders with seats. The large edifice was crowded in every part. Precisely at eleven o'clock the Prince and suite entered at the front door, and was received by the Churchwardens, the Bishop, the Archdeacons of York and Kingston, and the Cathedral clergymen in the porch. The Prince shook hands with the Bishop and walked up the aisle, the people showing great anxiety to see him, by standing up. The full tones of the organ pealing forth the voluntary, recalled their sense of propriety and the service began. Rev. H. J. Grasett, B.D., Rector, read prayers, Rev. J. G. Geddes, Rector of Hamilton, the Lessons, Rev. Archdeacon Bethune the Ante-Communion Service, the Rev. Mr. Boddy the Epistle, the Rev. E. Baldwin the Gospel, and the Rev. S. Givens of Yorkville the Offertory. The Bishop took for his text,

Psalm 72, 1st verse, "Give the king thy judgments, O God, and thy righteousness to the King's son."

THE SERMON.

In this prophetical prayer, the aged Monarch of Israel, about to resign the kingdom into the hands of his son Solomon, makes to God, for him, the request of a wise and affectionate father. He asks such a portion of wisdom and integrity from above as might enable the young Prince to govern aright the people of God, and to exhibit to the world a fair resemblance of that King of Israel who was, in the fulness of time, to sit upon the throne of his father David : to reign in righteousness, and to have all things committed unto him. This tender and affectionate prayer was afterwards more fully shadowed forth at Gibeon, where the Lord appeared to Solomon in a dream, and said : "Ask what I shall give thee;" and Solomon said : "O Lord, my God, thou hast made thy servant king instead of David, my father, and I am but a little child. I know not how to go out or come in; give, therefore, thy servant an understanding heart to judge thy people, that I may discern between good and bad, for who is able to judge this, thy so great people." And it pleased the Lord that Solomon had asked this thing. Such was the wise and manly answer made by a youth about twenty years of age. Now, reflecting on what almost all youths in his circumstances, with strong passions, a love of magnificence, and in possession of the proudest throne in Asia, would ask, we cannot but strongly admire Solomon's modesty and wisdom, and that diffidence in himself which turned him in confidence to God. Thus guided by heavenly principles, which can alone triumph in conflicts which monarchs have to undergo as well as others, he took upon himself the royal power as God's vicegerent upon earth, and as his appointed instrument of blessedness to his people. He was the predecessor of one far greater than himself, and prefigured who was to gather all the earth under his dominion. He was, as it were, riding in a glorious procession which his orderly conduct would bring happily towards its end ; and although great, he was only the harbinger in that mighty procession, and wore the livery of that heavenly Sovereign who, as in triumph, closed up the rear.

The principles which Solomon had chosen are like the soul of man, which cannot be affected by the elements of this world, but are enabled to defy their most violent assaults, and are like the wind which throws down palaces, but is itself unassailable; while on the other hand, worldly principles, like the body of man, yield before the assaults of kindred elements, and break up and waste away by being exposed to stronger and more corrupt principles of the same world. Solomon proved himself by his choice to be filled with that spirit which became him who had been anointed by God prophet and priest ; and the inward grace bestowed on that outward unction had been put to such good use that it carried more grace, and the wisdom shown in this petition obtained the gift of more wisdom. God gave him a wise and understanding heart,—so that there was none like him before him, neither should any arise like unto him. God also proved in him the rule which his blessed son Jesus Christ afterwards laid down, when he commanded to seek first the Kingdom of Heaven and its righteousness, and then all earthly blessings shall be added to it.

Because Solomon had asked this heavenly gift only, and mentioned none that were earthly, God gave him the earthly also,—"I have also given thee that which thou hast not asked, both riches and honour, so that there shall not be any among the kings like unto thee all thy days. And if thou wilt walk iu my ways, keep in my statutes and my commandments, as thy father did walk, then I will lengthen thy days." From the Tabernacle at Gibeon, Solomon returned to Jerusalem to offer sacrifice before the Ark of the Covenant of the Lord. Thus he consecrated the first days of his reign, and commenced his course under the most happy auspices. He made God the beginning, happy if he had also made him the end, of all his doings.

It is not, however, my desire on the present auspicious occasion to touch upon the last and melancholy years of King Solomon's life, but rather to connect the few observations I shall offer at this time with the youthful and more early portion of his reign,—while his heart was as yet pure, and the Lord preserved him.

I would observe in the first place that there is not, perhaps, in the history of mankind a more beautiful picture than that which is here represented. A young man in the bloom of life, when every thing was gay and alluring around him, in the moment of ascending to a brilliant throne where pleasure and ambition were before him, betaking himself to God and imploring of him that wisdom which might enable him to resist the temptations with which his situation surrounded him, and to fulfil the duties to which he was called. Had it been in the latter periods of his reign, when satiated with pleasure and disappointed ambition; when fatigued with the cares and pageantry of a throne, he looked abroad for better comforts—had it been at such a time, when Solomon directed his soul to heaven, much of the merit of his piety would have been lost. It would then have appeared only as the last refuge of a discontented mind which interest, not disposition, had led to devotion; and which only sought for repose in piety, because it had been disappointed in every thing else. But at such a season to be guided by such sentiments, in such an hour to betake himself to God, bespeak a mind so humble and yet pure; a disposition so ardently, and yet so rightly inclined; a soul so well fitted for every kind of excellence, that no language of praise seems too strong.

It is not, however, from the peculiar situation of Solomon that the beauty of this memorable instance of devotion arises. Its charm chiefly consists in its suitableness to the season of youth in its correspondence to the character and dispositions which distinguish that important age, which we eagerly desire to see in the young. Piety, or the fear of God in youth, has in it something singularly graceful and becoming—something which ever disposes us to think well of the mind in which it is found, and which better than all other attainments of life appears to promise honour and happiness in future days. It is suited to the opening of human life, to that interesting season when nature in all its beauty opens on the view. It is suited still more to the tenderness of young affections,—to that warm and generous temper which meets every where the objects of gratitude and love. But most of all, it is suited to the innocence of the youthful mind,—to that sacred and sinless purity which can lift up its unpolluted hands to heaven; which guilt hath not yet torn from confidence and hope in God, and which can look beyond this world to that society of kindred spirits "of whom is the Kingdom of Heaven." The progress of life may, indeed bring other acquisitions; it may strengthen religion by experience, and add knowledge to faith. But the piety which springs only from the heart,—the devotion which nature and not reason inspires,—the pure homage which flows unbidden from the tongue, and which asks no other motive for its payment than the pleasure which it bestows: these are the possessions of youth alone.

I would, in the second place, remark that the feelings of piety are not only natural and becoming in youth, but they are still more valuable as tending to the formation of future character. They spring up in the first and purest state of the human mind; when the soul comes fresh from the hands of its Creator, and no habits of life have contracted the use of its powers; they come in the happy season when life is new and hope unbroken, where nature seems every where to reign, to rejoice around, and where the love of God rises unbidden in the soul. They come not to terrify or alarm, but to present every high and pleasing prospect in which the heart can indulge. They come to withdraw the veil which covers the splendours of the external mind, and to open that futurity which awakens all their desires to behold and attain, and in the sublime occupations of which they feel already, as by some secret inspiration, the home and destiny of their souls. At such a period religion is full of joy. It is not an occasional, but a permanent subject, of elevating their meditations,—a subject which can fill their solitary hours with rapture, and which involuntarily occurs to them in every season when their hearts are disposed to feel, and to which they willingly return from all the disappointments or follies of life, and resume again their unfinished joys. If there be a moment of human life in which the foundation of a virtuous character can be laid, it is at this period. If there can be a discipline which could call forth every noble faculty of the soul, it is such early exercises of piety. They not only suggest, but establish a tone and character of thought, which is allied to every virtuous purpose; they present those views of man and the ends of his being, which awaken the best powers of his soul; and they afford prospects of the providence of God, which can best give support and confidence to virtue. But again there is no man, perhaps, who in some fortunate moments of thought, has not felt his soul raised above its usual state by religious considerations. There are hours in every man's life when religion seems to approach him in all her lovliness, when its truths burst upon his soul with a force which cannot be resisted, and when in the contemplation of them he feels his bosom swell with emotions of unusual delight. In such moments every man feels that the dignity and purity of his whole being is increased. The illusions and temptations of the world appear beneath his regard; his heart opens to nobler and purer affections, and his bosom regains for a while its native innocence. In the greater part of mankind, however, these moments are transient; life calls them back again to their usual concerns, and they sometimes relapse into all the folly and weakness of ordinary mortals. Now it is the tendency of early piety to fix this character of thought and endeavour to render that temper of mind permanent, which in many is only temporary and transient. By the great objects to which it directs the minds of the young, by its precedence to every other system of opinions which might oppose its influences, by its power to arrest and retain their attention, it tends gradually to establish in the soul a correspondent dignity in every other exercise. While yet the world is unknown, and the calm morning of life is undisturbed, it awakens desires of a nobler kind than the usual purposes of life can gratify, and forms in secret those habits of elevated thought which are, of all others, the most valuable acquisitions of youthful years, and fit it for future attainments in truth and virtue beyond the reach of ordinary men

Once more: another fruit of early piety is, that it presents those views of man and of the end of his being which will call forth the best powers of our nature. We readily accommodate our acquisitions to the opinions we entertain of the scenes in which they are to be employed, and take expectations which are formed in respect to us. It is hence that the different situations of human life produce so great diversity of character and improvement. The poor man whose life is passed in obscurity, and on whose humble fortunes the regard and observations of the world are never likely to fall, is seldom solicitous to distinguish himself by any other acquisition than those which are suited to the humility of his station, and which the exigencies of his station demand of him. The great and the opulent, on the contrary, who are born to be the objects of observation and attention, feel themselves called upon to suit their ambition to the opinions of mankind; and if they have the common spirit of men, usually accommodate themselves to these expectations. It is in this manner that early piety has an influence in forming the future character. It represents man as formed in the image of God, "as but a little lower than the angels," and as crowned with glory and honour. It represents life, not as the short and fleeting space of temporary being, but as the preparation only for immortal existence; as a theatre on which he is called on to act in the sight of his Saviour and his God, and of which the rewards exceed even the powers of his imagination to conceive. It represents all this in the season when no lower passions have taken the dominion of his heart, and when his powers are all susceptible of being moulded by the ends which are placed before him. In such views of man all the best qualities of his nature arise involuntary in the soul,—the benevolence which loves to diffuse happiness and to be a fellow worker with God in the designs of his providence,—the fortitude which no obstacles can retard and no dangers appal in the road to immortality,—the constancy which reposes in the promises of heaven presses forward in the path of strenuous and persevering virtue, such views have always the tendency to fortify the mind against all those narrow and unjust conceptions of life, which are the source of the greatest part of the follies and weaknesses of mankind. They level all those vain distinctions among men, which in one class of society are productive of oppression and pride, and in the other of baseness and servility. They silence that feeble and greviously complaining spirit which is so often mistaken for sensibility and superior feeling, and which, from whatever cause it springs, gradually poisons the source of human happiness and undermines the foundations of every real virtue. They dispel those dark and ungenerous views of man and of his capacity for happiness and virtue, which are in general only the excuses for indolence or selfishness, and which, wherever they have prevailed, have so often withheld the arm that was made to bless, and silenced the voice that was destined to enlighten them. "Whatsoever things are just, whatsoever things are pure, whatsoever things are lovely and of good report," these are the objects at which the spirit of early piety points the mind to aim, wherever the production of happines or virtue is to be acquired, or by the performance of duty praise is to be won. It is true that we sometimes find the pious and the wise, to whom religion ought to have taught better things, complaining under the unequal distributions, and nourishing in their hearts those secret murmurs against Providence which unnerve every virtuous purpose of the soul, and cover religion itself in gloom and melancholy.

It is the piety of the youthful days which can afford the best preservation against those dark and unjust conceptions. Before the experience of life has made any impression on the mind,—before they descend to the wilderness through which they are to travel, it shews them from afar "the promised land." It carries their views through the whole course of their being, and while no narrow objects have yet absorbed their desires, shows them its termination in another scene, in which the balance of good and evil will be adjusted by the unerring hand of God. Under such views of nature the system of Divine Providence appears in all its majesty and beauty. Beginning here, in the feeble state of man, it spreads itself into forms of ascending being, in which the heart expands while it contemplates them, and closes, at last, in scenes which are obscured only from the excess of their splendour. With such conceptions of their nature, life meets the young in its real colours,—not as the idle abode of effeminate pleasure, but as the school in which their souls are formed to great attainment,—not as the soft shade in which every manly and honourable quality is to dissolve, but as the field in which honour, and glory, and immortality are to be won. Whatever may be the aspect which it may assume, whatever the scenes in which they are called to act or suffer, the promises of God still brighten in their view, and their souls, deriving strength from trials and confidence from experience, settle at last in that humble but holy spirit of resignation, which, when rightly understood, comprehends the sum and substance of religion; which, reposing itself in undoubting faith on the wisdom of God, accepts, not only with content but with cheerfulness, every dispensation of his providence; which seeks no other end but to fulfil its part in his government, and which, knowing its own weakness and God's perfection, yields up all its desires into his hand, and asks only to know his laws and to do his will.

Such are some of the natural effects of youthful piety upon the formation of human character, and to which more might be added'; and especially the certainty which it affords of the favour of God, and of the continued assistance of his Holy Spirit as appears in our Heavenly Father's dealings with the young throughout the whole of Revelation. Rejoice then, O young man, in thy youth, —rejoice in those days which are never to return, when religion comes to you in all her charms, and when the God of Heaven reveals himself to thy soul, like the mild radiance of the morning sun when he rises amidst the blessings of a grateful world.

I would offer my young hearers, of both sexes, a parting word of loving kindness, for God is the Creator and Father of us all. If, then, piety hath already taught you her secret pleasures,—if, when revelation unveils her mercies, and the Son of God comes forth to give peace and hope to fallen man, if at such a time your eyes follow with astonishment the glories of his path, and pour at last over his cross those pious tears which it is a delight to shed,—if your souls accompany him in his triumph over the grave, and enter, on the wings of faith, into that heaven "where he sat down on the right hand of the Majesty on high, and beheld the society of angels and the spirits of just men made perfect," and listen to the everlasting song, which is sung before the throne ; if such be frequently the meditation in which your youthful hours are passed, renounce not, for all that life can offer you, these solitary joys. The world that is before thee—the world which thine imagination paints in such brightness—has no pleasures to bestow which can compare with these ; and all its boasted wisdom can produce, has nothing so acceptable in the sight of Heaven as the pure offering of youthful souls.

The following selections of music were performed under the leadership of Mr. Carter, the organist, during the service:—
  Venite—Chant—Gregorian.
  Glorias—Chant—Goss from Bethoven.
  Te Deum.
  Jubilate.
  Anthem, "Bow down thine ear, O. Lord."
  Introit—Sanctus—Spohr.
  Responses—John Carter.
  Gloria—(before and after the Gospel)—Tallis.
  Before Sermon—"But the Lord is mindful of his own."—Mendelsohn.

While the collection was being made, "Handel's Sampson" and "We worship God and God alone," from "Judas Maccabeus," were executed, and on His Royal Highness leaving, the "National Anthem" reverbrated through the massive building.

After the service the organ of the cathedral was at length heard thundering out the "National Anthem," and immediately afterwards the Prince appeared. Those inside the cathedral grounds doffed their hats as did many in the general crowd. His appearance was the signal for a cheer, and it was given with a will. His Royal Highness bowed several times to the persons in the crowd, and also to the ladies and gentlemen who filled the windows of the houses from Church street to West Market Square. A large number were also on the house tops.

Just as the carriage left the Church, the Duke of Newcastle and Earl St. Germains were observed to look back at the Orange arch, with the flags of the lodges upon it. On the arrival of His

Royal Highness at Government House he was cheered by the persons assembled in front of the gates, which he gracefully acknowledged.

Between six and seven o'clock in the evening the Governor General and Duke of Newcastle, with two other gentlemen belonging to the suite, walked along King street and examined the Orange arch.

Shortly after the Governor and the Duke of Newcastle left, a number of Masters of Lodges met and ordered the Orange flags to be taken down, as they did not want them left out. The flags were accordingly taken down and deposited in the halls of the different lodges to which they belonged.

The streets presented the usual quiet appearance in the evening. A large number of persons visited the arch and amphitheatre at the foot of John street, during the day and evening.

THE PRINCE IN TORONTO.

From an American view, than which nothing could be more cordial :—

We have often read with pleasure the letters of "Sentinel," the travelling correspondent of the New York *Courier* and *Enquirer*. He is truthful to a degree to which no other correspondent of an American paper, whose letters we have yet seen, can lay claim. Let our readers judge for themselves in the extracts from "Sentinel's" letters, which we subjoin :—

Now then we have him in an English town. Here the associations of the land of the lillies have ceased and the lion roars his loyalty in his native growl. The prosperous young city that is capital to Canada West desired its Sovereign's son to witness what Englishmen undisturbed by any admixture of races could effect, and the very progress and condition of their city is evidence. A rich land of sure harvest is the back-ground,—a wide blue sea is the highway over which all the markets of the world can be reached. These wharves see the rigging through which the breeze of the Atlantic whistles, and if the ocean is too distant, the merchants of Oswego willingly indicate to the Canadians the convenience of the inland navigation to New York. The graceful harbour of Toronto would shelter a navy. Its guard against the storm is better than any break-water coming from an unwilling government. Nature seems to have believed it constitutional to give protection to the mariner.

The Prince finds his idea of his dominions increasing. Can all this territory be under the shadow of the Crown, from the wild Belle Isle Strait to the Detroit? He may, if at his tender years, such tough regimen is allowed him, sometimes have read the debates of the Commons, and if he remembered the figures of rhetoric, has heard the sentence our own Daniel Webster so eloquently phrased,—of the ceaseless roll of the English drum's morning beat,—but did he believe that he possessed a domain so fair as is this Canada West, at Toronto,—sister in all her beauty of culture to our Ohio and Illinois?

He is entering the proudest of his provinces. Here is the land where law and loyalty move together,—where just as much freedom in labour and freedom from tax is enjoyed as is good for mortal man to possess.

His superb car may roll for many a mile through this land of plenty. The tireless tyres of the swift wheels have almost an empire for the length of their journeying.

Of Toronto harbour, the narrator has often written. It has been one of those protections to commerce which seemed as near the perfect as could be imagined. Its long and narrow and curving point, which was a screen from the storm and yet showed the pressing canvass,—this was inimitable. It is of the past. Ontario, by its wild waves, has seemed envious of the safety of the wharves of Toronto, and has broken in and over, so that keels go safely now where but a few years since waggon wheels ran merrily on a pleasure drive. The tremendous power of water!— even the Temperance Societies don't fully understand it—it makes or unmakes a barrier which no human hand defend or repair.

Toronto's beautiful bay has its proudest page to inscribe in its annals on the 7th of September, 1860. It has seen the sails of a hostile fleet, and has witnessed the coming of successive Governors-General; but of the Royal House, none until this hour. The reception was worthy of the guest.

The scene at the Amphitheatre was sublime,—it deserves just that word. Let us tell the story.

Never trust the weather. However brilliant the smile of the

day, let the quick coming shadows and clouds of the next be dreaded. If there is any climate where an umbrella is not one's "next friend," it is not within the range of civilization.

Friday's veil of cloud grew denser. The sunshine had but a faint resemblance to a glorious gush of light, but the hope of fair hours did not desert us. The city finished its banner dress,—the last wreath was placed on the arches,—the last cup in the device of illumination—the last ladder was kicked away—the painter gave his final colour. Cars and boats brought in the Canadians in great array, and the silver maple leaf, the badge of the native-born, was conspicuous.

The arrangements of the Amphitheatre was in divisions, and in numbered seats on those, so that in finding the letter corresponding with the letter on one's ticket, the seat was secure. But doors A, B, C, and others of the alphabet, were remorselessly shut long after the promised hour of opening, and the crowd good-naturedly waited, consoling themselves with many just reflections on the stupidity of all officials, conveying some very impressive lessons which would have been very profitable, if the door-keepers and managers would but have listened. The afternoon waned, and at last the portals unclosed, and the multitude who possessed tickets found rapidly their lettered places. The area was of enormous size—a Canadian Coliseum—and it seemed at first as if the emptiness on the benches was to indicate a cold reception. Soon a change was found. The schools in great numbers, in multitudes poured in, and ranging themselves on either side, prepared for their performances of the song of welcome embodied in the air of the national anthem.

And then the Societies, and then a gay company of Highlanders, and of Riflemen, and of grave Professors of the University, and Bishop and Archdeacon, and most decorous Judges, and concentrating the look, a soldier of Waterloo and the Peninsula, covered with the brilliancy of honourable medals, and yet in soldier duty, and the seats became thronged, and the area began to wear the dignity of a great mass of human beings.

Time told that the day would soon wane, and just then the keen sight of an acute Scotchman discovered a group of vessels, and the word was passed on, and ladies before dolorous smiled again, and the skies in the influence of the parting sun, seemed to surrender their right to showers, and as the steamers grew more and more distinct, and showed their proportions through the foliage of the Island, the arrival of the Prince seemed assuming reality. Suddenly three quick cannon told the official signal that he was coming, and by some such rapid movement, as with which Roderick Dhu brought up his soldiers out of brake and glen, the Amphitheatre filled, and a quick pulsation of excitement was felt every where. The steamers rounded a point near the lighthouse, and the forward vessel was found to be the *Kingston*, the Royal standard at her mast head and a brilliant scarlet group on her deck. Slowly she passed the wharves, and up from that great crowd went the long deferred shout, sending its voices over the blue of Ontario, till the depths stirred with it.

The *Kingston* came to the landing,—the officials, with the Mayor at their head, proceeded to the welcome. The Prince stepped on the wharf,—and landed in Toronto. The danger was over, and this Chief City of Canada West received its Royal Guest. From that moment there was such a scene of wild, enthusiastic, joyous, uncontrolled excitement in that grand multitude,—that enormous concourse of human beings,—as few shall ever again see,—few have ever seen. The danger and delay, the doubt, had all heightened the present outburst. It was Canada's voice to her Prince, that rolled up with the frenzied delight of that moment. The dais was crowded,—the thousands of children, and men and women, and decorated officials, and scarlet and plaided soldiers had voice of tremendous power then, and something that was either hospitality or affection, or loyalty, —whatever its precise name—something in great and glorious fact was there, and no one that witnessed that enthusiasm,—that kindled Amphitheatre,—will forget it while his senses live to paint the pictures of the past for him.

Of arches, Toronto showed a variety, and in this respect was superior to Montreal. The ornamental structures were in variety and in completeness, that was admirable to the enterprise of the citizens. From that which was nearest the place assigned to the landing of the Prince, banners were waving in the sun which played in glitter on the points of the staffs—while on that nearest the Rossin House there was a crown so gay and grand that it rivalled all that the most fertile of Arabian story tellers ever imagined for their Thousand and One Nights of romance.

Beautiful Bay of Toronto! On those shores there ought to be the fairest of towns. A street on the water's edge would be beyond the beauty of Venice. The lake has made invitation to architecture, but the invitation has not been accepted. There is no rival to Michigan Avenue here.

There was opened on Saturday evening, 8th September, Osgoode Hall, the place of session of the Higher Courts of the Province, and a beauty it is, surprisingly so. The centre hall was like a room of Alhambra,—indeed, it possessed what Moorish genius never attained, a transparent ceiling, through which the light was shed. The ceiling is magnificent. No eastern fatalist, out of the easy texture of fiction, ever framed one where form and colour were in more grace and wealth. It is a very broidered garment for the wear of Justice.

Pillars of Caenstone—floor of many-hued tesselate,—balustrade of elaborate carving,—there lawyers and judges dwell in luxury while they are in attendance at the gates of Themis.

The Court room itself is a delight. Oh, if our Court of Appeals could possess such a room, one so convenient, comfortable, elegant, not ostentatious—this grandest power in our State,—the "last resort," as our peculiar phraseology declares it, would have a seat, in whose fitness for the tribunal the people would rejoice. I say the people, for they approve of things appropriate. It is only demagogue in their name misrepresenting them who oppose and prevent wise liberality.

If ever our Court rooms are to be remodelled, the person in charge may profitably examine the arrangements of Osgoode Hall.

The illumination of this building was as brilliant as ruby and emerald and crystal could effect in combination, and the multitude seemed to enjoy it hugely, as a look of something real—something like a fulfilment of the promises made of bright occurrences on the occasion of the Prince's visit. It was a superb spectacle. This beautiful building, with its outline kindled into rich colouring of living, flowing light, and the dark town in background, while in the distance the Aurora's heaven-touching columns of the strong radiance, were pointing the way to the better world above us.

EXCURSION TO COLLINGWOOD.

The principal feature in the programme of Monday's proceedings was the excursion to Collingwood and the Georgian Bay. It was in every way desirable that the Prince, by travelling over the Northern road, should have the opportunity of seeing with his own eyes the rapid progress made by an important section of country, a large portion of which but a few years ago was an uncultivated wilderness—and that at the same time by visiting the Georgian Bay and taking a short cruise on its waters, he should be assisted in forming some definite notions with respect to the route over British territory which will at some future time, for purposes of travel and traffic, connect the waters of the Atlantic and Pacific.

A special train departed from the Amphitheatre at half-past eight o'clock on the morning of the 10th. At that hour the train was waiting the Prince's arrival. It consisted of four cars, of which two were for the special use of the Prince and his suite. One of these was the Grand Trunk car, prepared for the use of His Royal Highness during the railroad portion of his journey from Quebec. The other was an open car, built specially for the excursion by the Northern Railroad Company, under the direction of Mr. Grant, the Superintendent, at their works in Toronto. This car was of very elegant design, and sufficiently large to accommodate from fifteen to twenty persons comfortably. It was neatly carpeted, and fitted up with handsome ottomans. The exterior was decorated with embossed crowns, Prince's plumes, representations of the maple leaf, &c., and a number of banners waving over it gave it quite a gay appearance. Two other cars were provided for the accommodation of the favoured few who had received cards, inviting them to accompany the Royal party in the excursion to the north. Some of those who were thus invited came on at Toronto. Others joined the train at various points. Poppenberg's excellent German brass band of Buffalo also accompanied the train, and a few members of the Toronto police force, under the command of Deputy Chief Robinson. The train was under the charge of Mr. J. Harvie, who has seen about the longest service as a conductor of any man in Canada. The engines "Cumberland" and "Morrison" having been selected to draw and pilot the train, had been very tastefully dressed up

A 10

for the occasion. The "Morrison" took the train north, its driver being Mr. L. Williams. Mr. Tillinghurst, the Company's superintendent of moving power, ran the pilot engine. In returning, the places of the engines were reversed, the "Cumberland" drawing the train, and the "Morrison" preceding as a pilot engine.

The Prince was not quite punctual. Some two or three thousand people had collected in the Amphitheatre to see his departure. A body of police preserved the dais and platform free from the intrusion of the crowd, and as the hour approached when the Prince was expected to arrive from the Government House, the people were made to fall back to the right and left, to keep an open lane through which his carriage might pass to the platform. Those who were to go on the excursion, were collected on the platform to join in giving the Prince a cheer before they took their places on the train. The Mayor was also there, to see to the arrangements for keeping good order, and a few other prominent citizens obtained admission to the platform. The Hon. John Rose was down giving orders, and saw the train off, but did not accompany it himself.

It was a pleasant, genial morning. The sky, however, was partly covered by scattered clouds, and the sun was alternately visible and obscured. It was a little doubtful whether rain would keep off during the day or not. The probabilities, however, were that it would be dry, and the hope was entertained that the proverbial ill fortune which had attended the Prince's progress hitherto since his arrival in America, had taken its final flight, driven off by the splendid sunshine from a clear cloudless sky on Sunday. The day only partially justified the hope of its dawning. Some rain fell while the train was approaching Collingwood,—and again a little more at a later period, when the party were on board the *Rescue*. Fortunately, however, none fell on any of the occasions that the Prince was being welcomed at the stations along the line, and altogether the day was a most favourable one for a pleasant excursion.

A few minutes before nine o'clock, the appearance of the York Cavalry coming through the arch, indicated the approach of His Royal Highness. As his carriage, drawn by four bay horses, entered the Amphitheatre, the people cheered loud and heartily.

In the same carriage as the Prince were the Duke of Newcastle, Earl St. Germains and the Governor-General. In a second carriage were General Bruce, Major Teesdale and Captain Grey. Captain Retallick, and Mr. Engelhart, the Duke's Secretary, were in a third. General Williams, Commander-in-Chief of the Forces, and Col. Rollo had arrived at the station some time previously. They and Captain Retallick were the only members of the Prince's party who wore military uniform.

As the Prince stepped upon the platform and walked over it to the car prepared for his reception, he was greeted with repeated rounds of enthusiastic cheering. This demonstration he acknowledged, as was his wont, by lifting his hat and bowing to the crowds on either side. His Royal Highness wore a white hat, a blue frock coat buttoned over his chest, and grey pants. The costumes of the members of his suite were of various styles, such as members of the non-aristocratic classes would be likely to wear on a free and easy summer excursion. The Governor-General alone, of those in immediate attendance on the Prince, wore broad-cloth. The rest of the excursion party, those who went by special invitation, and not belonging to the inner circle immediately surrounding His Royal Highness, were in general much more punctiliously dressed, a few being in full dress or very near it.

The Prince appeared fresh and hearty, sufficiently recruited by the Sabbath's rest, to enter with zest on another week's exertions. During the greater portion of the journey north, he remained outside on the open car, which was the last one of the train.

Among the gentlemen upon the train when it left Toronto, besides those already mentioned, we observed Hon. J. C. Morrison, President of the Northern Railroad; Mr. F. W. Cumberland, its Managing Director; Mr. James Beatty, also a Director; Mr. J. L. Grant, the Superintendent; Dr. Beattie, Secretary; and Mr. S. Fleming, the engineer of the road; Sir E. P. Taché, Hon. J. H. Cameron, Mr. Angus Morrison, M.P.P.; Hon. W. B. Robinson, Mr. T. Galt, Mr. John Crawford, Major R. Dennison, Capt. Thos. Dick, Mr. C. Robertson, Capt. Armstrong of King, Mr. Elliott of New York, General Robinson, and Mr. W. H. Denny (these two gentlemen being a deputation from Pitsburg, Pa., to invite the Prince to visit that city;) several members of the Press, &c.

All the excursion party having got on board, the train moved off amidst the huzzas of the crowd, who had rushed over the dais and thronged the railway platform.

Passing Davenport, the train stopped a moment at Weston to take on the Hon. Messrs. Galt and Ross.

At Thornhill the train did not stop, but passed the station slowly. A considerable crowd collected at this point, and cheered the Prince.

At Richmond-hill the engine stopped for two or three minutes to take in water. A pretty arch had been erected over the track, bearing the mottes of loyal welcome. The people were there in large numbers, and enthusiastically cheered their future king.

The King station was passed slowly, amidst the loyal cheers of the assembled crowd.

Aurora was reached about ten o'clock. The preparations there were on an extensive scale. Platforms had been erected for the accommodation of spectators, and they were crowded by the villagers, and large numbers who had flocked in from the surrounding country to see the Prince. There were probably two or three thousand people assembled. Three arches, on which no little pains had been bestowed, spanned the track—A Mechanics' arch, a Masonic arch, and an Orange arch. The Masons' arch bore the inscription, "Welcome Grandson of a Grand-master."

The train stopped at Newmarket for a few minutes. Some two or three thousand people were assembled, waiting its arrival. A platform had been erected on the east side of the track. This was thronged, and masses of human beings were clustered on the house-tops near the station, the balcony of the Eagle Hotel, and other available points of view. As the train stopped, a salute was fired, and the people cheered. The Prince did not leave the train, but an address was presented, a joint address on behalf of the Council and the Temperance Society of the village. The address was read by Mr. Nixon, who was accompanied by Mr. Sutherland, the Reeve.

The Prince read the following reply:

"GENTLEMEN,—I thank you sincerely for the address which you have just presented to me.

" In the Queen's name I thank you for the expressions of your loyalty to her crown and person—and for myself, I am grateful to you for this welcome to your neighbourhood."

A reply exactly identical with the above in its terms was given to each address presented during the day.

The people of Newmarket had erected three very neat arches, through two of which the train passed before reaching the station, and through the third after passing the station.

The train passed Holland Landing at a sufficiently slow rate to enable the people to see and cheer the Prince. In a conspicuous position on the front of the platform, stood an Orange Lodge, headed by its Master and other officers in full regalia. The standard-bearers held aloft the lodge's banner, bearing the usual emblems and mottoes. As the train moved past, the scarlet-clad officers of the lodge led the cheers, with which the people saluted their Prince.

Bradford was reached at a quarter to eleven, the preparations made for the reception of the Prince were on a scale befitting the importance of the place, as the centre of a large and thriving agricultural district. An elevated dais, protected by a handsome canopy, had been constructed at a distance of twelve or fifteen yards from the track. To this the Prince proceeded, as soon as the cars had stopped, along a passage-way which had been neatly carpeted, and was preserved from the intrusion of the crowd by a number of special constables. His Royal Highness was accompanied to the place of honour under the canopy by the Governor General, the Duke of Newcastle, Earl St. Germains, and General Williams. All around, standing on the ground, seated on the structures which had been erected for the accommodation of spectators, and blackening the roofs of the surrounding buildings, the people of Bradford and its vicinity right loyally welcomed the Prince with enthusiastic cheers. Two large arches had been erected, one across the track, and the other across the main street bearing such inscriptions as "Welcome Albert Edward," "God save the Queen," &c. About three thousand people, including an assemblage of school children, were seated on the various erections, commanding a view of the ceremony, the number present might have been about five thousand. Three fire companies belonging to the village, dressed in their uniforms, were drawn up in front of the reception platform, and two instrumental bands joined in welcoming the Prince.

A joint address from the Reeves of Bradford and West Gwillimbury, was presented on behalf of those muncipalities. The Prince, in a distinct voice, read a reply, couched in the same terms as that at Newmarket. The two Reeves and their respective Councils had then the honour of being presented to the Prince. Mr. Ferguson, M.P.P., for South Simcoe, of which Bradford is the principal town, made his appearance here, and assisted in leading the cheers of the people. The ceremony was quickly over, and all again got on board the cars.

The stations of Scanlons and Gilford were passed with the train moving slow. Lefroy it passed slowly, allowing the Prince time to see a party of painted Indians with their squaws, who occupied a small raised platform, on which they were sufficiently conspicuous. An arch of evergreens here spanned the track, bearing the incription, "Long live the Prince." Throughout the village there was a large display of bunting and other decorations.

The train arrived at the Barrie station at a quarter to twelve. Here a splendid reception awaited the Prince. On the east side of the track, behind and south of the station, a very handsome pavilion had been erected in such a position as to command an excellent view of the town, the bay, and the lake extending away eastward further than the eye could see. A carpeted pathway led from the stopping place of the cars to the pavilion, which consisted of a dais overhung by a beautiful canopy of green boughs, surmounted by a floral crown. The pavilion was within twenty feet of the water. On the bay there were a large number of boats, a schooner, and two steamers, the *Victoria* and *Morning*, both of which—the former especially—were very beautifully decorated. The passage from the cars to the pavilion was under a remarkably tasteful arch, which called forth many enconiums from the Prince's party. It was an agricultural arch,—a very prominent feature of it, and one which appeared a novelty even to those who had been for the last month looking almost every day at arches of every size and pattern,—a splendid Prince's plume was placed on the summit of the central part of the structure, made entirely of sheaves of wheat. The two upper side compartments of the arch were filled with sheaves of wheat, prodigious specimens of mangold wurtzel, and other agricultural products. Three stands for the accommodation of spectators had been erected, one against the back of the the station, a second fronting the pavilion, and a third on the south side of the carpeted pathway. This last was occupied by the school children, but as a good deal of time was occupied with the presentations, the Prince could not stay long enough to hear them sing. Between the pavilion and the two stands facing it from the north, some space was left which was crowded by people standing. The members of the fire brigade formed a margin for this crowd, keeping them from pressing unduly forward. The Barrie Volunteer Rifles were stationed on the railway platform. A band was also stationed on the railway platform, and played as the Prince left the cars and walked along to the pavilion. Some eight or ten thousand people must have been present.

The Warden, Thomas D. McConkey, Esq., presented the address of the County Council of Simcoe, and Judge Gowan that of the magistrates of the county. The Prince read replies to both. The Warden, the Judge, and Sheriff Smith, were attired in their robes of office. They were presented by the Governor-General to His Royal Highness before the addresses were read, and after that ceremony was performed, the Warden, the County Judge, and Mr. Ferguson announced the names of the members of the council, the magistracy, and other gentlemen, as they were severally presented to the Prince. The following clergymen were presented; Rev. Messrs. Morgan, Jamot, Gray, Checkley, Slater, Wightman, Salter, Messmore, Lee, and Rey. Among the other gentlemen presented was Captain Hopkins, an old peninsular veteran, almost bent double by his infirmities. The presentation over, three cheers were given for the Queen, three for the Prince, and three for the Prince Consort. The Prince then returned to the train, and it once more got under way. The excursion party was joined at Barrie by the Hon. Mr. Paton, M.L.C., the Warden, the Judge, the Sheriff, and other gentlemen.

At Angus, about five hundred people were assembled to shout welcome to the Prince, and a salute was fired by a piece of artillery. A handsome arch had also been erected. At Sunnidale there was also a neat arch, and about a hundred people assembled. At Nottawasaga there were two arches, a piper playing the bag-pipes, and an enthusiastic crowd. Some amusement was excited by the precision with which a respectable looking old gentlemen mounted a stump, and, acting as bugleman, read off from a paper in his hands the successive cheers—first "three cheers for the Queen," then "the Prince of Wales," and lastly "Prince Albert and the rest of the Royal Family."

At Collingwood again the Prince had a splendid reception, scarcely if at all inferior to that at Barrie. The Collingwood people had not an arch equal to that at Barrie, but they made up for that by the number of their arches, there being at least a dozen within view of the pavilion where the presentations took place, and some of them quite handsome. The number of people assembled could not have fallen much short of the numbers at Barrie, but then the Collingwood people had the special privilege extended to them of their children being allowed to sing two verses of the National Anthem. The Mayor of Collingwood, Mr. John McWatts, and Sheriff Snyder, the Mayor of Owen Sound, having been presented to the Prince, read addresses on behalf of those municipalities, and received replies, and then announced the names of the members of their respective councils, as they stepped forward and were presented by the Governor-General to the Prince.

The train then steamed down to the wharf, and the excursion party followed the Prince on board the *Rescue*, where a first rate lunch was served, and a pleasant sail enjoyed for an hour. The *Rescue* was accompanied by two other steamers, the *Ploughboy* and the *Canadian*, crowded with passengers, who lustily cheered whenever they came sufficiently near the *Rescue*. They had come down from Owen Sound that morning with 600 passengers.

The Prince conversed freely with those on board. He had a conversation for some time with General Robinson and Mr. Denny, the deputation from Pittsburg. These gentlemen had a formal interview with the Prince on Saturday, and obtained a promise that he would visit Pittsburg about the 1st October. They informed him on Saturday that the people of the United States admire and love the Queen of England for her many virtues, and that they were prepared to love her son for the mother's sake. They expressed themselves much pleased with the affability and courteous demeanour of the Prince.

Captain James Dick, who had charge of the *Rescue*, and his brother, Captain Thomas Dick, were presented to the Prince.

Captain Thomas Dick was also introduced to the Duke of Newcastle, and had a lengthened conversation with His Grace on the subject of the route to the Red River, and ultimately to the Pacific through British territory. Captain Dick urged the propriety of a subsidy being granted by the British Government, and the Duke expressed much interest in the subject.

The sail over, the party again got on the cars a little before three. In returning the train only stopped to wood and water, and no particular incident occurred. At the principal stations considerable crowds had assembled, and cheered as the train passed. From Thornhill to Weston the train travelled at the rapid rate of 55 miles an hour. Toronto was reached at half-past six. A carriage was in waiting for His Royal Highness in the Amphitheatre. After the Prince, the Governor, the Duke of Newcastle, and Earl St. Germains had got into the carriage, the crowd pressed around cheering for the Queen and the Prince.

The Prince's trip to Collingwood on the 10th, made the strangers in town amuse themselves at the Grand Scottish Gathering, and in visiting the various places of interest in and around the city.

On the evening of the 10th, the display of fireworks took place in the area of the Amphitheatre, and was witnessed by thousands. The seats of the Amphitheatre were well filled, but the numbers outside far exceeded those inside, so that there could not have been less than twenty thousand persons on the ground. A great crush took place at the arch, which had been boarded across to prevent the crowd rushing in, but the pressure was so great that the framework gave way, and many persons, chiefly boys, were suddenly prostrated. Several then tried to gain admittance at the large entrance thus made, but a strong force of police was on the ground and frustrated the attempt. While the battle was raging between the police and the crowd, the Firemens' procession made its appearance, and entered through the arch. This was an excellent opportunity to gain admittance, and many took advantage of it. A number of the firemen seeing the course matters were taking, and that the police were likely to be overpowered, turned round and assisted the constables, to keep back the people, in which they succeeded, and the procession passed in, headed by the Union Maltese Battery Band, and Poppinberg's Buffalo Band.

A 11

This was the signal for the pyrotechnic display to commence. The night was very dark, and the expectations of all present were very high, as an extensive programme had been published. The performance commenced by a number of rockets being sent up, at which the people cheered and clapped their hands. Next came an illumination of Indian white fires of great brilliancy. This was followed by a large wheel and bouquet with smaller revolving wheels, having coloured centres, which produced a most brilliant effect, lighting up the vast Amphitheatre, and the faces of the thousands of spectators. The display occupied the whole front of the reception platform, and ended with a grand discharge of fancy rockets. This was following by "Dancing Jock," a figure life size, which was made to dance by a man pulling a string. While it was burning it afforded quite a fund of merriment. A grand illumination of Chinese fires was next made, followed by rockets and gold rain. Next came the army and navy, being two beautiful pieces specially dedicated to the soldiers and sailors of Great Britain now on this continent. This was loudly applauded and had a most brilliant appearance. A number of rockets and shells haveing been sent up, a large and magnificent piece, with various devices, was ignited, and elicited loud and prolonged cheering. It had hardly subsided when an immense piece was ignited. It consisted of large ornamented Roman fasces emblematical of union and strength, festooned with Union Jacks and surmounted by the Royal Standard. Between the firing columns was a bust of the Queen, encircled with the rose, thistle, and shamrock. The capitals of the columns on either side of the bust of Her Majesty were emblematical colours representing the several Provinces of British America, with the initials and seals of each in beautiful colours. The Royal Arms of Great Britain formed the base. This was a very large piece and at least thirty feet in height, and the colours were most gorgeous. When it was lighted up the crowd raised a cheer which made the welken ring. The sight presented was magnificent, and all seemed delighted. The crowd were a good deal surprised when Poppenberg's band struck up the National Anthem, and they were informed that the performance was over. They, however, gave three cheers for Mr. Sanderson, of Boston, the pyrotechnic under whose superintendence the display took place. Three right loyal cheers were then given for the Queen, three for the Prince of Wales, and three for the Prince Consort. The two bands on the ground performed alternately several pieces of music while the fire-works were being let off.

The firemen, who had been standing in the area during the display, were then formed into order of procession, headed by the Union Band, and marched up John Street. When the band reached King street the torches were lighted and the procession moved along King street. In front of the Government House a halt took place, and three cheers were given for Her Majesty, and three for the Prince, in the manner which only the firemen of Toronto can do. A large number of Roman candles were let off, and the balls of fire flying over the tops of the houses, with the torches in the hands of every man in the procession, presented a spectacle seldom witnessed in Toronto. Many persons were of opinion that the torch light procession was the finest ever seen in Toronto. First came the Hook and Ladder Company, with a beautiful transparency at their head, with appropriate mottoes. The other companies marched according to their numbers. No. 6 had the engine in the procession, and was followed by the Jackson Hose Company in their tasteful uniform. On the hose carriage was a large square transparency. A short distance in the rear of the firemen were the workmen of the Northern Railway, all of whom had their hands full of Roman candles, which they fired off without intermission, and in a most wanton manner. The candles were so elevated that a number of the fire balls entered open windows at which ladies were seated viewing the procession, and frightened them not a little. At the corner of Simcoe and King street, a great crush took place, and the crinoline suffered fearfully. The streets were crowded with spectators, and a number of public and private buildings, besides the Masonic and Orange arches, were illuminated.

The Prince having landed late on Friday evening the 7th, and with the exception opportunely afforded [of catching a glimpse of him when he went to church, the mass of the people still had no good chance of making themselves acquainted with the features of their future King. For this reason, principally, a visit to the Amphitheatre was planned ; and it was this reason which caused His Royal Highness to give so ready an assent to the proposition, when it was made, that he should again visit the scene of his reception into Toronto. It was to be emphatically for the people at large. The weather was most unpropitious, as the rain poured down in torrents, but the children attended in numbers, and were distributed right and left of the platform, the girls to the right, the boys to the left, by Mr. Boxal, ex-councillor.

The Temperance Societies were there also. Then came the Volunteer Rifles,—two companies commanded by Captain Macdonald and Captain James Smith, who took up their position in double line, extending from the dais nearly to the opposite seats. At eleven o'clock the Prince came, and folks grumbled at being kept in the rain, even under circumstances such as had been witnessed,—and when they had not the slightest explanation of the reasons which delayed His Royal Highness and did not get them, they presumed to compare Albert Edward's punctuality with that of his royal mother. When he did come, however, the rain was for a time forgotten. Every one in the vast assembly rose and cheer after cheer rolled along the semi-circular platform, shouted forth with vigour which none save a British people can manifest. When the Prince had taken his stand upon the dais, the gateway under the entrance arch was opened, and the pent up mass outside spread over the area within like a rapidly advancing wave. There was something grand in the mere sight of such a mass of people as that witnessed. His Royal Highness was evidently impressed by it. He must not only have felt pleased with the numbers who had gathered together and waited so patiently to do him homage; he must have felt also the importance and the solemnity of the position he holds, when so many of his fellow-creatures look up to him for example, and are ready to acknowledge and applaud the least of his virtues.

Besides His Royal Highness and suite, there were assembled upon the platform the Mayor and City Council in full dress, officers of Militia, the senior member of the city, and a number of favoured visitors. The members of the Royal Canadian Yacht Club were also there, dressed in a neat uniform of dark blue and gold—one or two of them having the courage, even to appear in white "duck." Having formed in line on either side of His Royal Highness, Commodore Durie advanced and read the address.

This concluded, Commodore Durie, in respectful language, requested His Royal Highness to become a patron of the club; to which the Prince graciously consented, and was accordingly presented with a copy of the rules and regulations. The children then sang the first and last verses of "God Save the Queen," under the direction of Mr. Carter, and very well they did it.

His Royal Highness accompanied by his suite, and having on each side the Governor-General and Commodore Durie, then left the platform and proceeded to the edge of the temporary wharf for the purpose of witnessing the Regatta of the Royal Canadian Yacht Club. The Prince was followed to the wharf by a large crowd of spectators, among whom were a number of ladies, all eager to get a glimpse of the Royal personage; meanwhile the officers and men belonging to the Club had embarked in small boats, and were busily engaged making preparations to get the several yachts under way. At this time, and while the Prince was standing at the edge of the water, a pelting shower came on. His Royal Highness quickly donned a Mackintosh, and kept his place watching the preparations. A stiff breeze was blowing at the time, and the rain descended in torrents, so that the Royal party were under the necessity of seeking shelter under the roof of the temporary railway depot in rear of the platform. While they were walking up His Royal Highness said to Commodore Durie that he was sorry the weather was so bad, for the arrangements of the Club seemed to be excellent. It had been arranged that the race for the first and second class yachts should take place at the same time, in order to make the display as grand as possible. Every thing being in readiness, Commodore Durie gave the preconcerted signal. A gun was fired and a most beautiful start was effected. Fourteen yachts of various tonnage took part in the race, and but for the rain the spectacle would have been one of the finest ever seen in Toronto. Notwithstanding the inclemency of the weather, however, the sight was a fine one, as the vessels slipped their moorings, and stood out into the Bay, while the crowd cheered lustily. The following were the yachts which started in the race:—*Rivet*, 17 tons, Messrs. E. & S. Blake; *Canada*, 25 tons, Alderman Sherwood; *Sea Gull*, 17½ tons, Mr. G. H. Mingaze, Hamilton; *Dart*, 14 tons, Capt. Robertson; *Water Lily*, 15 tons, Commodore Durie; *Arrow*, 17½ tons, Mr.

Walace, Cobourg. Second class—*Marian*, 8 tons, Mr. Stinson, Hamilton; *Fairy*, 4 tons, Mr. T. Bigley; *Phantom*, 9 tons, Mr. J. H. Perry; *Storm Queen*, 6 tons, Mr. C. B. Grasett and Mr. Morgan Baldwin; *Prima Donna*, 10 tons, Mr. J. Hamilton; *Expert*, 10 tons, Mr. Delany, Cobourg; *Surge*, 4 tons, Mr. J. Metcalf, Hamilton; *Glance*, 9½ tons, Mr. G. Oliver, Kingston. The gun was fired at seventeen minutes to twelve o'clock, and the *Rivet* took the lead in a gallant manner, followed closely by the *Prima Donna, Sea Gull,* and *Glance*. After the vessels had got fairly under way, His Royal Highness expressed his sorrow to Commodore Durie that his engagements would not permit him to wait the issue of the race. He then shook the Commodore cordially by the hand, and having entered the Royal carriage drove off, accompanied by the suite to open University Park, amid the loud and repeated applause of the thousands of spectators. As the rain was pouring down in torrents, the seats of the Amphitheatre were quickly vacated, and only a few spectators braved the pitiless storm and stood on the wharves to watch the race. A large number of ladies and gentlemen went on board the Yacht Club boat, where they partook of refreshments served up in the saloon in very tasteful style. Captain Robertson, in a few pertinent remarks, then proposed "Her Majesty the Queen," which was most enthusiastically responded to with three cheers. He then read the reply of the Prince to the address of the Yacht Club, amid loud applause, and announced that His Royal Highness had graciously consented to become patron of the Club. Captain Robertson then proposed the health of His Royal Highness, which was drunk with three times three and a cheer more. Dr. Hodder proposed the Commodore of the day, which was drank with all the honours, to which that gentleman replied. He then gave the "Army," which was received with three cheers. Dr. Hunt of the Royal Canadian Rifles, with whose name the toast was coupled, acknowledged the compliment. The health of Lieutenant Buckle, of the *Hero*, was next submitted by Mr. Wakefield, and warmly received. Lieutenant Buckle returned thanks in a few neat and appropriate remarks, and referred in pleasing terms to the hospitality of the Torontonians. Mr. Ord, in felicitous terms, proposed "The Ladies." The toast was briefly acknowledged on behalf of the fair sex by Mr. George Boomer, and the party went on deck, as the rain had almost ceased. While the party on board the Club boat were enjoying themselves, those on board the yachts were experiencing a gale from the south-east.

The prize for the winner of the race for the first class yachts was a silver cup, valued at $100, to which was added the sum of $100. The boats which entered and competed were the *Rivet, Canada, Arrow, Water Lily, Dart* and *Sea Gull.* The *Rivet* took the lead, and was closely followed by the *Water Lily*, the *Sea Gull* following a short distance in the wake of the latter, and the *Arrow* well placed. The cruise was from a buoy moored in the bay, opposite the Amphitheatre, to another moored opposite the eastern gap, thence to the Mimico River, back to Gibraltar Point, round a buoy in the lake and home. The distance sailed was twenty-one miles. The *Rivet* won the race at 4h. 40m. 50s., p.m., amid the loud cheers of the party of ladies and gentlemen on the Club boats and the crowds on the wharves. The *Arrow* came in second at 4h. 55m. 40s., p.m., and was also received with cheers.

The race for second class yachts was for a silver cup, valued at $64, with the sum of $61 added.

The yachts which started in the race were the *Marion, Fairy, Phantom, Storm Queen, Prima Donna, Expert, Surge* and *Glance.* The course was the same as for first-class yachts, with the exception of sailing up the Mimico river. The *Glance* took the lead, and gallantly kept it till the end, winning the race in splendid style. She rounded the buoy in the lake at 4h. 24m. 30s. p.m., having lost some time in finding the buoy. Her crew were enthusiastically cheered on landing. The *Expert* came in second at 4h. 50m. 4 p.m. The others were not placed. The *Prima Donna* gave up before rounding Gibraltar point, having carried away her peak halyards. This was an exciting race for some time, the yachts being well matched.

The next race was between the open boats for a purse of $30, but the weather was very rough.

The following boats entered and it was well contested:— *Widgeon,* Mr. H. Brown; *Dolphin,* Mr. E. Noverre; *Brother Jonathan,* Mr. A. Falkner; *Breeze,* Mr. A. Craik; *Midge,* Mr. E. Lee.

A good start was effected, and the boats got well away together.

After a short time the *Breeze* and *Widgeon* took the lead, and for some time they kept company. The *Breeze*, however, got the benefit of a slight gust of wind and shot ahead and won the race, coming in about twelve minutes ahead of the *Widgeon*.

This finished the day's proceedings, so it had been decided to postpone the rowing matches until the following day at twelve o'clock, owing to the inclemency of the weather. There were a number of boats from the United States and various parts of Canada, besides the champion boats of the lakes, and good sport was expected.

The following races would have taken place in the afternoon, if the weather had proved favourable:—for fishermen's boats, prize $20; for four oared boats, prize $60; for pair-oared boats, prize $20; for sculling match, prize $15; canoe race—for birch bark canoes, (two paddles,) prize $20; for duck hunt, prize $10; for tub race, (circular tubs only,) prize $10; for championship of the bay, $30.

Captain Stuppart; of the Royal Navy, acted as Commodore of the day, and the arrangements of the several committees gave general satisfaction.

After the regatta the next ceremony in the programme of the day was inaugurating the University Park, by laying the foundation stone of a pedestal for a statue of the Queen. An elevated stand had been erected, surrounding the foundation of the pedestal, and here at twelve o'clock the Mayor, the Rev. Dr. McCaul, Angus Morrison, Esq., M.P.P., A. Brunel, Esq., Ald. Carr, J. G. Bowes, Esq., and other members of the Committee had stationed themselves in readiness to receive the Prince. There were also on the platform General Williams, Commander of the Forces, Col. Rollo, Sir Allan MacNab, Sir E. P. Taché, and Hon. John Rose. The members of the City Corporation attended in full dress.

At twelve o'clock it was raining heavily. A canopy of canvass had been erected over the stand, but it did not happen to be water-tight, and the rain soaked and dripped through, making the position of those under the canopy even more uncomfortable than that of the *hoi polloi* in the Park. The latter were under umbrellas,—the former were in a situation where to hoist umbrellas was inconvenient. The central position of the stand, however, which was to be occupied by the Prince and those immediately beside him during the ceremony, was tolerably well protected. Notwithstanding the inclemency of the weather, large numbers assembled in the Park to see the Prince and the proceedings that were to take place. Many of them had driven or run up from the Amphitheatre, as the time approached when the Prince was expected in the Park. The number present amounted to five. or six thousand. If the weather had been favourable, this number would probably have been quintupled, but it is not every one who cares to stand out for an hour or two in Prince's weather. The crowd was kept back by a chain extending around the stand at some little distance from it. Within this circle the admission was by tickets, but the number who sought admission into this enclosed space was rather limited.

For the information of strangers it may be explained that the Park is a gift from the University to the city, not bestowed in fee simple, but to be retained for the free use of the citizens so long as the Corporation keep it in order as a Park and do not build on it. On the pedestal, of which the foundation stone was laid, it is intended to place a statue of the Queen, which will be a handsome object in the grounds, and serve perpetually to remind the citizens of Toronto of the visit of the Royal guest, and his assisting them to show their loyal and devoted attachment to the Crown and person of his exalted mother.

At a quarter past twelve, the arrival of the St. George's and St. Andrew's Societies marching in procession with their banners, was received with cheers by the crowds, as indicating the speedy approach of His Royal Highness. The Highland Brigade, Capt. Fulton, had before this taken its position on the ground, east of the platform, having been appointed to act as the guard of honour to the Prince on this occasion; also the York Field Battery of Artillery, under the command of Capt. Denison.

A few minutes after the arrival of the societies, the carriages of the Prince and his suite drove up, and a salute was fired by the Field Battery. His Royal Highness was received at the landing place by the Mayor, the Rev. Dr. McCaul, Mr. F. W. Cumberland, and Mr. A. Morrison, and being conducted along a carpeted pathway, passing between the two Russian guns presented by the Queen, took his place on the stand behind the stone which was about to be lowered to its permanent position. His Royal

A 12

Highness was accompanied by the Governor-General, the Duke of Newcastle, Earl St. Germains, General Bruce, Major Teesdale, Captain Retallick, and others of his suite. He was enthusiastically cheered by the crowd.

The Rev. Dr. McCaul addressed His Royal Highness as follows:—" May it please your Royal Highness,—I am deputed on behalf of the citizens of Toronto to request that your Royal Highness will be graciously pleased to lay the foundation stone of the pedestal for a statue of the Queen. Our object in erecting this statue is that there may be a permanent manifestation of our grateful sense of the manifold blessings which we enjoy under Her Majesty's benignant rule. I am deputed further to request that your Royal Highness will be graciously pleased to inaugurate that part of the University Park set aside for the use of the citizens, and I feel assured that I speak the sentiments of every individual in this community when I give utterance to the confident hope that this and succeeding generations, as they avail themselves of the opportunities which this public place of resort presents for healthful recreation, will ever associate their enjoyment with the reign of a Sovereign to whose Throne and person we feel devoted loyalty and attachment, and the visit of a Prince whom we welcome with enthusiastic joy."

His Royal Highness having graciously intimated that he would comply with the request thus made to him, Mr. Angus Morrison, M.P.P., presented to the Prince a glass bottle containing a sovereign, a half sovereign, a twenty cent piece, a ten cent piece, a five cent piece, an English shilling, and an English six-pence, all of the reign of Victoria, and copies of the *Globe, Colonist,* and *Leader* newspapers, published that morning, and also a copy of last week's *Mirror.* The Prince took the bottle and placed it with its contents in the cavity of the lower stone.

Alderman Carr then presented the plate which was to cover the cavity, and Dr. McCaul read the inscription on it as follows :—

    Hunc primum lapidem
      Basis Cui
     Cives Torontonses
    Statuam Victoriæ Reginæ
     Imposituri sunt
      Posuit
     Albertus Edoardus

Princeps Walliæ
VI. Id. Septembr. MDCCCLX.
Victoria
Annum Vices. et quartum
Regnante
Edmundo Walker Head Baronnetto
Vice-Regia Rerum summam
Per Provinc. Brittan. in America
Septembr.
Administrante
Eodemque die
Princeps Celsissimus
Agrum e Praedio Academico
In salutem oblectationemque
Civium Sepositum
Dedicavit.

His Royal Highness put the plate in its place, and then with a silver trowel, presented to him by the Mayor, spread some mortar on the stone, the mortar got another touch from Mr. James Worthington, builder, and then the support being removed, the upper stone was let down by pullies to its place. The Prince then applied the square and plumb presented by Mr. Cumberland and Mr. Patteson, and taking a mallet, handed to him by Mr. Brunel, gave the stone three blows, and pronounced the stone duly laid and the Park inaugurated.

The Rev. Dr. McCaul then announced to the people that His Royal Highness had inaugurated the Park, by declaring it open to the public under the name of the Queen's Park. The announcement was received with loud and prolonged cheering.

The trowel used by His Royal Highness has already been described. Not so with the other implements. The mallet was of black Canadian walnut, inlaid with various specimens of Canadian woods. The handle was of marble, ornamented upon the end with a mural crown in silver. The junction of the handle with the mallet was covered with a Prince of Wales' plume. The base was surrounded by a scroll of carved maple leaves. In the centre was a silver shield engraved with the plume. The level was open, carved scroll work, also inlaid with various specimens of Canadian woods. The plumb rule, in keeping with the rest, was of maple. The silver work was executed by J. G. Joseph & Co., the design by Jacques & Hay.

THE REVIEW.

A review of the active militia force followed. The various *corps* occupied positions on the open ground to the east of the platform, and all was ready for the review to commence, so soon as the proceedings connected with the inauguration of the Park were completed. The companies reviewed were No. 1 rifle company, Captain McDonald; No. 3 rifles, Captain James Smith, and the Highland company of rifles, Captain Fulton—the whole Rifle Force being under the command of Colonel Durie and Major Brookes; Major McLeod and Captain G. T. Denison, jr.'s troops of York cavalry, and the Field Battery of Artillery, Captain R. L. Denison, jr. The whole were under the command of Col. G. T. Dennison, commandant of the active force. His Royal Highness having advanced to the east front of the stand, with General Williams, the Governor-General, the Duke of Newcastle, General Bruce, and other members of the suite standing near him, the review commenced. The evolutions gone through were not very numerous. The falling rain made all desirous that the force should show their condition of efficiency in as short a space of time as possible. First the troops drawn up in line presented arms, and the bands played "God save the Queen." While this was being played a large proportion of the assemblage stood with uncovered heads, not heeding the pelting rain. Then the order was given, "shoulder arms," and forming fours right, the troops passed in front of His Royal Highness, marching in quick step to the air of "British Grenadiers," played by two bands, and the three pipers of the Highland company. After the review was over, Col. Denison was sent for, and His Royal Highness was pleased to express his high satisfaction with the appearance made by the volunteer force.

The rain kept pouring down all the time, but the ladies held on to their places, notwithstanding. His Royal Highness walked round the platform so that the people might have an opportunity of seeing him from every side. We are modest, most decidedly, but we do not shrink from stating the fact openly that the Prince of Wales is a favourite with the ladies. He pleases them much, and they are pleased with him. With the ladies on his side, who dare say a word against him.

THE UNIVERSITY.

From the park His Royal Highness proceeded to the University. As soon as he left the platform in the Park, there was a rush of the crowd to the University, that they might arrive there before the Prince, and give him a cheer as he entered. His Royal Highness having descended from his carriage at the door of the University was received there by the Hon. Justice Burns, Chancellor of the University; John Langton, Esq., Vice-Chancellor; The Rev. Dr. McCaul, President of the University College; and Hon. James Paton, President of the University Association, and conducted to the Convocation Hall, which was crowded with a fashionable assemblage of ladies and gentlemen, while the students and graduates formed a lane through which His Royal Highness passed to the dais at the further end of the hall. On this a throne had been placed, on the back of which was a raised Prince's plume of gold work, between the letters A. E. On the wall over the gallery at the other end of the hall, meeting directly the view of His Royal Highness, were inscribed the words—" Imperil spem spes Provinciæ salutat"—meaning that the Hope of the Province salutes the Hope of the Empire. On the dais, to the right and left of the throne, stood members of the Senatus, the Professors of University College, and other gentlemen.

The following address to the Prince was read by Chancellor Burns:—

To the Most High, Puissant and Illustrious Prince Albert Edward, Prince of the United Kingdom of Great Britain and Ireland, Prince of Wales, Duke of Saxony, Prince of Cobourg and Gotha, Great Steward of Scotland, Duke of Cornwall and Rothsay, Earl of Chester, Carrick, and Dublin, Baron of Renfrew, and Lord of the Isles, K. G.

MAY IT PLEASE YOUR ROYAL HIGHNESS,—

We, the Chancellor, Vice-Chancellor, Senate and Graduates of the University of Toronto, and the President, Council, and Members of the University College, desire to welcome your Royal Highness with loyal and dutiful respect on your visit to the capital of Upper Canada, and gladly avail ourselves of this auspicious occasion to renew the assurance of our devoted loyalty to the Queen, and to express our grateful appreciation of the manifold blessings which we enjoy under Her Majesty's benign sway.

Fresh from the advantages of England's most ancient University Your Royal Highness now honours with your presence the Academic Halls of this young Province. The pleasures and the profit united in the pursuit of collegiate studies have already been enjoyed by you, and we doubt not that our efforts to extend the same educational privileges among our Canadian youth will command your sympathy, framed as our system is upon the model of the institutions of the mother country, while adapted in its details to the special wants of this portion of the empire.

To this great work, which involves the intellectual advancement of Canada, our best energies have been directed. By its means the freest advantages of liberal culture, and academic honours and rewards, are placed within the reach of all who are prepared to avail themselves of their untrammelled facilities, and under the Divine blessing, our exertions have already been crowned with such success, as to anticipate a noble future for our Provincial University and College.

The high gratification which we feel on the coming of the Heir of the British Crown, the destined successor of our Royal Founder, is specially enhanced to us by the consideration that alike by study and travel, your Royal Highness is being trained for the duties of the exalted position you are born to occupy. In these halls, devoted to the training of the youth on whom the future hopes of Canada rest, we welcome you as the hope of this great empire. We rejoice to recognise in our Prince the promise of qualities which will render him worthy to inherit the Crown of our beloved Queen, whose virtues are associated with the glories of the Victorian era, and whose sceptre is the guarantee of equal liberties enjoyed in this, as in every Province of her world-wide dominions.

The Prince read the following reply:—

GENTLEMEN,—I rejoice to receive the assurance of your loyalty to the Queen, and your appreciation of the blessings enjoyed under her sway by every portion of her Empire.

I am at this moment a member of a more ancient University, but I am not on that account the less inclined to respect and honour those whose efforts are directed to the spread of knowledge and learning in a young country.

I sympathise heartily with the efforts which you are making on behalf of Science and Literature. I believe that much depends on your exertions, and I earnestly hope that the best evidence of the successful exertions of the University of Toronto may hereafter be found in the progress and prosperity of Canada.

Vice-Chancellor Langton then said,—His Royal Highness the Prince of Wales having been graciously pleased to express his willingness to enroll himself as a student of the University, I have the honour to move, seconded by the President of the University College, that His Royal Highness, Albert Edward Prince of Wales, be admitted a student of the second year in the University of Toronto.

The Chancellor put the motion, which was carried amidst the enthusiastic cheering of the students, and others assembled. The Register, Mr. Moss, presented the University book to the Prince, and His Royal Highness inscribed his name on its roll of students.

His Royal Highness and the members of his suite were then conducted through the building by the University and College authorities. In the gallery of the library the boys of the Upper Canada College were assembled, and cheered as the Prince entered. In the Museum Mr. Moss was specially presented by the Governor-General to the Prince, as a most distinguished alumnus of the University. The procession through the building was headed by the beadle, and the two Esquires Bedel, (J. A. Boyd, Esq., A. A., and J. T. Fraser, Esq., B.A.,) the two most distinguished graduates of the previous year. His Royal Highness did not ascend higher than the Mineralogical Museum. The state of the weather was such that the view from the tower was scarcely a sufficient temptation to induce him to ascend to its summit. When His Royal Highness left the building, the people outside who were waiting his egress cheered loudly for the Prince and for the Queen. A cheer for General Williams was also called for and heartily given.

From the University His Royal Highness proceeded to Government House to lunch, and then drove to the Botanical Gardens to effect the inauguration of the grounds. The horticultural people had been very busy at the Botanical Gardens for some days, and really achieved wonders. Not only were the grounds nicely sodded, the winding paths neatly finished, and the flower beds in full bloom, as if they had been planted at the usual season, but an arch had been put up at the entrance and a rustic pavilion erected in a central position, entirely of cedar, calculated to hold at least 1,000 persons. This pavilion was very tastefully decorated, festoons of evergreens drooped from its lofty roof, and its pillars were wreathed round with bands of cedar sprigs in which were put bouquets of flowers and branches of fruit trees laden with their luscious crop. Two or three bowers, much smaller but similar in character, were also built at proper points. The show of fruits, flowers, garden vegetables, and field crops was however not in these, but in less solid structures, as four large canvass tents were put up for their display.

The tent under which the show of flowers was held was circular, and instead of tables there were beautifully sodded concentric terraces within it, on which the plants and blossoms for exhibition were placed. This arrangement was exceedingly tasteful, and elicited the warmest approbation of all qualified judges. These grassy stands were covered with choice bouquets, the envy of the ladies, with gorgeous phloxes, ever pleasing verbenas, old fashioned stocks, staring China asters, stately begonias, upstart and glowing cockscombs, rare and tender greenhouse plants, and laboriously got up floral designs. One of these latter was specially noticeable, as it represented a country seat in a pleasant shrubbery, surrounded by well trimmed gardens, and having dwarf flagstaffs in various parts of the miniature grounds, whose flags were embroidered with such mottoes as "Welcome Prince of Wales," and "God save the Queen."

There was also a fine show under the fruit tent. On the central tables there were tempting plums, juicy grapes, luscious pears, and here and there a few long kept currants. On the tables which ran around were peaches, big as apples; apples huge as pumpkins, and small as peas; melons sweet to scent and taste; more red, green, yellow, and blue plums, grapes and pears, nectarines, filberts, and every other imaginable fruit that was in season.

Under the vegetable tent were big squashes, enormous cabbages, turnips, carrots, potatoes, salsafy, beet roots, and all sorts of garden produce of that kind.

There was, however, not so good a show under the tent set apart for field corps. The samples of wheat, a few mangold wurtzels, carrots, corn and pumpkins were not by any means so attractive as they might have been made, while there were but few specimens of poultry there. In all of these tents the exhibitors were busy at an early hour, and at about noon the judges commenced their labours.

At three o'clock, the rain which had been persistently pattering against the pavilion and oozing through the canvas of the tents, to the detriment of the petals of the flowers, the injury of the "bloom" on the fruits, the disgust and discomfort of the judges, suddenly ceased. The sun shone brightly for a short while, the sanded paths dried up, the flags fluttered gaily in the pleasant breeze and sunshine, and His Royal Highness entered. Accompanying him was the whole of his suite. Arrived at the platform under the pavilion, (which had been covered with *green* cloth,) the Hon. G. W. Allan presented an address and received a very gracious reply—both being textually as follows :—

To His Royal Highness, Albert Edward, Prince of Wales, Prince of the United Kingdom of Great Britain and Ireland, Duke of Saxony, Prince of Saxe Cobourg and Gotha, Great Steward of Scotland, Duke of Cornwall and Rothsay, Earl of Chester, Carrick and Dublin, Baron of Renfrew and Lord of the Isles, Knight of the Garter.

MAY IT PLEASE YOUR ROYAL HIGHNESS,—

We, the Directors of the Toronto Horticultural Society desire, on behalf of the Association, to express our grateful sense of the high honour conferred upon the Society by the visit of your Royal Highness to our Gardens.

In prosecuting the work of laying out these grounds, now for the first time to be opened to the public, the Society have been actuated by a desire to promote the interests of Horticulture and at the same time to prove a new source of healthful recreation, and rational enjoyment for their fellow citizens.

The encouragement which has always been accorded to undertakings of a similar nature in our fatherland, both by Her Majesty and the Prince Consort, have emboldened us to hope for the countenance and favour of your Royal Highness upon the present occasion, and we now, on behalf of the Horticultural Society, most respectfully request that your Royal Highness will be graciously pleased to inaugurate these gardens, and at the same time to leave a lasting memorial of your visit, by placing in our grounds a Canadian Maple, which may long continue a living monument both to us and to our children, of the gratifying events of the day, as well as of the honour conferred upon our country by the visit of the Heir Apparent to the British Throne.

G. W. ALLAN, *President.*

GENTLEMEN,—I shall have great pleasure in doing any thing which will tend to encourage amongst you a taste for the cultivation of gardens, such as may increase the comfort and enjoyment of the citizens of Toronto. I shall be content if the tree which I am about to plant, flourishes as your youthful city has already done.

The tree which the Prince planted was a fine young Canadian maple, about eight years old, in full leaf, its roots being undisturbed, so much earth being taken up with them. It hung from a four-legged set of shears by a pully over a hole. His Royal Highness having proceeded to the spot, the tree was lowered into its destined position, and the Prince, with a beautiful silver spade, shovelled a spadeful of earth around it; then three vociferous cheers were given, and the gardens being proclaimed open, His Royal Highness went through the tents in which the fruit and flowers were, examining them with careful attention.

As soon as the Prince had left, a photograph of the President and Directors, who stood in front of the tent, was taken, and they then, along with the press and fifty guests who were honoured with an invitation went to lunch.

The Hon. G. W. Allan was, of course, by virtue of his presidental office, at the head of the table, and on his right and left were Col. Thompson and Hon. Wm. Cayley. After excellent justice had been done to the colation, the President proposed "the Queen," and after that toast had been duly honoured, he gave the next in the following terms:

I propose the health of Prince Albert and the royal family, more especially that distinguished member of it who has honoured us by visiting these grounds to-day—a day which we shall always consider a proud one in the history of our society. The inaguration of these gardens by His Royal Highness will make the Toronto Horticultural Society better known in our fatherland, and I have no doubt that if we have to apply for assistance in completing our collections to any of the institutions there, which are favoured by Royal patronage, we shall find ourselves treated with increased consideration on account of the occurrences of to-day. (Hear.) I trust the tree which His Royal Highness has planted will flourish and be a gratifying momento of his visit in years to come. (Cheers.)

The next toast, also from the chair, was "the Governor-General."

This was followed by a speech from Professor Croft, who proposed the health of Hon. G. W. Allan, and suggested that he should plant an English Oak at a place near the spot where the Prince had planted the maple. Then there would be the emblem of Canada, planted by a true born Briton, and that of England planted by a true Canadian, emblems of the intimacy which existed between the two countries. Prof. Croft also alluded to the generosity of Mr. Allan in presenting so fine and valuable a property as the gardens for the use of the city.

Mr. Allan replied, intimating his readiness to plant the tree, and thanking the company for the very hearty manner in which the toast had been received. Mr. Allan then proposed the Judges, Hon. Mr. Cayley, the Secretary, Mr. Small.

Appropriate replies were made, and, after several more toasts had been given and replied to, the company dispersed.

Mr. Humphreys sang "God save the Queen," at the request of the company, with the addition of the following verses :—

> Victoria's heir we meet,
> With loyal welcome greet,
> To love our Queen.
> Trained by her Royal care,
> May he her virtues share,
> And with us long join in prayer—
> God save the Queen.

Oh! Thou that ruls't the wave,
Mighty alone to save,
    God bless the Queen.
Perils and dangers o'er,
Her princely son restore,
In safety to Britain's shore—
    God save the Queen.

At half-past three o'clock the Prince, accompanied by his suite, visited the Normal School. Notwithstanding the unfavourable state of the weather thousands of persons assembled around the entrance leading to the building. On alighting from his carriage, the Prince was received by the members of Council of Public Instruction, among whom were Dr. Lilley, Dr. Barclay, Dr. McCaul, Rev. Mr. Grasett, Dr. Ryerson, Hon. Judge Harrison, Chairman of the Council. There were also present Sir. Allan MacNab, Sir E. P. Tache, Hon. J. C. Morrison, Hon, J. H. Cameron, Hon. Mr. Mills, Messrs. J. G. Hodgins, Secretary of the Council; J. Howard, G. Ridout, T. Hodgins, Rev. Mr. Ellerby, Mr. Robertson, Head Master of the School; Mr. Cockburn, and many others. Upon entering the door he was presented by Miss Dixon, one of the pupils, with a very handsome boquet, which he accepted and for which he returned thanks to the young lady. The Prince was accompanied by the Governor-General, the Duke of Newcastle, Lord St. Germains, Generals Bruce and Williams, Colonel Rollo, Captain Retallick and others of the staff.

The Prince was at once conducted to the theatre of the institute, the body of which was filled by the pupils, male and female, to the number of perhaps 500. All the girls were dressed in holiday attire, and several of them threw boquets to the Prince when he appeared, for which he bowed his thanks. The galleries were thronged by ladies and gentlemen, who were admitted by ticket. Immediately after the Prince was conducted to his place, the Hon. Judge Harrison read the following address, to which His Highness replied :—

To the Most High Puissant and Illustrious Prince Albert Edward, Prince of the United Kingdom of Great Britain and Ireland, Prince of Wales, Duke of Saxony, Prince of Coburg and Gotha, Great Steward of Scotland, Duke of Cornwall and Rothsay, Earl of Chester, Carrick and Dublin, Baron of Renfrew, and Lord of the Isles, K. G.

May it please your Royal Highness—

The Council of Public Instruction for Upper Canada beg to unite with the many thousands of our fellow subjects in welcoming you to a country just selected as a home by United Empire Loyalists of America. To us as a body has been assigned the task of establishing Normal and Model Schools for the training of teachers, of making the regulations for the government of Elementary and Grammar Schools throughout the country, and of selecting the text books and libraries to be in them, while on one of our number has been imposed the duty of preparing and administering the school laws. It has been our aim to imbibe the spirit and imitate the example of our beloved Sovereign in the interest and zeal with which Her Majesty has encouraged the training of teachers, and the establishment of schools for the education of the masses of her people, and we have been nobly seconded in our efforts by our Canadian fellow subjects at large.

At the commencement of our labours in A.D. 1846, our meetings were held in a private house, the number of our schools was 2,500, and the number of the pupils in them was 100,000. At the present time we have the educational buildings honoured by the presence of your Royal Highness, where teachers are trained, and maps, apparatus, and libraries are provided for the schools; and those schools now number 4,000, attended by 300,000 pupils. In the songs and text-books of the schools, loyalty to the Queen and love to the Mother Country are blended with the spirit of Canadian patriotism; and christian principles, with sound knowledge, are combined in the teaching and libraries of the schools.

With all our Canadian fellow-countrymen our earnest prayer is "Long live the Queen;" but whenever, in the order of Providence, it shall devolve on your Royal Highness to ascend the throne of your august ancestors, we trust the system of public instruction now inaugurated will have largely contributed to render the people of Upper Canada second to no other people in your vast dominions in virtue, intelligence, enterprise and christian civilization.

Gentlemen,—The progress of Canada has excited my admiration, but there is no subject in which your efforts appear to have been more zealous than in the matter of public education. You have had, I know, the assistance of an able administrator in the person of your Chief Superintendent, and I hope that public education in Upper Canada will continue to inculcate the principles of piety and obedience to law, and christian charity, among a thriving and industrious people.

Accept, gentlemen, my thanks for the welcome now offered to me within the walls of this great and important establishment.

After the reading of the reply, the pupils, under the direction of Mr. Sefton, Music Master of the Normal School, sang the National Anthem. Three cheers were then given for the Prince,—after which the children sang "Hurrah for Canada," which was received with applause.

The Prince then left the theatre, in company with his suite, and was conducted over the Institute by the members of the Council present. In the Library, those gentlemen were presented to him by the Governor-General. The Prince examined attentively, the various objects of art in the Museum, Model School, and other departments in the building, and expressed himself pleased with what he saw. In the Library, he signed his name in the visitors' book, as also did the Duke of Newcastle, Earl St. Germains, and Generals Williams and Bruce. Those, therefore, who have a curiosity to see the autographs of such a bevy of great personages may indulge it by a visit to the Normal School. However, even if this attraction did not exist, there are enough of others to make a visit both pleasant and instructive.

While the Prince was making the tour of the building, hundreds of persons were congregated in the hall to catch a glimpse of him as he passed into the various rooms. There was no cheering when he appeared on those occasions,—but the ladies were loud in their admiration of his handsome face,—and paid him many compliment, which he pretended not to hear, but passed along, his head slightly inclined forward,—his usual way of appearing in public.

At half-past four o'clock the Prince left the building. An immense crowd had gathered around the gates, and his appearance was the signal for a repetition of that hearty applause which had rung in his ears ever since he landed in the city. Making his way with a little difficulty, through the crowd who would jostle and crush to catch a near glimpse of him, and who would cheer so heartily, the Prince reached his carriage. The horses then plunged forward and scattered the multitude right and left. The enthusiastic populace did not let him get off so easily, for they ran alongside of the carriage waving hats and handkerchiefs, and manifesting their intense delight with all the power of their lungs. The Prince, as he always did, acknowledged those hearty demonstrations by bowing, and what the people think a great deal more of, by repeatedly smiling and looking pleased.

After leaving the Normal School, His Royal Highness, accompanied by the Duke of Newcastle, the Governor-General and several others of his suite, paid a short visit to Knox's College, where the party were received by Principal Willis and several members of the College Senate. Dr. Willis, in a few words, gave a brief history of the institution and of its results. After inscribing his name in the register of visitors to the College Museum, His Royal Highness took his departure amidst the cheers of those who were present. A boquet was presented by Mrs. Willis, which His Royal Highness graciously accepted.

A state dinner was given at Government House on the evening of Tuesday. Besides His Royal Highness and suite, the following gentlemen were present:—Hon. Mr. Cartier, Hon. Mr. Ross, Hon. A. T. Galt, Hon. Mr. Rose, Hon. W. B. Robinson, Mr. Justice Burns, Mr. Justice Richards, Rev. Dr. McCaul, Rev. Dr. Willis, Rev. Dr. Ryerson, Dr. Connor, M.P.P., George Gurnett, Esq., William H. Boulton, Esq., and W. A. Baldwin, Esq.

THE BALL.

To say that the ball room presented a magnificent spectacle is to use merely common place language, which conveys no adequate idea of the reality. Such a spectacle was certainly never before presented in Toronto. On first entering the Palace, after the company had assembled, one felt dazzled and bewildered by the sight of the moving masses of life and gaiety, the brilliant colours and elegance of the costumes, the immense proportions of the building, the endless variety of its decorations and the splendour of its illuminations. For a time the mind was so occupied with the brilliancy of the spectacle as a whole, that it was incapable of noting the details of which it was composed.

At half-past ten the word flew through the joyous party that

His Royal Highness was about to enter the ball room. Ladies and gentlemen consequently ranged themselves along the length of the room, leaving a space between for His Royal Highness to pass through. This he did, accompanied by the Governor General, the Duke of Newcastle, Earl St. Germans, Major Gen. Bruce, Major Teesdale, and several gentlemen of the suite.

The arrangements in the ball room were of the most perfect kind. It was very cold, but how could it be avoided, as the several passages to and from the supper and other rooms produced a current of air which in warm weather would have been delightful, but then was the reverse. In the centre of the room a fountain played a small jet of water, which dripping over various coloured lights ranged round the edges of the fountain had a very pretty effect. In order to accommodate the dancers, and to give them an opportunity of meeting engagements, the several pillars in the room were numbered, which proved of the greatest convenience. The music was every thing that could be wished. In the main orchestra, Poppenberg's excellent band did the needful, and the Rifle band in the gallery opposite. The assembly was brilliant beyond compare; not too large to make dancing unpleasant, but large enough to fill the hall comfortably. There were several of the gentlemen dressed in uniform,—as was also the Prince.—which was a relief to the sombre but genteel black. To describe the ladies? Better leave such a subject untouched. But in one word we may say nothing was wanting to make the display as brilliant, as charming, as lovely as the most exquisite taste could desire. No attempt to describe the dresses of the *beau sexe* could be made,—they were of all hues and of every description— such as the Toronto belles know "how to do it." That is enough in itself. It is estimated that the assembly numbered over 3,000.

The dancing was kept up with spirit, and with but a very slight intermission, until a quarter past four, when the programme of 21 dances being concluded the Prince left. Such clapping of hands, such waving of handkerchiefs, such rousing cheers as greeted him on his departure are not often seen, and plainly manifested the delight of the whole assembly. And well might they feel pleased. The son of their Queen had spent the whole night among them. He had made one of their number, and acted like one of themselves. He did not confine himself to a few dances ; he did not restrict his movements to one section of the room,—he was every where ; now here, then there,—so that every one had an opportunity of seeing him.

One feature of the dance must not be allowed to pass unnoticed. It was a pleasing feature indeed. There in the same set of quadrilles, bearing through their lovely partners, were the Hon. the Premier, M. Cartier, and the Hon. George Brown. As they have often stood before, so they stood then—they were *vis a vis*, smiling and bowing in a polite manner. Who knows what good consequences may result from the pleasing *re-union?* Another incident noticed briefly. In one of the waltzes the Prince fell on his knees, but did not bring his partner to the ground, and was soon righted.

The following is a complete list of the ladies who were honoured with the Prince's hand during the night:—

1, quadrille, Mrs. Wilson, wife of the Mayor; 2, polka, Miss DeBlaquiere; 3, gallop, Miss Blackwell; 4, quadrille, Mrs. M. C. Cameron; 5, valse, Miss Kilally; 6, galop, Miss Julia Ridout; 7, lancers, Miss Cayley; 8, galop, Miss MacNab; 9, valse, Miss Helen Gzowski; 10, quadrille, Mrs. J. B. Robinson; 11, polka, missed; 12, Miss Wallace; 13, lancers, Miss Young, daughter of the Chief Justice of Newfoundland; 14, valse, Miss Moffatt; 15 polka redowa, Miss McCaul; 16, quadrille, Miss Harris; 17, galop, Miss Shanley; 18, valse, Miss Denison; 19, lancers, Miss Spragge; 20, valse, Miss S. Jarvis; 21, galop, Miss Murney, Miss Agnes Stewart, and Miss Powell.*

The following address was presented to the Prince of Wales in Toronto:—

---

*To LADIES WHO HAVE DANCED WITH THE PRINCE.—What an event among crinolinedom—to have danced with the Prince of Wales! We are afraid he will have much to answer for. Young men who were formerly considered paragons of perfection by these same young ladies, will doubtless be snubbed incontinently. A hand that has been grasped by a live Prince, will not be bestowed on every chance comer, depend upon it. Have a care, girls! Don't carry your heads too high, or at least not so high that you may not have the pleasure of telling your children "all about the Prince." In short don't be so puffed up that one of these days somebody else will exclaim, incredulously, in your hearing—"What! the Prince dance with *her!* Well, truly, there is no accounting for tastes!" Not the consolatory "Oh, but she was very pretty *once*"—will take the sting from the rejoinder —"*Is it possible?*"

FANNY FERN.

A 14

To His Royal Highness, Albert Edward, Prince of Wales, Prince of the United Kingdom of Great Britain and Ireland, Duke of Saxony, Prince of Saxe Coburg and Gotha, Great Steward of Scotland, Duke of Cornwall and Rothsay, Earl of Chester, Carrick and Dublin, Baron of Renfrew and Lord of the Isles, Knight of the Garter.

MAY IT PLEASE YOUR ROYAL HIGHNESS :—

We, the Commissioned Officers of Military District Number Five, Upper Canada, joyfully embrace this auspicious occasion to approach your Royal Highness with the assurance of our devoted loyalty and attachment to Her most Gracious Majesty, and with our hearty expressions of welcome to Your Royal Highness on your arrival in this portion of Her Majesty's dominions.

The period is not distant when this military district contained but one battalion of effective militiamen, whilst it now includes within its limits upwards of forty battalions, each averaging one thousand effective men; and whilst we have cause for congratulation in this large addition to the number of the defenders of our soil, we are proud to be able to assure Your Royal Highness that the patriotic and courageous spirit which animated the militiamen of Canada when they were but few in number would be found to pervade the numerically increased force, should their services be required—whether in maintaining the laws of the land in their integrity, or in protecting their homes, and the institutions of their country, against the foreign invader. That the martial spirit of Canada is not extinct is shown by the fact of many of her sons having enrolled themselves in the active force of the country, and of her having sent forth the 100th, or Prince of Wales regiment, to take its share in the general defence of the empire.

We hopefully regard this visit of Your Royal Highness to the colony as the inauguration of a long, happy, and lasting connexion with it; and that the impressions of it which you will carry away with you to your native shores may be as favourable as our reminiscences of it will always be gratefully cherished, is the heartfelt wish of the officers of this loyal district.

The following reply was received :—

Toronto, Sept. 8, 1860.

SIR,—I have the honour to convey the thanks of His Royal

Highness the Prince of Wales, for the address presented to him the Commissioned Officers of Military District No. 5, Upper Canada.

I have the honour to be, sir, your ob't servant,

NEWCASTLE.

Here the Belleville Address, of which the following is a copy, was presented to the Prince of Wales, by a large and respectable deputation from Belleville, on Tuesday, 11th September:—

MAY IT PLEASE YOUR ROYAL HIGHNESS,—

We, the inhabitants of the town of Belleville, beg to express to your Royal Highness our loyalty and devotion to the throne of Great Britain, and our heartfelt regret that when your Royal Highness condescended to visit us, untoward circumstances, deeply deplored, deprived us of the long and eagerly looked for opportunity of meeting your Royal Highness with an expression of our devotion to our beloved Queen and the Royal Family.

From earliest infancy we have been taught to regard our title to the time-honoured name of British subjects as a heritage dear to us as life. We feel deeply humiliated, and we pray your Royal Highness may, by forgetting the circumstances alluded to, enable us again to exult in the unfolding of that flag around which cluster the historic glories of ten centuries.

Do not leave Canada without testifying, in some way, the faith of your Royal Highness in our devotion,—without bearing home to your Royal Mother, our beloved Queen, the assurance that, notwithstanding the unfortunate events of the 6th of September, Her honour and Her interests,—reverential love for Her person and Crown,—pride in the power and glory of Britain, and an undying determination to preserve the integrity of the Empire, are most dear to us. We entreat your Royal Highness, if possible, again to visit her Majesty's loyal subjects in Belleville, and to relieve us from the unhappy position in which we are placed, thus restoring the right to feel that we are in the opinion of the world, but more especially in the sight of your Royal Mother, and your Royal Highness, lovers of peace and order, and loyal British subjects.

On behalf of the inhabitants of the town of Belleville,

W. HOPE, *Mayor.*

Dated at Belleville, this 8th day of Sept., 1860.

The following reply was graciously given:—

Gentlemen,—It gives me the most sincere pleasure to receive this very numerous and influential deputation from Belleville, and to hear from your lips the assurances and explanation contained in your address. All painful feelings occasioned by the proceedings in your town on a recent occasion, which I knew were heartily disapproved of by the great majority of the inhabitants, are now entirely removed.

The only regret which I now experience, is that I am unable to comply with the strongly expressed wish of your citizens and those of Kingston, that I would go back and pay them that visit which was so unhappily prevented last week. My engagements to other places would not admit of such a change as to return so far eastward, and I cannot break faith with those who have so kindly made preparations to receive me, and it causes me real sorrow to leave Kingston and Belleville behind unvisited, but I will not fail to inform the Queen of your protestations of loyalty and devotion, nor to add my own conviction of their entire sincerity.

The members of the Corporation present were personally presented by the Mayor.

At an early hour on Wednesday morning, the citizens and strangers who had been in the city for the past few days, were early astir to witness the departure of the Prince of Wales from Toronto. It had been announced that His Royal Highness would leave at eleven o'clock in the forenoon, but long ere that time, thousands had congregated on Front street and in the Amphitheatre to get another glimpse of our future King before he left the city.

About a quarter to eleven o'clock the various regular companies under command of Captains Fulton, Smith and Macdonald marched into the area of the Amphitheatre, headed by the Union Maltese band, to form the guard of honour, under the command of Col. G. T. Denison, the Commandant of the Active Force. This produced a good deal of excitement, and hundreds rushed to the reception platform and temporary railway depot for the purpose of getting a good look at the Prince as he passed into the train on the Grand Trunk Railway which was in waiting to convey him to Sarnia.

The struggle between the police and the populace was a fierce one, the former endeavouring as much as possible to keep the crowd back, and urgently advised them to take seats in the Amphitheatre, where a better view could have been got of the whole proceedings. The crowd refused the advice, and still pushed forward and the pressure became so great the police were obliged to give way, and in an instant the platforms were crowded with persons, both male and female. Then followed a scene which it is impossible to depict. The men tried by every means in their power to get to the front of the platform, but the fair ones who were standing on the edge bravely held their own. The multitude swayed to and fro until the crush became so great that a number of ladies were precipitated head foremost from the platform into the railway track, which elicited roars of laughter from all those who saw them rolling in the sand. In a few moments, however, they were on their feet and tried to regain their former position, but the "lords of creation" were masters of the place and dead to every thing in the shape of gallantry; the fair ones, many of them pretty and nicely dressed, were obliged to stand among the crowd in the track and have their crinoline smashed to pieces in the crushing which from time to time ensued.

The Royal train consisted of three carriages with baggage car. The first and second carriages for the members of His Royal Highness' suite, the members of the press, and the band of the Royal Canadian Rifles. The third, divided into handsome compartments, was especially set apart for His Royal Highness, the Duke of Newcastle, the Governor General, Earl St. Germains, General Williams, Major General Bruce, &c. A temporary pathway had been run out from the platform, covered with carpeting.

At eleven o'clock the field battery under the command of Capt. Denison, stationed in the field west of the Parliament Buildings, commenced firing the royal salute, announcing that the royal cortege had left Government House. This was the signal for the crowd to rush to the front of the reception platform,—all were aware by the firing of the guns that His Royal Highness was *en route* for the train. The police were again called to clear the way for the Prince, but this time they were assisted by the military, and in a few minutes a wide lane was formed from the front of the platform to the pathway leading to the Royal car, lined by the militia. The fourth gun had only given forth its loud report when the York Cavalry, who formed the escort, entered the triumphial arch at the foot of John street. Then the thousands of spectators rose *en masse* from the seats in the Amphitheatre and gave His Royal Highness a most soul-stirring cheer, which was again and again repeated.

The Prince gracefully raised his hat, bowed to the multitude, and the ladies waved their handkerchiefs. The cheering was then taken up by those on the platform, and when the carriage containing His Royal Highness, the Duke of Newcastle, the Governor-General, and Earl St. Germains drove up in front of the platform, the scene was beyond description. The morning was fine and the Prince in excellent spirits, and to judge from his appearance, no one could have imagined that at day-break he was "treading the mazy dance" in the Crystal Palace, and the "observed of all observers." When His Royal Highness stepped on the platform he was received by his worship the Mayor, the Lord Bishop of Toronto, and a number of the leading citizens, all of whom he greeted in the most cordial manner. Captain Smith then gave the command "present arms," and as His Royal Highness passed up the open column into the Royal car, followed by the gentlemen in attendance, the troops gave him a Royal salute, and the crowd cheered in the most lusty manner.

Then followed another fearful crush, as the spectators in front rushed suddenly to the rear after His Royal Highness. Hundreds were pushed down on the track until the space between the Royal train and the platform was one solid mass of human beings, and those on the platform were obliged to stand and brave the great pressure from without. The Prince waited only about a minute in the car and then came out and took his station in the rear platform. The crowd raised another heart-stirring cheer, which His Royal Highness gracefully acknowledged. He then entered into conversation with General Williams, and from time to time watched with much interest the fun which was going on below, and seemed to enjoy it vastly. The amusement was somewhat heightened by General Williams tossing an apple among a bevy of ladies who were stationed immediately in rear of the Royal car, and the scramble which ensued to get possession of the apple caused His Royal Highness to laugh heartily.

At this juncture the Lord Bishop of Toronto walked up the pathway, when the Prince stepped forward to meet him, and seemed highly pleased when he grasped His Lordship by the hand, which he did in the most cordial and loving manner. A few words passed between them, and the venerable Bishop bade His Royal Highness an affectionate farewell, and retraced his steps. When His Lordship was walking down the platform he was seen to brush away a tear from his eye. The Bishop also shook hands with the gentlemen composing the immediate suite of the Prince, and as he left the car platform the crowd gave him a cheer.

Three cheers were then given for General Williams, which the "Hero of Kars" acknowledged by lifting his cocked hat and bowing. Cheer after cheer then arose for the Prince, and it seemed as if he could never stop bowing. His Royal Highness observing some photographers on the ground with their cameras, stood still for a few seconds in order that they might take his portrait while he was on the platform of the car which was to convey him from Toronto.

His worship the Mayor, the Rev. Dr. McCaul, William H. Boulton, Esq., Col. R. L. Denison, and other gentlemen went forward and bade the Prince adieu, and every thing being ready, Mr. Christie gave the signal to the engine-driver, and the train moved slowly past the temporary station, amid the most vociferous cheering and waving of handkerchiefs by the ladies, and the Maltese band playing the National Anthem, which His Royal Highness acknowledged as long as the train was in view of the vast multitude. Before leaving the platform the crowd gave "three right loyal cheers for His Royal Highness the Prince of Wales."

After leaving the Amphitheatre in Toronto on September 12, 1860, the Grand Trunk Railway which bore the Prince of Wales and suite running rapidly along the smooth track soon passed the city limits, and whirled its Royal freight into the open country, where well-tilled fields and noble forests again diversified the scenery. At each station—almost, indeed, at every crossing—there were numbers of farmers and their wives determined to see the Prince's carriage, if they could not see the Prince. It would make the report too long to mention the names of all these places. Only those places where some remarkable display occurred can be recorded.

At Brampton, the first note-worthy turn out was made. There a company of militia were drawn up in a line, and about a thousand people assembled.

At the iron bridge over the Credit, near Georgetown, the train stopped, and the royal party went down the steep slope to have a good look at the the beautiful structure, which is 954 feet long, and is supported by seven stone piers, at the height of 126 feet above the level of the river below. The scenery in the neighbourhood being very picturesque.

At Georgetown, a large number of people, with bands and flags, were gathered together.

At Guelph there was a delightful scene. A long carpeted platform, on each side of which lines of militia were posted—thus ensuring perfect order—led from the cars to a pretty pavilion nearly in front of the handsome new Town Hall. Around this pavilion an amphitheatre of seats occupied by about 6,000 people had been erected, while 4,000 or 5,000 more were closely packed together all around on the market square, and on the house roofs even. A Royal salute was fired by the local battery of artillery as the train drew up, and as it moved away again. As the Prince walked to the centre of this assemblage the people cheered enthusiastically, and the ladies waved their handkerchiefs. A thousand school children sang the National Anthem in capital style, and the Prince and people seemed alike delighted. Several of the royal party thought the reception the prettiest they had seen at any town. Addresses were presented to the Prince by the Mayor, John Harvey, Esq., on behalf of the town, and by the Warden, William Whitlow, Esq., on behalf of the County of Wellington. In reply, His Royal Highness expressed his gratitude at receiving an address from the centre of so fertile a district, more especially as it bore the name of his family. The leading inhabitants of the town and neighbourhood were there presented, and the Prince returned to the cars, remarking as he did so the beautiful arch which spanned his path. After leaving Guelph lunch was had on board the cars.

At Berlin, where the train stopped for wood and water, there were about 1,000 people assembled.

At Petersburgh, a German settlement, an address in German handed in, and His Royal Highness having no written reply answered it verbally in the German language, telling them he thanked them—was delighted to hear of their prosperity, and hoped it would continue.

At Stratford the Prince went to the front of the railway station, and received and replied to an address presented by the Mayor, Mr. John McCullough. Here there were at least 1,000 spectators and a company of rifles. In default of artillery the people had bored holes in logs and stumps and cramming them with powder were shooting them off in every direction. At St. Mary's there was a somewhat similar demonstration. Near London, Mr. Christie, the superintendent of the western district of the Grand Trunk was presented to the Prince by Earl St. Germains. The road was certainly in such good order as to render the compliment deserved.

The royal train arrived at London at four o'clok. In spite of the biting cold wind some 10,000 people had congregated around the platform on the common, to which, as it was a hundred yards or more from the train, the Prince was driven in a carriage, escorted, as also subsequently, by Capt. River's fine troop of cavalry. At the platform he stood under the pavilion while J. Moffatt, Esq., the Mayor, and the Warden of the County, presented their respective addresses. The ceremony was hurried through as much as possible, owing to the cold ; and a procession was formed, which accompanied the Prince through the principal streets of the city to the Tecumseth Hotel, where he stayed.

Three hearty cheers were given for the Prince, and also for the suite and Governor-General, who was called for, and both bowed their thanks from the balcony of the hotel.

Dundas street was almost roofed in with bands of coloured calico stretched across, and was ornamented with several arches.

The procession was most orderly. The finest feature in it was the fire companies from Port Huron, Sarnia, Ingersoll, St. Thomas, St. Mary's, Stratford, &c., numbering, in addition to the London companies, at least 1,000 men, uniformed chiefly in scarlet, some however in pink, some in blue, and some in invisible green, setting off the prevalent colour. There was a large number of Indians feathered and painted, some of them being magnificent specimens of their race, though some of them had the weak constitutions and woe-begone look of the semi-christianised red men.

A 15

The following is the address of the Corporation and the Prince's reply :—

MAY IT PLEASE YOUR ROYAL HIGHNESS,—

We, the Mayor, Aldermen, and Committee, of the city of London, in Upper Canada, do, in the name of the inhabitants, most cordially welcome your Royal Highness. We rejoice that our city should be thus highly honoured by the presence of the son of our beloved Queen, and the Heir Apparent of the powerful and glorious Empire over which Her Majesty has for so many years so wisely and auspiciously reigned. It has given us unmingled satisfaction to be made acquainted with the enthusiastic reception accorded to your Royal Highness during your progress westward, from the day of your first landing in these provinces ; but less than such a welcome we never imagined you would receive, for the North American Colonies are peopled by those who will yield to none in their attachment to the British Crown and in affection to the reigning Sovereign. The fact, that at most, it is only forty years since in the locality where you now stand none but the red Indian once stood under the shade of the primeval forest, will sufficiently explain to your Royal Highness why we can conduct you to no magnificent buildings ; to no sacred historic monuments such as those which are familiar to your eye ; but we are persuaded you can well appreciate the results of an industry which, in our circumstances, are necessarily more marked by the useful than the ornamental. We trust that your Royal Highness may return home in safety, gratified with your visit to these colonies, and retaining pleasing recollections of their inhabitants. Do us the distinguished favour to convey to Her Majesty assurance of our most devoted loyalty to her crown and person. We pray the Almighty to guide and bless you through life.

(Signed,)

JAMES MOFFATT, *Mayor.*

GENTLEMEN,—I accept with great satisfaction the address in which you proclaim your deep attachment to the person and government of the Queen, and offer me so kind a greeting in your loyal city. You do no more than justice to the other parts of this splendid province when you speak of the enthusiastic reception which has been every where accorded to me as the son of your Queen. I know the attachment to the British Crown of the people of the North American Colonies, but all the expectations I had formed of their devotion have been more than realized by the demonstrations I have witnessed. The country through which I passed this day presented the spectacle of a population prosperous and happy. Its progress excites alike admiration and astonishment, and the industry evinced on every side having supplanted the trackless forest of past generations by smiling fields and pastures, reminding you of those which so many of you have quitted in your youth. That this prosperity may continue, and this industry meet with its fair reward, will ever be the constant prayer of your Sovereign, of myself, and of the people who share with you the blessings of free institutions, and are bound to you by identity of interest and by affection.

There was a very fine and general illumination in the evening, and a beautiful torch-light procession. A number of fireworks were also displayed by private citizens. There were upwards of 20,000 strangers in the city, and as beds were therefore difficult to be obtained, the compliment the city paid to the members of the press in considering them its guests was by no means an empty or valueless one.

FROM AN ENGLISH VIEW.

Who can follow the transatlantic "progress" of the Prince of Wales without arriving at the conclusion that the Queen's son is a young man with whom any other young man in the kingdom might well be pleased, at this moment, to change places? His career, indeed up to the present time, has been far from unenviable. He has been nurtured in the lap of luxury; he has had all the heart of man could crave for, or the tongue of man demand; he has had tutors to instruct him in the sciences, to expound to him the philosophy of Greece and Rome, to recount to him the tale of universal history, to store him with wisdom accumulated during centuries of thought and investigation, to teach him the languages of modern Europe. He has studied in Edinburgh and Oxford, and has paid homage to learning in the Eternal City. He has journeyed hither, he has journeyed thither; he has seen foreign land and foreign people under more favourable circumstances than Prince ever saw them before; and now, while still a

mere stripling, he is in the distant West, representing the majesty
of his august Mother in the midst of a loyal and delighted colonial
population. And what a very agreeable occupation it must be to
the fortunate youth who is thus employed. He may be new to
the work, but it is easy to see that he takes to it like a youthful
Louis XIV. Only one little mishap do we hear on the record of
the jubilant proceedings at Halifax. His Royal Highness made
a "slight mistake" in reading his address to the President of the
Council, and "coloured" at his awkwardness. But the blush of
annoyance did not long suffuse his cheek, for we are told that he
at once regained his self-possession and went on with his harangue.
It would seem, almost impossible, indeed, for even a passing cloud
to dim the brightness of his Nova Scotia sky. Albert Edward's
life is, for the time being, one continuous *fete*. The moment he
enters port, his long expected arrival is welcomed by the discharge
of cannon and the sound of stirring cheers. Ere he can step on
shore smiling deputations have boarded the vessel he voyages in,
to tell him of their devotion in exuberant prose. The moment he
lands crowds gather round him, all eyes are strained to catch a
glimpse of his person, officials press forward to bask in the sunshine of his glances, fair maidens look lovingly in his face, and,
as he passes onwards, he finds the streets lined with eager thousands, flags waving from windows, festoons linking house to house,
and triumphal arches erected along his path, every step of which
is strewn with roses. No wonder that Victoria's son looks gratified
and happy. No wonder that he captivates all hearts by his genial
bearing, and by the evident interest he manifests in every thing
that takes place around him. It would be hard, indeed, for him
to be otherwise then gratified with the attention showered down
upon him on every side. And then the night is even more
delightful than the day. For there is the ball-room alluring him
with its dazzling animation, and he knows beforehand that youth
and beauty in their most seductive aspect will strive there for the
honours of his hand. Who can tell, indeed, what havoc the
Prince may have already committed among the hearts of our fair
colonial sisters? For Albert Edward is an ardent devoted Terpsichore, and enters into the spirit of her mazy evolutions with the
ardour of another St. Vitus. His polking is pronounced by
colonial authorities to be superb, while his superiority in the
"Valse à Deux Temps" is nothing short of marvellous. As for his

"Mazurkas," eulogy has no terms to express her admiration of them, and even the Goddess of Grace herself would be delighted with the finished elegance of his quadrilles. Then, too, ask the special correspondent of transatlantic journals, as a partner, who can equal him? Not only does he dance to perfection with the lady whom he honours with his choice, but he continually gives her graceful "rests," and fills up the interval with the most entertaining and animated conversation. Evidently, the Prince is made happy by the reception accorded to him, the colonists are rendered even more so by the graciousness and urbanity with which he responds to their loyal demonstrations.

So we offer our warmest congratulations to Albert Edward, and wish him a hearty God speed on the journey he has still to perform. According to the latest advices he was soon to leave for Quebec, and probably before this, has been received with acclamation in that important Canadian city. If he is to be envied as Heir Apparent to the English throne, upon whom an entire colony is just now lavishing its enthusiasm, he is still more to be envied as the ambassador who is charged by his Sovereign with a mission of peace and good-will to the distant possessions of a great empire. He is in Canada as the representative of a country powerful by its physical strength and its material resources, but still more powerful by the progressive spirit of its rule and the freedom of its institutions. He goes with a message of sympathy to a vast and important colony subject to its sway, and he must be proud indeed when he feels that his mere presence on those American shores cannot do otherwise than sow seeds of affection and harmony between people and people, which will bear good fruit in the immediate present as well as in the remote future.

It would be hard to say whether the Prince of Wales' visit to British North America is more a matter of congratulation to himself or the colonists. The benefit is so great all round that no one can wonder at the fervour of expressions of gratification in the Queen's speech last week. The occasion is indeed one of singular instruction to the Prince. He had before seen a good deal of the world for a youth of eighteen. He was familiar with the sea and land exercises of travel at home; and his visit to Rome answered much the same purpose that "the grand tour" of the last century was supposed to accomplish in the case of noblemen and gentlemen finishing their education. But this travelling in Canada is a different affair altogether. The relation between the guests and the host is so close and peculiar—in truth so solemn—that all the hilarity of youth on the one side and gratified loyalty on the other—all the cheering and dancing, and roving and fun, are no more than enough to enlighten the seriousness of the occasion. It must be a daily astonishment to the English party to see what the country and people are who have ranked as a very subordinate part of the empire. It must be truly imposing to pass from one to another of those wide colonies which we group together, as we might speak of a group of islands, and to perceive that each might be, for space and capabilities, a kingdom in itself. After skirting hundreds of miles of shore on which a human dwelling is scarcely seen, it must be most striking to find in the towns, and in the rural settlements, an advanced civilisation equal to any thing that the provincial cities of the mother country have to show. To contemplate at once such public works as the admirable telegraph system connecting our colonies with the United States, and the railways, great bridges, and steam service on the lakes and rivers, and the prodigious area of country yet almost unexplored, extending across the whole continent, must be sufficiently stimulating to the imagination; but when the visitor sees all this under the constant impression that the millions of people occupying these vast spaces will hereafter depend much for their welfare on the rule for which he will be responsible, he must be impressed with a new sense of responsibility. They are, as he sees, ready and willing, with slight exception, to attach themselves more and more to British rule; and it must be clear to him that nothing more than simple justice and natural respect are needed to sustain a hearty friendship between the colonies and the mother country; and he, as the future trustee of the national polity, (for that is in fact the function of constitutional sovereigns,) must now be daily learning much of what the claims of the North American colonies are, and must continue to be. It is not a quarter of a century since Canada was miserable, mischievous, and a cause of grave apprehension to sovereign and people. This was from misgovernment. Now, not only when gratified by the presence of a Royal guest, but when we have been too busy or too careless to recognise the fact as we ought, the colonists have shewn a zeal, and dutifulness, and hearty attachment to England unsurpassed by any of the Queen's subjects, from her volunteers to the school children who greet her with the National Anthem as she passes on her journeys. Witness the noble subscriptions in money on any occasion of pressure or mishap. Witness the Canadian Regiment, landed at Liverpool in aid of the last war. The change is owing to the good government provided for them—the self-government permitted to them—during the present reign. The Prince must know enough of Canadian history to be aware of the change and its causes. Some painful incidents just reported from Montreal may be highly instructive in this direction. The outbreak of feeling on the part of a few ill-blooded representatives of the old French residents must show to all observers what the state of the country must have been formerly, and what it would have been now, as a scene of perpetual conflict between two races, not self-governing, but ruled over by a close oligarchy, in the name of the British Sovereign, all now happily allayed.

To the colonists the occasion may be no less profitable in instruction. They have always evidenced a strong loyalty to the British connexion amidst the incessant talk that is always going on, on the other side of the Atlantic, about their absorption into the great neighbouring republic. It is not at all known or imagined in England how entirely it is taken for granted by political men generally, and a large proportion of the citizens of the United States, that the Canadians would like to join their Union if they could. This assumption, and the constant discussion of the point, seem to have had no effect on the loyalty of the colonists hitherto; and now that they have met face to face both our Colonial Minister and the representative and heir of the Sovereign, they will perceive that their interests are considered important, their attachment valued, and their share in the blessings of our polity as complete as our own. Perhaps the passionate and perverse malcontents at Montreal may grow somewhat wiser and happier when they see what the home authorities are actually like—willing to hear (as the Duke of Newcastle always is) whatever they have to say, and anxious to see them satisfied. If this may not be hoped, their incivility need not be thought too much of. We see elsewhere how it is with any people who make or keep themselves peculiar, and shut themselves up and stand stock still when the rest of the world are expanding and moving on. There are still aged Irish persons in the United States who cast ferocious glances at every Englishman, and weep scalding tears while they rate him for the wrongs of '98. There are Germans in the Western States who will not learn English, and who carry flags with the inscription "no schools." These old-fashioned folks must be borne with. They will go to their graves in time, and a generation or two hence their children will know better. The Montreal malcontents do not know France any more than they know England. They live among old associations. Even the passing spectacle of a British Prince employed in opening so very modern a kind of a bridge may let in some light among their prejudices; and the consequent increase of the general prosperity must sooner or later modify their mood.

If we put ourselves in the position of the citizens of the United States for a moment, we shall see how remarkable an event the Prince's visit must appear to them. While even our eldest generation has almost lost sight of the American war of independence, the subject is perpetually in view in every American mind from the statesman's to the infant-school child's. While an Englishman travels there as in other foreign countries for observation and gratification, the inhabitants suppose him to be always looking at the country as a lapsed colony. This is inevitable, and neither blameable nor absurd; and it should be remembered through all we hear of the Prince's reception. We must remember how singular must be the pride and triumph with which such a nation must receive as a guest the great-grandson of the King from whose rule they withdrew. There is no quarrel between them and us about that act of theirs; and their prosperity is more gratifying to us than to any body but themselves. As for the instruction that the occasion may yield, it must be good for any constitutional Prince to obtain even a bird's-eye view of the great domain of a democratic republic. We must hope that he is aware that the genuine results of popular government are not to be seen among the aristocracy of capital cities and great seaports, but among the landowners of the interior and the industrial classes generally. Whatever his impressions may be of what he sees, he will not have seen, in so short a visit, the most characteristic, the soundest, and the happiest part of the population.

On the other side, some beneficial impressions may be left behind. There are multitudes in the United States who believe that to live under a hereditary sovereign is to be somehow enslaved to that sovereign; and it is a common remark in the country itself that the citizens have unconsciously grown up in a notion that Royal people are somehow visibly and entirely different from other folk. An American author tells us how an intelligent fisherman talked after seeing the Prince de Joinville land unexpectedly, repeatedly remarking that he should not have remarked the Prince as different from any other gentleman. It is not so much the childish feeling which makes a little boy or girl from India enquire whether our Queen rides about all day in a buggy with a crown on her head, as the notion that there must be some air of despotism distinguishing a Prince among ordinary people, as a planter moves in a distinguished way among his slaves. There is more of this notion, unconsciously held, than is commonly supposed; and we may hope that there will be less of it after the appearance among the republicans of one who is in training for the noblest throne in the world.

There will scarcely be time for them to perceive one fact of the strongest interest to them. The main characteristic of the young Prince's mind, as shown in his studies, in his love and justice of fair play—his enthusiasm for rectitude in human dealings, under all temptations, and through all sacrifices. He must be aware of the moral basis on which the republic was founded. His judgment of its present condition will be formed from the fact of its fidelity to, or desertion of, that basis of morality. The sympathy between the guest and his entertainers as to their condition and prospects as a nation may be measured by the consideration how faithfully the principles of the republic of eighty years ago now work in the policy of the American Union. So much for the impression on the judgment. About the mutual kindliness of feelings between all the hosts and all the guests, there is happily no doubt.

The Prince left London on September 13th, for Sarnia. The train stopped no where on the route; as it runs almost entirely through the woods he saw no crowds of people from the time he left London till he reached his destination. The day was charming, and the fine forest was seen to great advantage. Arrived at

Sarnia, the Prince left the cars and walking along the scarlet cloth which covered the platform for a hundred yards, he reached one of the prettiest pavilions he had yet seen. Around it on the slopes of the railway cutting, and in the station grounds some 5,000 people were seated, and, strangest sight of all, some 200 Indians from the Manitoulin Islands sat on long straight benches in front. Behind was the beautiful, clear, St. Clair river. The white houses of Port Huron on the other side glittering in the sun, and several steamers crowded with people lying at the wharf. The first part of the ceremony was the least interesting, consisting as it did of the presentation of addresses, in the usual routine manner.

The Mayor, Thos. W. Johnson, presented his address, and then the Councillors, standing in a semi-circle around the Prince, were severally introduced.

The Warden of Lambton next came forward, with the County Council's address, and the County Councillors were then presented as their brethren from the town had been.

A third address was then delivered by the St. Andrew's Society, and the President and office-bearers also had the honour of an introduction.

Then commenced one of the most interesting proceedings which had yet taken place.

The Indians, real red savages, majestic in mein, painted as to their faces, adorned with hawks' feathers and squirrels' tails as to their heads, with silver spoons in their noses, moccasins on their feet, and many of them ignorant of English, came forward, and one of them, a magnificent specimen of his tribe, named Kan-wa-ga-shi, or the Great Bear of the North, advancing to the front, stretching out his right hand yelled out an Indian address to the Prince, which was translated to him by the Indian interpreter, who, as the red man finished each phrase and folded his arms, gave the meaning of what was said. The whole harangue was as follows:

BROTHER, GREAT BROTHER—The sky is beautiful. It was the wish of the Great Spirit that we should meet in this place. My heart is glad that the Queen sent her eldest son to see her Indian subjects. I am happy to see you hear this day. I hope the sky will continue to look fine, to give happiness both to the whites and to the Indians.

GREAT BROTHER—When you were a little child your parents told you there were such people as Indians in Canada, and now, since you have come to Canada yourself, you can see them. I am one of the Ogibbeway chiefs, and represent the tribe here assembled to welcome their Great Brother.

GREAT BROTHER—You see the Indians who are around you; they have heard that at some future day you will put on the British Crown, and sit on the British Throne. It is their earnest disire that you will always remember them.

The Prince replied verbally that he was grateful for the address; and hoped the sky would always be beautiful, and that he should never forget his red brethren.

As each phrase was interpreted to the Indians, they yelled their approbation—the sound they uttered seeming like "nee wugh."

Then the name of each was called out by the interpreter from a list handed him by the Governor-General, and each one advanced in turn. Some had buffalo horns upon their heads; some had snake skins around their waists; most of them had feathers on their legs. Almost all had bands around their waists embroidered with coloured grass or porcupine quills. The Chief shook hands with the Prince and the Governor, the others bowed, and to each His Royal Highness gave a medal with the likeness of Her Majesty on one side—the Royal arms on the other. The Chiefs' medals were as large as the palm of your hand—the other Indians received smaller ones, the size perhaps of half-crowns. Then the red men brought forward a box and gave it to the Prince. It contained a tomahawk, bow and arrows, wampums, pipes of peace, and other Indian curiosities. His Royal Highness graciously received the present. This interesting ceremony over, the Prince went through the town of Sarnia, passing under three very fine arches, and was driven in a carriage drawn by four bay horses, and attended by a cavalcade of gentlemen and ladies on horseback to Point Edward to the Grand Trunk railroad station. Here a splendid lunch was prepared, and the Royal party partook of it. After the three usual toasts, which were given with great enthusiasm, the Prince

proposed "Prosperity to the Grand Trunk Railway," which was
enthusiastically honoured. Then the Prince went to the balcony
of the depôt, whence a fine view of the St. Clair was obtained,
and embarking on the G. T. steamer, Michigan, running up the
river into lake Huron, which was studded with sailing craft, and
returned at a rapid rate to the Great Western railway station,
where he embarked for London again.

ARTEMUS WARD SEES THE PRINGE OF WALES.

At larst I've had an intervu with the Prince, tho' it cum purty
nere costin' me my valcrable life. I cawt a glimpse of him as he
sat on pizaro of the hotel in Sarnia, and elbode my way through a
crowd of men, children, sojers, and Injins that was hangin' round
the tavern. I was drawin' near to the Prince when a red faced
man in millingtary close grabd holt of me and axed me where I
was going all so bold.

"To see Albert Edard, Prince of Whales," sez I, "who be you?"

He said he was Kurnel of the Seventy-fust Regiment, her
Majesty's troops. I toled him that I hoped the Seventy-Onesters
were in good health, and was passing by when he ceased holt of me
agin, and said in a tone of indignant cirprise:

"Impossible! It can't be! What sir! did I understan' you to
say you was actocaly goin' into the presents of his Royal Incss?"

"That's what's the matter with me," I replied.

"But sir, it's onprecedented. Its orful sir! Nothing like it
hain't happened sins the Gunpowder Plot of Guy Forks! Ow-
doshus man, who air you?"

"Sir," sez I, drawin' myself up and putin' on a defiant air,
"I'm a 'merican sittuzin, my name is Ward, I'm a husband, an'
the father of twins, which, I am happy to state look like me.
By perfeshun I'm a exhibiter of wax work and sich."

"Good gracious!" yelled the Kurnel, "the idea of a exhibiter
of wax figures goin' into the presents of Royalty! The British
Lyon may well roar with rage at the thawt!"

Sez I, "Speakin' of the British Lyon, Kurnel, I'd like to make
a bargin with you fur that beast for a few weeks tu add to my
show." I did'nt mean nothin' by this. I was only gettin' orf a
goak, but you orter to hev see the old Kurnel jump up and howl.
He actooally foamed at the mowth.

"This can't be real," he showted. "No—no, It's a orrid dream. Sir, you air not a human bein'—you hev no existens—yure a myth!"

"Wall," sez I, "'old hoss, yule find me a ruther onkomfortable Myth ef you punch my inards in that way ag'in, I began to get a leetle riled, for when he called me a Myth he puncht me purty hard. The Kurnel now commencet showting for the Seventy-onesters. I at fust thought I'd stay and becum a Martar to British Outraje, as sich a course mite git my name up and be a good advertisement for my show, but it occurred to me if some of the Seventy-onesters should happen to insert a bayonet into my stummick, it mite be onpleasunt, and I was on the pint of runin' orf, when the Prince hisself kum up and axed me what the matter was. Sez I, "Albert Edard, is that yu?" and he smilt and sez it was. Sez I, "Albert Edard, hears my keerd. I cum to pay my respeks to the futhur king of Ingland. The Kurnel of the Seventy-onesters hear is ruther smawl pertaters, but of course you ain't to blame for that. He put on as many airs as tho' he was the Bully Boy with the glass eye."

"Never mind," sez Albert Edard, "I'm glad to see you Mr. Ward, at all events," and he tuk my hand so pleasant-like, and larfed sweet that I fell in love with him at once. He handed me a segar and we sot down on the Pizaro, and commenct smokin' rite cheerful."

"Wall," sez I, "Albert Edard how's the old folks?"

"Her Majesty and the Prince are all well," he sed.

"Duz the old man take his Lager Bier reg'lar?" I inquired.

The Prince larfed, and intermatid that the old man did'nt let many kegs of that beveridge spile in the cellar in the course of a yere. We sot and talked there sum time about matters and things, and bimeby I axed him how he liked bein' Prince as fur as he hed got.

"To speak plain, Mister Ward," he sed, "I don't much like it. I'm sick of all this bowing & scrapin & crawling & hurrain over a boy like me. I would rather go threw the country quietly & enjoy myself in my own way, with the other boys, and not to be med a show of to be garpen at by everybody. Wheh the people cheer me I feel pleased, fur I know they meen it, but if these one-hos offishuls cood know how I see threw all their moves and understan exackly what they air after, and knowd how I larft at em in private, they'd stop kissin my hands & fawnin over me as they now do. But you know, Mister Ward, I can't help bein' a Prince, and I must do all I kin to fit myself fur the persishun I must sumetime ockepy."

"That's troo," sez I "sickness and the doctors will carry the Queen orf one of these dase, sure's yer born."

The time haven arove fur me to take my departer, I riz up and sed, "Albert Edard, I must go, but previs to doin so I will obsarve that you soot me. Yure a good feller Albert Edard, & tho Ime agin Princes as a general thing, I must say I like the cut of yure Gib. When you git to be King try and be as good a man as yure muther's bin. Be just and Jenerous, espeshully to showmen, who have allers bin aboozed sins the days of Noah, who wus the fust man to go into the Meenagery bizness, & ef the daily papers of his time are to be bleeved Noah's colleckshun of livin' wild beests beet enny thing ever seen sins, tho I make bold to dowt ef his snaiks was ahead of mine. Albert Edard, adoo!" I tuk his hand, which he shook warmly, and given him a perpeteooal free pars}to my show, and also parses to take home for the Queen & Old Albert, I put on my hat & walkt away.

"Mrs. Ward," I solilerquised, as I walkt along, "Mrs. Ward, ef you could see your husband now, jest as he prowdly emerjis from the presents of the future King of Ingland, youd be sorry you called him a Beest just becawz he come home tired I night and wanted to go to bed without taking orf his boots. Youd be sorry for trying to deprive your husband of the priceless Boon of liberty Betsy Jane."

A. WARD.

The Prince returned to London from Sarnia at half-past three. The interesting ceremony with the Indians there occupied so much longer time than was anticipated, that the special train had to run very fast to enable His Royal Highness to hold his levee there. It stopped nowhere on the route, and ran 61 miles in an hour and twenty minutes. On board were, in addition to the Prince and suite, Messrs. Cartier, Vankoughnet, Sidney Smith, Morrison and Sherwood, Mr. Bridges, Managing Director of the Great Western Railroad, Mr. Stephens, Secretary to the Company, Mr. Reynolds, Financial Treasurer, &c. Mr. Eaton, Locomotive Superintendent, was on the engine. There were three cars besides the Prince's, all filled, one of these having the London City Council on board, who had escorted the Prince to Sarnia.

The Indians were all drawn up in line as the royal train moved away. They yelled a farewell whoop, and a salute was fired.

Arriving at London an immense concourse of people gathered at the station, completely blocking up the broad street in front of the Tecumseth Hotel. There must have been 8,000 or 10,000 there. Shortly after alighting, a path was cleared, and the Prince having put on his uniform went to the City Hall to hold a levee. It was very numerously attended. Addresses were presented from the National Societies, and among them, from the Welchmen of the City and neghbourhood. A rifle, manufactured by Mr. Philo Soper, of this place, was also presented to the Prince, by a committee of citizens, as a specimen of the perfection which the mechanical arts have attained in so youthful a city.

It is quite true that the Prince, the Duke of Newcastle, and others who are now visiting the Province, have witnessed scenes in the countries of Europe which for magnificence of military and naval display have far exceeded any that Canada can hope to produce. But it may be questioned if there has ever been so thoroughly a people's demonstration as that which was awaited the Prince in all parts of Canada. That at Toronto, especially, entirely surprised the royal party, and presented an aspect to which they—habituated as they had been to dense populations— were entire stangers.

The magnificence of the celebration in Toronto is admitted to have surpassed every thing else of the kind that has been seen since the Prince arrived in America.

Not the least remarkable attraction in the history of the doings, was the striking appearance of the aborigines of this portion of Canada. They assembled in great muster, and decorated in the panoply of their tribes, looked exceedingly grotesque, with their faces painted, and their georgeous plumes of feathers decorating their caput. The chief and his lady led the van, while the subordinates, the greater portion of whom were minus the inexpressibles, created many a merry laugh to the white folk, as they defiled in line. They had their tomahawks and other weapons, making them look as fearful as in the days gone by, without the horrible results which followed them.

September, 14.

The Royal party left London at ten o'clock, by special train, preceded by another engine, and was under the special charge of Mr. Eaton, locomotive superintendent, Great Western Railway.

The first stopping place was at Ingersoll, where great crowds assembled. His Royal Highness stepped out upon the platform of the car, and was loudly cheered.

At Woodstock there was a very interesting spectacle. There was an immense gathering at the station, and great enthusiasm prevailed. Here the Prince and his party got into carriages, and drove to the mayor's residence, passing through the principal streets of the town, which were prettily decorated, and which were spanned by three pretty arches. At Mayor Cottle's, a fine brick house, a couple of miles from town, was a platform in front of the verandah, where could be seen the well trimmed lawn, the pleasant shrubbery, the close cut hedges of the mayor's residence, and a fine vista of well tilled fields. On these beautiful grounds were at least 5,000 people, and on a platform close beside the garden where a number of ladies and little girls. The arrangements were excellent in every way. There were the usual addresses from the warden, Mr. Harrington; from the mayor, Mr. Cottle; from the Baptist College ; and from the mayor of Ingersoll. Then there was the usual *levee* or presentation of the principal personages present. Next the singing of God Save the Queen by the girls. Next the shouting and hurrahing for the Queen, the Prince Consort, the Prince of Wales, and the Governor-General, which was led by Hon. Mr. Alexander, member for Gore Division. Afterwards the Royal party partook of a *dejeuner* in the mayor's house, and then left for the cars again.

The next stopping place was Paris, where Captain Patton's Company of Rifles had been drawn up. A pretty arch was erected, and an address read by Mr. Charles Whitlair, the Mayor. Here the party changed cars and were delivered by Mr. Brydges to Mr. Carter, General Manager of the Buffalo and Lake Huron Railway.

The Buffalo and Brantford railway had built a state car, which was almost as beautiful as that of the Great Western inside, and more handsome without.

A rapid run brought the Prince to Brantford, where the train halted inside a green arch quite massive in its proportions, and he stepped upon a platform carpeted with crimson, on each side of which was an array of handsome ladies, who showered boquets under His Royal Highness' footsteps. At the end of this were the carriages which were to take him to the Kerby House, where lunch was ready. On the way he was escorted by a procession, in part composed of firemen, in part of Mohawk Indians, dressed in their picturesque habiliments, painted and armed. These Indians, like those at Sarnia, presented the Prince with clubs, tomahawks, arrows, and other weapons. There were several beautiful arches on the line of procession, one of them being in the form of H. R. H. The H's at the sides—the R. above them, while a bevy of young ladies were arrayed upon the crosses of the letters. There was some crowding at the door of the Kerby House, owing to defective police arrangements and a lack of military; but once inside the scene was really magnificent. The lunch was prepared by Mr. Bloomer, of Buffalo, who being a little jealous of Mr. Sanderson of New York, who had been chosen for the Prince's steward, therefore tried to outdo his rival. The tables looked splendid, for, in addition to the choicest meats and fruits, there was a great profusion of beautiful bouquets. Mr. Clement, the Mayor, who had previously presented the address of the town, to which, as well as to that of the county, His Royal Highness had graciously replied, sat at the table with the Royal party, and the Rev. Mr. Nelles, who acted as chaplain and said grace, was similarly distinguished.

Lunch over, the party returned to the cars, and a rapid drive brought them to Dunville, where Captain Amsden's company of rifles and a crowd of some seventy-five people had turned out.

From Dunville the train went to Port Colborne and thence to Fort Erie. Here the party got into carriages and went to the old Fort, where some 5,000 people, chiefly Americans from Buffalo, had congregated. Here His Royal Highness had the first look at Lake Erie, whose blue waters were almost waveless. Delay there was out of the question, so the Prince quickly returned and passed across by the Buffalo and Lake Huron Company's great transit steamer *International* and embarked on board the *Clifton*. An hour's steaming took him to Chippawa; on each side of the creek, into which the steamer entered, were huge bonfires which lighted up the whole as clear as day, and made the spray, which drifted up from the Falls close by, assume a rosy tint.

The Magistrates of the County, headed by Sheriff Hobson, were at the landing to receive the Prince. The Members for Welland and Niagara having come up to fort Erie for that purpose, and as it was quite dark the firemen lit their torches and ran all the way beside the Royal carriage to the Pavilion Hotel, near the Clifton House, where the platform was on which the county address was to be presented. This was lit up with Bengal lights, and the scene was both novel and beautiful. Presenting the address was, however, performing ceremonies under difficulties. From the Pavilion the Prince drove to his temporary home, the late Mr. Samuel Zimmerman's house.

September 14.

The Prince danced in London with Mrs. Small, the Misses Beecher, Lawrason, and Moffatt, Mrs. Rivers, Mrs. Moffatt, Mrs. Beecher, Miss Prince, Miss Gzowski, Miss Lawford, Miss Dalton, Miss Hope, Mrs. Taylor, and Miss Goodhue. While dancing with Miss Lawrason the Prince caught his spur in a lady's dress, and slipped. He took the spurs off.

On arriving at Niagara the Prince was escorted up the avenue by a number of American ladies with torches, who jumped out of their carriages for the purpose.

A cavalry volunteer was thrown from his horse. His Royal Highness was very anxious about him, and sent Lord St. Germains to make enquiries. The man was taken to Zimmerman's, and reported but little hurt.

The following notice appears under date of 14th September, 1860. The inauguration will appear hereafter:—

MUSTER AT QUEENSTON HEIGHTS.

"Militia Officers of the active and sedentary force from Toronto and neighbourhood, intending to be present at Queenston Heights when the address to His Highness the Prince of Wales will be received from the survivors of the war of 1812, to form part of the accompanying escort, are requested to appear in uniform, and place themselves on arrival at Queenston under the direction of the Marshal, Lt. Col. R. L. Denison, who will attend to placing them in the order of procession, to the foot of Brock's Monument, where the address will be presented.

The presentation will take place on Tuesday, 18th Sept., at 11 o'clock, a. m.; and we are requested to state, that it would be most agreeable to the Committee acting on behalf of the men of 1812, to witness a very general muster of all militia men, to whom a place will be assigned in the procession by the Marshal. Similar arrangements are in progress in other places for ensuring a general attendance, and for marshaling the procession; and we hope that the display will be a most imposing one. The address has more than a thousand signatures attached to it; names of " good men and true," who took part in the glorious contest to which it refers. Let one and all then do them honour by joining them in full muster before the Prince at Queenston Heights.

THE ILLUMINATIONS AT THE FALLS.

The illumination of the Falls on the night of the 15th was superb. The great gulf, horribly dark a minute before, became clearly visibly in all its features, as soon as the long lines of fires were lighted, which extended near the water's edge all along the cliff on the Canada side. The seething waters seemed now white as milk, then red as liquid lava. As the colour of the lights changed, the Falls themselves seemed like cascades of moonlight or of liquid mother of pearl. The Royal party slipped quietly out of their house and went to Table Rock to see the sight. The Prince went so close to the brink that the Duke of Newcastle laid a warning hand upon him. From the rock the party went to the edge of the Horse Shoe Falls. The Prince and the Governor-General went out upon the rocks or stand which lie in the shallow water near the shore, and while holding by the log which there juts out, the Prince lost his finger-ring. Captain Harris, of the Hamilton Artillery, brought a lantern, and he was fortunate enough to find it just in the water. He gave it for His Royal

Highness to the Governor-General. Soon afterwards the Royal party went to their quarters.

On the 17th, the Prince's movements were nominally private, and in spite of the numbers of carriages and crowds of people which attempted to follow him wherever he had been, he succeeded in eluding their pursuit exceedingly well. It was announced that a boat with the figure of a man in it would be sent over the Falls, and great crowds assembled on Goat Island and in the prominent points of the Canada shore, but they were disappointed in their expectations, and after waiting a long time in vain, dispersed.

In order to view the Falls, the party put on water-proof clothes, hats, overcoats, trowsers and over-shoes, and except General Bruce, all went under the falling sheet of water as far as practicable. On their return they went up the same stairway, pausing at the windows to look at the beautiful rainbows and at the Falls themselves in their ever varying aspect.

At the top they inscribed their names in a register book on a clean page. Albert Edward, Prince of Wales, was the first signature, then the Duke of Newcastle's, then Sir Edmund Head's, afterwards General Bruce's and the others.

The lady at the museum considered it a high honour to have their names in her register book, and took pride in showing them to visitors, with particular instructions not to blot the page.

Afterwards the Prince and suite, on horseback, went to Blondin's enclosure, near the Suspension Bridge, and witnessed the successful feat of Blondin carrying a man over the rapids of Niagara on a rope; also walking the entire length of his narrow pathway on stilts. The Prince was very much pleased with the exhibition. About 5,000 people were present, and every thing passed off pleasantly.

The Prince, in returning, was every where received with enthusiastic cheers.

The most intensely exciting part of Blondin's performance on the 15th was, when he was going across the rope on stilts, he slipped and fell, catching the rope by his thigh. Some said it was done for effect; but, if so, the manœuvre was admirably executed, inasmuch that many ladies actually averted their eyes that they might not see the man fall into the rapids. After enjoying the sight much, and staying to see the whole of the rope walker's performance, for which the Prince gave him a cheque for one hundred pounds, and the suite something more, the Royal party left.

Just at dusk the Prince went on board the *Maid of the Mist*, and ran up into the spray of Niagara Falls. After dinner he went to the alley at the Clifton House and enjoyed the exercise of bowling, his side beating the Duke's completely.

On Sunday His Royal Highness drove to Chippawa Church, a distance of some three miles, and listened to a sermon from the Rev. Mr. Leeming, the incumbent.

The first appearance of the Prince on the 17th was on his way to the ferry. It was not expected that he would cross, so there was only a small knot of people collected on the Canadian side, and there were very few more on the American. The Royal party crossed in the open ferry boat, and on the other side were drawn upon the inclined railway. As they stepped out upon the green, this being their first appearance upon American soil, there was a slight cheer but no enthusiasm—hardly even a cordial greeting—and a photographer took a view of them. They went rapidly towards Goat Island, and the Prince walked round it, stopping at each projecting point whence a good view could be obtained. He went across the bridge which leads from Goat Island to Terrapin Tower, and ascended this. He did not go into the Cave of the Winds, but stood near it on a rock, whilst some twenty of the guides and others loosed a log a score of feet long, and sent it over the Falls. He returned by the same means of conveyance he used in going, employing a common hackman to drive him up the road from the ferry to his residence.

The next thing His Royal Highness did was to drive to the Suspension Bridge, where the Great Western state car was in waiting to take him across. Before entering it, the Hon. W. H. Merritt read him the address of the Bridge Directors, setting forth the length, height, cost, and other particulars connected with the structure. On the centre of the Bridge, the train paused to give him an opportunity of looking at the falls and at the rapids. The party drove to the whirlpool, and after having a good look at it, came back crossing the lower platform of the Bridge and returned to their quarters.

Subsequently the Prince rode on horseback into Thorold township towards the Welland Canal, examining the country, which is well settled, fertile, and very picturesque. He did certainly do Niagara and its neighbourhood thoroughly.

Queenston Heights.

Queenston Heights! It is not long since Brock's monument there was finished—since the remnants of the brave men who preserved to Great Britain her North American possessions assembled to celebrate its completion. Few among them then thought that on the 18th of September, 1860, the Heir Apparent to the British Throne would stand upon the scene of former strife, and for himself and for the Queen of England too, thank the veteran band for the part they had taken in the contest so long gone bye. Yet so it was.

At five o'clock on Tuesday morning the steamer *Peerless* started from Toronto, with a numerous company of military, old and young.

Many of the militia officers embarked their horses duly caparisoned the evening previously; amongst the foremost might have been observed the charger of Col. R. L. Denison, the marshal for the day.

Queenston was reached at half-past nine o'clock, and the St. Catharines band having formed in front, the Rifles of St. Catharines, and Highland Companies of Toronto, fell in, and those of the staff of the militia present also fell into the rear of the troops, and thus marched to the top of the eminence on which the monument is erected to the memory of Major General Brock.

On their way thither several arches were encountered and passed. While making no great pretensions to beauty, they were pretty rustic affairs, serving very well for the occasion. Many of the houses on the road were ornamented with flowers, and from the windows looked down the very prettiest of girls upon the gallant soldier boys below.

Around the base of the monument a large number of people collected. They hung in clusters upon the steep hill sides, blocked up the carriage way, and stood in dense firm masses upon the level grass. They were in a state of commotion. Col. Denison was labouring to produce order out of the chaotic mass of human beings gathered together. In the first place a large square platform, covered with crimson cloth, was erected, on three sides of which were placed tiers of seats for the accommodation of the ladies; who by no means rejected the opportunity thus offered. The fourth side faced the carriage way. To the left were placed the Toronto Highland and Volunteer Rifle Companies; to the right the St. Catharines Rifles. Down the centre of the lane thus formed were the Veterans. And there were a great many of them, all old men; dressed for the most part in a blue uniform, with steel epaulettes and glazed caps. It was for them the display was made—they were the observed of all observers. Old friends met there, men who had fought side by side in the olden times—and who had thenceforth been endeared to one another by the recollection of common dangers shared. Many a hearty shake of the hand was given; many a congratulation uttered that life should be yet left in some almost forgotten acquaintance of the past. Notes were compared, localities pointed out, comments in general upon the Yankees of the present day, and upon the Yankees in particular of 1812 indulged in—generally by no means complimentary to the citizens of the United States, for the old veterans are no republicans. And so amid the noise and confusion of successive arrivals and the general " hullabaloo" always attendant upon an unoccupied crowd, the time was wiled away.

The Committee for the reception consisted of Sir John B. Robinson, Sir Allan N. McNab, A.D.C., Colonel Street, Hon. W. Merritt, David Thorburn, Esq., and the Hon. E. P. Tache, A.D.C.

But the Prince arrived sooner than was expected—half an hour sooner. Things had very nearly been got into apple-pie order, but not quite. He immediately ascended the platform, and took his stand in such a position that the best view of him could be obtained by the surrounding multitude. But so quickly was the whole thing done, that it was almost impossible to say who were there, and who not. It is almost unfair to publish a part of the of the names of the veterans present. A list would willingly have been made out of the whole had time permitted, but the early arrival of His Royal Highness rendered this impossible.

Better a part perhaps than none at all. Among the veterans then who faced the platform, were:—Col. E. W. Thomson, commanding district No. 5 ; Col. T. G. Ridout ; Col. the Hon. Henry Ruttan, Cobourg, commanding district ; Col. McLean, Scarboro'; Capt. McLeod, Oak Ridges ; Isaac White, Detroit Medal ; John Ross, Detroit Medal ; William Higgins, George Bond, Archibald Macdonnell, Hamilton ; Major William Cawthra, Major Benjamin Milligan, John Perkins, Capt. Hiscott, 1st Lincoln ; William A. Thompson, Scarboro'; William Strain, Toronto township ; Charles Cameron, Toronto township ; Andrew A. Thompson, Scarboro'; John A. Thomson, Toronto township ; Philip Whiteman, Markham ; John Butts, Markham ; Cornelius Plummerfelt, Markham ; David Bridgeford, Vaughan ; Jacob Snider, York ; Major Miller, 1st Lincoln ; Alex. Thomson, Markham ; Major John Button, Markham ; Francis Button, Major George Bond, Yonge Street ; and James Fortier, Provincial Navy, Detroit Medal ; Majors D. Rolph, John Boulton, and Captain McLeod.

Of those militia officers present, were observed:—Lieut.-Col. R. L. Denison, 4th Battalion, Marshal of the day ; Col. G. T. Denison, Commandant of the Active Force ; Lieut.-Col. Durie, Commanding Rifles ; Major McLeod, York Volunteer Cavalry ; Major Nickinson, Toronto Rifles ; Major Brooke, Toronto Rifles ; Capt. Denison, York Volunteer Cavalry ; Capt. Fulton, Toronto Rifles ; Capt. D. G. Macdonald, Toronto Rifles ; Lieut. Patterson, Toronto Field Battery ; Lieut. Patterson, Toronto Rifles ; Lieut. Gardener, Toronto Highlanders ; Ensign Brown, Toronto Rifles ; Capt. J. O. Heward, Capt. Green, Capt. R. L. Denison, Capt. Goodwin, Capt. Cellem, Capt. Wilson, Lieut. Maughan, Lieut. Taylor, and Coronet L. Denison.*

The 1st Welland Companies, as near as could be ascertained, were represented by :—Lieut.-Col. T. C. Street, Major John Thompson, Major Samuel Strange, Capt. Archibald Thompson, Capt. Hiram Maclett, Lieut. Joseph Reavelly, Lieut. Hugh James, Ensign John Grenville, Ensign James Vanalstine, Ensign Hyatt Summers.

The arrival of His Royal Highness, you may be sure, was the

---

* In the second edition, any names forwarded to the publisher will be willingly inserted.

signal for many hearty cheers. The old gentlemen saluted with their swords; and all joined with their voices in welcoming the Prince to Queenston Heights. The instant he arrived Sir J. B. Robinson, surrounded by the members of the committee, advanced and read to him the following address :—

To the Most High, Puissant and Illustrious Prince Albert Edward, Prince of the United Kingdom of Great Britain and Ireland, Prince of Wales, Duke of Saxony, Prince of Cobourg and Gotha, Great Steward of Scotland, Duke of Cornwall and Rothsay, Earl of Chester, Carrick, and Dublin, Baron of Renfrew, and Lord of the Isles, K. G.

MAY IT PLEASE YOUR ROYAL HIGHNESS,—

Some of the few survivors of the Militia Volunteers who assisted in defending Canada against the invading enemy during the last American War, have assembled from different parts of the Province in the hope that they may be graciously permitted to offer to your Royal Highness the expressions of their loyal welcome upon your arrival in this portion of Her Majesty's dominions.

In the long period that has elapsed, very many have gone to rest, who have served in higher ranks than ourselves, and took a more conspicuous part in that glorious contest.

They would have delighted in the opportunity, which we now enjoy, of beholding in their country a descendant of the just and pious Sovereign, in whose cause they and their followers fought, and whom they were from infancy taught to revere for Her many public and private virtues.

We feel deeply grateful to Her Majesty, whose condescension to the wishes of Her Canadian subjects has conferred on us the honour of a visit from your Royal Highness; and we rejoice in the thought that what your Royal Highness has seen and will see, of this prosperous and happy Province, will enable you to judge how valuable a possession was saved to the British Crown by the successful resistance made in the trying contest in which it was our fortune to bear a part—and your Royal Highness will then be able also to judge how large a debt the Empire owed to the lamented hero Brock, whose gallant and generous heart shrank not in the darkest hour of the conflict from the most discouraging

A 18

odds, and whose escapes inspired the few with the ability and spirit to do the work of many.

We pray that God will bless your Royal Highness with many years of health and happiness, and may lead you by His providence to walk in the paths of our revered and beloved Queen, to whom the world looks up as an example of all the virtues that can dignify the highest rank, support worthily the responsibilities of the most anxious station, and promote the peace, security and happiness of private life.

To which His Royal Highness made the following gracious and very sensible reply :—

GENTLEMEN,—I accept with mingled feelings of pride and pain the address you have presented to me on this spot—with pride in the gallant deeds of my countrymen, with pain in the reflection that so many of the noble band you once belonged to have passed away from the scene of the bravery of their youth, and of the peaceful avocations of their riper years. I have willingly consented to lay the first stone of this monument. Every nation may, without offence to its neighbours, commemorate its heroes' acts, their deeds of arms, their nobleness. This is no taunting boast of victory, no revival of long past animosities. A noble tribute to a soldier's fame is the more honourable, because we readily acknowledge the bravery and chivalry of that people by whose hand he fell. I trust that Canada will never want such volunteers as those who fell in the last war, nor her volunteers be without such leaders. But none the less and most fervently pray that your sons and grandsons may never be called upon to add other laurels to those you have so gallantly won. Accept from me in the Queen's name my thanks for your expressions of devoted loyalty.

At the conclusion of the reply, his Royal Highness was conducted by Sir John B. Robinson to the monument itself. He ascended to the top, and from thence enjoyed the magnificent view which stretches far and wide below—a scene, perhaps, unrivalled in Upper Canada. From thence he proceeded to the foot of the hill to the spot where General Brock fell. Here a square stone pedestal four feet square, had been placed upon a grassy bank, three feet six inches high. Suspended by ropes and pullies, over the pedestal was a stone obelisk, four feet three inches high, and weighing about three and a half tons. On one side was the following inscription :—

" Near this spot Major-General Sir Isaac Brock, K. C. B., Provisional Lieutenant-Governor of Upper Canada, fell on the 13th of October, 1812, while advancing to repel the invading enemy."

On the opposite were the words :—
" This stone was laid by His Royal Highness Albert Edward, Prince of Wales, on the 18th September, 1860."

Some few have spoken about the absence of arrangement in the proceedings for the Prince's reception, and the following paragraph would seem to give colour to the rumour :—It is by no means the case. The marshal had barely time to disembark his charger, much less arrange a procession before the excitement of the Prince's arrival, and absence of adequate aid, prevented a proper arrangement of the *lermidnies*. It was however with the aid of Colonel T. C. Street, and some others of the militia officers, order was observed to a certain extent, and the exuberance of spirit on all sides, although interfering with the arrangements, was not unworthy of the occasion which brought together so many of our home protectors.

In reference to the inauguration of the obelisk, it may not be uninteresting to our readers to peruse a copy of the inscription on the reverse of the monument, erected by voluntary contribution after its destruction in 1840, and the following has been kindly furnished by the Custodian :—

A monument was originally erected on this spot by a grant from the Parliament of this Province, and subsequently destroyed in the year 1840. The present monument was erected chiefly by the contributions of the MILITIA and INDIAN WARRIORS of this Province, aided by a grant from the Legislature. The authority for erecting the same being delegated to a committee consisting of the following gentlemen :—

Sir Allan McNab, Chairman ; Sir John B. Robinson, Bart., Hon. Justice McLean, Hon. Wm. H. Merritt, M.P.P., Colonel The Hon. James Kirby, David Thorburn, Esq., Colonel Robert

Hamilton, Sir James B. Macaulay, Kt., Hon. W. H. Dickson, T. C. Street, Esq., Lieutenant-Colonel D. McDougall, Lieutenant Garrett, late 49th Foot; Captain H. Monroe, Secretary; Thomas G. Ridout, Esq., Treasurer; William Thomas, Architect; John Worthington, Builder; George Playter, Custodian.

No sooner was the ceremony of laying the stone completed, than His Royal Highness sought his carriage,—proceeded at once to the *Zimmerman*, and embarked for Niagara, the St. Catharines Volunteer Rifles forming a guard of honour. The distance between Queenston and Niagara was quickly passed. Upon the wharf a very nice arch was erected—the product of a night's labour—bearing the motto, "God save our noble Prince." Through the arch, from the vessel, could be perceived an open pavilion of spruce, with streamers gaily flying. The floor was carpeted, and upon it stood three handsome chairs. On the Railway Car Works were several large inscriptions. Among others were these side by side—"Prince Edward, Duke of Kent, August 22nd, 1792." "Albert Edward, Prince of Wales, September 18th, 1860." The railway station and several of the houses in the city were decorated. The Fire Companies turned out in full force, and guarded the way from the boat. A large number of people thronged the wharf, on one side of which stood a platform, occupied by ladies and children. Two addresses were presented. One from the Council by Mr. F. A. R. Clench, the Mayor; another from the Magistrates by his Honour Judge Lauder, Chairman of the Quarter Sessions. The scene was very gay, and from the strenuous efforts made by the people to see the Prince, somewhat exciting. While the presentation of the addresses was being proceeded with the *Peerless* arrived, loaded with passengers, who joined their enthusiastic cheers with those of the thousands upon the land. When His Royal Highness regained the boat he was presented, through Mr. G. F. Nash, the President of the Electoral Division Horticultural Society, with a large quantity of beautiful fruit, each separate basket bearing the name of the gentlemen in whose garden it was grown. Some of the peaches measured nine inches in diameter. The Prince was also pleased to accept from Miss Miller, daughter of Major Miller, a jar of peach preserves and a bouquet, and from Miss Mary McMullen a second bouquet. Wherever he goes, His Royal Highness is overloaded with presents. He gets huge canoes, quivers of arrows, big bows, and ugly tomahawks from the Indians, all sorts of things from some sorts of people, and fruit and bouquets from the ladies. If he were to stay much longer, the *Great Eastern* would have to be chartered to carry the load home. But Royal Highness though he is, he does not get all the good things. His Grace the Duke of Newcastle and General Williams came in this time for a share, at least they did upon this occasion, for two baskets of most luscious peaches and grapes were presented to them by Miss Powell, of Niagara. It was quite amusing to see the care with which they were packed up by one of the Prince's servants, so that no harm might befal them.

The *Zimmerman* started from Niagara at twenty-five minutes to one o'clock, and had got very near Fort Missipaya, when an alarm was raised. Mr. Purveyor Sanderson had been left behind. Imagine the distress of all—no provisions on board. Yes! there was Sanderson in the rigging of the *Peerless* making frantic gesticulations with his coat tails. He was first seen by the Prince, who ordered the boat back, and very soon the rescue of Mr. Sanderson and his supplies was effected. It appeared that the purveyor had been delayed by an accident. He had started in a train from Suspension Bridge to meet the *Zimmerman* at Niagara, but when some distance on the road, a poor fellow had been run over, both his legs had been cut off, and the train had to return. Hence the delay.

Port Dalhousie was reached after a short run, and an address presented by the Mayor, at the railway station. The train soon placed the Royal party in St. Catharines. The Volunteers were out in great force; the Fireman were there with their red coats and tastefully ornamented engines, and a general turn-out of the inhabitants took place. From the railway the Prince was conducted to the centre of the town, where a very large and handsome pavilion stood, and here His Worship Mayor Currie read the Corporation address, to which His Royal Highness replied. St. Catharines made a brilliant display. Quite a number of arches were erected of very excellent design, and the loyal fervour manifested by the people in ornamenting their houses was second to none in the province. One of the arches consisted of flour barrels, and looked very well. Unfortunately the stay was so short that any thing more than a mere mention of the fact of the excellence of the display made by the people is impossible.

The Great Western Railway station, being at a very considerable distance from that of the Erie and Ontario, a very fatiguing race for the cars in the hot sun had to be made. The conductor of the train in which the Prince took his seat, was Mr. W. Patchin; the Engineer Mr. George Lomas. Mr. W. Seward ran the pilot engine. A stoppage was made at Grimsby at a quarter to four o'clock. There over a thousand people were assembled, an address was presented to the Prince on behalf of the Loyal Canadian Society by Col. Clarke. The ceremony was soon over, and progress towards Hamilton continued.

In reaching Hamilton the train was two hours later in arriving than had been expected. The place of reception was at the usual landing place, in front of the principal entrance to the station. A space had been enclosed here, the Mayor and members of the Corporation and other personages, chiefly official, were in waiting to receive His Royal Highness. On either side of this an additional space had been enclosed, to which the admission was by tickets, issued to as large an extent as the available room in front of the station would accommodate spectators. The number of these who were thus favoured with a view of the Prince at his landing, and during the presentation of the Corporation address, could not exceed fifteen hundred or two thousand persons. It could not have been otherwise, unless, as at Toronto, a special station had been fitted up for the Prince's landing, with accommodation for many thousands of spectators. The railway authorities, however, made the best use possible of the facilities at their command ; and the reception, even at the station, was sufficiently creditable to the city. A temporary staging had been erected across the railway track running nearest to the depot, and the whole of the enclosed space in front of the station was thus made one level platform, with the exception of an elevated dais which the Prince was to ascend by two or three steps, on leaving his car, and there receive the address of the Corporation. The dais was overhung by a handsome canopy, which was found of substantial service, as a protection against the hot rays of the sun. An evergreen arch had been erected in front of the entrance to the station, having the motto " Welcome to Hamilton," constructed of flowers, ornamented with Prince's plumes, and trophies of flags, &c.

Precisely at five o'clock the pilot engine reached the station, and a minute afterwards the Royal train arrived, and as the cars stopped at the landing place, the Guard of Honour presented arms, and deafening cheers from the crowd welcomed the arrival of the Prince at Hamilton. When His Royal Highness stepped out and ascended the dais, the cheers were again most enthusiastically renewed, and were echoed with hearty good-will by the vast crowds on the streets and the heights behind the station, who were shut out from a view of the ceremony inside. The Governor-General and the Duke of Newcastle stood one on each side of the Prince, and near them were Earl St. Germains, General Bruce, General Williams, Mr. C. J. Brydges, Managing Director of the Great Western ; Mr. Rose, Mr. Cartier, Mr. Vankoughnet, Mr. John Ross, Sir Allan MacNab, Sir E. P. Tache, and other gentlemen who had accompanied the Prince in the Royal train.

The Prince having taken his station, the Mayor and City Clerk advanced to the foot of the dais, the Clerk bearing the address which His Worship was to read. But at this moment the Field Battery commenced to fire their salute, which made such a racket, that the Mayor could not venture to begin reading the address till the 21 guns were successively fired. This over, he read the address of the city.

The Prince read a reply, expressing the satisfaction he experienced in witnessing the marked signs of progress evident in this province, and his pleasure at receiving such warm assurances of the loyalty of its people.

Cheers for the Prince and for the Queen having been called for and given in the most enthusiastic style, His Royal Highness passed through the station to the carriage in waiting for him. It was not without some difficulty, however, that he got through. A terrific crush was one of the principal features of the Hamilton reception, and it was at this point it commenced. The Prince had scarcely advanced two or three steps beyond the dais, when those behind and at the sides began to rush forward and close together, so as in a very few moments to make an almost complete dead lock. Before the Prince had reached the door entering the station the crowd were upon them. Squeezing through with a few members of his suite, he got inside the station, and the door behind him was closed, to give him a chance of getting to his carriage. Although it was opened again almost immediately, it had been closed for a sufficient time to make the pressure in the crowd still more dense, and as each one neared the entrance his chief struggle was so to get carried through the door-way, that he should not run the risk of getting squeezed to a jelly against either of the side-posts. Generals, Ministers of the Crown, Corporate dignitaries, Knights, Clergymen, and unofficial citizens, were indiscriminately elbowed and jammed together, every one carrying out the maxims, "sauve qui peut."

The pent up excitement of the crowd outside, when the Prince at length made his appearance, burst out with such violence, that all efforts of the Marshals to get an orderly procession formed were unavailing. The following was the order of procession :—

Assistant Marshal.
Police.
Band.
Guard of Honor.
Abolition Society.
Temperance Societies.
Band.
Fire Brigade.
German Society.
Canadian Order of Odd Fellows.
Band.
St. Andrew's Society.
St. Patrick's Society.
St. George's Society.
Highland Society.
Band.
Sedentary Militia.
Officers of Militia.
The Magistrates of the County.
The Registrar, the Treasurer, the Clerk of the Peace, and other County Officers.
The County Council.
The Warden.
The County Judge.
The High Sheriff.
Members of the Reception Committee.

(flanked left by "Assistant Marshall." and right by "Assistant Marshall." printed vertically)

Officers of the Corporation.
The High Bailiff and the Chief of Police.
The City Clerk and Chamberlain.
The Aldermen and Councillors.
The Recorder and Police Magistrate.
The Mayor.
Members of the House of Assembly.
Members of the Legislative Council.
HIS ROYAL HIGHNESS AND SUITE.
The Commander of the Forces and Suite,
mounted.
Mounted Officers of the Army and Militia Field
Battery of Artillery.
Police.
Chief Marshal—Major Gray.

Cavalry. ... *Cavalry.*

The above order of procession had been all very nicely planned out and duly announced beforehand by the Committee of Arrangements, but it was almost entirely upset by the citizens at large rushing in and filling up the spaces assigned to the National Societies, the Fire Companies, &c. Gradually, as the first violence of the loyal excitement of the multitude abated, a procession was formed, but its component parts were oddly mixed up. A portion of the German Society might have been seen marching under the banner of the St. Andrew's Society, while the St. George's banner was being carried without a following alongside the Prince's carriage, and further on the St. Andrew's and St. George's Presidents might have been seen walking arm in arm, with some dozen or so of the rank and file of their respective societies endeavouring to keep within hail of them. The procession had reached King-street before it had assumed any thing like orderly form, and even then it differed as widely as well could be from the programme given above.

As the Prince's carriage emerged from the station and passed up Stuart-street, the spectacle which met his gaze would be in the highest degree gratifying to him. The heights behind the depot were covered with thousands of spectators, the street ascending the hill in front, up which the carriage had to pass, was crammed with a dense mass of human beings, every spot from which a view of the Prince could be obtained was occupied, and from all those thousands of loyal subjects went up shout after shout of enthusiastic welcome. A fine arch, somewhat in the style of the John-street arch in Toronto, had been built by the Great Western Railway Company at the top of the hill, spanning Stuart-street at its junction with Bay-street. A little before this arch was reached, the pressure of the crowd on the Royal carriage had become so great, that it was brought to a dead halt for a minute or two, until the cavalry escort made good a position in front of it and alongside, and cleared a passage. The procession turned out of Stuart into James-street, and as it got near the centre of the city, fresh interest was given to the spectacle by the bevies of fashionably attired ladies who thronged the windows and balconies of the splendid buildings in that portion of the route, waving their handkerchiefs and throwing bouquets, while the gentlemen accompanying them cheered. But the grandest spectacle of the whole was in the spacious Gore of King-street, flanked by as fine buildings as are to be found in Canada, the fronts of which, their windows and balconies being crowded with spectators, seemed one mass of life and animation. Between the two fountains, both of which were in full play, a stand had been erected, for the accommodation of three or four thousand children, who sang a stanza of "God Save the Queen," and a piece composed for the occasion, "Hurra! hurra! All hail the Prince of Wales," while the Prince halted in front of them. The procession passed along round the eastern fountain, and back by the south side of King-street to James-street, the Prince's carriage again halting in front of the children's stand, that those on its south side might enjoy the pleasure of getting a good view of him. The remainder of the route was by James and Hannah-streets to John-street, on which is situated the mansion of R. Juson, which was the residence of His Royal Highness during his stay in Hamilton.

On the evening of the 18th the city was illuminated. The effect was very good. Several of the Toronto illuminations re-appeared in Hamilton. That of the Post-office was transferred to the Post-office there. The Royal Hotel had the illuminations of the Romain Buildings, and the fine store of McInnes & Co., those of Osgoode Hall. The Canada Life Assurance Company's offices, the various banks and other public buildings and many private stores and dwellings were also very handsomely illuminated. So too were some of the arches and the fountains on King-street. In the course of the evening there was a display of fire-works and a torch-light procession.

The first public act performed by His Royal Highness the Prince of Wales was to visit the Central School. Twelve hundred children sat waiting for the arrival of His Royal Highness, all wrought up to the highest pitch of excitement at the prospect of seeing him. At eleven o'clock the note of alarm was given that His Royal Highness had arrived. At the door of the spacious edifice he was met by Dr. Billings, Chairman of the Board of School Trustees ; by A. McCallum, Esq., Head Master; by Egerton Ryerson, Esq., Chief Superintendent of Education ; by His Worship the Mayor of Hamilton ; by Isaac Buchanan, Esq., M. P.P., and by Sheriff Thomas. Conducted by Dr. Billings and Mr. McCallum, His Royal Highness proceeded to the library, and was there presented with the usual address. It was not read, neither was any reply given, the time at the disposal of the Prince being very limited.

As soon as he had received the address, the Prince passed through the different class rooms, in which were assembled the children. The boys' department was first visited, and then came the turn of the girls. Positively, Sir Edmund Head tried to convince the Prince that there was not time to look at the girls ! But Albert Edward P. (as he signed himself in the visitors' book) could not understand the force of the argument at all. If Sir Edmund was in a hurry, why did he not take the Prince through the girls' department first, and let the boys wait till he paid another visit to Hamilton. There would have been some sort of sense in such an arrangement—but there was none in the one proposed. So the Prince was right—as he always is—in looking at the girls. It did not take him long, for his stay in the building altogether did not exceed one quarter of an hour. Leaving the Central School, he drove at once to the Royal Hotel, and there held a levee, at which a very large number attended. The double staircase leading to the drawing-room was as crowded as Drury Lane on boxing night. Everybody wanted to be first. One pushed another up the stairs, trampled on one another's toes, and it may have been that a free fight would have been indulged in by the many among the assembly possessed of tender corns, had not the sight of the Water Police keeping guard cooled their sense of wrong.

His Royal Highness afterwards proceeded to the Exhibition

building, surrounded all the way by an immense crowd, who rushed along after the carriage, and alarmed quietly disposed people upon the sidewalks with prospects of overturning. The Prince entered the building, and walked about for a short time, but so great was the pressure that he had to leave before a quarter of an hour had expired. Finding it impossible to pursue his investigations inside the building, His Royal Highness sought the outside, and went to take a look at the pigs and cows. But his efforts were attended with no better success. He was penned in by the loving subjects of his Royal mother, and was scarcely able to move a pace. In this dilemma the carriages were sent for, and a drive round the grounds effected. During his short stay His Royal Highness was loudly and enthusiastically cheered. Returning to the Royal Hotel about two o'clock lunch was served. It was an informal affair, but the usual toasts, the Queen, the Prince Consort, and the Prince of Wales, were given and duly honoured.

The great event of the day however had still to come off. The water-works had to be inaugurated—and the Prince was required for the occasion. Who living in Canada has not heard of the Hamilton water-works—of the large amount of money spent upon them, and of their final success as an engineering work. Upon the shore of the bay, about six miles from Hamilton, stands the engine used for pumping the water from the lake, that it may be distributed into the city, and to this point the Prince was conveyed by the good steamer *Peerless* to the railway wharf. Matters were so arranged that no admittance could be gained to the *Peerless* without passing through the railway station. Sir Allan McNab arrived, and so did Adam Brown, Esq., the Chairman of the Water Commissioners, followed by several gentlemen of the Board, Mr. Isaac Buchanan, and Mr. Brydges. The appearance of an Aide-de-camp brought word that His Royal Highness had gone round by land, and he desired to meet the *Peerless* at the engine-house. Thither she at once proceeded, and when she got there, it was found that the Prince had arrived long before. The *Peerless* had Mr. Adam Brown on board, and without him business could not proceed. Who altered the arrangement, is the question ?

The *Bowmanville* left Hamilton crowded with pleasure-seekers, all of whom were exceedingly disappointed at the non-appearance of the white hat and blue coat on the deck of the *Peerless*, which ran as near as she could to the shore, and landed her passengers by means of the little steamer *Young Canadian*—a concern warranted to carry twelve without sinking. Proceeding at once to the engine-house, there was His Royal Highness. To the left of the double flight of broad stone steps giving entrance to the building, a square platform had been erected, ornamented with cedar and with wreaths of flowers. Over it stood a canopy of a very handsome design. The floor was nicely carpeted and furnished with chairs. There on behalf of the Water Commissioners, an address was presented by Adam Brown, Esq., the Chairman, but no reply was given, though one was forwarded in writing. The reading over, His Royal Highness crossed to the other side of the steps into the engine room, followed by a crowd of City Councilmen and others; he started the engines simply by turning a small handle. The steam passed into the cylinders, and they immediately commenced working—the task for which His Royal Highness had been brought, so far successfully accomplished.

Then a return to the boat had to be effected. Carriages were in waiting, and by their aid the Royal party got down to the beach. A long carpet had been laid across the sand, and passing over it to the small floating wharf near the *Young Canadian*, was reached. By her aid the party were placed on board the *Peerless* and Hamilton was regained.

Before concluding the notice of the inauguration of the Water Works, it must be stated, that the grounds around the engine-house were very nicely laid out, and that a fine arch had been erected over the entrance gateway. The engine house itself made an excellent appearance. It is built of white brick with stone facings, and both inside and outside was decorated with festoons of cedar boughs. The engines, of which there are two, are fifty-horse power each. They rest upon substantial stone foundations, and so strongly is the whole place built that, when working they cause scarcely any vibration. They move with great smoothness, and are very well finished. There is little display about them. The pillars supporting the beams are of fluted iron; the whole is painted green and black. Altogether they present a very substantial and satisfactory appearance.

On the morning of September 20, His Royal Highness went to the Exhibition grounds, in Hamilton. At noon there was an immense crowd gathered together there, variously estimated at from 20,000 to 50,000. Upwards of 18,000 tickets had been sold during the two days, but the weather prevented many from attending. There was such a perfect sea of heads that it was impossible to calculate the precise number. A Royal salute announced that the Prince was *en route et aliel*, and Capt. Bull's troop of Cavalry preceded the Prince's carriage, and cleared a road for him. He ascended the platform and was presented with the following address from the Provincial Agricultural Association, by John Wade, Esq., President :—

To the Most High Puissant and Illustrious Prince Albert Edward, Prince of the United Kingdom of Great Britain and Ireland, Prince of Wales, Duke of Saxony, Prince of Coburg and Gotha, Great Steward of Scotland, Duke of Cornwall and Rothsay, Earl of Chester, Carrick and Dublin, Baron of Renfrew, and Lord of the Isles, K. G.

MAY IT PLEASE YOUR ROYAL HIGHNESS,—

We, the Agriculturists, Artisans, and Manufacturers of Upper Canada, beg to approach Your Royal Highness with our expressions of devoted loyalty to Her Most Gracious Majesty's Crown and person, and to offer to your Royal Highness a most cordial welcome to this exhibition of the products of our soil and our labour.

This is the fifteenth exhibition of the Agricultural Association of Upper Canada, and we think it demonstrates to those who have witnessed the successive exhibitions from year to year, that they have been successful in stimulating the industrial classes in the improvement of all those productions upon which the prosperity of this portion of Her Majesty's dominions mainly depend.

Blessed with a fertile soil and healthful climate, and forming a portion of that extensive empire over which Her Majesty's benign rule extends, and in which it is exercised in the maintenance of the religious and civil rights of all classes of her subjects, we hail with delight the auspicious event of Your Royal Highness' visit to this colony, and rejoice that we have this opportuntiy of exhibiting to Your Royal Highness, as we take what we hope we may call an honest pride in exhibiting, as to our future Sovereign, such proofs of the industry, skill, and intelligence of the inhabitants of this country.

We gladly embrace this opportunity of expressing our ardent desire to maintain the connexion of this Province with that great and glorious empire of which we rejoice in forming an integral part, and from which we have in great part derived our agriculture as well as our existence; and whilst availing ourselves of the example and improvements of the older portions of the Empire, and of the many natural advantages we possess in our soil, climate, and navigable waters, we trust that our efforts may result in affording convincing proof that this Province is really a valuable jewel in the crown of our beloved Sovereign.

We hopefully pray that the intercourse of Your Royal Highness with the inhabitants of Canada, and the opportunity you have had of witnessing the efforts we are making to advance the material interests of our country, may, during your future life, leave a pleasing impression in your memory.

That your Royal Highness may be placed in possession of statistical and other facts connected with the rise and progress of this association, we beg that your Royal Highness will condescend to accept these volumes, containing a record of the transactions of this association from its establishment."

His Royal Highness replied as follows :—

GENTLEMEN,—I return you my warm acknowledgments for the address you have just presented upon the occasion of opening the fifteenth Exhibition of the Agricultural Society of Upper Canada, and I take this opportunity of thanking the agriculturists, artizans, and manufacturers who are now assembled from distant parts in the city of Hamilton, for the more than kind and enthusiastic reception which they gave me yesterday, and have repeated to-day.

Blessed with a soil of very remarkable fertility, and a hardy race of industrious and enterprising men, this district must rapidly assume a most important position in the markets of the world, and I rejoice to learn that the improvements in agriculture, which skill, labour, and science have of late years developed in the mother country, are fast increasing the capabilities of your soil, and enabling you to compete successfully with the energetic people whose stock and other products are now ranged in friendly rivalry with your own, within this vast enclosure.

The Almighty has this year granted you that greatest boon to a people—an abundant harvest. I trust it will make glad many a home of those I see around me, and bring increased wealth and prosperity to this magnificent province.

My duties as representative of the Queen, deputed by her to visit British North America, cease this day,—but, in a private capacity I am about to visit before my return home, that remarkable land which cliams with us a common ancestry, and in whose extraordinary progress every Englishman feels a common interest.

Before, however, I quit British soil let me once more address through you the inhabitants of United Canada, and bid them an affectionate farewell.

May God pour down his choicest blessings upon this great and loyal people.

Just as this ceremony was being performed it came on to rain, and the Royal party were not sorry to enter the Exhibition Building, which had been cleared for the purpose of allowing them to see the very fine show it contained. Subsequently it grew fair for a time and they went to look at the prize animals which had been let out of their stalls, and arranged in rows, as also at the agricultural implements scattered about the grounds.

The Prince was unwell and did not stay long; he with his suite went off to lunch with Sir Allan McNab at Dundurn.* The Duke of Newcastle, however, returned to the grounds after the departure of the Prince, and accompanied by the Hon. Mr. Alexander, Hon. Mr. Christie, and Mr. E. W. Thomson, made the round of the show ground. He showed an intimate knowledge of cattle and sheep, and was very much pleased with the display. His specialities are short horns and Leicesters and Southdowns. He sells 500 sheep off his farm every year, and understands the points of a good animal as well as Mr. Millar, of Markham, himself. He also took a good deal of interest in the horses, pronounced heavy Clydes not the thing for this country, but was

---

*It was admitted by one and all that Sir Allan's entertainment was worthy of a Royal guest's reception.

rather favourable to the Punches. The Prince's suite were in much better humour than yesterday.

A set of the transactions of the Agricultural Society, beautifully bound in red morocco, enclosed in a handsome case of the same material, was presented to the Prince before he left the ground.

Before taking leave of Canada the compiler presents to his readers an English view of the Prince's reception, and it may be that the account will be as acceptable to many of the colonists as to their friends at home.

ENGLISH REMARKS.

The progress of the Prince of Wales through the colonies has been responded to with a heartier and heartier welcome at every fresh colonial capital. The interest and excitement indeed have gained an impetus and a swing which carries people quite away; they cannot express themselves adequately, and when every thing had been done that could be done, by voice or symbol, by salutes and flags, by crowded streets, windows crammed with faces, and "yards fringed with sailors," by triumphal arches and festooned streets, by processions, addresses, and reviews; by welcomes from Governors, welcomes from Legislatures, welcomes from Corporations; by banquets, balls, illuminations, fireworks,—when heraldry had exhausted all its waving honours, the gardens all their colours, and leaf and flower, wreath and banner, lamp and evergreen, had converted the colonial capital into a fairy city, there was still an unexpressed longing in the colonial heart, which would fain do something to embody itself in outward shape if it could. Halifax did not know itself on the 30th of July. It was completely buried in green leaves and flowers, and metamorphosed into a gigantic bouquet. Every street, house, and window looked at its neighbours from under an overshadowing bower, which allowed openings, however, for waiving handkerchiefs and outstretched heads. Never since old Sebastian Cabot landed on its shore had Nova Scotia had such a holiday. It was a gala day, indeed, was more than a gala day, it was an event in history, a day which concentrated an age and created a mass of solid associations which will long survive the passing impression, and support the old hereditary connexion of the colony with the British Crown. From the moment that "two steamers were seen like dots on the entrance of Halifax Bay," to the farewell on the 1st,

A 20

the whole of Halifax was in a state of perfect and universal jubilee, triumphing in its temporary possession of the Heir Apparent of the English Throne. Nothing was done, even the mails were not despatched, and the very newspapers, whose business time is every other person's holiday, stopped work. The Prince, upon his very first stand upon the beach of Halifax—and a stand it was, for it was that motionless stand of due duration which is required for a photographic likeness—fixed all the hearts of Halifax by the perfection with which he bore this rather awkward ordeal, which constituted the first step of his introduction to the assembled and gazing colony, and inaugurated while it immortalised on the magic paper the first tread of a Prince of Wales upon Nova Scotian soil. And His Royal Highness, it need not be said, well sustained this first impression, and won more and more popularity every hour of his stay. His manners, "which blended a native dignity with the most winning courtesy and frankness," charmed everybody, and, whether it was the graceful ease with which he saluted the lines on each side of the streets and bowed amid the prancings of his spirited horse, or whether it was his observation at a review, or his ready flow of conversation at a ball, his whole address won unmixed admiration. He seemed to have given pleasure to everybody. The English public will read these descriptions of His Royal Highness' progress through his future colonial dominions with the greatest satisfaction; and the colonists will congratulate themselves on their connexion with a Royal family the Heir of which combines the grace and loftiness of a Prince with all the public sympathies of one of the people.

It adds to the strength and the native and spontaneous character of these demonstrations that they are responses to a visit which does not pretend the least utilitarian object, but which is simply paid for the sake of the visit itself,—for the sake of seeing and meeting the colonists. The Prince has no inquiries to make and no political business to transact. All that is done through the proper channels. This is a visit simply that the Prince of Wales may see the colonists, and the colonists may see the Prince of Wales. It is a friendly visit, it is a social visit, it is a visit of pleasure. It is on that very account a most advantageous and beneficial visit, and one which will produce the most lasting results.

It is these friendly meetings, which aim at nothing else but the natural pleasure of the meetings themselves, which touch the heart of a people most sensibly and most deeply. It is that best kind of compliment which is treasured up in the person's mind, and appealed to again and again in recollection, and yields a perpetual gratification. It is that kind of compliment which confers an inward rank upon the recipient of it, and is rested on as a guarantee that a true estimate is formed of him. It is these appeals to the heart and the feelings of a people that do most, that last longest, and that cement and bind a national connexion in the most effective and solid way. These meetings of a young Prince with his future subjects are not business proceedings, but they are an advance upon business; they are more efficient than business; they as much surpass any thing the Colonial Office can do as an act of feeling surpasses a bargain; they do the work of a hundred business-like and official benefits—they concentrate years of mere conscientious statesmanship. Such a visit is imprinted in the mind of a colony by a force of its own, it has a record in the natural register of every heart and memory, and it becomes a date for a thousand histories to go back to. The whole younger generation receives a bias and a stamp from such an event which is retained through life, and the mother country and the British Crown have the advantage of that bias.

It cannot, indeed, but occur to anybody as the very first idea which such a visit suggests, that our colonial society is no loser, in comparison with a neighbouring and kindred people, from its connection with the society, the Government, the Court, and the Royal Family of the mother country. It must be seen that, *cæteris paribus*, there cannot be, at any rate, any disadvantage in relation to an intercourse with the highest form of human rank. If Royalty oppresses, shackles, degrades and impoverishes a country, let it by all means be abolished; but if it does not, and if a country is quite as free with Royalty as without it,—if Royalty is not a disadvantage, then even every mere calculator must see on the plainest common-sense grounds that it is an immeasurable advantage. That whole conventional ascent of society which culminates in the highest form of human rank is an undoubted gain to the men which occupy the level. It is so much clear and palpable addition to their interests in life, so much ground gained for imagination and sentiment to work upon, so much additional field even for the occupation of that natural and intuitive instinct of self-elevation in our nature which leads us to value a proper connexion with those who are above us in rank. So long as men are men, this instinct never will be eradicated from the human heart, and those who pretend to despise it, are generally just the men who are under its yoke, and indulge it to any extent. But, if this instinct is a genuine part of human nature, the most effective and successful means of gratifying it, is clearly a system of definite and formal rank, ascending up to a crown. A polity which provides the very highest form of rank; provides the highest gratification for that instinct in human nature which desires definite rank to look to, and to lean upon, and values relation to it. The loyal desire to be noticed by Princes supposes that we have Princes to notice us. That is a truth which must be obvious to our loyal fellow-subjects of North America, it is a truth which nobody need be ashamed of seeing, it is a truth which the tastes, instincts, and sympathies of human nature require to be seen, and it is a truth which will aid in binding every sensible and well-disposed colonist to the English Crown.—*From the London Globe.*

The Prince reached Windsor at 8'oclock in the evening of 20th September, by special train from Hamilton.

After presentation of addresses by the Mayor and citizens of Windsor, the Royal party were escorted on board the Detroit and Milwaukee ferry steamer *Windsor*, which had been gorgeously fitted up for the occasion. On board were the Governor of Michigan, the Mayor, Councilmen, and about fifty prominent citizens of Detroit, who were presented to His Royal Highness, and when the steamer had reached American waters, Mayor Buhl, on behalf of the city, formally welcomed Baron Renfrew to the United States.

ON BOARD THE STEAMER.

On board, the members of the Detroit and Zephyr boat clubs, who were in their respective uniform—similar to sailors in the regular United States service—formed a line on either side, through which the Prince and his party passed to the stairway, and thence to the cabin.

The steamer had been put in bright array. Arches of red lanterns were made over each gangway, the decks were covered with red cloth, and colored lights were hung in various places. The cabin was decorated tastefully, and at the rear end a sofa with two chairs at either side, designated the peculiar place assigned to His Highness.

The Detroit Light Guard Band, on the arrival of the Prince on board, played the national air, "God save the Queen."

Arranged in the river, and covering a space of nearly a mile in length opposite the city, was a large fleet of river and lake vessels; their rigging hung with variegated lamps, and decorated with banners and emblems inscribed with words of greeting. As the steamer bearing the Royal party made its circuitous passage through the fleet, each vessel threw a shower of rockets and fireworks. The warehouses fronting the river were splendidly illuminated. Fireworks went off from the docks, and the whole river was a perfect blaze of light, making one of the grandest displays ever witnessed.

After the steamer had left the dock, and when across the line that divides the two countries, his honour Mayor Buhl addressed the Prince, now simply Lord or Baron Renfrew, in these words:

"The Mayor, Council, and citizens of Detroit—the commercial metropolis of the state of Michigan—bid you a most cordial welcome to the United States of America, and earnestly hope that your tour through the country, and your visit to the capital of the nation, will be pleasant and satisfactory."

The Baron acknowledged the address by a courteous bow, and simple expression of thanks.

The Mayor presented some of the members of the city government and other citizens to the Baron, mentioning their names simply. The Baron acknowledged by a bow, standing during the time, with his hat in hand, and with the Duke of Newcastle on his left.

This ceremony was completed in a few minutes, and the Baron and his suite complied with the request of Mayor Buhl to step upon the forward deck to view the display in the river and on each side.

Many a day, or rather many a night, may elapse before the people of that locality may witness so grand and so brilliant a display as was made that night. The scene, as viewed from the deck of the steamer, was beautiful in the extreme. On the one side was Windsor, from the mill to Sandwich point one blaze of light; around and about were the various steamers and sail vessels of the port, at anchor and in motion, covered on every spar, and on every line, with coloured lights; and on the American side were the buildings at the foot of Woodward Avenue and the warehouse of Hutchings & Co., illuminated, and six hundred torches glaring in line from the dock to Jefferson Avenue. From every point of view rockets were being sent up, and darkness was almost turned into day.

The Royal party landed at the foot of Woodward Avenue, where, and the adjoining streets, 30,000 people were gathered. An escort for the Royal party, composed of the firemen of the city, bearing torches, and most of the city military, had been arranged, but the crowd was so great that it was found impossible for the procession to form. After some delay, and the greatest confusion, the Prince was spirited away to a close carriage, and driven to the Russell House unrecognised by the crowd. His suite followed in carriages.

The Royal party remained until ten the following morning, when they left for Chicago by the Michigan Central Railroad in a special train. A gorgeous car, for the Prince's use, was provided by Mr. Rice, the superintendent.

September 21.

From an early hour in the morning the streets in the vicinity of the Russell House were densely packed with people, anxious to catch a glimpse of the Prince when he should appear to take his departure for the cars. Just before ten o'clock he made his appearance with two of his suite, accompanied by Mayor Buhl, intending to take a drive through the city before proceeding to the cars. A magnificent open barouche, drawn by four white horses, had been provided for the purpose, in which the party seated themselves. The crowd gathering about the carriage and blocking up the avenues, made it almost impossible for the carriage to proceed. Cheer after cheer was given, and the wildest enthusiam prevailed. The carriage was followed by immense crowds on foot, many hanging to the wheels, while the streets and sidewalks on the route were literally blocked with people, who intercepted the Royal party at every turn. Such a scene of confusion was never before witnessed. After driving through a few of the principal streets, followed by crowds at every step, the party proceeded to the depot and took their departure for Chicago, amid the firing of cannon and other demonstrations.

The Prince of Wales had left the dominions of his mother and was delivered over to our American cousins. His visit to Canada was pronounced a success.

At the time of the departure of the steamer *Windsor* from the American side, the opposite bank of the river was one blaze of light, every window from near Sandwich Point to Walker's Mill, a distance of three miles, were completely illuminated. Rockets and Roman candles were fired off in a continuous stream, and the whole country, so to speak, was a blaze.

The train with the Prince and suite arrived at the depôt just before 8 o'clock. The depôt grounds presented a dense mass of people, and the bank for a long distance was lined with loyal subjects. The best of order was observed.

On the appearance of the Prince, a shout arose from every voice, which was continued for several minutes with a vehemence and will, seldom known on this side of the ocean outside of "the provinces." The Prince, accompanied immediately by the Duke of Newcastle, and followed by the Earl St. Germains and the other gentlemen of the suite, stepped from the car upon a moveable platform covered with red cloth, and thence into the covered way. He paused but a moment there to receive the addresses of his honour Mr. Dougall, Mayor of Windsor, and Col. Rankin of the Canadian Militia, and replied in return. The ceremony was accomplished in haste, and consisted simply in the handing of a piece of parchment, in roll, which was taken by the Duke of Newcastle, and of the handing back a similar document on the part of the Royal party.

The mere desire of gratifying an idle curiosity by seeing the Prince of Wales at Detroit was not all the people cared for; though of course they had a great wish to look upon the future Monarch of the "old country," which so many of them love and reverence—they had also a far deeper and more exalted feeling. The object was to give his Royal Highness a most enthusiastic reception, that they might manifest their respect for him as the representative of Great Britain, and as the son of a noble and virtuous Queen. They were not thwarted, because they have cultivated the love of order as ardently as they have cherished the love of liberty.

THE JOURNEY TO CHICAGO.

As regards the facilities received upon the Michigan Central Railroad, and the comforts for His Royal Higness and His attendants had been well provided for by the fitting up of the directors' car in costly style. An engine preceded the Royal cars on the way to Chicago. The directors offered a special train free of charge, but the offer was declined. General Bruce insisted upon their receiving full compensation. and $400 was at last agreed upon as the sum to be paid. This, for a distance of two hundred and eighty-four miles, was little enough. The start was made at ten o'clock, and Chicago was reached at ten minutes to eight. The line was in beautiful order, and every thing which forethought could do had been done to ensure complete safety.* Throughout the whole length of this great railway, rapid progress, unceasing industry, and inimitable perseverance were seen on every side. From Detroit to Chicago scarcely a pine tree is visible, yet but few miles of unbroken forest were passed. Huge fields which a week or two before were covered with Indian corn; lately cleared patches with the blackened pine stumps unpleasantly prominent; immense orchards, the boughs groaning under the weight of fruit, which bore them down to the ground; numerous small rivers, hundreds of miles of snake fences; white farm houses of uniform type, backed by the luxuriant many-hued foliage of the hardwood trees, rendered doubly beautiful by the summer's sun, where the general features of the landscape which met the eyes of the travellers. For the first eighty or a hundred miles the ground is undulating, past that, it degenerates into a dead, monotonous level. There is little variety in the scenery—it differs nothing from that of Western Canada, save in the absence of the dark, sombre-looking pines. There is no object of marked interest throughout the whole route—nothing to enable the mind

---

* This is no exaggeration, and for the information of our English readers it is inserted.

to fix upon one spot, and recollect it distinctly from the others. One may as well try to describe each ocean wave—various in shape and size though they be, as to tell the difference after a ride upon a railway train, between one Michigan town and another. At every station people were gathered together, waiting to see the Prince, but no large crowds were assembled. The women presented an interesting spectacle.

At every point crowds of people lined the road, at Kalamazoo, Ann Arbor, and Marshall, there were immense gatherings, salutes, music and excitement. The Prince, who was very much fatigued, spent the greater part of the day on the bed in his sleeping apartment, and could, in no instance gratify the curiosity of the crowd.

The trip was a long, tiresome, tedious affair, and all were glad when the lights of illuminated Chicago burst suddenly upon the sight.

The scene from a distance was very fine, and the illumination was exceedingly brilliant. Arrived at the spacious depot, the throng inside numbered thousands, while outside the rush was fairly awful. The police kept admirable order, and the party were enabled to walk slowly through a large open space, giving all present a fine view of the Prince. In reply to the oft-repeated cheers, the Prince gracefully raised his white beaver and returned the salutations of the multitude from side to side. The Duke remarked that the scene was the most imposing he had yet witnessed, and they were all highly gratified at the enthusiastic and orderly welcome.

The British Consul met the Prince at the depot, escorted him to the carriage, and left him at the hotel, immediately after which they partook of a good substantial dinner.

The determination of Baron Renfrew to ignore all Royal state in passing through the American continent was respected by the people of Chicago to the very utmost. The Royal party received no annoyances—they were suffered to go on their way as they chose. There is no doubt, however, that the citizens, if allowed, would have given them a right Royal reception. They were somewhat disappointed and piqued at the privacy demanded. "A public demonstration, he shall not have," was the sentiment of many, "if he does not wish one," and such a feeling to a great

A 21

extent aided Baron Renfrew and his advisers in the end they desired to gain. The Americans wished to make a grand demonstration; they were refused, and abstained from making any demonstration at all. Very few remarks have been made by the newspapers; no editorials have been written upon the "auspicious event."

Chicago, 19th September, 1860.

The folllowing official demonstration was addressed to Lord Lyons by the citizens of Chicago as British Minister and cordially replied to :—

RICHMOND HOUSE, Sept. 22, 1860.

To Lord Lyons, Minister of Her Majesty, the Queen of Great Britain, to the Government of the United States.

MY LORD,—The city of Chicago have deputed the undersigned to welcome Baron Renfrew to our young city.

As a representative in a very high sense of our mother country —that country to which we are allied by so many and varied interests and sympathies; to which we are bound by so many common ties of blood, and by our common customs, laws, literature, language, and love of liberty ; Baron Renfrew's presence among us awakens in the bosom of our people no common interest; an interest which receives additional force from the earnest desire which is felt by our people to cultivate such relations of friendship and amity with the people of Great Britain, as shall for ever obliterate the slightest traces of jealousy and unkindly feeling.

As the son of the most admirable of Monarchs, the best of women, and the noblest of Anglo-Saxon matrons, Baron Renfrew challenges our most affectionate and kind regards.

These, among other considerations not less marked, would have rendered it highly gratifying to our fellow-citizens to have received Baron Renfrew in a different capacity, and to have exhibited their respect for his country, for his Royal mother, and for his Lordship's self, in a manner, if less demonstrative, at least not less cordial than that stimulated by the loyalty of his future subjects in British America.

But learning that his Lordship's fatigue, arising from the exciting scenes through which he had so recently passed, would render such attentions onerous to him, we have forborne from every demonstration calculated to disturb his privacy and repose. But we have ventured to solicit your Lordship, so well and favourably known to the American public, to assure Baron Renfrew; that under proper circumstances the people of Chicago would have cheerfully made every suitable demonstration on the occasion of so distinguished an arrival. As it is, my Lord, with this assurance, we have but to tender a cordial welcome to Baron Renfrew and suite to Illinois, accompanied by the hope that he and they will find on our broad prairies the recreation and repose which they seek.

With every high respect and consideration, permit us, my Lord, to subscribe ourselves,

      WM. B. OGDEN
      JOHN WENTWORTH,
      WM. BROSS,
      E. W. McCOMAS.
         Committee.

At Chicago he showed himself on the balcony of the hotel for a few minutes, and then disappeared. There was little crushing. There was room for all who came to see—room for many more had they desired to come. Every thing passed off quietly. A carriage was drawn up at the door, and Lord Renfrew entered it. He was driven down the broad and beautiful street until the court house was reached. It has a remarkably fine appearance, surrounded with large stores and hotels, most of them five stories in height. At the top there is a lofty dome from which a birdseye view of the city can be gained, stretching far and wide, the New York of Western America. Perhaps a couple of thousand people had gathered in the square waiting the return of the Prince. He stayed but a few minutes "up aloft," and then passed through some of the principal streets of the city at a rapid pace.

His next appearance was upon the balcony at two o'clock. The assemblage was far larger than before—numbering not less ten thousand people. When Lord Renfrew stepped forward he was greeted with a series of loud and hearty cheers. He bowed several times, and then, as before, descended to his carriage. The people made way for him respectfully, and many followed him a considerable distance along the streets, until the pace of the horses quickened from a walk to a trot, and then to a gallop. Few knew that he was bound for the railway station at Bridgeport, two miles distant. His Royal Highness followed as described, started at 3 o'clock, by the St. Louis, Alton and Chicago Railway for Dwight. The train stopped in the grassy plain where no station exists, and the party were accommodated in the house of a gentleman residing there.

September 24th.

While in Chicago, Lord Renfrew proceeded to the grain elevator of Messrs. Sturges, Buckingham & Co. There he saw something really deserving of admiration. Their warehouse, when full, holds no less than 1,500,000 bushels of wheat. It is an immense oblong brick building, of enormous strength, standing close by the water's edge, where lie vessels ready to receive their loads. The process of emptying the cars was exhibited to Lord Renfrew. A train was brought into the building and the elevators set to work. In a very few minutes the whole of the grain had disappeared. Of the rapidity with which this was done some idea may be formed, when the other day 22,000 bushels of grain were loaded in eighty minutes. There are thirteen elevators in Chicago of greater or lesser power, but all capable of doing an immense amount of work.

Afterwards the proprietors of the "Richmond House" were surprised to receive a letter from the Duke of Newcastle, containing $25, and stating that some little things had been omitted from the hotel bill. They were quite pleased about it, and the expressions of approval tendered by the Royal party for the arrangements made for their convenience, being known, were received by the Americans as a tribute to their hotel system, of which they were pretty proud. Before leaving, Lord Renfrew presented Mr. Sargeant, the able manager of the Michigan Central Railroad at Chicago, with a diamond breast-pin, which will be much valued by a most staunch republican.

The impression made upon the English visitors to Chicago were very favourable. They were astonished at meeting so far west a city of such magnificence. They had heard of its population, of the greatness of its commerce, of its rapid growth, and of its increasing importance. But they were not prepared to find, instead of a collection of wooden houses and unpaved streets, a vast city with stores and warehouses presenting a more imposing appearance than any town of equal size in Great Britain. John Wentworth, the mayor, made the most of the opportunity afforded him. He was exceedingly assiduous in his efforts to impress upon the Duke of Newcastle the fact, that by English capitalists the greater part of the stock in all the larger undertakings was owned, and thus that it was manifestly to the advantage of English people that they should continue to direct their efforts towards the development of American traffic rather than that of the Canadians. His Honour the Mayor treated the Prince well, secured him no small share of comfort and privacy, and did not allow the rest of the city fathers to come within a mile of his Royal person. He may be somewhat grateful to him on that account.

The Chicago Zouaves are a splendidly drilled corps, and the reports as to its efficiency are not at all exaggerated. The English soldiers perform all the manœuvres required of them with great exactitude and precision. So far, no body of men in the world excel them. But of the Chicago Zouaves much more is required than in the regular service. They go through their movements at a most rapid pace; with a speed that is perfectly bewildering. Col. Ellesworth, the officer in command, and to whom belongs the greater share of the merit which attaches to the corps, frequently issued his orders as fast as he could speak, and the men changed their positions so quickly that none could see how they accomplished it. There was not the slightest hesitation among them; they had confidence in one another; they worked with one accord. The word was given for them to form into two lines. Then they were told to lie down, and down they went. When commanded, they turned over upon their backs, and while in a horizontal position loaded their rifles. The first line fired. No sooner done than the second line leaped to the front and also fired; those behind loading at the same time. They formed in squares to receive cavalry, separated and appeared with levelled rifles back to back. They performed the musket exercise,—an exercise specially adapted to enable them to guard against sabre strokes should their ranks be broken,—with most admirable skill. They fired so well together, first in twos, then in threes, then in fours, that the hammers were brought down upon the nipples with such exactitude that no difference in time was perceptible to the ear. In short, there can be no doubt of this that they are the most perfectly drilled company of men in the world. Of course much that they have learned would be useless in active warfare; but still the strength of muscle and power of endurance their performance requires alone render it particularly valuable. In the present state of public opinion at home, if Col. Ellesworth would visit England, he would, probably, create quite a *furore*. It would strengthen the confidence of the people in the voluntary system, and create a spirit of rivalry which would be attended with the most beneficial effects. An invitation was forwarded to the Baron to attend a review of the Zouaves, but unfortunately previous engagements precluded the pleasure he would have enjoyed in such a pleasing sight.

Perhaps a few words may be said about Chicago itself. It is a magnificent city, the very embodiment of American enterprise and skill. The streets laid out at right angles; wide and well paved. The stores exceedingly lofty, and built either of white stone or red brick faced with stone, all with highly decorated fronts and of great architectural beauty. The public buildings, the churches, and schools, have been erected with some regard to splendour of appearance. The sidewalks for the most part of large flag-stones. Chicago itself being somewhat lower than the lake, caused many difficulties to be encountered. The stupendous work of raising the whole city has been commenced. Some of the largest blocks of stores in the place have been lifted up several feet; and the sidewalks themselves in a state of transition, the difference in the height between the portions which have been lifted and those which remain at their old level, necessitates the use of steps or slanting boards. Railways run along the principal streets; the number of vehicles large; no attribute of a large city inhabited by an energetic population wanting. Each one of the hundred and ten thousand people seem to have some business in hand, and bent upon discharging it in the quickest way possible.

In acknowledgment of the hospitality of Mr. Juson and Mr. McLaren of Hamilton, in placing their residences at the disposal of the Prince and his suite, His Royal Highness left portraits of himself, bearing his autograph, to be presented to Mrs. Juson and Mrs. McLaren on their return from Europe.

Just before the Prince retired from the lunch, at Brantford, a Bible presented to the Indians by Queen Ann, and containing her autograph, was laid before the Prince, with the request that he would enter his name on the same page, to which he graciously acceded, recording his name in a full, bold hand.

Here the following document was presented to the Prince :—

The following characteristic address was presented by the raftsmen of Upper Canada to the Prince of Wales during his short stay at Arnprior.

TO HIS ROYAL HIGHNESS THE PRINCE OF WALES :

We, the raftsmen of the Upper Ottawa, constitute a body of 13,000 men, the bone and sinew of Canada.

We take advantage of meeting your Royal Highness upon a raft to offer you our hearty welcome, and to express our loyalty, our devotion, and our affection for the Queen. God bless her.

May your Royal Highness long remain the Prince of Wales.

September 22*nd.*

Lord Renfrew and suite arrived at Dwight, and was the guest of J. C. Spencer. Mr. Spencer's accommodations not being sufficiently ample for the entire Royal party, the others were the guests of Mr. Roadright, and Mr. R. P. Morgan.

DWIGHT'S STATION, ILL., Tuesday, Sept. 25.

The day was most charming. All were up and at breakfast at $5\frac{1}{2}$ o'clock. At seven o'clock they went by special train to Stewart's Grove, as at that point there is always a great abundance of quail. For a few hours no game was found, and the party separated in squads. The Prince, Spencer, Isdale, and three others, went together.

By 12 o'clock game was plentiful. The Prince was in great spirits, and shot frequently, always successfully. He had great fun after the rabbits.

Lunch was taken at two o'clock by a brook, and the time was spent in relating experiences and comparing results.

At seven o'clock the party returned to the cottage laden with spoils. The total result of the shooting of the whole party was $91\frac{1}{2}$ brace of quail, $1\frac{1}{2}$ brace of prairie chickens, and two couple of rabbits. The Prince shot, with his own gun, 14 brace of quail, and two couple of rabbits, with which success he was delighted beyond measure. The hot sun bronzed his face; his eye was clearer, and he seemed more manly than at any other time before. They all regretted that their time was so limited, and that they should so soon go. The Duke of Newcastle enjoyed the quiet and rest. Gen. Bruce took delight in the Prince's happiness; Lord Lyons, in a quiet way, charmed all by his quaint remarks, and the rest dropped state and care, and were up to their eyes in jollification.

On the following day the sport was as follows:—

The Prince, thirty head of quail.

The Duke of Newcastle, twenty head of quail.

Mr. J. Clinton Spencer, ten head of quail.

Captain Retallick, twenty head of quail.

On the previous day the Prince shot fifteen brace of prairie fowl; the Duke of Newcastle, twelve brace; Captain Retallick, five brace, and Mr. Spencer, two brace. The excess on the side of His Royal Highness may be accounted for by the fact of his having always the first shot.

The grand total of birds shot by the entire party amounted to a hundred and ninety head, and on the previous day to a hundred and thirty head.

These figures may be interesting to sportsmen.

A rabbit was shot by one of the party, and the equerries, Major Teasdale and Captain Grey, hit a deer yesterday, but did not succeed in bringing it down. It fled in a fright, from which it has likely not yet recovered.

The accomplished lady of the house, Mrs. Le Duc, rendered the in-door visit extremely pleasant, but 9 o'clock was bed-time for all hands.

This shooting part of the Prince's visit charmed and delighted him and the whole party, more than all the attentions that had been showered upon him.

The Prince of Wales left Dwight, September 26. Before his departure he expressed his regret that he could not make his stay longer, and presented his hosts with several beautiful gifts, among which was a Manton gun, &c. Several of the suite also exchanged presents with their entertainers.

A few people collected to see the Prince, who departed amid hearty cheering.

The train made no stoppages but for wood. Every station was crowded with people, who cheered as the Prince flashed by.

At Alton he took the steamer for St. Louis, and crowds followed his carriage to the wharf.

A FRENCH VIEW OF THE PRINCE OF WALES IN AMERICA.

From a French pamphlet headed "The Emperor in Algeria," is extracted the following:—

"While Algeria proposes to disguise her sufferings by displaying her hopes, the son of the Queen of England, heir to the British crown, has crossed the ocean. He goes to a rich colony which his ancestors conquered from France, whose language and usages have not been forgotten. On the frontiers of that rich country flourishes a power whose expansion seems unlimited. It was founded by men who shed their blood to wrest it from the tyranny of their forefathers, and whom the aid of France enabled to convert a revolt into a triumphal revolution. The son of the Queen of England will traverse many a battle-field where the English arms were covered with glory, and where the blood of the insurgents flowed in torrents. Nevertheless, every where will the young Prince be welcomed with the same enthusiasm and cordiality. He will hardly perceive the passage from his mother's dominions into the neighbouring States. The descendants of Frenchmen will forget their origin to do homage, in his person, to the government which allows them to enjoy a liberty so complete that emancipation is no longer to be desired. The republicans will not think they are betraying their principles, by applauding the representative of a liberal monarchy, which has profited by the lessons they inflicted on it. He may even forget that he is a Prince, for no body will ask him for any thing. No accusing voice will be uplifted against slowness of administration and abuses of power, and against functionaries faithless to their duty. None will implore increased liberty, or subsidies from the English Parliament. In no town will he find scandalous trials and burdened finances and urgent need of reforms. Gigantic monuments will attest the power of a nation which attains the age of virility, and which exercises its productive strength in the construction of prodigious bridges and of railroads of immense length. Every where he will find steamboats, manufactures, and agricultural improvements. The uncultivated land of Canada belongs to nobody, and those who desire to fertilize it, find help, credit, and protection. No formality shackles the cultivator's energy, no vexatious clauses prevent him from selling, or paralyses his energy. An incessant current of emigration flows to those fertile shores, and enriches them with the surplus population of the encumbered states of old Europe. Those who once set foot on this fruitful land for the most part remain there, and induce friends and relations to follow their example. They do not recross the Atlantic, cursing the day when they first thought of confiding their families, their fortunes, and their future to the country which prospers under the reign of British laws. What has produced these marvels ? Is it the sacrifices the mother country has imposed upon herself ? By no means ; two very simple things, two inexpensive virtues—liberalism and tolerance—have sufficed. Such is the talisman perfidious Albion has employed in Canada."

September 27.

On the Mississippi river, thirty miles above St. Louis, is the city of Alton in the State of Illinois. The population is seventeen or eighteen thousand. It is here that the Terre Haute line in conjunction with the Illinois Central terminates, thus giving the Illinois people a river port on their own side of the Mississippi. The progress of the place was rapid, but it was not likely to ruin its gigantic rival, St. Louis, as was once threatened by the railway men. At Alton point, Lord Renfrew found a fine steamer in waiting for him, and at once went on board, thus finishing his journey to the west by a voyage down the far-famed Mississippi. There were about fifty people on board, including a number of ladies, and Lord Renfrew viewed from the pilot house the river and the scenery on its banks. He remained there during the rest

of the voyage, with the exception of a moment when he left it at
the request of the captain to look at the engines. Returning to
the pilot house the objects of interest were pointed out. About
ten miles below Alton lies the *T. B. Chambers*, a large river boat,
which the previous week struck on a snag and sank with all on
board. About three hundred lives were lost. Of this terrific
calamity little was heard in Canada. The boat as she lay with
her hurricane deck above water, was pointed out to the Prince.
The junction of the Mississippi and Missouri rivers passed, he
arrived at St. Louis about half-past six o'clock, p. m.

St. Louis, like almost all the towns and cities upon the banks
of the Mississippi, has in front a large levee, or an esplanade. The
ascent from it to the top is very precipitous, paved with very
hard stones—much in the same way as the southern portion of
Yonge-street, Toronto—and altogether as nice a place for accidents as you can well imagine. As the *City of Alton*—the name
of the steamer in which Lord Renfrew crossed—approached the
wharf, cannon were fired from the magnificent steamboats lying
in the river. His Royal Highness had arrived half an hour earlier than had been expected, and hence so many people had not
gathered together as would otherwise have been the case. But
the noise of the guns brought them to the levee, and in a very few
minutes upwards of two thousand came rushing on. The Baron
was met by the Mayor, Mr. O. G. Filley, upon the wharf, and
the way being kept clear by about fifty men of the City Guard,
the carriages were soon reached, and Barnum's Hotel gained.

The proprietor of the hotel, Mr. Barnum, is not *the* Barnum,
but a cousin of that celebrated individual. His hotel is considered
the best in St. Louis, and he succeeded in making the Royal
party very comfortable during their stay there. A suite of apartments was fitted up expressly for their accommodation, and the
rooms will henceforward be used solely as bridal chambers. Won't
the house have a run of custom? Until a late hour in the evening, the hotel was surrounded by crowds of people, gazing eagerly
at balconies in the expectation that Lord Renfrew would show
himself on the outside. Some sort of serenade was also got up,
but the Prince did not appear. He was too tired.

The Prince's stay upon the prairies considerably improved his
appearance. He lost the look of fatigue which he wore upon

leaving Canada, and appeared to be in most excellent spirits. The other members of the party were likewise much benefitted by breathing the pure country air.

At daylight St. Louis was up and doing. The pouring rain did not perceptibly interfere with the preparations for business and pleasure. Attracted by the Fair and by the presence of the Prince, thousands upon thousands of strangers came in by the trains, while all the avenues leading to the city were choked with miscellaneous vehicles of all descriptions. A great portion of the people were German, French, or Irish, and the jargon of these folk, mixed up with all the known dialects of the American language—produced a state of things by no means favourable to the continuation of perfect sanity. Around the doors of the hotels the public gathered in crowds waiting the moment when along the horse railroad should pass a car in which room would be left for their conveyance to the Fair Grounds. It had been announced that Baron Renfrew would pay the Exhibition a visit at twelve o'clock; but before ten o'clock thirty thousand people had gathered together there, and at the appointed time there could not have been less than seventy thousand upon the grounds. The road from the city was packed close with vehicles, rendering travel difficult and dangerous, and all around the place itself stood acres of cabs and carriages, unable to return towards the city, so thoroughly were the streets leading to it blocked up. The cars on the horse railway, which carry passengers three miles for five cents, alone could go backwards and forwards as the conductors chose. The ordinary avenues of entrance to the grounds were found entirely insufficient to admit the pressing throng. Openings in the fence had therefore to be made, and ticket-takers placed at each. Even this, however, did not satisfy the turbulent mob; they threw down the boards, and several hundreds forced their way in without paying any thing at all.

The Prince and suite, accompanied by a few citizens, left Barnum's hotel in seven carriages, for the Fair Grounds, at half-past ten o'clock. The Prince, Mayor Filley, Lord Lyons, and the Duke of Newcastle, took the lead in an open carriage drawn by four coal black horses. The rest of the suite followed in the six other carriages. The procession was viewed from the widows along the route by a great many ladies and gentlemen. Every thing passed off quietly and in an orderly manner.

The Chamber of Commerce passed a resolution to transact no business that day. The stores and banking houses, in accordance with the resolution, generally closed, and the employees had an opportunity to visit the Fair.

The Baron and his suite arrived at the fair at half-past twelve o'clock. In some places they were recognised and room made, but the greater portion of the route was passed without their rank being suspected. Arrived inside the grounds, Lord Renfrew was conducted to the amphitheatre. The amphitheatre of St. Louis was round, and about the same size as the Toronto structure. All the seats were covered, the roofs being slightly ornamented and painted white. From the centre rose a sort of Chinese tower, with two galleries, in the upper one of which was placed a band; in the lower one the Royal party went, after they had been driven slowly round the ring. A careful estimate of the number of people seated gave twenty-eight thousand eight hundred as the result. The calculation was rendered easy from the fact that the pillars supporting the roof divided the seats into compartments, the average of which could readily be taken. Besides these, the promenade circling the gallery was full of people, who for lack of seats were standing, so that there could not have been less than thirty thousand people inside the amphitheatre. The ring was kept clear by a number of persons on horseback, so that out of the immense mass of spectators there was not one of them who chose to look that did not see the Prince. The people did not cheer altogether as he was driven round, but in small sections as he passed each compartment. When the circuit had been made, the party dismounted from the carriage, and went into the gallery of the central tower, the band above playing, "God Save the Queen" first, and "Yankee Doodle" afterwards—both of which tunes were vigourously cheered. When His Royal Highness passed through Canada, knowing that many American gentlemen were among the visitors, the authorities were careful to elevate the stars and stripes out of respect to them. It might have been expected that the compliment would have been reciprocated, but nothing of the sort had been done except at Detroit. From the tower at the St. Louis Fair, where Baron Renfrew stood, waved the American flag. The committee had it in contemplation to raise by its side the Union Jack; but an active search throughout the city revealed not a single square inch of British bunting. The fact becoming known to the merchants on 'Change, eighty dollars were in a few moments subscribed to purchase a banner, but none could be had.

Many gentlemen from the neighbouring states were there, and presented by the Mayor. Certainly the Prince and the noblemen with him found much worth looking at. In the first place, the cattle which had taken the several prizes in their distinctive classes, were brought from their sheds and placed in a circle round the centre tower. There were some most magnificent animals amongst them. The Royal party descended from the gallery and examined the stock. From the questions asked, and the remarks made, especially by the Prince and the Duke of Newcastle, shewed that they knew a great deal more than was at first suspected. But the best part of the exhibition was the competition between stallions in harness for a $600, $300, and $400 prize. About thirty splendid horses were brought into the ring. They were all examined with much attention by the Prince, and the greatest interest manifested by him, while the judges were deciding upon their respective merits. They were trotted round the spacious ring, first to show their action, and finally a series of regular trotting matches took place. The judges called out those horses they considered best, four or five at a time, and when they saw that certain among them had no chance, called them. By degrees the contest was narrowed down to a few, and it became evident that the first prize would either be taken by "Silver Heels," belonging to General Singleton, of Quincey, Illinois, or by "Royal Oak," from Medonta, Illinois. "Silver Heels" a majestic stallion, large and most beautifully proportioned—too heavy for a race, but just the build for a trotter, a glossy jet black, with the exception of heels, which are white. "Royal Oak" smaller than his rival, and younger. The perfect symmetry of "Silver Heels," and so far as appearance decidedly an inferior horse, yet he beat every thing in the field.

So interested was His Royal Highness in the proceedings that he stayed in the ring three hours and a half witnessing these trotting matches. He was invited to take lunch in a little wooden shanty prepared for the directors, to which he accordingly repaired.

Lord Renfrew and his party left the amphitheatre about half-past four o'clock and drove through the Fair Grounds, which cover more than forty acres. Owing to the immense crowd but little could be seen by the Royal party. No attempt was made by any of them to enter the numerous isolated sheds wherein were exhibited the different specimens of manufacture.

The whole exhibition was, as usual in the States, a most pleasing evidence of the energy and enterprise of its inhabitants, and will be impressed upon the memory, and be remembered as a pleasing incident of the Prince's visit to St. Louis.

Baron Renfrew advanced to Cincinnatti, Ohio, in safety on his tour though the United States of America. He left St. Louis at nine o'clock on Friday, the 28th of September, by the Ohio and Mississippi Railway, under the charge of Captain McLellan, the able superintendent of that long line. The gathering on Friday morning around the hotel, and at the *levee* at St. Louis, where waited the boat to convey Lord Renfrew to the railway station on the opposite side of the river, was very large. Shortly before starting the firemen sounded an alarm, and the whole brigade, bringing out their splendid steam engines, rushed down to Barnum's. When the Prince left he was saluted with louder cheers than he had elsewhere heard in the United States.

The distance from St. Louis to Cincinnati is three hundred and forty miles. The train conveying the Royal party proceeded with speed and safety to Vincennes—one hundred and ninety-two miles from the starting point. Here a junction is formed with the Evansville line. A freight train passing over the Ohio and Mississippi, had in some way or other got off the track and damaged it for a space. The repairs thus caused a delay of four hours, during which time His Royal Highness had time to learn that near the spot where he then was once stood a fort which was ceded to the British by the French in 1763, and afterwards taken from them by General Clark during the revolutionary war. It was therefore not until two o'clock on Saturday morning that Lord Renfrew and suite arrived in the city. At the railway station His Lordship was met by the Mayor, Mr. Bishop, Judge Hilton, and other gentlemen. The crowd, late though the hour was, numbered four or five hundred people. The hotel was speedily gained, and the Baron, much to the disappointment of the assemblage outside, by slipping in at a private door, evaded the unpleasantness consequent upon having to force his way through an impressibly curious crowd.

The Burnet House, at which the Prince stayed, is one of the most magnificent hotels in America. The entrance hall is of a very large size, and paved with squares of red and white marble alternately. Consequent upon the visit of His Royal Highness, every room in the house was crowded with people ; three or four beds in every room, and the very corridors were furnished with cots for the use of those for whom no better bed-rooms could be found. The ladies in the hotel—and there were a great many,— on Friday evening all dressed themselves in their most brilliant array and gathered together in the drawing room with the intention of receiving the Baron when he came. But the detention of the train spoiled their pretty plan, whereat they were greatly vexed, and after staying up until twelve o'clock, gradually retired to bed.

When in St. Louis his Lordship had accepted, through Mr. T. D. Hall, of the Grand Trunk Railroad, Chicago, an invitation to a citizens' ball, to be given in the O'Hern House. This same O' Hern House was erected and is owned by Mr. Pike, one of the most enterprising and spirited citizens of Cincinnati. It stands upon Fourth-street, near the Post office, measures one hundred and ninety feet, by one hundred and thirty-five feet, and cost nearly half a million of dollars. The front is of sandstone, elaborately decorated. It is five stories high, and, as is the case with buildings of this description in America, has on the ground floor a series of large stores. The theatre itself is said not to be excelled in beauty upon the continent of America. There are two galleries, the boxes and the pit, or—in American parlance— the dress circle and the parquette, are in reality one, rising gradually from the foot of the stage. From the floor of the parquette to the top of the dome is a height of eighty-two feet. The interior is one blaze of gilt and gas. The arms from which hung the chandeliers spring from the centre of shields supported by cupids, their wings tipped with gold. On both sides of the stage were six colossal female figures with lighted torches in their hands, while the roof and the walls had been painted with figures of gods and goddesses. Around the base of the dome, and around the base of the lantern in the dome, were hundreds of small gas jets, which shone like so many diamonds. The pillars supporting the galleries were wreathed with gilded flowers, while the foot lights upon the stage were partially hidden with evergreens, that the flaunting crinoline might not be endangered. The scenery was so arranged, that from the boxes the appearance of a large hall, with numerous marble pillars, was gained. The theatre was splendid. It was one blaze of light, one mass of colour—in fact the designer succeeded in making an exceedingly brilliant and a really beautiful place. There was no quiet for the eye, no relief from the blaze of light. In ideas upon these matters, we might differ much from Americans. Mr. Pike's theatre was greatly applauded. Had any architect ventured to erect it in England, the crisis might have been sadly different.

The Prince arrived at half-past nine o'clock, after running the gauntlet through a crowd which lined the streets all the way from the hotel. Upon entering he was conducted to one of the private boxes, where he remained a few minutes looking at the house, and the company numbering about five hundred. At length one of the committee advanced and said—"Ladies and gentlemen, the Prince will dance—choose your partners." Lord Renfrew was introduced to Mrs. Pike, and the first quadrille commenced. Our readers will perhaps be surprised to learn that the people there despite their republicanism, gave themselves aristocratic airs. Some of the fair ones actually presumed to censure Lord Renfrew for dancing with the wife of the "manager of the theatre." He did—and one would like to know what better woman he was likely to meet in his tour through the United States. Mrs. Pike stands at the head of society in the city of Cincinnati,—she is a well educated woman, wears diamonds, knows how to dance, and knows how to conduct herself with propriety. Besides Mrs. Pike, the Baron danced with four or five other ladies. It must not be supposed that he was left to enjoy himself without remark, or without being looked at. Upon one occasion a waltz was called, and when he led off with the lady he had honoured with his hand, the whole company looked on with admiration, and formed themselves into a circle round him, leaving him and his partner to dance alone, while they looked on. His Lordship when he saw that no one joined him, very speedily stopped, and it was not until some of the suite came to his rescue that he was relieved from

A 23

his embarrassing position. For the remainder of the evening quadrilles only were danced.

Another very curious episode occurred which created great laughter. The Americans are accustomed, it appears, to have a master of ceremonies, whose duty it is to direct the movements of the dancers. The ball was commenced without this aid, but the greatest confusion was the result. At length a stalwart fellow, in a white waistcoat, was captured and stuck up in the gallery, where for the rest of the night he occupied himself in calling out :—"Ladies chain," "set and turn partners," &c., much to the amusement of His Royal Highness and other Englishmen present.

The Duke of Newcastle, Lord Lyons, Earl St. Germains and others, were objects of great attraction; little crowds gathering round them all the evening. The following conversation, which took place between the first mentioned gentleman and a citizen of the United States is too good to be lost. The Duke was leaning against one of the pillars which supported the gallery, looking upon the gay throng, when up came the aforesaid citizen, who grinning his politest, said—"Yeu're one of the soote (suite) ain't yew?" "Yes sir, I am;" blandly replied his grace, "Might I ask who yew may be?" "Oh, certainly, my name is Newcastle."—"Oh, yew're the Dook of Newcastle air yew?—who'd a thought neow?" —and after a pause, and looking up in the nobleman's face, he observed—"My! yew scared them Orangemen, didn't yew!!" What his grace replied is not on record.

Not only are these noblemen objects of great attraction, the footmen also come in for a share. One of them was very much bothered by an American, who mistook him for Lord Lyons or somebody else of equal importance. John did not think it worth while to undeceive the inquisitive individual, and let him talk on. At length Jonathan spoke something in this style : " This is a mighty fine country ain't it ? No poor folks here. You've got nothin like it in England 'ev yew? How fur 'ev yew bin? From De-trite to Chicago and St. Lewis, etc. My! Come now, ain't it a fine country; don't you like it?" John thus addressed, assumed his most aristocratic air, pulled down his waistcoat, stroked his chin, and in the most serious tone possibly said— "Like it, certainly. If it's all as good as the portion we have passed through, I will buy it before I go home!" Jonathan subsided.

Lord Renfrew attended Divine Service in the Cathedral, on the 30th of September. The sermon was preached by Bishop McIlvaine. The church is rather a fine building, erected at a cost of $80,000. The congregation was large, but not so large as it would have been had the weather been favourable, the rain pouring down all day long. His lordship started at nine o'clock for Pittsburg. He went first to Columbus, and then to Crestline on the little Miami road, and from thence to Pittsburg, by the Pittsburg, Fort Wayne, and Chicago Railway, a distance of 310 miles, and in accordance with these arrangements Baron Renfrew and party left Cincinnati at seven o'clock, a. m., and arrived at Pittsburg at forty-five minutes past eight o'clock. The journey was a most pleasant one in every respect save the length. A fourteen hours' ride in a railway carriage, smooth though the road was, and entirely free from dust, could not be made without fatigue. The state of Ohio is one of the most beautiful of the union. Monotonous scenery had been left behind in the western wilds. That which now met the eye of the travellers abounded in hill and vale, in cultivated fields free from blackened stumps, in pleasant vistas of forest trees bordering the numerous streams and rivers over which the train rushed. When the Prince landed in Newfoundland and visited the lower provinces, he found summer in all her glory. The foilage of the trees was fresh and green, the grass unmown, the wheat uncut. Now this had passed away, autumn was there, the harvest had been housed, nature had assumed a different but more beautiful aspect. All along the line of railway, the diverse and brilliant colours of the trees shone gloriously in the sun, those in the forest being more directly exposed to the sun's rays, standing out in vivid contrast to the darker hued masses behind. At the commencement and at the termination of the journey, more particularly through deep valleys, were passed the hills pressing close on either side, the line sometimes running along mere ledges of rock, with the Ohio on one side, and a towering darkly covered precipice above. It was not until darkness closed in, until thick clouds gathered overhead and poured down their contents upon the earth, that the travellers sought other employment than that of gazing upon the beautiful prospect which every where met their view. Then the chess board was brought, and His Royal Highness was soundly beaten by the "Dook."

As the Prince travelled eastward the enthusiasm of the people seemed to increase. The crowds at all the railway stations larger, the cheers more frequent, the excitement evidently greater. But those things to a certain extent amused the Prince.

At Alliance, eighty-three miles from Pittsburg, the Royal party were met by a Committee of citizens from the latter place, who, entering the train, pointed out many objects of interest to the English visitors. They were exceedingly pleased with the affable manner in which they were treated by the Royal party, and loud in the praises of the Prince.

RECEPTION AT PITTSBURG.

At Pittsburg, the railway station and the streets adjoining were of course crowded with thousands of people, who shouted out an enthusiastic welcome. The Duquesne Grays—a fine company of men, together with the police, kept the platform clear. There was somewhat of a rush when the Baron stepped from the car, but he was not incommoded. The streets from the railway station to the hotel were lined with thousands of people; banners, British and American, were hung from the windows, and a bridge spanning the river opposite the Monongahela House, was illuminated by a large number of wide-awake torches. The entrance door was kept clear by the men who had done good service at the railway station. A committee of reception conducted the Prince and suite to their rooms in the hotel, and by the excellent arrangements made, the utmost privacy was secured. A band played underneath the windows several American and Canadian airs; but as His Royal Highness did not show himself upon the balcony, "God Save the Queen" was omitted. The crowd, numbering five or six thousand people, after waiting nearly two hours, gradually and quietly dispersed. The reception given to the Prince in Pittsburg was the best he had met with in the United States— the most orderly, the most respectful.

The apartments prepared for the Royal party at the Monongahela Hotel were all that could be desired. The rooms were re-carpeted, and supplied with oaken furniture. The bed provided for the Prince presented a very elegant and most comfortable appearance.

The Baron visited a coal mine, and afterwards started in the afternoon for Harrisburgh. The people were gathered in crowds at the railway stations and cheered heartily. The car constructed for the Prince by the Pennsylvania Central Railroad Company, besides being fitted up with the ordinary conveniences, had an extended covered platform behind, securely railed in. Upon this platform, during a great portion of the journey, Baron Renfrew sat, and enjoyed the noble scenery through which he passed. Pittsburg itself is surrounded by hills of no mean height, but as the east is gradually gained the hills become lofty mountains, their heads among the clouds, clothed from base to summit with foliage beautiful in variety of colour. The ascent of the Alleghanies commences at Conemaugh, about eighty miles from Pittsburg. From thence the road runs along a succession of mountain ridges, gradually increasing in height, until the summit of the mountains, 2,160 feet above the level of the sea, is gained.

In crossing the Alleghanies the sight is grand, but terrific. Far down in the valley below is the Conemaugh river, looking in the distance like a winding line of silver thread, scarcely perceptible from the railway train, though so directly beneath that a stone might be thrown into it from the cars. Towering many hundred feet above the highest point attained by the railway are other mountains, while now and then glimpses are gained of an immense sea of hills below, spreading around for miles their rounded tops, looking like the billows of the sea. And when darkness drew nigh, and the mists began to ascend from the valleys, hiding from view the little white farm houses which here and there dot the green expanse, there seemed no limit to the depth of the awful precipices along whose edges the train thundered. When near the highest point attained, away, hundreds of feet below, a freight train was seen creeping slowly up the steep incline. Sometimes, as it wound in and out along the sides of the hills, it appeared close at hand. Now it disappeared in some deep cutting, with solid walls of rock on either side, and now emerging, looked farther off than before. With the brakes pressing hard upon the wheels, the cars containing the Royal party descended. Upon a ledge of rock, which, looked at from below, appeared scarce wide enough to afford foothold for a goat, the trains met and passed each other. The precipice was here of as precipitous a descent as along any portion of the route. Its base was lost in the mists below, its summit was hidden in the clouds. Cloud above and cloud below, the line of rail appeared like a road built in the air by other than mortal hands. The Prince and his party travelled long and travelled far, but no where else upon the American continent could they have seen nature wearing a more sublime aspect. The journey across the Alleghany mountains must live in their remembrance as long as life lasts.

To enable Baron Renfrew the better to enjoy the scenery, the train was stopped at the little town of Willmore on the western slope, and he, together with some of the younger members of the party, mounted the engine. But the Prince, not satisfied with the platform used by the driver, placed himself in front of the smoke-pipe. Had he by any means managed to fall from thence his guardian, the Duke of Newcastle, would have found it extremely difficult to find him afterwards. There is no saying how far he would have tumbled. At a rough guess it would have been between eighteen hundred and two thousand feet. By the side of his lordship stood Mr. Smith, one of the engineers engaged in the construction of the road. The work occupied three years and cost an immense sum of money. The steepest grade being ninety-five feet in the mile. The railroad has a double track throughout its entire length, and is one of the best built, if not the best built, in the United States.

Numerous deep cuttings through solid rock in many places had to be made, and in some of them through thick seams of coal, and along the line numerous holes leading to cuttings from which the coal is taken. The people who gathered at the railway stations looked like those of Staffordshire or Monmouth, black and dirty, covered with coal dust, while the air was full of sulphur from the smelting furnaces of the coke ovens. Surely his Lordship must have occasionally fancied himself back in England.

After remaining upon the engine for the space of twenty-five miles, the Baron returned to the car provided for his especial accommodation, and a tunnel of 3,750 feet in length having been passed, Altoona was gained in safety. There a stoppage was made for the purpose of telling the Chief Superintendent of the road, that as the train was behind its time, the dinner he had provided in his office for the Royal party could not be tasted, unless he chose to put it on board. This was accordingly done, and amid the cheers of some thousands of people, the journey was again resumed. Altoona is a little town with a very big hotel, nearly as large as the place itself. It is the seat of the machine shops of the Pennsylvania Central Railroad Company, to which fact it owes all its importance.

From this point to Harrisburg, the capital of the state, and the stopping-place for the night, is a distance of one hundred and thirty miles. Of the remainder of the route little more may be said but that it was hidden in the darkness. A tunnel at Barre, 1,950 feet in length, was passed, and, before entering Harrisburg a bridge, 3,680 feet long—over the Susquehanna river—was crossed. The Prince slept, or perhaps it would be more correct to say lay down, during the latter part of the route in one of the beds with which his car was fitted up. When he arrived at his destination he looked very much wearied.

Upon arriving at the Harrisburg railway station, he was conveyed in a carriage provided by the Mayor and a committee of citizens, almost before he knew any thing of it. He was then left to get his supper of oysters and go to bed in peace.

A SERENADE.

Fast asleep he was, indeed. There below his window was thundering away a brass band—serenading, as they called it. And because the Baron, after a ride of two hundred and forty-seven miles, and of the three hundred and something on the previous day, would not go on to the verandah outside and make a speech, as Abe Lincoln or Stephen Douglas would do, if they had the chance, the folks below were getting excited.

October 3rd.

Baron Renfrew left Harrisburg this morning at thirty-five minutes past nine o'clock, and arrived at Baltimore at three minutes past one, travelling by the Northern Central Railway to Harrisburg. Entering a town at eleven o'clock at night, and leaving it next morning at nine o'clock, was not the way to gain an acquaintance with its people, or to become intimate with the objects of interest it might afford. It possesses a population of about twelve thousand, and judging from so much as was seen of it, appears greatly to resemble Belleville in Canada. The capitol is an imposing building of considerable size in the south east part of the town. Before proceeding to the railway station, the Baron, accompanied by the Mayor of the city, paid a visit to it, and passed rapidly through the principal rooms; he then drove at once to the railway station, and at the time already mentioned started for Baltimore.

Before his arrival at Baltimore, an immense crowd gathered to receive him. The railroad passes through a considerable portion of the city before reaching the terminus, and along both sides of the route thousands of people were collected. They were perched on the fences, they roamed all over the numerous vehicles which were grouped together, they were laid down flat in long rows upon the low sand hills bordering in some places on the line, at the iminent danger of breaking their necks, they hung half out of the windows, and ornamented the roofs of the ricketty shanties which in the suburbs abound. At and around the railway station an immense crowd assembled, and when the train stopped, it was only by the most strenuous exertions that the police were able to keep a way clear for the carriages procured for the Royal party. The roofs of the cars were covered with some hundreds of boys, who, when the band present for the occasion struck up "God save the Queen," kept time with their heels and toes.

Amidst the tremendous din occasioned by this curious combination of sounds, the Prince and the Duke of Newcastle got into a barouche large enough for the two only. The Mayor of the city, Mr. Swann, with despair depicted to a most terrible extent upon his countenance, besought the Royal youth to descend, for he, the Mayor, was desirous of riding with him in a four horse vehicle to the station of the Baltimore and Ohio Railway Company. Lord Renfrew had not got it in his heart to refuse. He probably thought of the many sleepless nights his honour had spent in anticipation of the honour he was so near losing. The Prince and Duke lept from the barouche, transferred themselves to the carriage provided for them, and with a smile of contentment mounting his vehicle the Mayor took his seat by the side of the Royal visitor. Then the cortege started straight for the railroad station, passing through crowded streets, and saluted by the waving handkerchiefs of hundreds of ladies who filled the numerous balconies along the line of route. At twenty minutes to three the train started on its way to the capital of the United States.

The distance from Baltimore to Washington, thirty-eight miles, was accomplished in an hour and a quarter. The scenery all along the road was uninteresting. Before arriving in Washington, Baron Renfrew was met upon the platform by Secretary Cass, and two of the President's nephews, both bearing the name of Buchanan. Mr. Cass, having been introduced to the Baron by Lord Lyons, the British Ambassador, invited him to the White House, which invitation was accepted. Thither they accordingly adjourned, and were lost to public view.

At eight o'clock a Cabinet dinner was given. All the members of the Executive with their wives were present.

October 4th, 1860.

If his Royal Highness the Prince of Wales was given to making reflection, there was plenty of matter for him in Washington, the capital of that immense country which was wrested from the rule of his fathers by a people determined to be free; the future Monarch of the British Empire, by special invitation, appeared under the roof of an elective magistrate, the descendant of a long line of kings. The time was when antagonistic principles existed, the one of the popular voice, the other of absolute power. But now, though the Presidents of the United States are elected, they have greater authority during their term of office than the Prince of Wales can ever have sitting upon the English throne. The allegation may be sneered at as savouring of republicanism, but the fact remains nevertheless, that the British monarch is dependant upon the people; without their aid he were as impotent to rule as the candidates for the Presidency now are. Never before in the history of the world have the representatives of two nations, occuping at the same time such similar and such dissimilar relations to their people, before met. What extravagant prophecies may not henceforth be believed in, what predictions may not be fulfilled! Britain's future King, the guest of the American Republic! What next—and next!

But the event has been brought about after so much talk, it has

A 24

been so long mooted, so certainly fixed, that now it has occurred it excites no surprise. It has been taken as a matter of course, and so done with at once. The Americans think it necessary to find excuses for the curiosity they manifested to see His Royal Highness. Numbers of them went to the railway station "only to see the car." Others were "just passing and thought they might as well wait," while those who did go purposely were " old country people." Many of them, too, did not hesitate to throw in a word expressive of their opinion, that an elective chief was best for a nation—such opinions not being changed by the view gained of the Baron. Should he be a republican with whom you conversed, he would mildly suggest that in all probability His Royal Highness would make a better King for England than Douglas or Breckenridge would a President for the United States, throwing in at the same time a reference to Joe Lane's spelling ship with two p's, and the man is with you directly. Meet a democrat in a similar manner, and the like result is obtained. Whatever be the end of the approaching contest we may be sure of this, that the Queen of Great Britain reigns over a people far more united in her favour than any candidate who may be elected chief officer of the United States.

The city was crowded with visitors, the greater part from the south. They manifest far more interest in the doings of Baron Renfrew than their brethren of the northern states through which he had passed. With their wives and daughters, very richly dressed, they drive about the city, lounge in the avenues, and seem generally to be afflicted with *ennui*. The visit of the Prince did them all good.

The Baron, accompanied by the Mayor of the city and Secretary Floyd, ascended the noble steps leading to the dome, and quickly turning to the right passed down a long corridor to the new Senate Chamber, the doors being closed behind him to prevent any crowding. Passing entirely through the right wing, he returned along one side of the corridor surrounding the chamber, and entered the rotunda through the door by which he had left it. Here, those who were present, numbering about five hundred, had a good opportunity of seeing him, while he looked at the pictures and sculptures with which the place was decorated. The people did not press upon him very closely as he passed round, though sometimes a mob of ragged little boys, who, one after the other, got between the legs of the Duke and Colonel Grey, caused considerable annoyance. In the rotunda eight large pictures, representing events in the history of America, were placed. The subjects—the embarkation of the Pilgrims by Weir, the landing of Columbus by Vanderlyn, De Sotos' discovery of the Mississippi by Powell, and the Baptism of Pocahontas by Chapman. Opposite were four pictures painted by Colonel Trumbull, one of Washington's aides-de-camp. They represented the authors of the Declaration of Independence, the surrender of General Burgoyne at Saratoga, the surrender of Lord Cornwallis at Yorktown, and General Washington resigning his commission to Congress. These pictures the Prince looked at with considerable earnestness, and asked Mr. Floyd the names of many of the originals whose portraits were delineated. He appeared greatly pleased with them, and would have stayed much longer had he not been hurried to be in time for the levee.

From the rotunda the party passed down the left hand corridor to the old Senate Chamber, soon to be occupied by the Judges of the Supreme Court, and to the House of Representatives. From thence to the library, where after staying a few moments he entered his carriage and drove to the White House.

The Capitol of the United States, familiar as it must be to many of our readers, stands upon the site of that building which in 1814 was destroyed by the British army. The Americans hold that the deed tended to cast a slur upon the British arms, but whether that be the case or not, they ought to be much obliged, for had it not been pulled down the probabilities are, it would be there still, instead of the magnificent building now erected. The centre of the Capitol is of yellow sandstone, painted white; the wings which were lately added, are of marble. The total length is 745 feet. Built in the Corinthian style of architecture, it abounds in lofty columns, and affords ample opportunity for the display of the magnificent works of sculpture with which it is ornamented. The rotunda is not yet complete. At present it is covered with a temporary roof, affording but a poor light for the exhibition of the aforementioned pictures upon the walls. When finished it will rise 241 feet above the top of the building, and 396 feet above the level of the grounds at the foot of the terrace upon which it is built.

The Senate Chamber and the House of Representatives are similar in design, but differ to a considerable extent in the ornaments adopted. The ceilings are flat, and though a great distance from the floor, make the rooms look low. They are very richly decorated with coloured glass windows and an enormous amount of gilded work. "Republican simplicity" here entirely vanishes. The pillars supportiug the galleries are of richly polished Italian marble. The seats of the members arranged in a sort of semicircle opposite the chair, are of carved oak. The President's room is a mass of brilliant colours. Upon the panels are portraits of eminent republicans, over the entrance door a representation of Peace, another of two Peaces on each side lying down on the floor revelling amidst fruit and flowers. The floors throughout the entire building are laid with encaustic tiles of varied colours, but all of rich patterns. The grounds around the building boast some avenues of beautiful trees, and many large series of sculpture. It is as difficult to say what the Capitol has cost as to tell how much money has been spent on the English House of Commons. It is supposed, however, that $10,000,000 will pay for what has so far been done. Had the money been properly laid out, it would have been finished for about half that sum.

Previous to visiting the Capitol, Baron Renfrew had been to the Post-office, the Patent-office, and the Treasury department— the two last mentioned places having been closed by order of the President, and a holiday in honour of the Prince having been given to the employees. All these buildings are of white marble, and have a most magnificent appearance.

The levee was held by the President, not by the Baron, although he was there for all that, and took his stand under the chandelier in the reception room, by the side of Mr. Buchanan, in democratic style. The doors were opened at twelve o'clock. Such a crush scarcely ever was before, ladies and gentlemen were packed closely together in the ante-rooms, and as soon as the opportunity was afforded they crowded in tumultuous order into the presence chamber as though their very lives depended upon gaining instant admission, and to render the confusion worse, those who were presented had to take their exit by the door at which they entered. Few, however, attempted this until the chamber was crammed full. The ladies jumped upon the chairs which were placed round the walls, and did violence to their pretty necks in endeavouring to catch a glimpse of the personages within the small circle underneath the chandelier. And those who could not get chairs, manifested decided symptoms of climbing the shoulders of the gentlemen who accompanied them. A small number only who got into the room were presented—they were in too great a hurry for that. Who can blame them? They were anxious to see the Prince—a very pardonable weakness. If Mr. President Buchanan had desired to keep order he would have admitted only one or two at a time, and would then have caused them to pass out of the room. Nominally the people were presented to him alone, but numbers of them continued to shake hands with the Prince. The ladies were especially active. When they held out their hands to His Royal Highness and gave him the very sweetest smiles they could bring to their faces, how could he refuse them? No, he braved the scolding he may get from his Queen Mother for disobeying her orders, and squeezed the fingers of the girls in right Royal style. Some of them, at least one of them, complained of his grip. But there is no need to believe her; for she was not very good looking, so that it is scarely likely the Baron was guilty of the offence complained of. No cards were necessary to gain admission, or entering of names in books was required. The free and independent citizens of the United States crushed in, whispered their names in the ear of the usher, took hold of old Buck's fist, viewed the Prince, and took their stand as near to him as possible. At length tired of this method of proceeding, and seeing from the sea of heads, visible through the doorway, that before all had passed midnight would be near, Albert Edward complained of fatigue, and the levee was instantly declared at an end by Mr. Buchanan. However, to satisfy the disappointed republicans—all of whom had come to pay their respects to the President and to see the Prince—His Royal Highness appeared at the window over the balcony, where he stood for some moments "the admired of all admirers."

The other day Lord Renfrew sent for Mr. Davis, the artist of the New York *Illustrated News*, and asked to be allowed to look at his sketches. Mr. Davis of course complied, and was highly complimented by his Lordship on the skill and taste manifested in his drawings.

October 5, 1860.

His Royal Highness the Prince of Wales, having seen all the larger sights at this time to be seen in the capital of the United States, was under the necessity of paying a visit to a ladies' school. Yes, to a ladies' school, conducted by a certain Mrs. Smith? Why was he taken there? Was it that he might be able to form some opinion upon the future mothers of America? Not at all. No such object was in view. He went there simply to have a game at ten pins with Miss Lane. Rather extraordinary, some uncivilised people in Canada may think, that a lady would play at ten pins. But not at all extraordinary is it thought there. To be a good ten pin player is a necessary accomplishment of the present age, and not at all an unworthy one either, as professors of calisthenics will be most ready to argue. It affords an opportunity for exercise which otherwise would not occur, and besides strengthening the muscles, it gives great bodily strength to the women, and places them beyond all fear of ill-treatment from brutal husbands. Perhaps to this training the ladies of America owe it, that they are frequently enabled to cowhide an offender of the opposite sex, and thus manifest their superiority over their sisters on the other side of the Atlantic. Whether from any anxiety with regard to future matrimonial experiences the President's niece has thus trained herself, it is impossible to say, but at any rate she understood the game of ten pins well, and beat Albert Edward nearly every "string." They were engaged in the contest for two hours, during which time the Baron showed that he was possessed of considerable muscular strength, but of little skill. He improved, however, greatly towards the end. A few more lessons, and he would become nearly as great a proficient as his fair preceptress.

The Patent Office visited by the Baron, is one of the finest buildings in Washington. Standing upon a high plinth, built principally of marble, with double columns supporting the projecting roof, it presents a most imposing appearence, and to admirers of Grecian architecture appears almost perfect. It is of an immense size, measuring four hundred and ten feet by two hundred and seventy-five feet. The ground floor is occupied by offices for the transaction of public business; on the upper story is a large apartment, having a total length of thirteen hundred and fifty feet, running entirely round the quadrangle. Here are kept models of all the machines patented by citizens of the United States. Although the space is so great, there is little room to spare, and it is perfectly evident, if the Americans go on at their present rate of inventing, that in a very short time from this they will want a second building as large as the present one for their accommodation. The Baron during his visit was shown several objects of peculiar interest. Among others, Franklin's printing press, which the Americans do well religiously to preserve. A pair of breeches worn by General Washington during the revolutionary war were also exhibited, with the cut and make of which His Royal Highness expressed himself well pleased, and proposed having a pair made like them on his return home. But Washington's sword was of most interest.

———

October 5.

The Prince of Wales was highly pleased with his inspection of public buildings. During his visit to the Patent Office he remarked that the revolutionary relics should be placed in a separate room. They must have appeared very simple to him after the vast number of the relics of the past which he saw in the Tower of London, and must have impressed him with a new sense of the enterprise of a nation which is so young as to have few relics beyond a uniform, a printing press, and a few flags, and which has yet attained such an immense growth and power.

The Prince seeing several brass rings suspended from the ceiling, inquired their use, and feeling decidedly on his muscle, caught hold of them and swung himself by a usual gymnastic feat, from one to the other across the room. The Hon. Mr. Elliott exhibited himself upon a rope ladder, and the whole party indulged in hearty and merry laughter. The Prince called a little girl to him, inquired her name, and in every way seemed so gay and light-hearted that his suite could not suppress ther surprise, and even the grave Duke joined in the fun.

The Prince was very particular about his presents. When the photograph of the home of Washington was offered to him, General Bruce inquired if any duplicates could be obtained, adding that the Prince would accept of no presents which could be purchased by him.

A crowd of about eight thousand persons witnessed the fireworks on the first evening. It was composed of not only residents of Washington, but people from Georgetown, Alexandria, and the circumjacent counties in Virginia and Maryland. The fireworks were not entirely successful on account of the rain, which prevented the largest pieces being displayed. The united arms of America and England was a superb piece, and elicited enthusiastic applause.

Miss Lane's reception was a most successful affair. About six hundred persons, the *elite* of Washington, were assembled.

When the fireworks began, Miss Lane, escorted by the Prince, appeared on the south balcony, with the President, and were received with hearty cheers. The marine band, stationed in the east room, gave the music.

At eleven o'clock supper was served for the entire company, and in the finest style. During the conversation, which became quite general, and of which the Royal party were the leaders, Queen Victoria's visit to Prussia was mentioned, and one of the distinguished members of the suite said laughing. that England must take care of itself, as all the Royal family were deserting it. The party broke up late, and was most successful.

At ten o'clock in the morning the Prince, with Miss Lane, the President and Lord Lyons started for Mount Vernon, the suite, among which was Sir Henry Holland, the Queen's physician, following in carriages to the dock, where the cutter *Harriet Lane* had been prepared for the party. About forty-five persons embarked, among whom were several members of the Cabinet and Mesdames Slidell, Gwin, Ledyard, Riggs and others, and Hon. Augustus Schell, of New York.

The voyage up occupied only an hour and a half. Upon landing the party inspected the entire grounds and gardens most attentively. The Prince and the Royal party were deeply observant, asking many questions, and apparently much impressed with the feelings natural to the occasion. Mrs. Riggs, Vice-Regent of the Mount Vernon Association, acted as chaperone, and the rule excluding all other visitors, although Friday was the regular visiting day, was rigidly observed, the regular steamers postponing their trips to the following day.

The day was all that could be desired—the finest that the

Indian summer could give. Having carefully inspected the house the Prince stood reverently uncovered in the room in which Washington died, looked at the piano which he presented to Mrs. Lewis, and examined the key of the Bastile and the other curiosities there. The party expressed their gratification at the taste and neatness displayed in the arrangement of the place, and then proceeded to the tomb of Washington.

The marine band had arrived before them, and concealed by a neighbouring thicket, begun playing a dirge composed by the leader. The scene was most impressive. The party, with uncovered heads, ranged themselves in front of the tomb, so simple, yet so grand in its associations, and looked in through the iron grated door at the sarcophagus which contains the remains of the Father of his Country. Then retiring a few paces, the Prince, the President, and the Royal party, grouped in front, silently contemplated the tomb of Washington.

Around were the representatives of that aristocracy, which once proclaimed every republican a traitor, now doing homage to the great representative republican. Next to the Prince stood the President of the United States, reverently bowing before the resting place of the first of rulers. Besides him were those who, in the last battles between England and this country, had taken a not unprominent part, while he himself had once borne arms against the very country whose future ruler was now his honoured guest. What lessons all must have learned from this visit—what thoughts must have occurred to each—how all must have felt that, above all, and over all, God reigns supreme, ordering events for His own wise purposes, and working miracles, not at once by His instantaneous word, but by the slower process of time.

At the request of the Mount Vernon Association, the Prince planted a young horse chestnut tree, to commemorate his visit to the place. The tree was planted upon a beautiful little mound, not far from the tomb.

This ceremony being over, the party again stood for a few moments before the tomb, and then turning away in the thoughtful silence, slowly and silently retraced their way to the *Harriet Lane*, which during their absence had been transformed, by means of canvass and gay flags, into a beautiful dining saloon, with covers laid for the entire party.

The steamer went slowly up the Potomac until dinner was over and the deck cleared for dancing, the Marine Band furnishing the music. The Prince opened the dance with Miss Lane, and during the passage up danced with Misses Slidell, Gwin, Riggs, and Ledyard. The whole party were in such excellent spirits, and so enjoyed the voyage, that their intended visit to Fort Washington was altogether forgotten until the fort was passed, and it was too late to return.

Four hours were consumed in the passage to Washington, and upon landing the party were greeted with salutes from the Navy Yard and Arsenal, neither of which, as it was past six o'clock, they had time to visit.

The party immediately drove to the residence of Lord Lyons, and soon after dinner was served in the large square dining-room, with its heavily curtained windows. Upon the side-board and rich dressers Lord Lyons' splendid service of silver plate was displayed. In the centre of the table stood a large golden tray, with three ornamental golden vases, and these and two porcelain vases at the extremities of the table were filled with flowers. This tray is the pride of the family plate, and even its blemishes from the sea voyage were pointed out with pride. Lord Lyons sat in the centre of the left hand side of the table, and on either side of him were Miss Lane and the Prince. Opposite Lord Lyons sat the President, supported by the Cabinet and diplomatic corps The dinner was a superb and *recherche* affair.

The Prince passed the night at the White House.

October 6.—The anxiety on the part of the public to obtain a view of His Royal Highness seemed to have undergone no abatement as the period of his stay in Washington shortened. This was clearly evidenced by the crowds which assembled at various points anxiously awaiting the approach of the Prince on his way to the cutter which was in readiness to convey himself and party to Acquia creek, from whence they went to Richmond.

In anticipation of securing a glimpse of the Prince as he should make his exit from the executive mansion, large numbers began to assemble about the White House at an early hour, and it was not long before the crowd had so augmented that the mansion might well be said to have been literally besieged by anxious and curious spectators. Large numbers had assembled at different points along the avenue.

Shortly before, the Prince and suite took an affectionate leave of the President and Miss Lane. In this final interview mutual regret was expressed that the pleasant hours that had been spent at the White House during the Prince's stay in the city, should be so shortly terminated, and wishes for the future health and prosperity of the President and niece, and the Queen and the Prince, as well as for the prosperity and harmony of the two respective countries, were mutually expressed.

The carriage of the Prince, followed by those of the members of the Cabinet, in which were those officers, with some others, left the mansion about ten o'clock, surrounded by numerous vehicles and a large crowd of pedestrians, eagerly gazing at the Prince. The line of carriages drove slowly down Pennsylvania avenue to Four-and-a-half-street, and thence to the Arsenal, where a large crowd of spectators was gathered on the wharf where lay the steamer. On the arrival of the party a salute of twenty-one guns was fired from the Arsenal, which was responded to by a like number from the Navy Yard.

The vessel loosed her moorings at precisely eleven o'clock, and proceeded down the noble Potomac, amid the plaudits of the vast concourse assembled, with the British ensign floating at her foremast and the American at the stern.

The Prince having gone, Washington again assumed its usual "recess" look, and the fashionable quarter its aspect of solitude.

The parting of the Prince and his companions from the President and his family was marked by genuine feelings of regret, and the public functionaries on both sides showed more emotion than usual at any mere ceremonial of leave taking. To the last "the Mount Vernon day" was the subject of pleasant conversation.

Sir Henry Holland remained until Monday, the guest of the President. Dr. Ackland, of the University of Oxford, of the Prince's suite, went on Friday morning, in company with the Hon. William C. Rives, of Virginia, to visit that gentleman at his seat, Castle Hill, but joined the Royal party at Richmond.

The cutter *Harriet Lane* proceeded directly to Amboy, N. J., for the purpose of meeting the Prince on his way from Philadelphia, to land him at Castle Garden.

The Royal party looked forward with undissembled anticipations of delight to the grand ovation in New York.

The Prince was decidedly a "heart smasher," the young ladies say ; and, indeed, he has won some of the old fellows of the rougher sex too.

Southern gentlemen, now that they have seen him and his suite, regret that he could not extend his journey to that part of the country.

During the stay of the Prince the diplomatic corps made no personal calls, but left their cards, according to etiquette.

October 6.

The *Harriet Lane* had a fine run to Acquia Creek, on the Potomac. As she passed Mount Vernon, the ship's bell was tolled, and after a momentary hesitation all the Royal party removed their hats. The day was beautiful, and the south never better deserving the epithet of "sunny." The whole party were in great spirits.

At Acquia Creek the Royal party landed, bade good by to the gentlemen who had accompanied them, and took a special train for Richmond.

The first part of the journey was over a road laid with the dangerous strap rail, the only road of the kind in the country, past woods gay with autumn's livery, past golden fields, past lanes, so shaded and tree-arched that the Royal party compared them with those of England.

The train then crossed the Rappahannock, and stopped a few moments at Fredericksburg. The Prince was told this was the only finished city in the United States. He could not understand the jest, and said he had seen finer. It was explained that the city had not gained in population in forty years. The Prince appeared deeply interested when he was told that there Washington became a Freemason, and there Washington's mother was buried. A great crowd of people were assembled at the depot, cheering and shouting, the negroes bowing and courtesying to the ground, praying "God bless massa!" The Prince came out and bowed, curiously inspecting the slaves, as if he expected to see some badge upon them.

The train started off again, and passed wide-stretching plantations, with central white houses. There are few villages on the route, as if all the ground was used for cultivation, and none could be spared for building lots. In comparison with the rich prairies which the Prince had seen, the land looked poor.

At Ashland, about a mile from which Henry Clay was born, the train was detained for some time to await the arrival of the regular train.

The Prince and suite were received at the fair ground, two miles distant from the city, in the evening, by the Mayor and a committee of citizens. The Prince and suite were conveyed to the city in barouches.

When the party reached Richmond it was nearly seven o'clock. There was a tremendous crowd at the depot, who cheered greatly, and blocked up the street leading to the hotel. The people crowded into the passages and stairways, and it was with much difficulty the party got through. There was no formality and no procession, but continual cheers. There had been no such popular demonstration since the Prince reached the States, and the arrangements were satisfactory.

The ball had been given up, partly on account of the Prince's fatigue, and partly on account of financial difficulties.

A great crowd stood in front of the hotel, but the party did not appear.

On Sunday the party went to St. Paul's Church, where a very fine sermon was preached by Dr. Muneigerde, the pastor, from first Corinthians, first chapter, 8th verse :—" Who shall also confirm you unto the end, that ye may be blameless in the day of our Lord Jesus Christ."

No allusion was made to the Prince in the sermon. The Prince was introduced and shook hands with the Doctor at the close of the service, but could not stay to communion.

The Prince, after service, instead of going to his hotel, as he ought perhaps to have done, at the invitation of Governor Letcher and of the Mayor, Mr. Mayo, bent his steps toward the Capitol, situated one hundred and fifty or two hundred yards from the church. On his way he stopped to look at an equestrian statue of Washington in bronze, which, besides its great beauty, is additionally interesting on account of its being the last finished work of the great Crawford.

A crowd chased the carriages to the Capitol, through which the Prince was taken. He then made a formal call of a few minutes upon Governor Letcher. He said he must positively leave on the 20th, and had hardly time for his journey; and he must give up his trip down James' River, the inspection of plantations, and reluctantly his visit to old Jamestown. The Prince was very talkative and pleasant.

As usual, another crowd awaited the party at the hotel, where they were received with more cheers.

All day long the staircase and halls were filled with curious spectators, among whom were many ladies.

In the Senate Chamber several objects of interest were shown to the Royal visitor and his friends. Among other things was the chair occupied by Patrick Henry in the House of Burgess. On one wall hangs a portrait of the great Earl of Chatham, to whose gout the Americans are so deeply indebted. The portrait was painted for the County of Westmoreland, in Virginia, while yet the people were loyal to the British Crown, and by them presented to the State after the successful termination of the War of Independence. Opposite to this portrait hangs one of Jefferson, said to be a remarkably good likeness. The table used in the chamber is another curiosity. It is made of oak, and once like the chair before mentioned, stood in the hall of Burgess. At the junction of the legs with the table proper, are carved portraits of eminent men, among which is a likeness of Sir Philip Sidney. Then there is the celebrated statue of Washington, by Houdin. While the great man, so justly revered by Americans, still lived, it was conceived desirable that a statue of him should be made, and for that purpose Houdin was sent for from France. He stayed with Washington about two months, and took casts from his body that he might execute his task with the greater accuracy. These facts were told by Governor Letcher to Lord Renfrew, who said something indicative of great interest in Washington. Governor Letcher was evidently vexed at the conduct of his constituents, took Lord Renfrew by the arm, and endeavoured to divert his attention by pointing to a bust of Lafayette, also by Houdin. He was then taken towards a large iron stove, once used in the hall of Burgess, bearing the arms of Great Britain and Virginia in friendly connexion. He was then conducted to the Governor's House, and was guarded to the hotel.

After his trip to the Capitol the Baron partook of dinner. The Exchange Hotel in Richmond boasts the possession of the best compounder of cooling drinks in the world. The name of this celebrated man is Jim Cook, a negro, worth it is not known how many hundred dollars. His fame having been bruited abroad it at length reached the ears of the Prince. The day was warm, and the said cooling drinks in some sort necessary. Baron Renfrew did not send for Jim. Far from it. Jim went to the Baron, and so with his black skin shining, his white teeth glittering, his dark eyes sparkling, and his back-bone bent, proffered his Lordship a large lump of ice. Yes—of ice—upon a silver salver. But the ice was hollow. Jim first took a tumbler capable of holding a pint and a half of water. In this tumbler he compounded a mint julep, mixing the cooling ingredients requisite in due proportions. Next taking a mould in the shape of an obelisk, he filled it with ice very thinly shaved, which being compressed, soon formed itself into a solid mass. The base being accordingly rounded, was fitted into the tumbler, and decorated with a boquet of flowers at its summit. Then the glass itself was surrounded with ice, formed into on ornamental shape. Holes communicating with the interior of the tumbler being bored through the crystal surroundings and straws placed therein the mint julep was ready for use. This it was Jim brought to His Royal Highness, Albert Edward, Prince of Wales, who by the process common to all mortals took a suck, and started back astonished at the luscious taste of the liquid. He looked at the negro as though he expected to find in him a philosopher who had at last discovered the elixir of life. "Why Jim, how did you make this?" he inquired, and while Jim explained, "Massa" sucked and sucked away until it was all gone; and then ordered another, which other, by the aid of the Duke of Newcastle, Earl St. Germains, and Major General Bruce was quickly dispatched. By common consent Jim was told to have a third in readiness for the next morning before the party started. This proved Mr. Cook's masterpiece. It was a very large one; was furnished with thirteen tubes, out of which an equal number of the Royal party pulled at one and the same time. Jim Cooks are not to be found every where.

After the Sunday dinner and the mint julep, the Baron paid a visit to St. John's Church, the edifice in which Patrick Henry roused the people to resistance against the British Government. From thence he went to Hollywood cemetery and to President Munro's grave. The hotel was left privately, and the trip passed without interference, the crowd which had gathered round the hotel taking it for granted that the Prince was inside, because none of them had seen him go out. At nine o'clock this morning he started by rail for Acquia Creek, on the Potomac. No noticeable incident occurred during the journey. There was a considerable gathering at the Creek, but the few steps to be taken from the railway station to the *Harriet Lane* admitted of no demonstration. In Washington the party were met by the President, Miss Lane, and General Cass, and by them accompanied to the railway station. Final good byes were given, and mutual regrets at parting expressed. The Prince became, if all reported true—not only a favourite with the President, but with Miss Harriet also. And as for General Cass, you will hear little more in future of his rabid anti-British propensities.

The Royal train arrived in Baltimore much later than was expected. Six o'clock was the time named, but the adieus already spoken of lasted so long a time, that it was not until half-past six o'clock Washington was left behind. At eight o'clock the train stopped in the Camden depot, and the Baron alighted. The people had long been most patiently waiting, not only at the railway station, but at the Gilmour House, and all along the line of route. Many ladies were out without their bonnets, for the evening was especially warm; the windows were all filled with fair faces, and every point from which a view could be obtained was seized upon by the enterprising citizens. No outsiders were allowed within the railway station—the doors were locked, and a strong force of police detailed to keep order. The volunteers of the city, too, rendered good service. Two companies, numbering about one hundred and twenty rank and file, kept the way clear, marched by the side of the carriage, formed an avenue through which the Baron passed into the hotel, and saw generally that good order was kept. Both the militia and the police deserved the greatest credit for the arrangements made. Baltimore has had the name of being the most disorderly city in the Union, and doubtless at one time deserved it. That, however, was when the police force was in the hands of the city. Now, the State Government control it. The change, similar to that made in Canada, has in every way been beneficial.

Baron Renfrew was enabled to pass from the railway station to the hotel without annoyance, a band playing "God Save the Queen!"

The ride from Baltimore to Philadelphia, a distance of ninety-eight miles, is a pleasant one. The road runs along the western banks of the Chesapeake Bay and Potomac River. In its progress a series of small bays are crossed, and being too wide to be bridged, the track was built on piles and afterwards filled in. Many scenes of remarkable beauty presented themselves. The country is well cultivated, farm houses present themselves on all sides, and the general appearance of the landscape denotes long settlement. Ornamental grounds here and there appear; the houses are surrounded with gardens in which many flowers in full bloom delight the eye; the fences well kept and nicely whitewashed; neat churches here and there lift their tall spires, and numerous villages necessitate the frequent stoppage of the railway trains. At Havre de Grace the Susquehanna River was crossed by means of a huge steamboat. Once on board the boat, the immense strength of the pillars supporting the upper works attract the instant attention of strangers. After walking about for ten or fifteen minutes backwards and forwards along the three hundred feet of deck, a stair-case may be found leading to the upper deck, whereon are placed the baggage car and express van. A little bell rings, the immense mass moves quietly away from the wharf, and with a motion perfectly imperceptible to those within, reaches the other side. No noise—no bumping—no confusion. The railway track on the boat, and the railway track on the land are brought exactly opposite each other; a draw-bridge is lowered, over which the people pass and take their seats in the cars; the train is backed, the waggons hitched on, and away they go. Here is something for the Marquis of Chandos to study, a triumph of engineering skill, no where of its kind surpassed. The correspondent of an English paper, who two or three nights previously had travelled from Philadelphia to Baltimore in a sleeping car, said that he knew nothing of the crossing of the river. So quietly was the transfer managed that he and the other passengers with him were not disturbed in the slightest degree. The Prince himself was not called upon to leave his carriage. The whole train, locomotive and all, was placed upon the boat, and it was not until she began to move that the party were aware of their situation.

The locomotive, by means of which the party were conveyed to Philadelphia, bears the name of "George Washington." The Americans do not like the idea of "the Father of his Country" being made to do such work, but the feeling is a blot on American courtesy, as the Prince gave Royal Honours to Washington's greatness by visiting his tomb.

After he had taken his dinner at the hotel, darkness having closed in, the Prince, with one or two attendants, passed by a private door into the streets of this, the second city of the Union, where a great many people were outside waiting for him to make his appearance, so he had the pleasure of mingling in the throng, and of listening to their remarks.

Baron Renfrew during his sojourn in the United States made many inquiries and endeavoured to gain acquaintance with the politics of the people. Although all sides of the great question have been presented to him, it is well known towards which his sympathies lean. It was a curious coincidence that he should arrive in Philadelphia on the very day when the death knell of the slave party rung—for such was hoped the victory in Pennsylvania would really prove. As the different republican clubs of the city passed the Continental Hotel with their torches lit and their bands playing, they cheered for the British Prince, while no democratic huzza resounded on his behalf.

From eight o'clock until a quarter past twelve His Royal Highness was in the street, unrecognised and unknown. But he doubtless listened to some of the speeches which were made, mingled in the throng of enthusiastic politicians, and cheered with the rest at the successful termination of the contest. No British Prince ever before had such an opportunity of examining the working of universal suffrage. The conduct of the people of Philadelphia was most creditable, most praiseworthy and most exemplary. Although wrought up to the highest pitch of excitement, few rows occured and good order prevailed. The impression produced upon the Royal party must in every respect have been most favourable. The people of the United States could not wish better representatives than the citizens of Philadelphia by which to be judged ; the people of Philadelphia can never appear to greater advantage than they did then, at the termination of the great contest in which they were engaged. And the Prince himself could not have had a better lesson. Would that other Princes could have been there too !

As has already been said it was not until a quarter past twelve that he entered at the public door, and was recognised by many. The ladies were all up waiting for him, and were highly pleased at the view they obtained. Way was made for him as he passed, the gentlemen took off their hats and the ladies curtsied as he went along. The behaviour of all was most exemplary. In the morning he left the hotel in a carriage for a drive through the city, and paid a visit to the race-ground, five miles distant.

On this day, October 10th, His Royal Highness the Prince of Wales occupied the greater part in driving about from one point to another of the great and beautiful city of Philadelphia.

Philadelphia rejoices in the possession of magnificent streets, bordered with large trees, whose spreading branches afford a most welcome shade to the over heated pedestrians. Houses and stores of great size, upon which much architectural skill has been spent, abound ; not so regular in appearance, not so monotonous in style as those of the western cities, but still agreeable in their diversity, and speak of wealth and prosperity in the solid and substantial appearance they present. The system of horse railways is the most complete of any city in the United States, and the extent to which they are patronised proves their great usefulness and efficiency. From many of the buildings flags and banners hung, not in honour of the Baron, but as symbols of different parties now waging active political war one with another. The population of Philadelphia is about six hundred thousand, so that the traffic is immense, and most cheering to the eye of the Englishman accustomed to the turmoil, confusion, and constant uproar of the great cities of his native land.

By a circuitous route, best adopted to give him a good idea of the size of Philadelphia and of its principal characteristics, Lord Renfrew was conducted first to Girard College, a noble educational institution, founded and endowed with $2,000,000 by Stephen Girard, for the education of youth; it is built entirely of stone, and is one of the finest architectural buildings in America. When the Prince entered the children were all engaged in their studies, and he would not allow them to be interrupted, requesting the teachers to proceed with the lessons as they would do if he were not present. Unable from want of time to visit the whole of the building, the central portion was alone examined. But the ladies engaged in the neglected portion of the building were not thus to be "done" out of a sight of the Prince. They left their classes, and Albert Edward soon found himself surrounded by a fine phalanx of crinoline. Fearing the consequences, he hurried forward to the steps leading to the roof and mounted to the top. A splendid view of the city was thus obtained. Much interested in the sight, he asked many questions about it, and pointing out the largest buildings which appeared, enquired what purposes they served. Among others he hit upon Independence Hall, the place from whence the Declaration of Independence was issued, and where now is enshrined the bell which rang out the first notes of defiance from the American people. While this was being told to him a sudden gust of wind carried away his hat into the grounds below. An American gentleman present with great courtesy offered his own to the Prince, who smilingly placed the proffered chapeau upon his head. Upon descending the lost hat was recovered and the borrowed one returned. Mr. J. Micheson, to whom it belongs, will take care to retain it in safe keeping for the admiration of future ages. Once more upon *terra firma*, His Royal Highness picked up a couple of chestnuts and placed them in the ground opposite the house of the principal, Professor Allen. The compliment was appreciated. Should mother earth prove propitious and allow trees to spring therefrom they will be carefully preserved as a memorial of the Prince's visit.

From the college at a rapid pace the Royal party drove to the Penitentiary, a very large stone building, with seven wings radiating from a common centre, built upon the "solitary system" plan. His visit had been anticipated, and many ladies, friends of the Warden, had voluntarily consigned themselves to imprisonment for a time, with a purpose perfectly clear. Several hundred convicts were in confinement. When opportunity offered they peered through the bars of their cells as the party passed, and manifested much anxiety to make themselves well acquainted with the personal appearance of His Royal Highness. The strictest silence was enjoined and observed. Several notorious criminals were pointed out to the Prince, and with one, Judge Vandersmith, he held some conversation. He next proceeded to a cell once occupied by a German mentioned by Charles Dickens in his "American Notes." The poor fellow during his confinement, to wile away his time, painted the walls very beautifully. The Baron made some inquiries as to his fate, but it appeared that since his discharge nothing had been heard of him.

At a considerable distance from the city is situated the race-course of Point Breeze. The overlooking of the prison accomplished, thither His Royal Highness proceeded.

Nearly two thousand people were present—*bona fide* sportsmen and sportswomen. A committee of one hundred gentlemen appomted by the citizens of Philadelphia to receive the Prince, and to take care that he was treated properly, were present, being for the most part good looking men, they were "worried out of their lives" by numerous lady friends, desirous of getting into the immediate neighbourhood of the Baron. The consequence was that the committeemen yielded, selected the best looking of the fair claimants, and brought them into the balcony, each and every one pledging herself to take up as little room as posssible. But by and by, so many had got together, that with the addition of a few black-coated individuals, Lord Renfrew found himself confined to one corner. And still they came, still ladies begged, as though their lives depended upon the issue, that they might be allowed to go into the balcony "just for a moment." At length the Mayor placed a couple of policemen at the foot of the stairs with strict orders to admit no one—not even a committeeman, should he once find himself on the outside. And by this means the confusion abated.

There were but two races, and except that the horses were in first rate condition, and very skilfully managed, little can be said in their favour. The first race came off at half-past two o'clock, between "Throgsmeck" and "Rosa Bonheur." The mile was made by the latter in one minute $47\frac{3}{4}$ seconds, to the complete discomfiture of her opponent. The second race took place an hour after the first. It was not until after four o'clock that "Rosa Bonheur" and "Fanny Washington" were brought up to the scratch. This was a two mile race, best out of three trials, and in the first heat was gallantly contested. Soon after the horses started, Fanny got about three lengths ahead, but Rosa, a few yards before the posts were gained put the best foot foremost, and was near coming in the winner. As it was, she lost by about half a neck. Her owner, however, insisted that she was the winner, inasmuch as she had rapidly caught up to her opponent, and would, if she had had time, have passed her. Of course the judges refused to entertain such an argument, and "Rosa Bonheur" not making her appearance for the second heat, to "Fanny" was awarded the prize.

Some citizen of Philadelphia rejoices in the possession of an old carriage, said to have belonged to General Washington. With six horses attached to it, he made his appearance on the race course, and asked Lord Renfrew to ride in it back to the hotel. Of course the offer was declined, the Baron preferring a vehicle of modern construction.

After a prolonged drive the Continental was gained about five o'clock, without any incident worthy of particular note occurring by the way.

Montreal may boast her concert, St. Louis her amphitheatre, Cincinnati her ball, but with one exception the most splendid entertainment upon this continent at which the Prince was present, was given in his honour in Philadelphia. The Opera House is one of the largest in the world ; and very nearly as large as that of La Scala in Milan. It has three tiers of galleries besides the dress circle ; is magnificently fitted up ; and was filled with three thousand people—the ladies sitting in diamonds, and attired in their richest dresses, presented an appearance of which Philadelphia might justly be proud.

The stair-case leading to the foyer, and the foyer itself, were ornamented with large stove plants, contributed by one of the citizens ; while the plume of the Heir Apparent "done in gas," and surrounded by prisms, gave out a most brilliant light. Over the proscenium box occupied by the Baron were placed the arms of England and America. Soon after he had entered, the curtain was raised, and Patti, Brignoli, and Formes advancing, "God Save the Queen" was given. The effect of the first notes was electrical. The whole house rose and stood until the conclusion of the anthem, when all cheered, waved their handkerchiefs, and clapped their hands most enthusiastically. Out of compliment to His Royal Highness the following words were sung as the second verse by Formes :

> "Long may the Prince abide,
> England's hope, joy, and pride,
>   Long live the Prince;
> May England's future King
> Victoria's virtues bring
> To grace his reign.
>   God save the Prince."

"Hail Columbia" was then played by the band, and after a round of cheers, the audience quietly composed themselves for the serious business of the evening.

The opera—selected by the Baron—was Flotow's "Martha." Of course with such a caste—Adelina Patti as Martha, Notali as Nancy, Formes as Plunkett, and Brignoli as Lionel,—it could not fail to be a success. The most charming feature of the whole was Patti's "Qui sola, virgin rosa," encored by the company, and answered by her with the "Last rose of summer." The air again occurs in the fourth scene of the third act named. Plunket sings, "I gather the young rose." He also received the compliment of an encore. There were other things comical, however, besides the opera. The Prince frequently applauded the performers, and when he clapped, the audience immediately followed, no one venturing to raise a hand until his kid gloves were in motion. The multitude of glasses through which he was eyed was very great; but nothing abashed, he returned stare for stare, and between the scenes occupied the greater part of the time in examining closely the beauties of Philadelphia. To do this the more effectually, he crossed over to the opposite side of the house, and from the box occupied by some members of the suite, ogled the ladies to their heart's content. As it was with the audience, so it was with the performers. They could scarcely keep their eyes from the Royal box. Both Martha and Nancy, when in the height of their distress at being entrapped into service, found time to eye, from under their handkerchiefs, Albert Edward; and he for his part seemed bent on mischief, for as often as this disposition was manifested, his lorgnette was brought fully to bear on the pretty faces of the actresses. And so the evening passed away, the members of the Royal party evidently enjoying themselves to the full. After the opera of "Martha," the first act of "La Traviata" was performed. It was soon concluded, but proved the most agreeable portion of the entertainment. By those who have frequently before heard her, Patti was pronounced at her best. The scenery was most artistically managed, and all the performers engaged "knew well their parts." There was no bungling; everything passed off as well as the most enthusiastic musical devotee could desire.

October 11.

In describing the progress of His Royal Highness the Prince of Wales through the British North American Provinces,—in attempting to do justice, so far as they have been able, to the enthusiasm of the people,—to the endeavours made to manifest in outward show their warm feelings of loyalty to the throne, and their fervent hopes for the prosperity of their future Sovereign,— the correspondents of the press have ever felt how unequal they were to the task. It may be that in other and older, and richer countries, the arches would, under similar circumstances, have been more costly, and the various displays altogether upon a grander scale; but in no past time have any, nor in future time can any people make plainer to be seen that there was no empty boast of loyalty, but a thoroughly deep-seated feeling, which will stand the test of the hardest trial and greatest misfortune. To this of all it has been most difficult to do justice. Let the matter be argued as it may,—let the best defences of monarchial institutions be logically annihilated, still the fact does remain patent, undeniable, unquestionable, that this same loyalty which defies analysis, and puzzles your mathematical, sternly practical philosopher, exists in the breasts of men, excites them to the bravest deeds, animates their every action, makes them to risk all and dare all. This to many who share not in the feeling may be unaccountable. But it is a great fact, nevertheless. A fact which demands attention and recognition,—which must be dealt with as a reality which cannot be set aside, for it has a world-wide interest, and controls the destinies of millions of mankind.

The people of the American republic know this well. The most confirmed sticklers for what are called equal rights, own that the subjects of an empire are as liberty loving as they,—not only pay a willing homage to the British monarch, but seek not to get rid of the duty; on the contrary, that they aim to preserve it with a steadiness, a constancy, and a determination that ensures its continuance. The citizens of New York have recognised this. They have seen fit to extend the right hand of welcome to the representative of a principle held dear by their brethren across the Atlantic. No difference of opinion held them back. Conscious that their republicanism could in no manner be compromised by honouring him whom the whole British nation honour, they have done right worthily towards their visitor as one who, in the providence of God, will be called to rule over the only really free people of the earth, save and except those who have themselves extended the welcome.

They may justly claim this, that Royalty has for once been brought into contact with a democracy able to control themselves; who can gather together in immense masses, behave orderly and peacefully; who obey the desires of those whom they have elevated to office quietly and constantly. The reception His Royal Highness met with in New York will live in his memory side by side with the scenes of the Philadelphia election. His confidence in the people and his belief in their good sense must be strengthened. Though he may not like the idea of being so dependent upon those of his own land, as some would have him to be, yet, be sure of it, he will contemplate such a fortune for the future with much less dislike than he or any of the Royal house have hitherto known. Such language may seem unwarranted from the shortness of the time by which experience could be gained; but it may be affirmed with safety, that never was so formidable a mass of people gathered together before, who almost without the aid of police or organized force of any kind, behaved themselves so well. Every man, woman, and child of the five hundred thousand gathered together in New York streets, acted as though the very existence of the United States depended upon their conduct. From mid-day until darkness obscured the sky, this vast mass of human beings, each one with his individual desires, his special thoughts, his distinct characteristics, waited patiently for the

A 27

arrival of him whom they desired to honour. Rich and poor were mingled together; the merchant prince, the hard-worked mechanic, the silk-attired lady, and the cotton-dressed drudge; all degrees and conditions of men of that great republic stood side by side in this unparalled congregation of humanity. No disturbance occurred to mar the scene. All was unanimity, all peace, concord and good-will. In vain might any such exhibition be sought for among any other people than those accustomed to self-government, knowing their own strength, and experienced in the use of it.

The Prince and suite embarked at Philadelphia on board the *Harriet Lane*, and about half-past one o'clock in the afternoon was observed approaching the wharf, at the foot of Broadway. The people who thronged the water's edge, at the appearance of a few police immediately left the open space called the Battery, and saw in silence the whole area covered with troops. All the ships in view, and there were some hundreds of thèm, ran up their colours, and the sailors ran the spars; while the decks of many were crowded with people, anxious as those on shore. And as the news spread through the city that the Prince had at last arrived, every window along the line of route was opened, every house top was speedily occupied,—no inch of vantage ground upon which the chance of foothold existed remained unseized upon. The sight was a most glorious and yet an awful one. Far as the eye could reach was one dense mass of human beings covering the whole expanse of Broadway, until the parallel sides of that noble thoroughfare appeared to commerge in a single point. No omnibus was allowed to intrude, no cart, dray or aristocratic carriage, made even a temporary opening. Each window of the lofty stores was brilliant with gaily dressed ladies, every balcony, every tressel, every roof was full. When the Prince landed, the roar of guns in the Battery was drowned by the tumultuous shouts of the people, which commenced at Castle Garden, and rolled round and round like thunder, gathering in force as it progressed, until lost miles away among the palatial residences of the Fifth Avenue. No sooner had the Prince put his foot upon the ground, than "God save the Queen" was played, and without delay or inconvenience he was admitted a few paces to the interior of that building which once resounded to the voice of Jenny Lind, but now used by the poor emigrants who seek work and wealth upon American soil. The Prince and his suite were taken behind a barrier, which served to separate him from those who had been privileged to enter the building, and Mayor Wood, in the name of the city of New York, gave him a cordial welcome, not as Baron Renfrew, but as Prince of Wales. He was then taken to a private room, and exchanged the civilian's dress which he wore, for that of his Colonel's uniform. This process he had so frequently before been compelled to go through in Canada took him but little time. He speedily emerged, and at once entered his carriage drawn by six splendid horses. Over the back of each white net-work had been thrown, the reins were also white, and the harness glittered with silver ornaments. Before the carriage walked fifty police in double rank, stretching across the horse road. The people gave way before them as they came forward, not stubbornly or sulkily, but with the greatest alacrity and good will. Too much praise for this cannot be awarded them. It was the same all the way, and though in some places the crush was very great, and the difficulty of wedging together upon the side-walks dangerous to ribs, and unspeakably destructive to crinoline, yet the feat was accomplished. After the police came a regiment of cavalry. They rode in single file along the edges of the road, and surrounded not only the carriage containing His Royal Highness, but those which followed with the gentlemen of the suite. Not a man attempted to cross. Instead of pushing forward the crowd held back, all combined to keep in the best possible order. The progress was purposely slow, so that every opportunity was given of seeing His Royal Highness. All heads were uncovered as he passed; from the windows the ladies waved their myriads of handkerchiefs, and a continual war of cheering was kept up. It never subsided for an instant. Those who could see the Prince cheered, and those who could not see him cheered also. The smile of enjoyment was on his countenance. He bowed to the ladies in the balconies, and to the people on the foot-paths, taking care to look out from both sides of his carriage that all might see him. Several times he rose in the carriage and gazed upon the sea of heads behind and before. He pointed to the various large buildings as he passed, and turning to Mayor Wood evidently asked what purpose they served. And as for the Duke, he actually appeared excited. Instead of sitting still as usual, he got up and down every half dozen yards, and pulled the Prince by the shoulder first to one side and then to another, waved his arms about, giving unmistakable evidence of his surprise and pleasure. The women were loud in his praise—indeed, wherever he goes, he excited their admiration. The Prince they regarded as a boy, as a "nice little fellow," but the Herculean shoulders of His Grace, his full chest, his height, and his noble bearing, met the feminine idea of a complete man. Slowly the cortege wended its way to the City Hall. There a platform had been erected, upon which His Highness took his stand, while the troops passed in review before him.

They numbered, exclusive of officers, upwards of six thousand men, and presented as splendid an appearance as ever was made by any body of military in the world. No better defence of the volunteer system could be offered than that which they presented. They marched in companies with the greatest precision, each regiment preceded by the staff officers, the drums and the band. There was no irregularity, no mistakes made. Through the long line of people they made their way, their colours flying, their drums beating, and their swords and bayonets, the bright brass cannons, showy uniforms, glistening in the sun. Two regiments of Light Infantry came first, followed by two regiments of Cavalry, the one Dragoons, the other Hussars. Then came two more Infantry regiments, and a battery of Artillery, followed by the celebrated seventh regiment, whose appearance fully bore out all the enconiums passed upon them. After them were two other brigades, amongst which was a Scotch regiment, glorious in kilts and tartans. The people cheered each corps heartily as it passed, and appeared highly proud of their citizen soldiery. And well they may be. Nothing could better illustrate the self-dependent character of the American people —one of the main characteristics to which they owe their rapid growth and present greatness.

Ere the review was over, darkness had set in, and it was apparent that before the Prince reached his appartments in the Fifth Avenue Hotel, little sunlight would be left. But this did not alter the determination of the people to see as much as they could of His Royal Highness. The Fifth Avenue was as crowded as the other streets had been. There New York had anticipated making her greatest show. There the "aristocracy" reside. There the republicans, who mount upon their carriages coats of arms contradicting all the laws of heraldry, have their domiciles. Large sums of money had been spent by their fair dames and daughters upon new silk dresses, in gorgeous opera cloaks, and in female finery generally. They had been seated in the balconies and at the windows for five or six hours, and had been the wonder and admiration of the plebeian crowd gathered in the street below. Never, according to report, was such a galaxy of female beauty before witnessed. Never did Prince lose such a chance as that which Albert Edward lost of being smothered in choicest bouquets, thrown by whitest of hands. He stopped looking at the soldiers too long. When he got to the Fifth Avenue nought was to be seen save the dim glare of the street lamps among the trees, the glimmer of lights at the windows, blocked up with the inmates of the houses, and the dense crowd of people who firmly held the positions they had taken hours before. Fifth Avenue was disappointed. Fifth Avenue was in a state of intense grief.

The Prince reached his hotel in safety, a little *ruse* having being practised by which he got in at a private door. He was not suffered to rest in peace long, for the Caledonia Club appeared with their fine band and played "God save the Queen," "Hail Columbia" and other favourite pieces. The Prince made his appearance upon the balcony, after some delay, and was loudly cheered.

Among the regiments possessed by New York is one composep of Irishmen, commanded by Col. Brien, who were ordered to turn out to welcome His Royal Highness, along with the other troops, but refused. A very strong feeling prevails against them, and it is said they will be disbanded. Americans condemn them in the most bitter terms. And properly so, I am ashamed of my countrymen.

On the morning of the 12th October, the Prince started on his tour of inspection of New York. Of course there was a crowd outside the hotel, there always was a crowd wherever he went. The first place to which he was driven was the New York University in Washington Square, a marble building of great size. It is built in what may be called the English collegiate style of architecture, with a large central hall, flanked by hexagonal towers, which with a pointed roof between them rise high above the castellated wings on either side. With the exception of a large Gothic window which admits the light into the central chapel, the windows are flat. The general appearanc of the building is rather plain but substantial. The Prince upon alighting was conducted to the Central Hall, and received by the Professors and a large number of students in their robes. Passing through them up a flight of marble steps, he was shown direct to the chapel, almost filled with ladies, who rose as he entered. The Chancellor of the University then advanced, and read to him an address of welcome, rather long but good withal. After which Professor Morse spoke a few words in acknowledgment of the assistance he had received from the Duke of Newcastle, then Lord Lincoln, in bringing his telegraph into use while yet the invention was but in its infancy. From the chapel His Royal Highness was led to the ladies' library and welcomed by Miss Powell, the librarianess. There were many ladies present—the real object of the Prince's visit to these institutions was not so much to see as be seen. To gratify the ladies every body else is sacrificed. The lords of the creation had to stand in the crowded streets, to suffer all sorts of inconveniences, and if by chance they got into any place visited by the Prince, they had to remain in the back ground where they would see nothing.

Having taken a rapid glance at some of the class rooms, the Baron was next driven to the Free Academy in Lexington Avenue—an institution answering to Canadian Grammar Schools. Nothing was done there besides exhibiting about a thousand students collected in the chapel, but the stay was very short.

Then the Astor Library was visited, so named after its founder, who endowed it with the munificent sum of $400,000. The value of the books contained within its walls must not be measured by number, for great efforts have been made to secure a collection of rare works, rather than a large one, although 100,000 volumes already stand upon its shelves. Dr. Coggswell, the librarian, explained to the Prince the mode of classification adopted, a plan similar to that in use at the British Museum, under the management of Monsieur Panizzi. The library itself is a very beautiful hall. It is about fifty feet high, and lighted with an immense skylight. Fourteen pillars of Italian marble sustain the roof. Between them are the galleries, by which the higher tiers of books are reached. From the floor rise eight compact and elegant spiral staircases. The Prince expressed himself much pleased with the institution, and complimented Mr. John Jacob Astor upon the liberality and spirit displayed both by himself and his father, in giving to New York so valuable a library—unquestionably the best upon the continent of America. Mr. Astor thanked His Royal Highness, and in return acknowledged the courtesy with which he and Dr. Coggswell had been treated by the British authorities in their efforts to secure a good collection of books, pointing out to the Prince at the same time the reports of the English Patent Office, which had been presented to the library.

The visit was very short, occupying not more than about ten minutes. The Royal party were then quickly whirled to another institution, which New York also owes to a public spirited citizen —Mr. Peter Cooper. The cost of the building was about $250,000. The ground floor is occupied by stores, by the rental of which a revenue is derived for the payment of lecturers and teachers. The stay of the Prince was very short. He was conducted rapidly through the reading room, the picture gallery, and the ladies' school of design, in which was assembled a great quantity of crinoline. From thence he mounted to the roof, took a view of the city, came down again and drove away, the whole operation lasting less than ten minutes.

The most interesting part of the day's proceedings was the visit to the central park. His Royal Highness arrived at the park about twelve o'clock. It contains no less than 750 acres of ground, well wooded, and exceedingly picturesque; hill, dale, and stream —presenting a most happy combination of natural scenery. A great deal of money has been spent upon it, and much more will have to be spent before all the beauties of the great area will be developed. Near the centre, a large parade ground, and some magnificent carriage drives and promenades are constructed. Rustic bridges span some of the streams, and, aided by the natural formation of the ground, a large lake will shortly lend additional beauty to the scenery. When the Prince arrived on the ground, he was conducted to the Mall, and immediately surrounded. At the request of Mr. Green, the comptroller, he planted an oak and and elm tree. No formalities were observed; no silver spade used or presented. When this was completed, he was driven away to a portion of the park called, "the Ramble"—a very pretty place—where he walked for a few moments, until overtaken by a number of carriages occupied by the "aristocracy," who had been in waiting on him the whole morning.

Mayor Wood's house was next sought and gained. It is situated a considerable distance from the city, upon the Bloomingdale road. Here a select party had the honour of lunching with the Prince. About five hundred carriages were gathered together on the road. None were admitted, save the Prince and his suite, with one or two New York gentlemen accompanying him. From Mayor Wood's the party went to Fort Washington, and inspected the Deaf and Dumb Asylum there. The pupils were examined, and the mode of instruction adopted, explained to him by Dr. Peet. The whole affair was intensely interesting. A number of slips of paper, upon which were written words of welcome by the pupils, including several practicable contributions of no mean merit were produced.

The journeyings of the day were completed by a voyage upon the river in the *Trumpeter*, a visit to Randall's Island, and a return to the hotel in the Fifth Avenue. The entry was easily effected, for the crowd was not large. His Royal Highness was cheered lustily as he escaped from public view.

THE GRAND BALL.

October 8th, 1860.

The event of the age transpired last night. That for which thousands of fair ladies sighed; which excited more envy than any other event that has happened for years; the grand ball at the Academy of Music came off amid a blaze of gas lights, the sweet perfume of thousands of exotics, the attendance and smiles of hundreds of the most beautiful women that New York can produce, and the richest display of gorgeous costume that was ever witnessed in this city.

The doors of the Academy of Music, where this grand *fete* took place, were open to the public at half-past eight. But long before that hour the streets and avenues leading thereto were lined with carriages bearing fair ladies and brave men, and waiting to discharge their living freight into the Temple of Euterpe, for the nonce a Temple of Terpsichore.

The decorations of the Academy heretofore described need but a single remark in conclusion, they were gorgeous in the extreme. The room was one blaze of gas light, and every preparation was complete.

As soon as the doors were opened, the stream of invited guests commenced to pour in, and proceeded to the retiring rooms prepared for the duties and pleasures of the evening.

Descending from the cloak rooms, the ladies with their partners gathered upon the floor, and after a brief promenade assembled at the upper end of the room, where the Prince was expected to make his appearance.

The movement was natural. Every one present had taken this occasion to visit the Academy for the express purpose of seeing the Prince. The ladies had donned their best and most costly dresses; had exhausted all their ingenuity and the patience of their milliners in providing the most elegant and chaste costumes for this ball, not because it was a ball simply, but because the Prince was to be there, and each flattered herself that some good fortune might enable her to be his partner in the dance—"just once."

To see the Prince, to be presented to him, to receive some *souvenier* of Royalty, no matter how trifling, was the height of ambition of at least half the ladies present. For this they visited the ball, and for this they gathered at the upper end of the room so that they might catch the first glance at the youthful Royal personage.

Viewed from an elevated point of observation, the scene was grand. Hundreds of ladies, adorned in the most gorgeous costumes, and of unmatched beauty; the gentlemen clad in the most faultless black, while here and there glittered a gay uniform—the whole combined to make it the most magnificent spectacle ever presented on any similar occasion.

Ten o'clock was the hour announced for the arrival of His

Royal Highness. At that hour the principal members of the Committee of Invitation assembled in the upper part of the room and patiently awaited the arrival of the Prince. Sufficient space had been reserved, and the arrangements were completed for a speedy presentation of every person upon the floor. Shortly after ten o'clock the Prince arrived, accompanied by his suite. The Seventh Regiment band struck up the British Anthem, "God save the Queen," when all who were seated arose and remained standing.

During the performance of the anthem, every eye was turned towards the quarter of the room in which was the Prince. Lorgnettes from the boxes were brought to bear on him, and elongated necks were prominent with eyes staring vigorously after Royalty. He was stationed upon an elevated dais and bore this battery of eyes and glasses unflinchingly. He was dressed in a black suit, and set the example of full dress by wearing a white cravat.

While crowding forward and straining to get a glance of the Prince, filling the upper part of the room so closely that no additional room could be obtained, a crash was heard, and immediately followed a scattering of the mass that had assembled at a point over the edge of the stage. The floor had given way beneath the immense weight, and fell a distance of about three feet. Fortunately no one was injured.

Instantly, the police took charge of the place, and carpenters were set to work to repair the damage. The Prince remained at his post, but the ceremony of presentation was imperfectly performed, owing to the break in the floor between the dais and the large majority of the persons present. Scarcely had the momentary alarm which had been occasioned by the crash subsided, when another crashing sound was heard and the flooring settled in another part, about twenty feet from the former. The police and committee now extended their efforts, and by desire the persons upon the floor accompanied the ladies to the supper room, to which the Prince retired, and the ceremony of presentation continued.

The scene upon the floor of the ball room became animated; the covering of the parquette was torn up, carpenters leaped in, stanchions were procured, and soon the sound of the hammer and saw were prominent. Among the most active participants in the labour of repairing the damage was Mr. Brown, the sexton of Grace Church, who divesting himself of his dress coat, leaped into the breach and worked away lustily. The members of the committee of arrangements hastening the labour of repairing, but not until two hours had elapsed was the work completed.

In the interval the company not in the supper room promenaded about the floor of the ball room, while a large proportion selected positions in the circles where they might see but not participate in the festivities. Conspicuous among the promenaders on the floor was Lieutenant General Scott who, with the Duke of Newcastle upon his arm, was leisurely sauntering through the crowd, greeting his friends and introducing the Duke. The members of the suite were similarly provided for, but the Prince was absent, and the presence of the members of his suite attracted but little attention.

At last, the breaches in the floor were closed up and the room was once more prepared for dancing. The Prince entered the the room and occupied his position. Every body crowded to the top of the room ostensibly to see the Prince dance, but possibly with a faint hope that they might be honoured with his hand. After much difficulty and a vast deal of ceremony, space was cleared near the spot where the first crash had taken place, but this was afterwards abandoned, and a vacant space near the head of the room was prepared.

At last the Prince opened the ball, selecting for his partner the amiable and accomplished wife of Governor Morgan. This lady was most richly and elegantly dressed, and acted her part with becoming dignity. The Prince in dancing the set merely walked through the figures.

At the conclusion of the first quadrille, the Prince and suite, under direction of Mr. Peter Cooper, promenaded through the room. After the promenade, he returned to the head of the room and led off the second dance with Miss Mason. The third lady honoured with his hand was Mrs. Hoyt, the youngest daughter of General Scott.

In addition to the above, the Prince danced with the following ladies: Miss H. Russell, Miss Jay, Mrs. Edward Cooper, Mrs. Belmont, Mrs. M. B. Field, Miss VanBuren, Mrs. Kernochan, Miss Butler.

While the Prince was dancing almost every body else in the room were motionless or unanimously peering at His Royal Highness. They crowded around the Royal set so that it was difficult to take the steps successfully.

This continued until the departure of the Prince about five o'clock. The scene was more of a levee than a ball; the immense assemblage promenaded around the room in the intervals of the dance, and during that operation crowded so close to the Prince that at last dancing was impossible. When the Prince left, the company left, and the Academy was abandoned to fading perfumes and departed glories.

Never before in New York were assembled so many beautiful women, wearing such gorgeous dresses, and displaying such a profusion of costly jewellery. Art and ingenuity seemed to have been exhausted in striving to produce something which would dazzle and adorn the natural charms of the person. Of material there were brocades, tulle, moire antique, and the richest descriptions of silks and satins.

For ornament, lace in all its variety and elegance was conspicuous, and of colours, white, trimmed with Solferino, Magenta or Mauve, also dresses composed of material of these colours.

The head dresses were magnificent, and included every variety of jewellery and wreaths in every conceivable form. The effect of this gorgeous costuming was magnificent, and hundreds ascended to the upper tiers to witness the *coup d'œil*, thence presented.

The supper room began to fill with hungered guests about one o'clock, and the throng passed in a continuous stream constantly after that hour. The arrangements were faultless, and under the superb management of Mr. Delmonico, every body that visited the apartment accorded the full meed of praise for the successful management of so difficult a thing as a ball supper.

The fruit was of the choicest variety, and the wines of the most superior green and blue seal brands. Music in excellent quality, and every thing contributed to the enjoyment of the occasion.

The evening will long be remembered by all who participated in the festivity, and will mark an epoch in their lives. Those who were so fortunate as to dance with the Prince or engage *vis-a-vis* in the same set with him, will have peculiar occasion for gratulation, while those who acted as a committee of arrangement, and provided the magnificent entertainment, will have the satisfaction of knowing that they discharged their duty to the best of their ability, and entitled to the thanks of the entire community.

Whatever of good resulted from the ball was due to their efforts and those of the persons employed by them. Whatever of evil resulted was not the fault of any of the committee.

It was fortunate, indeed, it may be considered providential, that the falling of the floor occurred at the period it did, and resulted in no more serious consequences. The accident had the effect to make the guests more cautious in their movements, and enabled proper precautions to be taken with the remainder of the floor. It was also a matter of great congratulation that the accident did not occur at the time when the Prince was upon the floor engaged in the dance, for with the motion that is usually given the floor, himself or his partners might have been thrown and seriously injured, which disaster would have ruined the entertainment, and been a by-word of reproach in this and other cities.

Whoever was charged with the construction of the floor, should have been more careful to see that it was properly supported, and of good material. However, the accident may have been the result of some unforeseen and possibly unavoidble cause; and while it resulted no more disastrously than the breaking of a few joists or the delay of two hours in the arrangement, we can afford to be charitable towards those who are responsible.

The thronging around the Prince by the people present, may well be pardoned, when the nature and extent of female curiosity in all its charming developments is considered. If their bright eyes did make the young Prince blush painfully, the heightened colour was pleasing to behold, and betokened a virtue that ladies should admire in young men.

The police arrangements under Superintendent Kennedy, assisted by Inspectors Carpenter, Dilks, and Leonard, were perfect, both inside and outside the building. The officers inside the room were polite and gentlemanly in their deportment, and outside the building the arrangements were as complete as possible.

In the course of the evening the Committee of Police proceeded to examine and count the tickets received at the door, when a rumour was circulated that an extensive fraud or collusion had taken place, and that a large number of persons not entitled to tickets had gained admission. This, however, proved to be untrue ; the whole number of tickets issued by the Committee was 3195, including the 2800 to the members of the general committee, 200 to invited guests, and the remainder to the members of the press.

Of these 3025 were received at the door, showing that 170 persons, who were provided with tickets, failed to avail themselves of the privileges they conferred. Each ticket was examined by four persons as it was received, and no opportunity was given to practise fraud. Among the entire number of guests in the house not one improper person gained admission.

The people of New York gave to the Prince as noble a welcome as he could have received did they owe to His Royal Highness that homage which the American subjects of the Queen willingly accorded.

The number of people brought to New York by the Royal visit was enormous. All the hotels were filled, and every place of amusement was crowded. Most of these visitors lingered about the Fifth Avenue, waiting there for many hours the incomings and outgoings of the Baron. Several large store keepers in Broadway were alarmed by the rapid collection of crowds before their windows, because a decent-looking carriage had taken its station opposite, and the Brooklyn ferry-boats were in danger of sinking from the rush of passengers who imagined the Prince would give New York the slip, and had taken to the City of Churches. It was only necessary in Broadway for an individual to stand still, to look forward with an air of interest, and he was sure to be surrounded by a knot of people anxious to know if the Prince was coming. That was the all-important question in New York; men, women, and children had concentrated all their attention upon it.

It was, indeed, exceedingly difficult to find out where His Royal Highness was. It was not until late in the day that the Prince left his hotel, and though near twelve o'clock, it was evident that he had not fully recovered from the immense amount of dancing he had been compelled to perpetrate the previous night. He bowed languidly to the people who had assembled, as the carriage dashed off, none among them knew where. As it afterwards turned out, they stopped at the celebrated photographic establishment of Mr.

Brady, on Broadway. At this place His Royal Highness and suite remained upwards of two hours. Notice of the visit had been given, and all and sundry were remorselessly excluded. Not even a lady managed to find an entrance. The Royal party had it all to themselves. They examined very minutely the numerous photographs of the celebrated men of the United States, asking for many whom they had not seen, and for others whom they could not see, as the grave had closed upon them. Among the latter was Secretary Marcy, for whose likeness the Duke asked. But a series of portraits were taken, not only of the Prince, but of all the members of his suite; of all sizes, in all positions, collectively, separately, and by twos and threes. He next visited Barnum's Museum. The hotel was sought and nothing remained to do beside eating and drinking until the firemen turned out. This they did about half-past nine o'clock, to the number of five thousand. Such a torch-light procession the Prince never saw before, and will in all probability never see again. He stood upon the balcony while it passed the hotel, and afterwards mounted the roof that he might take in at a glance the length to which it extended.

The engines, both hand and steam, were highly decorated with flowers and banners, many union jacks being interspersed among them. Rockets and blue balls were discharged during the progress, and each company cheered lustily as it passed. Many thousands of people were in the streets, and the best order was preserved.

The Prince had been very much magnified—a man, an Englishman and a democrat, rather freely expressed his opinion to some of the bystanders round the hotel, that as Americans they ought to abstain from demonstrations of respect to a Prince. A discussion was the consequence, the man being taken severely to task by the Yankees for his impudence. He got violently excited, abused the Prince and all the Royal family; threatened to "punch" Albert Edward's head, if he could get near enough, and launched out into a most furious eulogy upon republican institutions. The people about had tolerated his censure, and laughed at his threats, but when he got to the last stage, immediately came to the conclusion that he was insane, and gave him into custody. A berth for the night in a police office cooled his head considerably. He was discharged in the morning.

October 15th, 1860.

There was a great show on the 14th, at Trinity Church. For once in a way the edifice was crowded—an experience to which, if report be true, it is not often subjected—for the Prince attended divine service there. That he would do so was previously known; a fact sufficient to account for the assembling of large crowds outside the church door, and for the jam which took place inside. "Admission by ticket only" was the order of the day. Few but the members of "upper tendom" were favoured— the select of New York—the aristocracy of riches, of goodness, or of greatness. Before one o'clock the crowd began to gather around the church, and before the service was over, not less than ten thousand had assembled.

Then His Royal Highness the Prince of Wales entered— though the heir to the greatest crown on earth, the least self-important of all in that church. He was conducted by the beadle—for a wonder, actually a sensible-looking person—to a seat in the centre aisle, where three pews had been reserved for himself and suite. The service was performed by ten clergymen— prayers were intoned, the litany was intoned, the communion service was intoned, the psalms were intoned; the epistle and sermon were read. The service was very good. None, not even the most frivolous, could fail to be affected by the grandeur of that glorious old litany, displayed as it was in complete beauty. The sermon was preached by the Rev. Dr. Vinton. Great truths were told, great and important in themselves. But they were told in a way calculated to impress them upon the minds of the people. It was an easy style of sermon that was read. Dr. Vinton delivered it in a smooth and dignified manner. From the sixth chapter of Daniel and the 4th and 5th verses the text was taken. The reverend gentleman then concluded with the prayer as used in the English churches for the Queen and Royal Family; the Prince being especially mentioned in the petition. No other allusion to his presence was made.

The Prince found in the pew in which he sat two prayer books. The large one, bound in red morocco, bore a large gold clasp, engraved with the Prince of Wales' crest. The second prayer book was of smaller dimensions, fitted for the pocket. Inside was an inscription to the effect that the book was presented to the Prince by Francis Vinton, D.D., and Frederick Ogilby, D.D., the clergymen in charge of Trinity Church, "as a memorial of the nineteenth Sunday after Trinity."

The Baron dined with Mr. Archibald, the British Consul. Besides His Royal Highness, the host and suite, there were present Consul General Crawford, Mr. and Mrs. Cunard, Mr. Consul Kortright, Mr. Barclay, Mr. and Mrs. French, and Mr. Edwards, Vice-Consul.

The hour for the departure of the Prince of Wales and his party was fixed at nine o'clock a. m. Accordingly, thousands who had been disappointed of a view of the illustrious stranger availed themselves of the only remaining chance to see him as he left the Fifth Avenue Hotel. There, crowds gathered at an early hour, and remained patiently awaiting his appearance. At $9\frac{3}{4}$ o'clock the Royal party entered their carriages, and amidst the cheering of the assembled multitude drove rapidly to the revenue cutter.

The *Harriet Lane* was awaiting at her anchorage off the Battery at the appointed hour of the departure of the Royal guest. Capt. Faunce had been industriously at work day and night, to have every thing in apple-pie order. Dodworth's splendid band was engaged to accompany the party to West Point, and Mr. Stetson, of the Astor House, as on the former occasion, was to provide the collation on board. The weather, which on Sunday night was the stormiest of the season, and threatened to disappoint the hope every where indulged that the Prince would have a pleasant day in which to take leave of New York, happily cleared off at the right moment. The wind blew very chilly from the north-west, but the sun rose pleasantly. For the better convenience of the party, it had been decided that the Prince should embark from the foot of Hammond Street, instead of from the Battery, thus avoiding the drive and consequent excitement through Broadway. The *Harriet Lane* remained at her anchorage until 9 o'clock, waiting for the arrival of the band, but they did not appear, and the steamer was accordingly started for the place of the Prince's embarkation, up the North River. Meantime the baggage of the Royal party had been driven to Whitehall pier, under a written order from some one, and it was with considerable difficulty that the expressman, with the order in his hand, could be induced to go in pursuit of the steamer.

On the way to the place designated for receiving the Prince on board, the cutter was greeted with every demonstration of respect for the mission on which she was going. River steamers saluted her as she passed, by screams of their steam whistles, and dipping their flags. The shipping along the North River was decked out with all their colours, and the Cunard steamer at Jersey City, as well as the English steamers along the upper piers on the New York side of the river, were conspicuous for their display of bunting.

The Hammond Street pier was partly submerged, which obliged them to go to the foot of Perie Street. The appearance of the steamer was the signal for a sudden rush of people, who poured out of the streets towards the pier. A cordon of police was formed across the dock, but for which it would soon have been too full for the carriages of the Prince to drive upon. Shortly after ten o'clock a waving and cheering at the head of the pier announced the coming of the Prince. The yards of the *Harriet Lane* were manned, and in another moment the Royal party were at the landing. As the Prince went on board the English ensign was unfurled at the fore; but for once there was no band to strike up the stately national anthem of old England, and there was no salute. The yards were manned, the Prince shook hands cordially with Captain Faunce, and bowed to his officers. Lord Lyons, the Duke of Newcastle, and the other gentlemen of the suite followed him on board, and immediately after the baggage was passed in and the order was given to cast off.

The contrast in this embarkation of the Royal party with the joyous and stately character of the reception on board of the *Harriet Lane*, was very marked, and was due entirely to the meddling stupidity of the collector of the port of New York.

The circumstance was deeply regretted, as in addition to the compliment which it would have been to the distinguished guest, it deprived them of the pleasure of listening to an American band whose reputation is world-wide. The only compensation for this deprivation was the genial good humour of the Prince and his party, which never forsook them. As the *Harriet Lane* steamed away from the pier the Cunard steamer at Jersey City fired a salute, which was answered by dipping the English ensign on board of the cutter. The crowd on the deck cheered and waved their adieus to the departing Prince, who gracefully raised his hat and bowed his farewell to New York. The steamer *Thomas P. Way*, with a large party on board, and the *Flushing*, with a large number of excursionists, followed the steamer up the river. Vessels and steamers dipped their ensigns, and the yachts *Maria* and *Haze* fired salutes from their anchorage at Hoboken. These compliments were responded to on board the cutter in the usual way.

The Prince at first took his stand on the pilot-house, where he could have a good view of the objects and scenery along the river, and, at the same time, escape from the keen north-west wind. He soon emerged, however, and with his suite occupied themselves with what was to be seen. The orphan children from the Asylum at Seventy-fifth street came out, and ranging themselves along the bank of the river, cheered and waved their adieus to the departing Prince. The inmates of the Deaf and Dumb Asylum also came out and paid their silent respects to the passing steamer.

The scenery along the Hudson—which, decked out in the changing hues of autumn, never appeared more beautiful—interested the Royal party very much, and they expressed their admiration particularly of that portion of the river towards the approach to West Point. Sunnyside, the late home and now the resting-place of Irving, was pointed out to the Prince, as well as many other localities of historical interest.

At every village and landing-place flags streamed from house-tops and flag-staffs, and the villagers came down upon the piers opposite to catch a glimpse of the son of the British Queen.

The steamer *Thomas Powell* came round in the wake of the *Harriet Lane*, the captain, on getting within hail stating that a gentleman on board had despatches from Col. Delafield at West Point, for Gen. Scott, who was to be on board. The steamer was accordingly stopped, and Mr. Bidgelow, of the *Evening Post*, made his appearance, and joined the Prince's party. The letters related to the details of the reception at West Point. Gen. Scott had gone up by railroad.

The lunch, which, as on the former occasion, was served up by the popular host of the Astor House, was in the best style of the art. The bracing air gave edge to appetite, and the entertainment was evidently greatly enjoyed by the Royal, as well as by the more democratic portion of the guests. Mrs. Captain Faunce and daughter, and Mrs. Captain Ward and niece, graced the occasion with their presence.

THE RECEPTION AT WEST POINT.

At half-past two o'clock, p.m., the *Harriet Lane* approached the Highlands, and the Royal party prepared to land. On the landing were seen several officers in uniform, and a dozen horses saddled for the use of the Prince and his suite. Fifty dragoons were drawn up along the road at the bottom of the hill, and squads of people lined the road side. At the top of the ascent, however, there was to be seen a dense mass of people awaiting the arrival of the Prince. Col. Richard Delafield, Superintendent of the Military Academy and Commandant of the Post, accompanied by Lieut. Col. Reynold, were on the dock to receive the Royal visitor. The steamer having been made fast, the party stepped ashore, and the Prince, Lord Lyons, the Duke of Newcastle, and others of the suite shook hands with Col. Delafield, and immediately afterwards mounted their several steeds. As the Prince took his place at the head of the suite, a salvo of 17 guns was fired from the battery on the hill, and the *cortége* immediately moved on. The dragoons presented arms as the Royal party went by, and immediately closed in behind them, and all marched rapidly up the ascent. Cheers greeted them as they passed along. The procession rode directly to the quarters of Col. Delafield, (passing in review the Cadets on the way,) where the escort drew up, as the Prince dismounted the troops presenting arms. Entering the residence of the Commandant, the Prince was welcomed by Gen. Scott, who, with Col. Delafield, presented a large number of ladies and gentlemen. Profs. D. H. Mahan, W. H. C. Bartlett, Albert E. Church, Col. Reynolds, and other heads of departments. Gen. Scott presented Gen. G. P. Morris, and Col. Delafield presented Mr. N. P. Willis, Hon. Governor Kemble, Judge Parrott, Gen. John Ewen, of the Fourth Brigade of Artillery, New York. Many others were also presented. This ceremony occupied about half an hour, when the Prince and Lord Lyons, accompanied by Col. Delafield, proceeded to inspect the various Halls of Instruction. The Library was first visited, and the other institutions in order. Following this, there was a review of the Cadets, the Dragoons and Flying Artillery, which occupied three quarters of an hour. The Prince on this occasion wore a plain suit. The troops made a fine appearance, and were highly complimented by the visitors.

The review of the troops concluded the programme of the day, and at six o'clock the Prince and party returned to Col. Delafield's, where a supper was provided.

In the evening a ball was improvised by the Cadets, at which the Prince and his suite attended. At the conclusion of the ball they proceeded to Cozzen's Hotel, where elegant quarters had been provided for them. There the Prince became the guest of Gen. Scott.

October 16.

The Prince of Wales and suite left West Point at 11 o'clock, on board the *Daniel Drew*, which was handsomely fitted up for the occasion. Bulletins had announced that the party had left at 7 o'clock, and would be at Albany at half-past two. The streets were consequently filled with people at two, who had to wait till nearly five before the Royal visitors arrived.

The Mayor and Council went down the river in the *Young America*, and were taken on board the *Daniel Drew* at Stuyvesant.

The Mayor made a brief address to Lord Renfrew, who received it in silence, making no remarks.

The party arrived there at half-past four o'clock, when a procession was formed with two regiments of military, and some civic societies. The Prince rode in an open barouche, with Mayor Thatcher, Duke of Newcastle, and Lord Lyons.

The streets from the landing to Congress Hall were crowded with people, and no effort was made to press after the carriage, and commendable decorum was observed. Loud cheers were given as the carriage passed along, which the Prince acknowledged with quiet dignity and grace.

Flags were waiving from the Capitol, Delevan House, and Congress Hall, and a large portion of the stores and houses on the route were decorated with small flags. The apartments reserved for the visitors at the Congress Hall were very elegantly fitted up, and could not fail to gratify the guests. In the evening the Prince and suite dined with Gov. Morgan and staff. Among the invited guests was Hon. Wm. H. Seward.

A special car handsomely furnished was provided for the trip to Boston, and the Albany Burgesses corps, Captain Hale Kingsley, in the morning conducted the Prince to the cars.

The Prince arrived at Boston late in the afternoon. Extensive preparations had been made for the reception of himself and suite. On his arrival at the depot he was conducted to the Revere House, where quarters had been provided for the Royal party.

The rooms were in the L portion of the hotel, for the Prince's private parlour, dining room, and sleeping room were connected with each other, and a temporary partition rendered them private. The ladies' entrance was closed, and the ladies' drawing room was his reception room. The whole suite numbered about twenty rooms.

A grand military review, and reception of the school children took place. The Prince was presented to the Governor at the State House. The Ancient and Honourable Artillery Company of Boston then escorted the Boston city government to the common where the review took place. A visit was then paid to the Winthrop school, where one thousand girls sang a poem written by Longfellow. It is as follows, and was sung to the air of "God Save the Queen:"

OUR FATHER'S LAND.

God bless our Father's Land,
Keep her in heart and hand,
  One with our own!
From all her foes defend,
Be her brave people's friend,
On all her realms descend,
  Protect her throne!

Father, in thy loving care,
Guard Thou her kingdom's heir,
  Guide all his ways;
Thine arm his shelter be,
From harm by land and sea,
Bid storm and danger flee,
  Prolong his days!

> Lord, let war's tempest cease,
> Fold the whole world in peace
> Under thy wings!
> Make all thy nations one,
> All hearts beneath the sun,
> Till Thou shalt reign alone,
> Great King of Kings!

The ball came off in the evening, when an extraordinary entertainment was presented.

October 17.

Promptly at the hour appointed, the Burgesses' Corps of Albany waited upon the Prince, and after he had, in company with Governor Morgan, Senator Seward and his own party, taken his position, they escorted him through crowds of enthusiastic people to the cars. The Prince seemed delighted with Senator Seward, conversed with him for a long time, and extended a cordial invitation for him to visit England. The Duke was equally cordial towards Senator Seward, and the party seemed pleased and satisfied with the visit. The only *mal apropos* occurrence was the great length of the dinner, which lasted over three hours, completely wearying the Prince. He was obliged to endure presentations till a late hour. As the train left the depot, Mr. Seward called out to Dr. Ackland, that he would send him some works to Oxford, and the entire suite joined in a farewell salute.

At Chatham, Consul Archibald took an affecting parting from the Prince, and at the state line the Governor's staff resigned their formal charge, the Prince begging them to reassure Gov. Morgan of his great gratification at the attentions he had received in Albany.

At Pittsfield there was an immense outpouring of the people. No such enthusiasm or desire to see His Royal Highness had been manifested since his arrival. In compliance with their oft repeated request, he went to the rear of the platform and bowed several times to the cheering multitude.

At Springfield the spacious depot was jammed with a dense mass, all struggling to see the lion of the day. Lunch had been provided for the party, but no knives or forks or plates had been brought, so Bachmeyer was compelled to borrow a dozen of each from the saloon. Here Cols. Thompson and Sargent, Aids to Governor Banks, met the Prince. They presented their credentials, extended their invitations, and made part of the company. The Prince was very cordial to them, but was evidently tired and sleepy. Salutes were fired from the armoury and several private residences.

At Palmer, and other smaller but important towns, there were demonstrations, varying only in extent. As he neared Worcester, the Prince sent for Superintendent Gray, and thanked him for the skill and safety with which he had arranged and conducted the trip.

At Worcester there was a very great rush for the Royal car. Men, women and children vied with each other in the most frantic attempts to get hold of the Prince or touch his garments ; to all of which he paid but little attention, bowing occasionally to the right and left. Governor Washburn and the Directors of the road here joined the train. They desired to be presented, but the Prince was sleepy, and they were not introduced.

The train arrived at five o'clock in Boston. The idea had been inculcated that there would be nothing worth seeing beyond the city line running across the isthmus which connects the peninsula Boston is built upon with the main land. Most of those who were there had driven up in carriages, and these, together with the people who live around, formed the assembly who waited to receive the Prince. The doors of the station were locked, and the way was kept clear to the carriage by a strong detachment of mounted police. The mayor, Mr. Lincoln, met the Prince, and welcomed him to the city, and in a very short time the cortege was on its way. The first three miles was travelled at a quick pace, but shortly before reaching the line it was moderated, in order to give the people an opportunity of seeing His Royal Highness. All Boston was out—there is no mistake about that. Washington street, Baylstone street, Treemont street, Kent street, all the way to the Revere Hotel, were thronged. Washington street is lined with noble elm trees, which spread their mighty branches until in many places they nearly meet in the centre of the street. It has its large houses, with flights of stone steps in front, affording accommodation for hundreds of the softer sex, for whose use they were by general consent most gallantly reserved.

While some houses, too, have for the most part large bay windows, at which were seated the belles of the city and their mammas, waving white handkerchiefs innumerable—two to each lady in some cases—as the carriage containing the royal guest drove past. It had its large verandahs, also monopolised upon this occasion by crinoline, and its broad sidewalks. There were no soldiers to line the streets, and but few policemen. Yet no obstruction was experienced—a matter of little surprise in Boston. That the people should have been well behaved in Baltimore or New York was subject of remark. Those cities have obtained such a notoriety for disorderliness of their people that any thing to the contrary is unlooked for from them. But in Boston—the noble city of Boston—the Puritan city, *par excellence*—the whole Union would have been struck with amazement had any of the many thousands who assembled in her streets to do honour to the Prince, manifested any thing else than a most Yankee-like propriety of demeanour.

The order of procession was this:—first came a number of gentlemen on horseback, who dashed along the street on spirited horses, and cleared away the crowd. Then came a body of mounted police, shoulder to shoulder, keeping clear the cleared way. The royal carriages came next, surrounded by a troop of dragoons, dressed in red, having brass helmets and drawn swords. After them came about two hundred lancers, a remarkably fine looking body of men, evidently well drilled, good steady riders. A band played "God save the Queen," "Hail Columbia," and other airs, at different points along the route. The Prince was surrounded by soldiers, those who were nearest him most persistently keeping the heads of their horses opposite the doors of his carriage, so that the Royal visage was during the greater part of the route pursued, invisible. It is the Prince's custom always when cheered to bow in acknowledgment, and as he is the only one who raises his hat of those in the carriage, he is by that act recognised.

When he turned off Washington street on to Tremont street the huzzas were for a space loud enough. The large park which had to be passed was crowded with people, who got almost enthusiastic. The progress lasted but about an hour, and though the people remained a long time about the hotel, nothing was seen of the Prince after he had entered it, except by those who had

A 30

gathered upon the staircase, and by the servants who waited upon him at dinner.

The rooms occupied by the Royal party in the Revere House were fitted up in most sumptuous style. Much new furniture had been procured for the occasion, gorgeous in gold brocade. The room containing the bed in which the Prince was to sleep, we were glad to learn, met the motherly approbation of the ladies.

When Charles Dickens, in the course of his peregrinations, got to Boston, he was made happy by the crooked streets. They had a home-like aspect extremely refreshing. The Prince may have shared somewhat in this feeling. Boston is more like an old country city than any other in the States he has visited, not excepting Pittsburg. The stores look old and substantial; the stone of the buildings is brown, most of the houses are of red brick, and the streets are hilly.

In the evening there was a grand ball, at which the Bostonians endeavoured to outshine the New Yorkers.

THE PRINCE'S WELCOME.

Across the ocean's stormy deep,
There comes to us a nation's hope,
And here his princely keep,
All gracious, on our verdant slope.

A host of greetings here await
The Lord of Renfrew and the Isles;
And manhood's shouts, with joy elate,
Will rend the air 'mid woman's smiles.

His Saxon land is wide and far,
Where bards in magic strains have sung;
That naught this pleasing scene may mar,
Our welcome breathes his native tongue.

A kindred sense of Shakspeare's art,
Of Milton's verse, so grand, sublime,
Inspires the mind and fills the heart,—
Bright promise for all coming time.

For year's of brotherhood and love,
For stalwart work and golden lore,
With sweet permission from above,
To daily add increasing store.

Lo! she who sends her treasure here,
The wife and mother,—England's Queen!

Who finds no equal, knows no peer,
In all her measureless demesne.

In holding fast a Christian part,
Enthroned in majesty of birth;
No counterchange of soul or heart,
A sacred service renders earth.

And we, unheeding jewelled crown,
Supremacy and sceptred line,
In veneration bow us down
At gentle virtue's holy shrine.

With benediction on her name,
We laud again this Royal One;
And thus a second welcome frame
For good Victoria's favoured Son!

ONE OF THE BARCLAYS.

Boston Common, 17th October, 1860.

October 18*th*, 1860.

Yankee land may well feel proud of this day's hospitality. Boston has entertained the Prince of Wales in a judicious and pleasing manner, to his entire satisfaction and greatly to her credit.

After a late breakfast the Prince granted audience to Edward Everett, who introduced Ralph Farnham, the last surviving soldier who fought at Bunker Hill. He is one hundred years of age, and his youngest daughter, who accompanied him, is a sprightly maiden of seventy-six. The Prince was very kind to the old gentleman, and quite won his heart, as was evinced by his remark, that "if Princes allers acted like this to a body, there would be less wars."

In compliance with a proclamation of Mayor Lincoln making this a holiday, the stores were generally closed and the schools all dismissed at an early hour. The streets were thronged with people, particularly in the regions of the Revere House and the Common. The escort was drawn up in Bowdoin-square. The Cadets were stationed at the State House, and the rest of the troops were upon the Common waiting the movements of the Prince. Col. Reed, who, under Gov. Banks, had general charge of the militia, and to whom the New York reporters are greatly indebted, called for the Prince, and in carriages the entire Royal party were conveyed through the crowded streets to the Governor's head-quarters, in the Governor's room, where were the Governor and his staff, the Executive Council, the Chief Justice. Col. Reed presented the Prince to the Governor as "His Royal Highness," this being the only instance where the Prince had been willing to have an official reception. Governor Banks greeted him cordially and addressed him as follows :

"It is with great pleasure that I welcome your Royal Highness to the Commonwealth of Massachusetts, and extend to you the most cordial greetings of its people. They have regarded with profound gratification your visit to this continent, so auspicious in its opening, so fortunate in its progress, and now, I regret to say, so near its termination. Be assured, Sir, you will bear with you the united wishes of the people of Massachusetts for your safe return to your friends and to your country, to which we are attached by so many ties of language, law and liberty. In their name I bid you welcome. I welcome, also, with unfeigned pleasure the distinguished and honourable gentlemen of your suite. Permit me to present to you my associates in the Executive Department of the Government—His honour, the Lieutenant-Governor, the gentlemen of the Executive Council and the Secretary of State."

The several gentlemen referred to were recognised by the Prince, who shook hands cordially with the Aids, whom he had met before.

The Representatives' Hall was filled to overflowing by ladies. The Governor led the Prince through the hall, while the ladies rose *en masse*, greeting him with smiling faces and waving handkerchiefs. The Senate Chamber was occupied by some forty members of the Valuation Committee, who were also permitted to gaze on the face of His Royal Highness.

Horses, splendidly caparisoned, were provided for the Prince and suite, who, as well as the Governor and staff, were dressed in full uniform. The troops, numbering over three thousand, were drawn up so as to form three sides of a parallelogram. In the centre were stationed the parties above named, the whole forming one of the most beautiful spectacles ever seen. Sir Fenwick Williams was to have been one of the party, but as the Governor

General of Canada had sailed for Europe, and as General Williams had been sworn in his stead, he was compelled to forego the pleasure, and despatched Quarter-master Connelly and Capt. De Winton, his Aide, to apologise, and appear in the Prince's suite for him.

As the Prince rode up and down the lines, the vast crowds outside cheered continuously and lustily, to which he responded by lifting his plumed chapeau and bending his acknowledgments. The review reflected great credit upon the citizen soldiery, and elicited warm praise from the Prince and Gen. Bruce, who were in a body presented at the close of the review. Too much praise cannot be awarded to Gov. Banks and Mayor Lincoln for their admirable and systematic arrangements.

After the review a grand procession was formed, which wound around the crowded streets greatly to the joy of the populace, and which finally deposited a select few at the State House, where the Governor had prepared a lunch. The room in which it was given was very tastefully decorated, and the entertainment was truly a delightful one. The Prince's servant had been unable to obtain admittance with a change of raiment—so Colonel Reed quietly put the Prince into a covered carriage, in which he was speedily conveyed to the Revere, greatly to the astonishment of the countless outsiders.

The most unique and graceful compliment yet paid the Prince was the musical festival in the afternoon. The school children had been ranged in four triangular rows of seats, all verging towards a common centre—the boys on the inside, and the girls on the outside—the dark clothing of the former relieving the brilliant toilette of the latter. A platform had been prepared for the occupancy of the guests, while the spacious hall was densely packed with Boston's choicest set. On the platform, besides the Royal party, were Messrs. Everett, Hilliard, Agassiz, Emerson, Summer, Winthrop, Holmes, Longfellow, and others of the "Mutual Administration Society," besides the Prince's steady friends, the New York reporters. The entrance of Mr. Hamlin, candidate for the Vice-Presidency, was the signal for subdued applause. The programme was short and the execution superb. When "God save the Queen" was sung, all arose, and the allusion to the Prince's life and health was received with great applause. When he entered and when he retired, the boys clapped their hands and shouted in unison, while the girls waved their handkerchiefs. The Prince was delighted and gratified at the success of so novel and interesting an entertainment.

While at the State House, the Prince and suite, but particularly the Duke of Newcastle and Dr. Ackland, were very much pleased with an exhibition of ancient documents, charters of 1628, 1630, and 1691.

The photographers, Brady and Gurney, were there—the former to deliver certain pictures ordered by the Royal party at New York, and the latter by command of the Prince, who gave him a sitting, when pictures of the Prince and the rest of the suite were taken.

The Government ordered from Rossitor a historical picture of the Prince and Mr. Buchanan standing at the Tomb of Washington. The Prince had already granted Mr. Rossitor several opportunities for the progress of the work.

Every thing that is tasty, every thing that is lovely, every thing that is fashionable, every thing that is ambitious, every thing that is of good report, was represented at the ball. It was not aristocratic, in any sense, for aristocracy supposes a class which holds a position either by wealth or by talent, or by hereditary right. All classes had their representatives. The crowd was promiscuous. The company was a fair sample of the community of New England in its best array, with its loveliest women, its display of wealth and of extravagance, and under considerable excitement, but excitement that did not break through proper restraint.

The general appearance of the ball room at the hour of ten o'clock, when entered, was brilliant. The Prince had not arrived and there had been no dancing. The great floor was completely covered with ladies and gentlemen in elegant and varied attire, while the two tiers of boxes were completely filled. This was no diamond ball. There were doubtless jewels there, and jewels of price, too, but they did not dazzle by their light. Gilmore's Band was performing a march, and the company was promenading as they best might in that many-coloured and sparkling sea of crinoline. All eyes were kept towards the canopy which had been erected for the Prince's accommodation. The decorations were in good taste, and sufficiently profuse for the large area which they were intended to beautify. The stage was transformed into a large room, the ceiling being improvised from red cloth, and the walls decorated with large mirrors, which reflected the light. The floor was covered in the morning with a preparation of shell-lac, which has the property of drying almost as soon as applied, making new boards look like mahogany just waxed, and affording a smooth surface for the dancers. Directly opposite the stage, in the middle of the balcony, a canopy of heavy red velvet, surmounted by the American eagle, had been arranged as a spot from whence the Prince might witness the gay scene on the floor, as if in his box at the opera. Two retiring rooms, handsomely fitted with rich hangings and massive furniture, were ready for him on the same floor. In one of them was a large bust of Victoria. The rest of the balcony was draped with the velvet of the same colour as the Prince's tent, but with two stripes of gold lace at the bottom, which was continued all the way round. The first tier was draped with yellow cloth fringed with red and blue. Wreaths of evergreen entwined with red and white roses—the mottoes "Probitas," "Concordia," "Amicitia," "Fiducia," and American flags occurred at frequent intervals.

The upper part of the house was draped with red and blue, presenting a very tasteful appearance. The great chandelier seemed much better adapted for a ball room than a theatre, and added very much to the brilliancy of the scene. In the ladies' saloon some improvements had been effected by means of new furniture and fresh curtains, and the appearance of the apartment was decidedly pleasing. The floors of the lobbies were covered with green cloth, and a number of seats had been removed in the balcony, whereby the comfort of promenaders was considerably increased.

It was half-past ten o'clock before the scion of royalty made his appearance. Many minutes before that, the large company, numbering many thousand, had ceased their promenading, and stood in a mass on the floor gazing into the Prince's box, or crowded the boxes with the same object in view. A noise was hushed by the mysterious rustling of robes, and the still more mysterious impatient whispers. Presently the Germania Band struck the first words of "God save the Queen," and Mayor Lincoln's smiling face was first seen beyond the heavy drapery, then the innocent face of the Prince, and a huge sigh of relief swelled up from the floor to the dome, because now the dances would be ordered. After looking down upon the animated scene for a few moments, His Royal Highness descended to the floor in company with Mayor Lincoln. The crowd made a narrow passage for him, for all the ladies were dying to see his face in a near view. In a little while a space was cleared near the centre of the floor, hardly large enough for a quadrille, and preparations for dancing were made in earnest.

Mrs. Frederick W. Lincoln, Jr., the Mayor's wife, was the first partner.

The quadrille commenced, and a scene of indescribable excitement ensued. There was hardly any dancing on the floor. But a vast number enclosed about the set and kept gathering it in, in a smaller circle and still smaller, until there was scarcely room to turn a partner.

They did not pinch the Prince, as was done in New York, but they jostled him, and impeded his movements to such a degree that they might have been called any thing else with as much propriety as dancing. While this was going on upon the floor, another exciting scene was transpiring in the gallery. Ladies, with their protectors following after, hurried up stairs in flocks; nor did they stand much upon the order of their rushing up, so that the object could be gained—that of obtaining a satisfactory view of the Prince's dancing.

When the second dance was called, there was much speculation as to who would be the probable partner of the Prince. Mrs. Banks, the Governor's wife, was selected, although this was not in accordance with the programme. In the third dance, a waltz, the Prince had for a partner a daughter of Mr. Everett, and by this time he had thawed considerably. This waltz was the most curious dance ever seen upon a ball-room floor. There might have been space enough, heaven knows, but the room left for the waltzers was down to a small triangular piece, about twenty feet in length on its right angle. It was like waltzing in a cage, with thousands of spectators to witness the feat. They stood looking on from every side, from ten to twelve feet deep, and it was with the greatest difficulty that the limits of the cage were enlarged.

After this experience in the centre of the ball-room, the Prince

He next tried the stage with better success as to room, and danced with vivacity and spirit with ladies who were young and fascinating. Every dance that followed the Prince was joined in, and showed no signs of fatigue. He was certainly indefatigable on the light fantastic toe. But though the Prince danced every time, there was, on the whole, less dancing among the rest of the party than you would ordinarily find in a small social assembly. One reason for this was because of the crowd, and another reason, because more went to see and to be seen than to dance.

It was not until half-past 12 o'clock that any portion of the party adjourned to the supper table. This had been laid in the Melodeon, which was made fragrant and beautiful by floral decorations that were scattered with lavish profusion, banks and pyramids of flowers and wreaths, and bouquets without number were to be seen on every hand. The supper was worthy the occasion, and the appetites it was to satisfy were equal to the most liberal supply the caterer had furnished, at least it appeared so by the immense crowds that hurried to the supper room. But there was likely to be no lack, for every thing had been furnished on the most liberal scale; besides, the gentlemen's saloon on the third floor had been fitted up for refreshments, which were open to all for the whole night.

Recapitulation :—the Prince danced with Mrs. Mayor Lincoln ; 2, the Prince danced with Mrs. N. P. Banks, who was pushed out of the first set by Ward Eleven; 3, the Prince danced with Mrs. Lieut. Wise, (daughter of Mr. Everett,) whose husband is now in Japan; 4, the Prince danced with Miss Fanny Crowninshield ; 5, the Prince danced with Miss Susan Amory; 6, the Prince danced with Miss Carrie Bigelow, (daughter of the Chief Justice of Massachusetts ;) 7, the Prince danced with Mrs Col. Thomas E. Crickering; 8, the Prince danced with Mrs. Harrison Ritchie; 9, the Prince danced with Miss Lombard ; 10, the Prince danced with Miss Fanny Peabody; 11, the Prince danced with Miss Kitty Fay; 12, the Prince danced with Miss Mary Crane. After the dancing His Royal Highness went to supper.

October 19.

The Prince of Wales and suite to-day visited Cambridge, Mount Auburn Cemetery, and Harvard College. At the College he was welcomed at Doane Hall by President Felton and the faculty, and with hearty cheers by the students.

After visiting the library of the Scientific School and Observatory, the distinguished party had a collation in Harvard Hall.

The citizens of Cambridge were out *en masse*, and cheered the Prince heartily as he passed through the city. Mayor Green acted as his chaperon. In the evening the Prince visited the Boston public library.

October 21.

Prior to his departure from the Revere House the Prince expressed the perfect satisfaction which he and his suite felt at their accommodations and the attentions which had been quietly shown them. He had never seen or tasted such fruit before.

On the 20th, accompanied by the Mayor and at least twenty-thousand citizens, he was escorted to the superb car which was to take him to Portland, by a troop of lancers. He had been surrounded and completely occupied by Everett, Winthrop and others, from the time of his arrival almost to the entire exclusion of Governor Banks and his associates. The Duke had noticed this, and in a very quiet way put an end to it. He requested Mr. Hooper to make out a list of prominent state and national officials from whom he might obtain desirable information concerning the state of political feelings. The hint was taken, and Messrs. Banks, Sumner, Wilson, Burlingame, Rice, and Bigelow, were invited to accompany the Royal party to Portland.

The trip to Portland was a succession of popular ovations. The Prince, with unusual animation and wonderful gaity, entered into the spirit of the day, and at every place popped out upon the rear platform, and bowed smilingly and familiarly to the enthusiastic crowds. At Lynn three thousand school-children greeted him with cheers and flowers. At Salem the depot was decorated with flags and thronged with people. At Portsmouth the shipping was dressed and the crowd immense. Governor Goodwin took the Prince by the hand and said : " Fellow-citizens of New Hampshire, I present to you His Royal Highness the Prince of Wales, and in your name I bid him a hearty welcome!" And so it was every where—a cheerful, hearty recognition of his presence, and the most enthusiastic, unaffected demonstrations of kindly regard.

Lunch was served in the car, and during its progress politics were discussed. The certainty of Lincoln's election and the absurdity of disunion were demonstrated.

The Duke of Newcastle stated that the party felt under great obligations to the American Press, and that the full and accurate reports of their movements had cast a ray of light upon their pathway, which would disclose to the English people a view of this country such as they have never had, and which they could get in no other way. He expressed great regret that their copies of Friday's New York papers had been mislaid, and requested Gov. Banks to try and procure others; but it was too late and none were got.

The Prince said he was not weary of his experience but was delighted, and approached his departure with mingled feelings of pain and pleasure. General Bruce said his time had been so taken up with festivities that he had been unable hitherto to get at serious matters, and he was sorry he had so soon to leave.

Mayor Howard received the Prince at Portland with a large military escort, consisting of the 1st Regiment commanded by Col. Leavat, the Portland Blues, Light Infantry, Light Guard, Rifle Guard, Portland Rifles, the latter acting as a guard of honour. In addition the Norway Light Infantry, and Lewiston Light Infantry and Auburn Artillery, were paraded through the town, and thence to the Great Eastern wharf, where Admiral Milne and Commander Seymour met them.

There was no formality about the reception. The people were out in thousands, cheering and delighted, kind and respectful as every where, quite content if they only saw the Prince, and knew that he in turn saw and appreciated their welcome. There was a short drive made round the town, and then the party went to lunch at the Prebble House, for there was much leave taking to be gone through, and kind Canadian friends to whom to bid a last farewell. Mr. Rose, of whom all had so many warm recollections, was there, with M. Cartier, the Prime Minister, the Mayor of Montreal, and the leading gentlemen connected with the series of superb entertainments which that great capital of Canada gave the Prince. There were gentlemen too from Halifax and New Brunswick, Quebec and Toronto, London and Hamilton. All who had been in any way concerned in the magnificent displays and receptions of the great Canadian colonies were waiting to wish his Royal Highness a happy voyage back, and take a kind leave of their young visitor, who on that soil will always be remembered with pride and affection. A little before three o'clock His Royal Highness left the hotel to embark. Nearly two months previous it had been arranged that the departure should take place from Portland at 3 p. m., on the 20th of October. The day and the hour had come, and with the same perfect accuracy which had distinguished every movement of the long progress, this last appointment was kept. Crowds thronged the streets down to the wharf, the hill overlooking it was black with people, the ships in the bay were dressed with colours. There was great shouting, cheering, and waving of handkerchiefs as His Royal Highness, with the chief members of his suite, stepped into the *Hero's* barge, and one long shouted farewell seemed to fill the air as the boat shoved off from American soil, and the first Prince of Wales who had ever visited the United States, quitted it with the love and good wishes of all its people. There was a moment of ceremony as the *Hero, Ariadne, Flying Fish, Nile* and *Styx* manned yards and slowly thundered out a Royal salute. Another salute as the Prince's standard went up to the *Hero's* main. Then "boat's recall" was hoisted, and before five o'clock the Royal squadron was steaming out of the harbour. The last salute was given as the vessels passed the forts. It was returned gun for gun, dotting the hills with smoke, till the crowds were hidden and the land lay dim in a blue haze, which gradually sunk lower and lower in the horizon.

The departure of the Prince deeply affected Lord Lyons, who remained upon the quay. A very marked compliment was paid to the American flag. The Prince first saluted, then the American flag was raised on the ships of the *Admiral* and *Commodore*, and saluted by the same.

Every thing was conducted on a grand and effective scale, and was in perfect harmony with the entire tour.

How gratifying to know that all have been delighted with their reception, with the attentions paid them, and the reports made concerning them, and that one and all of the distinguished party carried away the kindliest feelings of regard and esteem for the American hosts of the Prince of Wales.

After a dull and tedious voyage of nearly twenty-seven days, His Royal Highness and suite completed their long American tour, and landed in England again at Plymouth, on November 15th, 1860. The length to which the voyage from Portland was protracted,—a length only equalling the average winter passages of sailing ships,—probably gave rise to apprehensions in the public mind as to the "rose and expectancy of this fair state" being buffetted about in all directions by the rudest of rude storms. Few winter passages across the North Atlantic lasted so long in which ships have fallen in with so few storms or heavy seas. It was especially desired to make a quick passage,—fourteen days was the outside spoken of at Portland,—but there was nothing but a long gloom average of fogs and head winds, relieved now and then by a gale in the opposite direction to which the ships were going, and in contending against which, that insatiable monster of the deep,—leeway,—soon swallowed up the previous day's hard steaming, and left the squadron to begin *de novo*, with increased impatience but diminished coal. To this and other causes must be ascribed the reason why Albert Edward was the first Prince of Wales who ever spent his birthday knocking about the Channel in a south-easterly gale, and to the same reason must be ascribed that the *Hero*, the crack steam line of battle ship in the the English navy, made, on the whole, rather a poor passage as compared with a sailing New York trader. The *Hero* made a bad passage, as compared with the *Ariadne*, which could have been in England in less than twelve days had it been required; but whether the *Hero* went fast or went slow (the latter was the rule) her consort was bound to keep her company, and it necessitated almost as much work on the part of her crew in shortening sail to keep behind the flagship as it would to have accomplished one of the fastest passages ever made by any frigate in the service.

Scarcely any thing remains to add to this transient record save the arrival and embarkation at Portland, and following His Royal Highness throughout "unto this last," a few words more will suffice to bring to a conclusion the narrative of the first great public colonial visit ever made by a Prince of Wales.

On board the *Hero* the Prince, with all the immediate members of his suite, was embarked. A winter voyage across the Atlantic is always a long, dull and comfortless affair. On this run, as in going out, His Royal Highness had his usual ill-luck with regard to weather. There were head winds, there were calms, there were fogs, and in the short intervals when the breeze was favourable there was so much of it and to spare, that on the whole one rather wished the calms and fogs were back again. For the first two or three days out both the *Hero* and *Ariadne* were under steam. The former was at full speed, the latter at less than half, and had to resort to every nautical artifice to keep her place behind the flagship. Now and then the *Ariadne* ranged up so close alongside that both parties could converse from their respective quarter decks by writing out their questions on black boards, and holding them up. Once, indeed, the *Ariadne* came so close that both could speak with ease. This experiment, however, was only attempted once, for a heavy swell was running, and the two ships were within a hair's-breadth of coming broadside against each other, when the consequences might have been serious. Their yards actually touched, and nothing but the speed of the *Ariadne* and the indomitable coolness of Captain Vansittart saved them from actual collision. Even as it was, many ran below, thinking that the masts and spars would be about their ears. After this slight escapade, open order was kept, except in fogs, when the *Ariadne* had to follow, almost touching the Prince's vessel. These fogs were as frequent as on the voyage out, and were a source of perpetual anxiety. The *Hero* used to go ahead, sounding her fog whistle, till the shrill alarm was faint in the distance, and stifled in the thick air. Then the *Ariadne* would follow, sounding hers, till close upon the flagship, when the *Hero* again took up the scream and went ahead; and in this manner, moving step by step, the nights and days would pass. The *Ariadne* carried coals enough for her voyage home, but the *Hero* only stowed some six or seven days' fuel, most of which, of course, was reserved in case, as it really happened, of their coming on this coast with easterly winds against them. But in spite of the care with which the coals were husbanded, it was evidently of no good lying becalmed some 600 miles off Portland, so on Thursday the 25th, both vessels got up steam, and went ahead, the *Hero* at full speed and the *Ariadne* keeping her place with ease at little more than one-third. On Friday, the 26th, the *Ariadne* took the *Hero* in tow, and actually dragged her along through a heavy rolling swell at the rate of nine knots an hour. Both vessels were rolling rather heavily, and the hawser kept tightening and vibrating like a harp-string. It went at last with a terrific snap at about 5 a.m. on the 27th. At that time the long-wished for wind had come at last from the north-west. The towing, therefore, was not renewed, but both went under plain sail. During Saturday the breeze freshened more and more, the sea got up as the glass went down, and the wind came in fierce squalls, driving showers of sleet and hail before it. On Sunday it blew more than half a gale, and hour by hour, reef after reef was taken in. About 3 a.m. on Monday this brief storm was at its worst, and struck upon both ships in a succession of angry squalls. The squall which the copper-coloured clouds foretold came on the *Hero* with a hoarse, loud roar, as if a mountain was in motion. At once it split both her foresail and her mainsail, and heeled her sharply over. The *Ariadne's* turn came next. With a loud premonitory rush of hail, and dash of sea up over her sides, the wind struck her, as the sailors say, "like a hammer." The reefed maintopsail split at once. Then the forestaysail went. With this squall the thickness of the weather increased, till even the dubious, greasy light of the moon was damped out. At last the clouds partially cleared, and then the *Hero* was no where to be seen. The last that had been seen of her was through the mist, when she was apparently heaving to to reef. So the *Ariadne* hove to also, till nearly nine o'clock, in the hope of her consort being still in the neighbourhood. At nine o'clock the gale was almost as bad as ever, but the sun was bright for a short time, yet still the flagship was no where visible. After a delay of two hours and more, Captain Vansittart came to the conclusion that the *Hero* must have run before the gale, and was still ahead. Acting upon this supposition, which proved to be quite correct, all the sail which the Ariadne could safely carry in such a heavy breeze was crowded on, and away she went; tearing through the waves at the rate of more than thirteen knots an hour. All troubles were forgotten when, though the gale still blew, the weather cleared, and the man at the masthead hailed that the

Hero was in sight, about 14 miles a-head. In less than five hours after first sighting her from the mast-head the *Ariadne* was alongside once more. With the night the wind—the only favourable wind she had—died away, and left both ships rolling helplessly to the bidding of the long, smooth swell. Then came calms by day, with fogs by night, then more idling and rolling, getting a start of winds for a few hours to raise momentary hopes of still making a fair passage; then came calms, and yet more fogs, till the chances of reaching England under 14 days waxed fainter and more faint with each long day's no progress. Then the *Ariadne* would tow again. Yet before the towing had lasted half an hour the shackle broke, and left the *Hero* adrift. A larger shackle was then got up, and with this the *Ariadne* again set to work, and pulled the *Hero* though the water some 200 miles, making every timber in the ship creak and work awfully under the strain. After 20 hours of this work the hawser parted on board the *Hero*, and as there was then a little wind, the towing was not renewed, but both vessels crept on under sail. In this manner, now creeping on for a few hours, with a faint wind, then steaming a little through calms and fogs, the 1st of November found the ships in that part of the ocean called "the beginning of the Chops of the Channel," with the sea like glass, fogs by night with a long fog swell, and a steady easterly wind against them during the day. On this, the 1st November, the ships were 600 miles from the Lizard, at noon on Monday, the 5th, 430. The *Hero* had not coal enough to steam, and the wind was too strong in the day, and the swell too much at night, for the *Ariadne* to tow. On Monday, the 5th, there was another attempt made to tow the *Hero*, but then there was a heavy swell on, and after some three hours the hawser parted again, and both ships jogged on as usual, creeping up slowly to windward, and passing many sail of merchantmen similarly situated. At last, on Monday, the 5th, the glass fell, and a strong south-westerly gale set in. Thus the 6th and 7th were passed with no sign of the wind abating. On Wednesday, the 7th, the ships were near Galway, and it was thought the *Hero* would have made for that port, filled up with coal, and then steamed home. Friday, the 9th, the ships were back again in the same place that they had been on Monday, the 5th, while on Sunday, the 11th, they were some

30 miles further off the land than they had been on Sunday, the 4th. On Monday, the 12th, both vessels were well into the Bay of Biscay, towards Ushant. Then came rain, then little puffs of fair wind, coquetting and flapping about the huge sails. Gradually it came round more from the west, till by 10 a.m. on the 13th, the 24th day out, there was, almost for the first time, a fair wind, and both ships at last making their course, stood towards England. The breeze, however, was but a poor one. In the night it almost died away, though the *Hero* still kept the double reef in her topsails to a light wind that scarcely moved her five knots an hour. A yacht would have gladly spread all her canvass to the wind which was keeping this crack line-of-battle ship under double reefed topsails. On the morning of the 14th, the wind came decidedly fair—a strong south-wester, under which, she rushed through the water at the rate of more than 12 knots an hour. This was all very well, but as some slight uncertainty existed as to where the vessels were, and consequently whither they were going, it was evident that they could not carry on long that way. There had been no observations for some days, and when there had been any, the *Hero's* differed from the *Ariadne's*, and the dead reckonings from both. Observations from stars only made matters worse again. So, as the weather was thickening and the wind in-shore, both ships shortened sail at one o'clock, and hove to, to sound; coarse gravel was got in 83 fathoms, which the chart said meant off Ushant, but this was almost doubtful, so soundings were taken again at six, and the bottom at 60 fathoms placed the first soundings above suspicion. The course of the vessels was, therefore, altered to east-north-east, and under shortened sail the *Hero* and the *Ariadne* stood across the channel for the Lizard light. This, the last night of the cruise, was as foggy as any, and once the *Ariadne* missed the *Hero's* red rockets, but the rockets were answered by the *Himalay*, which had been on the look out. At last the *Ariadne* put on full steam, and running up at 14 knots an hour, overtook the *Hero*, cautiously creeping towards the Lizard. Fortunately the light was soon made, and the cold gray morning at last showed the shores of Old England in the lofty, rugged, picturesque coast of Cornwall. The run to Plymouth was soon made, and before 10 a.m. the *Hero* and the *Ariadne* cast anchor inside the breakwater, the ships

in the sound, and in the harbour, and the batteries on shore saluting the Prince's flag. In a very short time His Royal Highness was ready to land. For the last time the ships manned yards, salutes were fired as the Royal standard came down from the *Hero* amid the cheers of the crews of the *Hero* and *Ariadne*. The Prince of Wales quitted the Royal squadron, and his long progress was brought to a close

His Royal Highness landed at the Royal William Victualling yard, where he was received by the Plymouth Volunteers, and a guard of honour of the 12th. At the station Colonel Lambrick and 100 Royal Marines formed a guard of honour on the platform.

The Royal train started from Plymouth at noon. His Royal Highness looked extremely well, and before departing conversed on the platform with Lady Mount Edgecumbe, the Hon. George Edgecumbe, Port Admiral Sir Houston Stewart, K. C. B., Admiral Superintendent Sir Thomas Pasley, Major General Hutchison, Commander of the Forces in the West, &c.

Precisely at half-past six o'clock the Royal train arrived at the Windsor station, where the Windsor Rifles formed a guard of honour.

His Royal Highness the Prince Consort came to the station to receive the Prince. The Prince proceeded to the castle amid the hearty cheers of the inhabitants, the firing of a Royal salute from the corporation ordnance, and the ringing of joyous peals from the bells of the Chapel Royal of St. George and St. John's Church.

THE ENGLISH PRESS ON THE PRINCE'S VISIT.

A new relation had to be established between two of the greatest empires in the world, members of the same human family, heirs of the same grand traditions, the same historic names, the same language, poetry, religion, and laws. For near a century the gulf of a bloody schism has gaped between them, and the triumph of success on the one side has been met with the sneers of disappointed dominion on the other. They have forgotten in the petty resentments of the hour that we are their elder brothers and fathers; and we have forgotten that they are but our young kinsmen, and that what is amiss in them must come of our breeding. Every tourist has had his fling at their freedom of manners, their laxity of opinion, and the stern reaction of their Puritan theology. Men who could know but little of their own country, and its still undigested heptarchy of dialects and manners, have made their sports of phrases and usages to be found in full vogue within six hours of this metropolis. The Americans have stood on their political dignity, and have resolved never to abate a pretension or lose an inch of ground. They have felt that they had to assert a rank which they did not inherit, and to stamp upon the world the measure they would be taken at. That they have been eminently successful, and that Fortune, as usual, has favoured the bold, will be admitted even by those who protest against their protest, and abhor the results. There can be no doubt that the United States form a very great nation, to be treated with quite as much respect, to say the least, as any other nation in the world. But, if we English have been slow to learn the lesson, the Americans also have acquired in the process of teaching something which they could now well afford to unlearn. In fact, we have to become brothers, as brothers ought to be. Already we call ourselves cousins and brothers, already we claim the monopoly of mutual criticism, and are proud of one another's achievments and progress when they do not interfere with our own. Yet there is much to unlearn on both sides of the Atlantic. What lingers as an expiring tradition, or the pang of an old sore, in the public action and language of the two countries, exists here and there in various exaggerated forms. Religious bigotry gives it a colour in one place, political fueds in another. The Orangeman, the expatriated Celt, the Slave-owner, the descendant of the Pilgrim Fathers—all have their separate quarrels, and find a ready response here.

The Prince of Wales has had to smile down all this. He has had to arrive, to be seen, and to conquer. The mild eye and the open palm, the errect bearing and the easy carriage, the good seat on horseback, the ready sympathy of tone, and the unshaken confidence of manner, have been the peaceful armory and the simple art by which he has had to win a people's good opinion. He has had to meet more variety and adapt himself to more situations than were likely to occur in twenty German States. He has been made much of; he has passed under a hundred arches of welcome, and been honoured with banners and devices; he has walked through miles of torches, and danced with hundreds of fair ladies amid acres of crinoline; he has received the cordial hospitalities of the Capitol, and visited the tomb of Washington; he has had to receive and reply to countless addresses, made by all manner of men on all sorts of occasions, and in a curious variety of allusion and style; he has had to review citizen armies glad to see and be seen, and equally pleased to show both their friendship and their power. Here and there he received demonstrations which it devolved upon him to interpret and make the best of. He had to laugh down ejaculations not meet for Royal ears. Thus he has had to act the Prince and the future King among those whose chiefest boast is that they will never be in subjection to any crowned head. That he has had an immense assistance in the great name of his mother, and the youthful son of a Queen could hardly fail to appeal to the natural loyalty of the hardiest politicians, all confess; but it was not the less to the Prince's credit that he has felt the tenderness of that position and discharged it to a nicety. Everybody cannot do that which is the most natural part, for it is the highest merit to be just what man ought to be. The commonest form of error is to attempt a part not one's own, or to combine two in one. The Prince of Wales not only showed himself in his own proper character as the head of the young British gentry, the future Sovereign of a constitutional country, and the representative of an empire whose best interest it is to be at peace with all the world, and which neither hopes for aggrandizement, nor fears any foe He expressed to the Americans the real sentiment of every true British heart to that great cognate nation. There is none in which we are all so interested; none the success and glory of which we all hear with such unmixed satisfaction; none with which we so identify ourselves. The Prince of Wales, while showing the feelings of a true-born Englishman, elicited the feelings of all true born Americans, and so brought the two face to face and made them feel they were brothers. That he took home, we are persuaded, a heart thrilling with affection for the mighty offspring of England, and a deep respect for that energetic freedom and expanding power,—an intellect sharpened and strengthened by contact with the vitality of a new civilization. He tested the life and destiny of the New World in the prairie, in the forest clearing, in populous cities, where but yesterday the pioneer plied his axe. He has seen a nation of soldiers without an army, civil order without a police—wealth, luxury, and culture without a court or an aristocracy. He learned to mingle with the busy crowd of men without the intervention of chamberlains and courtiers; he has found respect without ceremony, and honour without adulation. He dwelt, too, in England at sea; and no where can he have better learnt the secret of England's greatness than in his experiences on board the *Hero* on the Atlantic. It is only due to the Duke of Newcastle to say that the Prince has been singularly fortunate in the selection of a Secretary of State to attend him on his travels. It seems a happy coincidence that at the hour when the Royal squadron was making the English land on Wednesday night, the Prime Minister was eloquently acknowledging the hospitalities which the Prince of Wales had enjoyed in the United States.

December 8, 1860.

A grand masonic banquet took place in the Corn Exchange, Nottingham, yesterday, to commemorate the installation of his Grace the Duke of Newcastle as Grand Master of Nottinghamshire.

The Duke of Newcastle occupied the chair; and there were present the Earl of Zetland, Grand Master of England, Mr. Bass, M. P., &c.

The noble Duke said—One of their great principles, as Freemasons, was obedience to all constituted authorities and respect for the existing authorities of the realm. These were principles from which they could under no circumstances diverge. They supported those institutions not only because they were, but because they were such as they could wish them to be. It had been his good fortune recently to visit other portions of the globe, and examine the colonies in a distant part of the world, and in those colonies he might be allowed to say that he witnessed such devotion to the Sovereign of these realms as no one who had not witnessed it himself would be ready to believe. (Cheers.) The enthusiasm which he saw came from the inmost hearts of all those who displayed it; it was no mere noisy acclamation in the street; it was not a mere demonstration of the towns and populous places, but an enthusiasm exhibited in every back street and thinly populated locality. It was a demonstration of the attachment of the entire people to the throne of England, and of their veneration for the lady who at present occupied it. (Cheers.) It was a loyalty not of creed, nor of party, nor of race. After leaving that country he went to another, which, it was true, did not at present own the sceptre of Great Britain, and, therefore, throughout the many thousand miles through which he had travelled, there was not the same loyalty, because there was not the call for it in a country which was not subordinate to the Crown of England; but there was an amount of respect, of attachment, of veneration and love for the Queen of this country which far transcended any thing that could possibly have been expected. (Cheers.) It was a tribute on the part of the American people : it was a demonstration of their veneration for female excellence, and it was also a proof of their deep and lasting attachment to the mother country. He had no hesitation in saying that the feeling towards the Queen of Great Britain in the United States of America could not be designated by any other word he knew of but a passion. (Cheers.) He had the gratification in the Lodge that morning of seeing a brother—he did not know whether he was in the room at that moment or not—who came from America. (It was here announced that the brother in question was present.) He (the Duke) was delighted to find that he was there, and he should say nothing in his presence which he would not say even more strongly in his absence, when he stated that the impression made upon his mind by that journey was one which time would not efface. He was referring now to the general powerful influence which the excellent Queen of this country exercised over other nations, and more especially over those with whom we had a common origin; and he was certain they would not be wanting on the present occasion in that feeling which had been so generally exhibited elsewhere. Having now referred briefly to the attachment exhibited towards her Majesty in the colonies and in the United States of America, he might notice the fact that a no less striking demonstration of affection was recently seen in the anxiety and alarm which he had been told prevailed in this country respecting the safety of His Royal Highness the Prince of Wales. (Cheers.) From the manner in which that anxiety was displayed, her Majesty was fully convinced of the ardent attachment of her people. Nor was this less strikingly demonstrated when His Royal Highness reached these shores, for he met with a reception most enthusiastic in its nature at every railway station between Plymouth and Windsor. In conclusion, he asked them to drink "Health to the Queen and prosperity to the craft," and to give the toast all the masonic honours. (Loud and protracted cheering.)

His Grace, in proposing "The rest of the Royal Family," said that it had been the lot of the Prince of Wales, at the age of nineteen, to render to his country a great and essential service. Many a man born of a Royal family has descended into the grave rendering to his fellow men much less good service than has been rendered by this young Prince. Whatever has been the destiny which Providence reserved for him, it is a proud thing that he can reflect on this voyage across the Atlantic. He believed that nothing so much as that journey could have cemented the good feelings—he said cemented, mind, because he was convinced that they were previously entertained—which exist between the two countries on the opposite side of the Atlantic. But not only is it desirable that the existence of these good feelings should be known; it is singularly fortunate that they have already been placed on record and propagated by the press. (Cheers.) The feeling between the two countries just now is one of peace and good will, and woe be to us when the day shall come that that peace is broken up. He would not say that that peace is likely to be broken up, but he would say that it is less likely—that the likelihood of such an event has been greatly postponed by that which has taken place. (Cheers.) This he could say of this extraordinary visit, that they witnessed in New York and in every other city of the United States an amount of enthusiasm which was perfectly extraordinary from the moment at which they entered Detroit till their departure from Portland. (Cheers.) With one solitary exception, they met with nothing but enthusiasm; and, in fact, he did believe that the visit of the Prince of Wales to America had done more to cement the good feeling between the two countries than could possibly have been effected by a quarter of a century of diplomacy. The two great people on either side of the Atlantic disclosed those feelings of fraternity which they entertain towards each other. (Cheers.) His Grace concluded by proposing " The health of the rest of the Royal Family," with which he coupled the name of his Royal Highness the Prince Frederic William of Prussia.

The toast was drunk with great enthusiasm and the usual honours.

THE QUEEN THANKS THE PRESIDENT.

The following correspondence explains itself, and, says the New York *Herald*, will be read by every American with pride and pleasure:—

LETTER OF LORD LYONS.

Washington, Dec. 8, 1860.

SIR,—The Queen, my august Sovereign, has commanded that the earliest opportunity after the return of the Prince of Wales to England be taken to convey to the President of the United States the expression of Her Majesty's thanks for the cordial reception given to His Royal Highness during his late visit to this country by the President himself, and by all classes of the citizens.

One of the main objects which Her Majesty had in view in sanctioning the visit of His Royal Highness, was to prove to the President and citizens of the United States the sincerity of those sentiments of esteem and regard which Her Majesty and all classes of her subjects entertain for the kindred race which occupies so distinguished a position in the community of nations.

Her Majesty has seen with the greatest satisfaction that her feelings and those of her people in this respect have been met with the warmest sympathy in the great American Union ; and Her Majesty trusts that the feeling of confidence and affection—the existence of which late events have proved beyond all question —will long continue to prevail between the two countries, to their mutual advantage, and to the general interests of civilization and humanity.

I am commanded to state to the President that the Queen would be gratified by his making known generally to the citizens of the United States her grateful sense of the kindness with which they received her son, who has returned to England deeply impressed with all he saw during his progress through the States, but more especially so with the friendly and cordial good will manifested towards him on every occasion by all classes of the community.

I have the honour to be, with the highest consideration, sir, your most obedient humble servant,

LYONS.

The Hon. LEWIS CASS, &c.

DEPARTMENT OF STATE,
Washington, Dec. 11th.

MY LORD,—I have the honour to acknowledge the receipt of your note of the 8th instant, in which you have conveyed to this Government the expression of Her Britannic Majesty's thanks for the cordial reception given to His Royal Highness the Prince of Wales during his late visit to this country, by the President and by all classes of the citizens, and of Her Majesty's wish that her grateful sense of courtesies extended to her son may be made known generally to the citizens of the United States.

I am instructed by the President to express the gratification with which he has learned how correctly Her Majesty has appreciated the spirit in which His Royal Highness was received throughout the Republic, and the cordial manifestation of that spirit by the people of the United States which accompanied him in every step of his progress.

Her Majesty has justly recognised that the visit of her son aroused the kind and generous sympathies of our citizens, and, if I may so speak, has created an almost personal interest in the fortunes of the Royalty which he so well represents. The President trusts that this sympathy and interest towards the future representative of the sovereignty of Great Britain, is at once an evidence and a guarantee of that consciousness of common interest and mutual regard which have in the past, and will in the future bind together more strongly than treaties, the feeling and the fortunes of the two nations which represent the enterprise, the civilisation, the constitutional liberty of the same great race.

I have also been instructed to make this correspondence public, that the citizens of the United States may have the satisfaction of knowing how strongly and properly Her Majesty has appreciated the cordial warmth of their welcome to His Royal Highness.

I have the honour to be, my Lord, with high consideration, your Lordship's obedient servant,

WM. HENRY TRESCOTT,

Assistant Secretary.

The following autographs have been obtained with some difficulty, and are placed here on record as being the principal personages so often mentioned in this narritive:—

WASHINGTON, March 19th, 1861.

SIR,—In compliance with your request I send you an autograph of President Buchanan. It will be appropriate for your purpose, as it was written very near the time at which the letter to Her Majesty was signed. I beg you to be so good as to *return it to me* as soon as it has been copied for insertion in your compilation.

I am, Sir,
Your humble servant,

To Capt. ROBERT CELLEM.   LYONS.

QUEBEC, March 28th, 1861.

SIR,—I have the honour to acknowledge your letter of March 25th. I presume that the signature at the foot of this note will answer your purpose.

Your obedient servant,

To ROBT. CELLEM, Esq.   EDMUND HEAD.

The visit of the Prince of Wales having come to a conclusion, the compiler hopes that his labours will tend to its universal reception by the inhabitants of Upper Canada and also of the Lower Province, as well as our friends in the United States. No opportunity or expense has been spared to make a faithful record of so auspicious a visit, and its novelty is trusted to for a liberal contribution towards getting out the work in a pleasing and acceptable manner.

In introducing the name of the Publisher, it has been a great source of satisfaction to the Compiler that his name has been accepted as a guarantee of a proper production.

In every selection made from the various sources, there has only been the one desire, that of a faithful record of what took place during the period of the Royal reception, and if through inadvertence any omission occurs, it is not from any desire to suppress, but rather with a view to limit the amount of matter which naturally appeared at the time.

The Compiler cannot conclude his last remark without giving all honour and thanks to the local papers—principally the *Globe*, *Leader*, and *Colonist* of Toronto—yet much is indebted to the English journals for the favorable criticisms which they have shown throughout, and to Lower Canadian publications as well.

The event as related by the American journals will certainly be read at home with much pleasure.

The Compiler takes leave of his various subscribers with many thanks for the support he has met with in compiling the work, and trusts to the distribution of their patronage in bringing out another edition.

GOD SAVE THE QUEEN.

APPENDIX.

OTTAWA.

The address presented by the Mayor was as follows :—

To His Royal Highness Albert Edward, Prince of Wales, Duke of Cornwall, &c., &c.

MAY IT PLEASE YOUR ROYAL HIGHNESS,—

The Corporation of the City of Ottawa, in Council assembled, most respectfully approach your Royal Highness with the offer of a sincere and loyal welcome to this city, and beg to convey to your Royal Highness sentiments of profound devotion and inalienable attachment to our much-beloved Sovereign.

We consider it a privilege in being allowed to tender to your Royal Highness our hearty congratulations upon your safe arrival in this portion of the extensive empire of which this province forms an integral part, and to assure you of the satisfaction which your visit affords to every class of Her Majesty's liege subjects resident in the Ottawa valley.

We feel proud in having the opportunity of acknowledging, with gratitude, the act of your august mother, our most gracious Queen and ruler, in selecting this city as the future capital of Canada ; and your presence upon this occasion is viewed as a further indication of the great condescension and interest, manifested by our beloved Sovereign, in the welfare of her Canadian subjects in this portion of her Majesty's dominions.

We hail with the utmost delight the auspicious event of your Royal Highness' visit to Canada ; and sincerely hope, that a personal acquaintance with the resources and varied capabilities of this important part of the British possessions, may be found interesting as well as instructive ; and that the experience acquired during your sojourn in the country may satisfy you that its inhabitants are loyal, contented and prosperous.

In conclusion, allow us to wish you a pleasant and agreeable tour throughout the Province, with a safe voyage across the Atlantic ; and on your return to your native land, may you enjoy every comfort and happiness this world can bestow.

ALEX. WORKMAN,
Mayor of Ottawa.

To which the Prince made the following reply :—

GENTLEMEN,—I thank you sincerely for this address, and request you to convey to the citizens whom you represent, the expression of my gratitude for the very kind language in which it is couched, and the warm reception with which they have greeted me.

In this city, at your request, I am about to lay the first stone of a building, in which, before long, the deliberations of the Parliament of Canada will be held, and from which emanate the laws which are to govern the great and free people of these Provinces, extend the civilizing influences of British institutions, and strengthen the power of the great empire of which this colony forms an integral and most important portion.

I do not doubt, that, with its increase of population and influence, this city will prove itself worthy of the country of which it is now the capital, and will justify the selection which your Sovereign made, at the request of her Canadian subjects.

It has been most gratifying to me to witness the demonstrations which have met me on every occasion during my progress through this magnificent country, and which evince the feelings towards your Queen, entertained alike by all races, all creeds, and all parties.